STABILITY AND LEGITIMATE INTERNATIONAL ENERGY INVESTMENTS

This book assesses stability guarantees through the lens of the legitimate expectations principle to offer a new perspective on the stability concept in international energy investments. The analysis of the interaction between the concepts of stability and legitimate expectations reveals that there are now more opportunities for energy investors to argue their cases before arbitral tribunals.

The book offers detailed analyses of the latest energy investment arbitral awards from Spain, Italy and the Czech Republic, and reflects on the state of the art of the legitimate expectations debate and its relationship with the stability concept. The author argues that, in order to achieve stability, the legitimate expectations principle should be employed as the main investment protection tool when a dispute arises on account of unilateral host state alterations.

This timely work will be useful to both scholars and practitioners who are interested in international energy law, investment treaty arbitration, and international investment law.

Global Energy Law and Policy: Volume 6

Global Energy Law and Policy

Series Editors

Peter D Cameron
Pieter Bekker
Volker Roeben
Leonie Reins
Crina Baltag

Energy policy and energy law are undergoing rapid global transformation, characterised by the push in favour of decarbonisation. The 2015 Sustainable Development Goals and the 2015 Paris Agreement on international climate action have forged a consensus for a pathway to a universal just transition towards a low-carbon economy for all states and all societies.

This series publishes conceptual works that help academics, legal practitioners and decision-makers to make sense of these transformational changes. The perspective of the series is global. It welcomes contributions on international law, regional law (for example, from the EU, US and ASEAN regions), and the domestic law of all states with emphasis on comparative works that identify horizontal trends, and including transnational law. The series' scope is comprehensive, embracing both public and commercial law on energy in all forms and sources and throughout the energy life-cycle from extraction, production, operation, consumption and waste management/decommissioning. The series is a forum for innovative interdisciplinary work that uses the insights of cognate disciplines to achieve a better understanding of energy law and policy in the 21st century.

Recent titles in this series:

Decarbonisation and the Energy Industry
edited by Tade Oyewumni, Penelope Crossley,
Frédéric Gilles Sourgens and Kim Talus

*The Global Energy Transition: Law, Policy and Economics
for Energy in the 21st Century*
edited by Peter D Cameron, Xiaoyi Mu and Volker Roeben

The Law and Governance of Mining and Minerals: A Global Perspective
by Ana Elizabeth Bastida

*National Climate Change Acts: The Emergence,
Form and Nature of National Framework Climate Legislation*
edited by Thomas L Muinzer

*Governing the Extractive Sector: Regulating the Foreign
Conduct of International Mining Firms*
by Jeffrey Bone

Stability and Legitimate Expectations in International Energy Investments
by Rahmi Kopar

Stability and Legitimate Expectations in International Energy Investments

Rahmi Kopar

·HART·

OXFORD · LONDON · NEW YORK · NEW DELHI · SYDNEY

HART PUBLISHING

Bloomsbury Publishing Plc

Kemp House, Chawley Park, Cumnor Hill, Oxford, OX2 9PH, UK

1385 Broadway, New York, NY 10018, USA

29 Earlsfort Terrace, Dublin 2, Ireland

HART PUBLISHING, the Hart/Stag logo, BLOOMSBURY and the Diana logo are
trademarks of Bloomsbury Publishing Plc

First published in Great Britain 2021

First published in hardback, 2021

Paperback edition, 2023

Copyright © Rahmi Kopar, 2021

A catalogue record for this book is available from the British Library.

A catalogue record for this book is available from the Library of Congress.

Library of Congress Control Number: 2021021416

ISBN: PB: 978-1-50995-207-6
        ePDF: 978-1-50993-839-1
        ePub: 978-1-50993-840-7

Typeset by Compuscript Ltd, Shannon

To find out more about our authors and books visit www.hartpublishing.co.uk.
Here you will find extracts, author information, details of forthcoming events
and the option to sign up for our newsletters.

PREFACE

The stability concept has been considered a shelter by international energy investors against unilateral host state actions. Investors constantly look for ways to ensure a stable legal environment in host states in order to be able to secure profit from their investments. Stability provisions, as found under investment contracts or domestic laws, are the main tools that international energy investors employ in this regard.

Even though stabilisation clauses have been around for decades, the dispute regarding their efficiency is still ongoing. This book adds another perspective to the utilisation of the stability concept in investment treaty protection by assessing it through the prism of the legitimate expectations principle. The legitimate expectations principle, as the most important component of the fair and equitable treatment (FET) standard, plays a significant role in providing protection to investments. Despite this, the contours of the principle have not been defined well under investment treaty jurisprudence.

This book explores the relationship between the stability and legitimate expectations concepts in the field of international investment law. First, it analyses these concepts separately to identify their contours, then it brings them together to illustrate the interplay between the two concepts. The book finds that there is a close link between them, upon which investors might rely when arguing their cases before arbitral tribunals.

The analysis in this book identifies three main sources of legitimate expectations: contractual commitments, administrative representations of host states and the general legal framework prevailing in host states. It is argued that each of these sources, when analysed in conjunction with stability commitments, provides a stronger and more efficient protection framework to investors under investment treaties. The book shows that while stabilisation provisions create legitimate expectations to be protected, there is also a requirement arising from investment treaty law for host states to provide a stable investment environment, even in the absence of an explicit stability assurance.

This interplay between the stability and legitimate expectations concepts provides international energy investors with a strong means to ensure protection before investment arbitration tribunals. This book advances the debate surrounding the FET standard and the legitimate expectations principle, and provides a comprehensive analysis of the issue of stability in international energy investments.

The main aspiration of the book is to achieve the greatest use and effectiveness of the stability concept for international energy investments. In order to achieve the stability that is sought after, the book argues that the legitimate expectations principle should be employed as the main investment protection tool when a dispute arises on account of unilateral host state alterations.

This book is both timely and needed, as statistics indicate an increasing number of investment arbitrations in the energy sector. In particular, the latest regulatory changes in some European states, including Spain, Italy and the Czech Republic, have caused a spike in investment treaty arbitrations under the Energy Charter Treaty and highlighted the need for a holistic inquiry into these issues.

ACKNOWLEDGEMENTS

This book is an updated version of my PhD thesis, written at the Centre for Energy, Petroleum and Mineral Law and Policy (CEPMLP), University of Dundee. I wish to express my sincere gratitude to my supervisors, Professor Peter D Cameron and Mr Stephen Dow. Their intellectual guidance, continuous support and constructive comments throughout the whole time were of great help in developing and completing this study.

This work would not have been possible without the funding of the Ministry of National Education of the Republic of Turkey and therefore I am grateful to them for providing the scholarship that made it possible for me to pursue the PhD that resulted in this book.

I would like to offer my special thanks to Professor M Fatih Usan, the Dean of Ankara Yildirim Beyazit University Law Faculty, Associate Professor Musa Aygül, the head of Private International Law Department, and all of my colleagues at the department for their support. Professor Yusuf Caliskan and Professor Volker Roeben's insightful comments were really helpful in improving the study and I owe them a great debt of gratitude. I am grateful that Hart Publishing agreed to publish my work, and I would like to extend my thanks to Roberta Bassi and Rosemarie Mearns from Hart Publishing for their help during the preparation of this book.

This book would not have come about without the guidance and mentoring of my father, Fahri Kopar. My mother, Nesrin Kopar, deserves special thanks for always being supportive. They taught me, and made me never forget, that being a good person and being on the straight path are more important than anything else.

Last but not least, I must thank my wife, Tuba, for constantly being by my side throughout this entire journey. She has always been supportive and hence she deserves my highest appreciation. Our lovely children, Ayşe Hüma and Ömer Salih, will now get their well-deserved longer hours at the playground.

CONTENTS

LIST OF ABBREVIATIONS

BIT	bilateral investment treaty
CNE	Comisión Nacional de Energía (the Spanish National Energy Commission)
ECA	Export Credit Agency
ECT	Energy Charter Treaty
EU	European Union
FET	fair and equitable treatment
FiT	feed-in tariff
FTA	free trade agreement
GSE	Gestore dei Servizi Energetici
ICSID	International Centre for Settlement of Investment Disputes
IEA	International Energy Agency
IIA	International Investment Agreement
IMF	International Monetary Fund
LCIA	London Court of International Arbitration
LSA	Legal Stability Agreement
MIGA	Multilateral Investment Guarantee Agency
MIT	Multilateral Investment Treaty
NAFTA	North American Free Trade Agreement
NOC	National Oil Company
OPIC	Overseas Private Investment Corporation
PCA	Permanent Court of Arbitration
PRI	Political Risk Insurance
PSA	Production Sharing Agreement
PSC	Production Sharing Contract

PV	photovoltaic
RD	royal decree
SCC	Arbitration Institute of the Stockholm Chamber of Commerce
TNC	transnational corporation
UNCTAD	United Nations Conference on Trade and Development
UNTS	United Nations Treaty Series

TABLE OF CASES

TABLE OF LEGISLATION

1

Introductory Remarks:
The Quest for Stability

I. General Introduction and Background

According to the World Energy Investment Report of the International Energy Agency (IEA), energy investments amounted to 1.5 trillion USD worldwide in 2020.[1] This figure includes every subsector of the energy industry, from coal, hydro, solar and nuclear power generation to upstream and downstream oil and gas investments.

Several scenarios conducted before the COVID-19 pandemic indicated that total energy demand and consumption will continue grow worldwide over the two to three decades.[2] Electricity demand was expected to double by 2060,[3] while the demand for oil and other liquid fuels was projected to grow simultaneously, albeit at a lower and diminishing rate.[4]

This growing demand brings along with it an increasing need for investments. Until 2035, around $40 trillion of additional global investment was thought to be needed in relation to energy supply.[5]

Even though the full effect of COVID-19 pandemic on these projected investments is not yet clear, there are several scenarios presenting possible outcomes and, according to these scenarios, energy demand will continue to grow even if it is at a slower pace.[6] Thus, the need for further investments is still alive.

A significant share of these investments is and will be undertaken by international players. Most of the largest transnational corporations (TNCs) are

---

[1] IEA, 'World Energy Investment 2020' (International Energy Agency, 2020) www.iea.org/reports/world-energy-investment-2020.

[2] BP, 'BP Energy Outlook 2018' (2018) www.bp.com/content/dam/bp/en/corporate/pdf/energy-economics/energy-outlook/bp-energy-outlook-2018.pdf; World Energy Council, 'World Energy Scenarios 2016' (2016) www.worldenergy.org/assets/downloads/World-Energy-Scenarios-2016_Full-Report.pdf.

[3] World Energy Council, 'World Energy Scenarios 2016' (2016) www.worldenergy.org/assets/downloads/World-Energy-Scenarios-2016_Full-Report.pdf.

[4] BP, 'BP Energy Outlook 2018' (2018) www.bp.com/content/dam/bp/en/corporate/pdf/energy-economics/energy-outlook/bp-energy-outlook-2018.pdf.

[5] IEA, 'World Energy Investment Outlook: Special Report' (International Energy Agency, 2014) www.iea.org/reports/world-energy-investment-outlook.

[6] IEA, 'World Energy Outlook 2020' (International Energy Agency, 2020) www.iea.org/reports/world-energy-outlook-2020.

involved in energy-related projects, be it extractive industries or the power sector. Investments in the energy sector account for a large part of international invest-ment globally.[8] It is anticipated that, in parallel with the surge in investments disputes about energy investment will also increase in the following decades.[9]

Irrespective of whether they relate to energy exploration, production or construction, energy investments tend to be complex, long-term, capital-intensive projects.[10] Hence, these features make energy investment arbitrations of para-mount importance with respect to the amount of money involved in disputes.[11]

Alongside the high amounts at stake, 41 per cent of all cases registered or administered by the International Centre for Settlement of Investment Disputes (ICSID) until June 2020 pertain to the energy sector directly.[12] Other arbitral insti-tutions (such as the Arbitration Institute of the Stockholm Chamber of Commerce (SCC), the London Court of International Arbitration (LCIA[13]) and the Permanent Court of Arbitration (PCA)) also indicate a significant percentage of investment arbitration cases in the energy industry.

So, taking the amounts involved and the dispute numbers into account, it is incontrovertible that energy investment arbitrations constitute a significant portion of the investment arbitration portfolio.[14] One of the main underlying causes of this high dispute rate in the energy industry is closely related to the sector's heavy affili-ation with the government in many countries.

Since the energy industry is socially sensitive and considered strategically important for states from an economic, security and geopolitical aspect,[15] it is usually highly regulated and under the close scrutiny of host states.[16] This feature

[7] J Karl, 'FDI in the Energy Sector: Recent Trends and Policy Issues' in E de Brabandere and T Gazzini (eds), *Foreign Investment in the Energy Sector: Balancing Private and Public Interests* (Brill Nijhoff, 2014) 10.

[8] G Coop, 'Introduction' in E de Brabandere and T Gazzini (eds), *Foreign Investment in the Energy Sector: Balancing Private and Public Interests* (Brill Nijhoff, 2014) 1.

[9] M Scherer, 'Introduction' in M Scherer (ed), *International Arbitration in the Energy Sector* (Oxford University Press, 2018) 4.

[10] ibid 14; AT Martin, 'Dispute Resolution in the International Energy Sector: An Overview' (2011) 4(4) *Journal of World Energy Law & Business* 332, 332.

[11] Scherer, 'Introduction', 3.

[12] ICSID, 'The ICSID Caseload – Statistics' (2020) 2020-2 https://icsid.worldbank.org/sites/default/files/publications/The%20ICSID%20Caseload%20Statistics%20%282020-2%20Edition%29%20ENG.pdf.

[13] 22% of the LCIA cases in 2019 pertain to the energy and resources sector. For details, see LCIA, '2019 Annual Casework Report' (2019) www.lcia.org/media/download.aspx?MediaId=816.

[14] E de Brabandere, 'The Settlement of Investment Disputes in the Energy Sector' in E de Brabandere and T Gazzini (eds), *Foreign Investment in the Energy Sector: Balancing Private and Public Interests* (Brill Nijhoff, 2014) 130.

[15] RD Bishop, EQ Roché and S McBrearty, 'The Breadth and Complexity of the International Energy Industry' in JW Rowley, RD Bishop and G Kaiser (eds), *The Guide to Energy Arbitrations* (Global Arbi-tration Review, 2017) 6; Karl, 'FDI in the Energy Sector', 14; Coop, 'Introduction', 1; UNCTAD, 'World Investment Report: Transnational Corporations, Extractive Industries and Development' (United Nations, 2007) xvii.

[16] K Talus, *EU Energy Law and Policy: A Critical Account* (Oxford University Press, 2013) 72.

of the energy industry, when combined with the complex characteristics of energy investments, renders such investments vulnerable to political risk[17] and regulatory changes.[18]

While direct expropriations were more of a concern in the past, this concern has now shifted towards regulatory interventions.[19] Political risks are considered by foreign investors as among the most significant threats against their investments.[20] Investors have difficulty in intervening to prevent this type of risk from materialising. Rather, materialisation mostly hinges upon the unilateral and arbitrary acts of host states, to which investors are only exposed as passive recipients. Host states might introduce new measures at the constitutional, legislative or regulatory level, which, in turn, might affect the investment detrimentally.[21]

However, this does not mean that there are no tools that can be employed to mitigate or distribute those risks. There are several methods available to international energy investors, such as investment contracts, international investment treaties, domestic laws, political risk insurance, government guarantees and risk distribution strategies, that can assist in reducing or managing the political risk.[22] The stability concept often comes into play during energy investors' pursuit of protection against political risks.

An international energy investor will always look for a stable legal framework in a host state in which it is going to invest a substantial amount of money.[23] The tension between the political risks and the needs of the investors rises to the surface especially in the upstream petroleum industry, where the money at stake is very high and the duration of the projects is long.[24] This entails a heightened need for stability against potential regulatory risks.

Of course, this stability requisite does not solely belong to upstream petroleum investors; other investments in different branches of the energy industry also bear

---

[17] The term 'political risk' will refer to the regulatory risk, as explained in detail in s II.

[18] DW Rivkin, SJ Lamb and NK Leslie, 'The Future of Investor–State Dispute Settlement in the Energy Sector: Engaging with Climate Change, Human Rights and the Rule of Law' (2015) 8(2) *Journal of World Energy Law & Business* 130, 131.

[19] M Krajewski, 'The Impact of International Investment Agreements on Energy Regulation' in C Herrmann and JP Terhechte (eds), *European Yearbook of International Economic Law* (Springer, 2012) 368.

[20] P Bekker and A Ogawa, 'The Impact of Bilateral Investment Treaty (BIT) Proliferation on Demand for Investment Insurance: Reassessing Political Risk Insurance after the "BIT Bang"' (2013) 28(2) *ICSID Review – Foreign Investment Law Journal* 314, 315.

[21] PD Cameron, 'Reflections on Sovereignty over Natural Resources and the Enforcement of Stabilization Clauses' in KP Sauvant (ed), *Yearbook on International Investment Law & Policy 2011–2012* (Oxford University Press, 2013) 318.

[22] M Erkan, *International Energy Investment Law: Stability through Contractual Clauses* (Kluwer Law International, 2011) 7.

[23] T Childs, 'The Current State of International Oil and Gas Arbitration' (2018) 13(1) *Texas Journal of Oil, Gas, And Energy Law* 1, 14; G Bellantuono, 'The Misguided Quest for Regulatory Stability in the Renewable Energy Sector' (2017) 10(4) *Journal of World Energy Law & Business* 274, 274.

[24] Erkan, *Stability*, 6; A Al Faruque, 'Validity and Efficacy of Stabilisation Clauses: Legal Protection vs Functional Value' (2006) 23(4) *Journal of International Arbitration* 317, 318.

similar characteristics and therefore are exposed to similar risks (a power plant or transmission network, for example). This is also evident from the arbitration statistics given above. Therefore, it can readily be stated that stability has been a major quest for energy investors of all types.

Legal stability is sought by the utilisation of several tools: contracts, investment agreements, domestic laws and regulations. It might be pursued by investors at a domestic level by relying on the domestic legal framework or at an international level with the help of international investment agreements, or at the contractual protection level, which might have reflections on both sides. Often, more than one of these legal tools would exist together in an international energy investment setting.

Under certain circumstances, the stability tools would interact with other treaty protection mechanisms and produce a new layer of investment protection.[25] This is clearly visible in their interaction with the legitimate expectations principle under the fair and equitable treatment (FET) standards of international investment agreements. It can be seen from this interaction that there is a close link between the stability concept and the legitimate expectations doctrine in pursuit of investment protection. As stated by Voss, these two concepts are not severable; on the contrary, they are in a close relationship.[26]

The stability concept and the legitimate expectations principle are two constantly developing aspects of international investment law. They are both of paramount importance especially in the energy sector, where government interventions tend to be frequent and the amount of capital at risk from such interventions is unusually large.

With the help of globalisation and technological advancement, small-scale international energy investors are also becoming more active in the sector.[27] While this is happening, the energy sector itself has been going through a transformation too. Due to the newly arising international obligations connected with climate change, states are motivated to adapt energy policies that provide incentives for renewable energy.[28]

These new developments bring new problems too. It does not matter whether an investor is a large multinational corporation or a small one, since they both require a certain level of stability for their investments. However, their negotiating power might well differ at the beginning of the investment relationship and contractual stabilisation clauses that are granted to large investors might not be secured by smaller ones.

---

[25] PD Cameron, *International Energy Investment Law: The Pursuit of Stability* (Oxford University Press, 2010) 66.

[26] JO Voss, *Impact of Investment Treaties on Contracts between Host States and Foreign Investors* (Martinus Nijhoff Publishers, 2010) 212.

[27] PD Cameron, 'Stabilization and the Impact of Changing Patterns of Energy Investment' (2017) 10(5) *Journal of World Energy Law & Business* 389, 389.

[28] N Gallagher, 'ECT and Renewable Energy Disputes' in M Scherer (ed), *International Arbitration in the Energy Sector* (Oxford University Press, 2018) 252.

On the other hand, even though a contractual stabilisation clause might be secured by an international energy investor, this still does not prevent host states from altering the investment conditions and changing the rules of the game once a significant element of the investment has been made, or when they find it appropriate to do so.

It is also common for host states to regulate their energy investment frameworks as a whole under their domestic legislation without concluding separate investment contracts. This can be seen in the renewable energy sector. Therefore, the investment protection mechanisms available to investors against regulatory risks become significant. The legal value of the stability provisions also become more visible during the dispute resolution process.

Under any of these circumstances, whether there is a stability provision existent or not, the legitimate expectations principle plays a significant role in protecting the investor in the event of a dispute under the treaty framework. The legitimate expectations principle, when considered in conjunction with the stability guarantees provided under contracts, domestic legislation or administrative representations, is capable of providing an additional level of stability to the investment framework and a strong protection. When there is no explicit stability provision, investors might still expect a certain level of stability from the host states by relying on the legitimate expectations principle under investment treaties.

II. Objectives and Scope of the Book

This book presents an analysis of the stability concept and its interplay with the legitimate expectations principle, bearing in mind international energy investments. The particularities of this sector, as will be discussed in the next chapter, render such investments more prone to certain types of risks, especially political risks. Therefore, the stability quest has always been at the forefront of international energy investment planning. Even though there are several protection mechanisms against political risks, the focus of this book is only on the stability concept and the investment treaty aspect of it. While the term 'political risk' encompasses, inter alia, war, terrorism, civil disturbance, expropriation and convertibility restrictions,[29] this study will restrict the term to 'regulatory risks' only, where the main concern is the unilateral alteration of the investment framework by host states.

Energy investments have also gone through a significant transformation over the years, from being 'petroleum-centric' to becoming more inclusive of other large-scale investments, especially in the wind and solar sectors.[30] Therefore, in order to provide a holistic understanding, the focus of this book is not solely on the petroleum industry; rather, it also features other large-scale forms of energy investments that bear similar characteristics and that are exposed to political risks.

---

[29] See ch 2, s V.
[30] Cameron, 'Changing Patterns', 390.

Even though international energy investments and energy disputes have specific characteristics, these do not indicate that they should be held subject to a set of rules totally different from the ones present under general international investment law.[31] Findings on both sides would be applicable to one another.[32] This is the reason why protection against the unilateral interventions of host states in international energy investments is pursued under the international investment law regime. Thus, the scope of this book is limited to analysing the legitimate expectations principle only in relation to the international investment treaty law, and the principle will not be discussed within other frameworks such as the World Trade Organization, the European Court of Human Rights (ECtHR) and the European Court of Justice (ECJ). Domestic legislation is also outside the scope of this book.[33] However, in section III of chapter four, while discussing the roots of the concept, several references to domestic laws will be made in order to justify its recognition and application by investment treaty arbitration tribunals. This is only to present a superficial overview of the historical roots of the principle; an in-depth analysis of the concept under domestic legislation will not be undertaken.

It is true that energy disputes not only arise from the investment treaty relationship between states and investors – a large portion of energy arbitrations pertain to commercial disputes which fall under the scope of international commercial arbitration.[34] However, the focus of this book is only on investor-state arbitrations, with commercial arbitrations being excluded, because the central standard to be scrutinised, the FET standard, belongs to the international investment regime.

The study definitely does *not* involve a balancing approach. It is not focused on the issue of how to balance the legitimate expectations of investors and the regulatory needs of host states; rather, the investment protection aspect of the principle is emphasised.[35] Additionally, the issue of whether host states are

---

[31] For a detailed recent discussion on this issue, see O Varis, 'Constitutionalisation and Institutionalisation Applied to the International Investment Regime: Toward a Uniform, Consistent and Coherent International Investment Law' (PhD Thesis, University of Dundee, 2018).

[32] SW Schill, 'Foreign Investment in the Energy Sector: Lessons for International Investment Law' in E de Brabandere and T Gazzini (eds), *Foreign Investment in the Energy Sector: Balancing Private and Public Interests* (Brill Nijhoff, 2014) 260.

[33] The following studies have already dealt with certain aspects of these issues: N Muhammad, 'Legitimate Expectations in Investment Treaty Arbitration: Balancing between State's Legitimate Regulatory Functions and Investor's Legitimate Expectations' (PhD Thesis, University of Dundee, 2015); LM Nowak, 'Exploring the Limits of the Concept of Legitimate Expectations in Investment Treaty Law: a Study in Comparative Law and the Development of International Law' (PhD Thesis, SOAS, University of London, 2015); SJ Schonberg, *Legitimate Expectations in Administrative Law* (Oxford University Press, 2000).

[34] Childs, 'Oil and Gas Arbitration', 4.

[35] For recent discussions on states' right to regulate and balancing the interests, see T Thakur, 'Reforming the Investor–State Dispute Settlement Mechanism and the Host State's Right to Regulate: A Critical Assessment' (2020) *Indian Journal of International Law* https://link.springer.com/article/10.1007%2Fs40901-020-00111-2; FM Palombino, *Fair and Equitable Treatment and the Fabric of General Principles* (Asser Press, 2018); G Coop and I Seif, 'ECT and States' Right to Regulate' in M Scherer (ed),

:apable of having legitimate expectations or not is also beyond the scope of his study.[36]

This book is an attempt to present the potential ways in which an investor might protect its investment from the unilateral and arbitrary changes of host states. The aim is to show investors that reliance on a treaty principle – the legitimate expectations principle – might prove useful and protective, both in cases of the presence of an explicit stability provision and in the absence of such an explicit undertaking by host states. The legitimate expectations principle is formulated here as a means of securing a stable investment environment.

In this book, the legitimate expectations principle is considered as a significant investment protection tool for international energy investors in the event of a dispute, and it is argued that adopting a broader approach in evaluating the principle is the right way to ensure the stability to which investors aspire.

Although there have been scholarly attempts to detach legitimate expectations from the legal stability obligation of a host state under a treaty,[37] this book rejects that proposal and argues that they should be evaluated in conjunction with one another because the stability quest is one of the main underlying concepts of all investment treaties.

The legitimate expectations principle has also been analysed under the minimum standard of treatment provision, especially under the North American Free Trade Agreement (NAFTA) framework.[38] However, this book will only feature an analysis of the principle as a part of the FET standard under which the doctrine finds its widest application, in order to keep the study focused and manageable.

International Arbitration in the Energy Sector (Oxford University Press, 2018); P Bernardini, 'Reforming Investor–State Dispute Settlement: The Need to Balance Both Parties' Interests' (2017) 32(1) *ICSID Review – Foreign Investment Law Journal* 38; D Gaukrodger, 'The Balance between Investor Protection and the Right to Regulate in Investment Treaties: A Scoping Paper' (2017) OECD Working Papers on International Investment 2017/02; N Pusic, 'Balancing the Interests between TNCs and Host Developing States: The Role of Law' (PhD Thesis, Institute of Advanced Legal Studies, University of London, 2017); A Mills, 'The Balancing (and Unbalancing?) of Interests in International Investment Law and Arbitration' in Z Douglas, J Pauwelyn and JE Viñuales (eds), *The Foundations of International Investment Law: Bringing Theory into Practice* (Oxford University Press, 2014); Y Radi, 'Balancing the Public and the Private in International Investment Law' in HM Watt and DPF Arroyo (eds), *Private International Law and Global Governance* (Oxford University Press, 2014); A Titi, *The Right to Regulate in International Investment Law* (Nomos/Hart, 2014); OECD, 'Indirect Expropriation and the Right to Regulate in International Investment Law' (OECD Publishing, 2004).

[36] For a short discussion about this issue, see KP Sauvant and G Unuvar, 'Can Host Countries Have Legitimate Expectations?' (2016) 183 *Columbia FDI Perspectives* http://ccsi.columbia.edu/files/2013/10/No-183-Sauvant-and-%C3%9Cn%C3%BCvar-FINAL.pdf.

[37] S Maynard, 'Legitimate Expectations and the Interpretation of the "Legal Stability Obligation"' (2016) 1(1) *European Investment Law and Arbitration Review* 99.

[38] M Jacob and SW Schill, 'Fair and Equitable Treatment: Content, Practice, Method' (2017) Amsterdam Center for International Law Research Paper No 2017-20 https://ssrn.com/abstract=2933425; C Campbell, 'House of Cards: The Relevance of Legitimate Expectations under Fair and Equitable Treatment Provisions in Investment Treaty Law' (2013) 30(4) *Journal of International Arbitration* 361; S Fietta, 'The 'Legitimate Expectations' Principle under Article 1105 NAFTA' (2006) 7(3) *Journal of World Investment & Trade* 423.

While umbrella clauses are also relevant within the stability context,[39] they also remain outside the scope of this study for the same reasons.

Even though this book revolves around the stability concept in international energy investments, its analysis of arbitral awards is not confined solely to energy investment disputes. The main reason behind this is that the legitimate expectations principle is an ever-developing concept, and it is important to analyse all of the inputs from every arbitral tribunal in order to identify its limits properly. Most of the findings will not be exclusive to international energy investments; on the contrary, they are applicable to all disputes within the broader international investment law context, as already stated above.

There are two main problems on which this book focuses:

1. *Lack of stability* for international energy investments due to the presence of a high degree of regulatory risk in the energy sector.
2. *The ambiguous scope of the legitimate expectations principle* in international investment treaty arbitration jurisprudence.

The lack of stability in the energy industry is a key problem for foreign investors, which encourages them to take certain measures prior to making their investments, or to seek assurances from the host states as a comfort against adverse effects at some future date. The main reason underlying this lack of stability is the regulatory risks prevalent in the energy industry.[40] International energy investors are constantly seeking to enhance the stability of the legal framework under which they make their investments as far as possible. While stability remains one of their primary concerns, the methods that they employ to achieve stability in the legal and business framework are variable.

The stability concept in relation to investment has mostly been analysed through discussions of stabilisation clauses[41] in the literature.[42] However, there is one more dimension through which the stability concept could be scrutinised, which is the treaty protection aspect. If we take that route, the legitimate expectations principle under the FET standard could also provide a lens through which the stability concept can be viewed and assessed. Nevertheless, this is unlikely to be successful without some clarification of the principle with respect to investment treaty arbitration. There is an ambiguity in both the scope and content of the legitimate expectations principle which stands in the way of a rigorous analysis. Therefore, in order to solve the stability problem that investors face, it is vital to provide clarification of the legitimate expectations principle first.

In this book, I attempt to knit these two ostensibly different, yet essentially interrelated problems together, and to propose a protection framework for

---

[39] Cameron, *International Energy Investment Law*, 66.
[40] See ch 2.
[41] The following terms will be used interchangeably: stability provision, stabilisation clause, stability guarantee, stabilisation provision, stability assurance.
[42] See ch 3.

international energy investors upon which they can rely in the event of a dispute in order to secure a wider protection for their investments.

Herein is an analysis of the stability concept through the prism of legitimate expectations. While the interplay between the legitimate expectations principle under investment treaty law and stability provisions found under various legal sources is capable of creating an additional and broader layer of protection for the investor, the principle itself also acts as a means of securing a stable legal framework, even in the absence of an explicit stability guarantee given by the host state.

Accordingly, this book, by clarifying the scope of the legitimate expectations principle and revealing its interplay with the stability concept, attempts to present a new dimension and solution for the stability problem which international energy investors face.

There are two distinct sub-questions associated with each of the problems mentioned above. The first question, which is in relation to both problems, is: How are investors protected against political risks, thereby securing stability in international energy investments? The second question is associated with the second problem, and that is: What is the scope of the legitimate expectations principle under investment treaty arbitration jurisprudence?

Notwithstanding that these questions compose the two central pillars of the book, the main question of this study will be built upon them as follows:

How do the legitimate expectations principle and the stability concept interact with each other so as to provide investors with protection against regulatory risks?

Alongside this main question, several sub-questions will be discussed in various chapters of the book. Some of these questions are as follows:

- What is an international energy investment according to international investment law?
- What is the stability concept and why is it important in the energy industry?
- What are the sources of stabilisation provisions?
- What is a legitimate expectation, and how is it determined?
- Is it justified to include the legitimate expectations principle within the FET standard?
- What are the sources of legitimate expectations?

The main argument of this study is that there is a close link between the stability concept and the legitimate expectations principle under the FET standard which might be utilised by international energy investors as an effective protection mechanism against regulatory risks and unilateral alterations of host states once a dispute arises. While already existing stabilisation clauses in various forms play a role in creating strong legitimate expectations, there is also a duty for host states arising from the legitimate expectations principle itself to maintain a stable legal and regulatory framework, even in the absence of explicit stability provisions.

III. Justification and Significance of the Book

Rudolf Dolzer stated in a 2013 article that: 'The topic of legitimate expectations will likely remain in the foreground of the FET rule. The further definition of this central topic remains the most important component in the development of the FET standard.'[43] Indeed, his prediction has been proved true. This book is both timely and needed, as statistics indicate an increasing number of investment arbitrations in the energy sector. In particular, the latest regulatory changes in some European states, including Spain, Italy and the Czech Republic, have caused a spike in investment treaty arbitrations under the Energy Charter Treaty (ECT). Most of these cases include breach of legitimate expectations claims. Other than these ECT cases, there have also been numerous investment treaty arbitrations that have dealt with the legitimate expectations issue within the last decade.

It is also anticipated that a new wave of energy disputes will soon appear over the horizon, and therefore international energy investors should make good use of the available risk management tools in order to protect themselves from potential adverse effects.[44] International investment agreements are of capital importance in this regard.[45] Taking this point of view as its starting point, this study has identified the legitimate expectations principle as the principal protection tool whose importance grows persistently.

The divergent decisions reached by arbitral tribunals on the legitimate expectations principle have shown that there is an urgent and ongoing need to clarify its contours and content. In order to provide a certain level of consistency in the application of the legitimate expectations principle, there is a need to conduct comprehensive research and create a theoretical basis for choosing one approach over the other. By analysing the legitimate expectations principle in conjunction with the stability concept, this book is an attempt to fill that gap.

In 2018, Mistelis stated that: 'The more stability there is at the treaty level, the less stability is arguably needed at the contractual level.'[46] According to this, when stability at the treaty level is ensured by treaty standards, investors could still be protected even in the absence of a contractual protection tool. This is the stance taken in this book.

This study is an attempt to clarify the nexus between the legitimate expectations principle, a treaty protection tool and the stability concept. Establishing this link between legitimate expectations and stability could help investors to understand the protection methods available to them at the treaty level. Thereby, it will be shown that from these divergent arbitral approaches to the legitimate

---

[43] R Dolzer, 'Fair and Equitable Treatment: Today's Contours' (2013) 12(1) *Santa Clara Journal of International Law* 7, 33.

[44] Scherer, 'Introduction', 4.

[45] PM Blyschak, 'Arbitrating Overseas Oil and Gas Disputes: Breaches of Contract versus Breaches of Treaty' (2010) 27(6) *Journal of International Arbitration* 579.

[46] L Mistelis, 'Contractual Mechanisms for Stability in Energy Contracts' in M Scherer (ed), *International Arbitration in the Energy Sector* (Oxford University Press, 2018) 155.

expectations principle, the one that enhances the stability aspirations of investors should prevail. This is so because one of the substantial motives behind investment treaties is to build confidence in the stability of the legal framework and the investment environment of a host state.[47]

Returning to Dolzer's article, he signalled the nexus between these two concepts as follows:

> Whereas stability and predictability are more abstract concepts linked to the general contours of an investment-friendly climate, the notion of legitimate expectations concerns, in a normative operational mode, the affirmation and the limitations of stability and predictability in the light of the particular circumstances of a case.[48]

The need for clarification of the relationship between host state commitments and legitimate expectations was also emphasised by Cameron, when he commented that it was unclear whether a host state's commitment would lead to a successful claim before an arbitral tribunal in the absence of an explicit contractual stabilisation clause.[49] He also underscored the importance of the interplay between treaty standards and other protection mechanisms in ensuring stability.[50]

Taking these comments and recent investment arbitration developments into account, it becomes clear that there is a need to conduct an in-depth research into this matter; the aim of this book is to play a significant role in the development of both the legitimate expectations and stability concepts.

Until now, these two concepts have typically been analysed separately, with only a very few exceptions. While there are numerous works on stability provisions, the traditional literature mostly focuses on the types and sources of such clauses, their validity and effectiveness, and the analysis of international arbitration cases that deal with certain types of stability provisions.[51] Even though there

---

[47] JW Salacuse, *The Law of Investment Treaties* (Oxford University Press, 2015) 11; Bekker and Ogawa, 'Political Risk', 338; JW Salacuse and NP Sullivan, 'Do BITs Really Work?: An Evaluation of Bilateral Investment Treaties and their Grand Bargain' in KP Sauvant and LE Sachs (eds), *The Effect of Treaties on Foreign Direct Investment: Bilateral Investment Treaties, Double Taxation Treaties, and Investment Flows* (Oxford University Press, 2009) 118; SD Franck, 'The Legitimacy Crisis in Investment Treaty Arbitration: Privatizing Public International Law through Inconsistent Decisions' (2005) 73(4) *Fordham Law Review* 1521, 1525.

[48] Dolzer, 'Today's Contours', 32.

[49] Cameron, *International Energy Investment Law*, 418.

[50] Cameron, 'Reflections on Sovereignty', 316; Cameron, *International Energy Investment Law*, 66.

[51] C Partasides and L Martinez, 'Of Taxes and Stabilisation' in JW Rowley, RD Bishop and G Kaiser (eds), *The Guide to Energy Arbitrations* (Global Arbitration Review, 2017); M Mansour and C Nakhle, 'Fiscal Stabilization in Oil and Gas Contracts: Evidence and Implications' (2016) www.oxfordenergy.org/publications/fiscal-stabilization-in-oil-and-gas-contracts-evidence-and-implications/; A Umirdinov, 'The End of Hibernation of Stabilization Clause in Investment Arbitration: Reassessing Its Contribution to Sustainable Development' (2015) 43 *Denver Journal of International Law & Policy* 455; P Puscceddu, 'Contractual Stability in the Oil and Gas Industry: Stabilization, Renegotiation and Unilateral State's Undertakings' (2014) 2 *International Energy Law Review* 58; Erkan, *Stability*; J Nwaokoro, 'Enforcing Stabilization of International Energy Contracts' (2010) 3(1) *Journal of World Energy Law & Business* 103; A Shemberg, 'Stabilization Clauses and Human Rights: A Research Project Conducted for IFC and the United Nations Special Representative to the Secretary General on Business

is a good amount of recent literature on the legitimate expectations principle as well,[52] it is still a developing concept under investment arbitration jurisprudence, and its contours are being clarified by successive arbitral decisions.

This study is different from other studies with respect to its approach to the stability and legitimate expectations concepts. This is the first comprehensive

and Human Rights' (2009) www.ifc.org/wps/wcm/connect/0883d81a-e00a-4551-b2b9-46641e5a9bba/ Stabilization%2BPaper.pdf?MOD=AJPERES&CACHEID=ROOTWORKSPACE-0883d81a-e00a -4551-b2b9-46641e5a9bba-jqeww2e; P Bernardini, 'Stabilization and Adaptation in Oil and Gas Investments' (2008) 1(1) *Journal of World Energy Law & Business* 98; L Cotula, 'Reconciling Regulatory Stability and Evolution of Environmental Standards in Investment Contracts: Towards a Rethink of Stabilization Clauses' (2008) 1(2) *Journal of World Energy Law & Business* 158; JN Emeka, 'Anchoring Stabilization Clauses in International Petroleum Contracts' (2008) 42(4) *International Lawyer* 1317; AFM Maniruzzaman, 'The Pursuit of Stability in International Energy Investment Contracts: A Critical Appraisal of the Emerging Trends' (2008) 1(2) *Journal of World Energy Law & Business* 121; A Al Faruque, 'Typologies, Efficacy and Political Economy of Stabilisation Clauses: A Critical Appraisal' (2007) 5(4) *Oil, Gas & Energy Law* 1; AFM Maniruzzaman, 'National Laws Providing for Stability of International Investment Contracts: A Comparative Perspective' (2007) 8(2) *Journal of World Investment & Trade* 233; Al Faruque, 'Validity and Efficacy'; A Al Faruque, 'The Rationale and Instrumentalities for Stability in Long-Term State Contracts' (2006) 7(1) *Journal of World Investment & Trade* 85; PD Cameron, 'Stabilisation in Investment Contracts and Changes of Rules in Host Countries: Tools for Oil & Gas Investors' (AIPN, 2006) www.international-arbitration-attorney.com/wp-content/uploads/arbitrationlaw4-Stabilisation-Paper.pdf; AFM Maniruzzaman, 'International Energy Contracts and Cross-Border Pipeline Projects: Stabilization, Renegotiation and Economic Balancing in Changed Circumstances – Some Recent Trends' (2006) 4(4) *Oil, Gas & Energy Law* 1; MTB Coale, 'Stabilization Clauses in International Petroleum Transactions' (2001) 30(2) *Denver Journal of International Law & Policy* 217; TW Waelde and G Ndi, 'Stabilizing International Investment Commitments: International Law versus Contract Interpretation' (1996) 31 *Texas International Law Journal* 215; SKB Asante, 'Stability of Contractual Relations in the Transnational Investment Process' (1979) 28(3) *International & Comparative Law Quarterly* 401.

[52] See some recent studies: MW Lo, 'Legitimate Expectations in a Time of Pandemic: The Host State's COVID-19 Measures, Its Obligations and Possible Defenses under International Investment Agreements' (2020) 13(1) *Contemporary Asia Arbitration Journal* 249; S Faccio, 'The Assessment of the FET Standard between Legitimate Expectations and Economic Impact in the Italian Solar Energy Investment Case Law' (2020) 71 *Questions of International Law* 3; M Krzykowski, M Marianski and J Ziety, 'Principle of Reasonable and Legitimate Expectations in International Law as a Premise for Investments in the Energy Sector' (2020) *International Environmental Agreements: Politics, Law and Economics* https://doi.org/10.1007/s10784-020-09471-x; T Wongkaew, *Protection of Legitimate Expectations in Investment Treaty Arbitration: A Theory of Detrimental Reliance* (Cambridge University Press, 2019); SR Kethireddy, 'Still the Law of Nations: Legitimate Expectations and the Sovereigntist Turn in International Investment' (2019) 44(2) *Yale Journal of International Law* 315; CJM González, 'The Convergence of Recent International Investment Awards and Case Law on the Principle of Legitimate Expectations: Towards Common Criteria Regarding Fair and Equitable Treatment?' (2017) 42(3) *European Law Review* 402; V Poiedynok, O Kolohoida and I Lukach, 'The Doctrine of Legitimate Expectations: Need for Limits' (2017) VIII(5) *Journal of Advanced Research in Law and Economics* 1604; FD Simoes, 'Charanne and Construction Investments v Spain: Legitimate Expectations and Investments in Renewable Energy' (2017) 26(2) *Review of European, Comparative & International Environmental Law* 174; A Bazrafkan and A Herwig, 'Reinterpreting the Fair and Equitable Treatment Provision in International Investment Agreements as a New and More Legitimate Way to Manage Risks' (2016) 7(2) *European Journal of Risk Regulation* 439; N Teggi, 'Legitimate Expectations in Investment Arbitration: At the End of Its Life Cycle' (2016) 5(1) *Indian Journal of Arbitration Law* 64; Maynard, 'Legitimate Expectations'; C Annacker, 'Role of Investors' Legitimate Expectations in Defense of Investment Treaty Claims' in AK Bjorklund (ed), *Yearbook on International Investment Law & Policy* (Oxford University Press, 2015); F Dupuy and PM Dupuy, 'What to Expect from Legitimate Expectations? A Critical Appraisal and Look into the Future of the "Legitimate Expectations" Doctrine in International Investment Law'

attempt in the literature to analyse the stability concept through the lens of the legitimate expectations principle and vice versa. Even though there have been several attempts to discuss the two concepts together, they have either failed to cover the issue extensively by taking the latest arbitral developments into account together with all forms of stability guarantees, or have not analysed the subject from the same standpoint as the one used herein.[53] In this book, the stability and legitimate expectations concepts are first analysed separately, before being combined to present an in-depth understanding of the interplay between the stability concept and the legitimate expectations principle.

in MA Raouf, P Leboulanger and NG Ziadé (eds), *Festschrift Ahmed Sadek El-Kosheri – From the Arab World to the Globalization of International Law and Arbitration* (Kluwer Law International, 2015); N Monebhurrun, 'Gold Reserve Inc v Bolivarian Republic of Venezuela: Enshrining Legitimate Expectations as a General Principle of International Law?' (2015) 32(5) *Journal of International Arbitration* 551; Muhammad, Legitimate Expectations in Investment Treaty Arbitration; Nowak, Exploring the Limits; L Reed and S Consedine, 'Fair and Equitable Treatment: Legitimate Expectations and Transparency' in M Kinnear et al (eds), *Building International Investment Law: The First 50 Years of ICSID* (Kluwer Law International, 2015); S Hamamoto, 'Protection of the Investor's Legitimate Expectations: Intersection of a Treaty Obligation and a General Principle of Law' in W Shan and J Su (eds), *China and International Investment Law: Twenty Years of ICSID Membership* (Brill Nijhoff, 2014); T Wongkaew, 'The Transplantation of Legitimate Expectations in Investment Treaty Arbitration: A Critique' in S Lalani and RP Lazo (eds), *The Role of the State in Investor–State Arbitration* (Brill Nijhoff, 2014); Z Asqari, 'Investor's Legitimate Expectations and the Interests of the Host State in Foreign Investment' (2014) 4(12) *Asian Economic and Financial Review* 1906; SA Bandali, 'Understanding FET: The Case for Protecting Contract-based Legitimate Expectations' in IA Laird et al (eds), *Investment Treaty Arbitration and International Law*, vol 7 (JurisNet, 2014); Z Meyers, 'Adapting Legitimate Expectations to International Investment Law: A Defence of Arbitral Tribunals' Approach' (2014) 11(3) *Transnational Dispute Management* 1; O Osasu, 'Legitimate Expectations and Political Risk: Lessons from Investment Arbitration for Energy Investors' (2013) 6 *International Energy Law Review* 249; M Potestà, 'Legitimate Expectations in Investment Treaty Law: Understanding the Roots and the Limits of a Controversial Concept' (2013) 28(1) *ICSID Review – Foreign Investment Law Journal* 88; Campbell, 'House of Cards'; DLF Shamila, 'Rationalize of Host State's Regulatory Measures and Protection of Legitimate Expectations of Foreign Investor: Analyzing the State of Necessity in the Investment Treaty Context' (2013) 2(3) *South East Asia Journal of Contemporary Business, Economics and Law* 34; FM Téllez, 'Conditions and Criteria for the Protection of Legitimate Expectations under International Investment Law: 2012 ICSID Review Student Writing Competition' (2012) 27(2) *ICSID Review – Foreign Investment Law Journal* 432; APG Pandya and A Moody, 'Legitimate Expectations in Investment Treaty Arbitration: An Unclear Future' (2010) 15(1) *Tilburg Law Review* 93; C Schreuer and U Kriebaum, 'At What Time Must Legitimate Expectations Exist?' in J Werner and AH Ali (eds), *A Liber Amicorum: Thomas Wälde- Law beyond Conventional Thought* (CMP Publishing, 2009); E Snodgrass, 'Protecting Investors' Legitimate Expectations – Recognizing and Delimiting a General Principle' (2006) 21(1) *ICSID Review – Foreign Investment Law Journal* 1.

[53] D Zannoni, 'The Legitimate Expectation of Regulatory Stability under the Energy Charter Treaty' (2020) 33(2) *Leiden Journal of International Law* 451; J Gjuzi, *Stabilization Clauses in International Investment Law: A Sustainable Development Approach* (Springer, 2018); Maynard, 'Legitimate Expectations'; AV Kuznetsov, 'The Limits of Contractual Stabilization Clauses for Protecting International Oil and Gas Investments Examined Through the Prism of the Sakhalin-2 PSA: Mandatory Law, the Umbrella Clause, and the Fair and Equitable Treatment Standard' (2015) 22(2) *Willamette Journal of International Law and Dispute Resolution* 223; R Supapa, 'The Protection of Upstream Energy Contracts under Investment Treaty Arbitration: A Study of the Interaction between Contract and Treaty Instruments' (PhD Thesis, University of Aberdeen, 2014); M Hirsch, 'Between Fair and Equitable Treatment and Stabilization Clause: Stable Legal Environment and Regulatory Change in International Investment Law' (2011) 12(6) *Journal of World Investment & Trade* 783; PD Cameron, 'Stability of Contract in the International Energy Industry' (2009) 27(3) *Journal of Energy and Natural Resources Law* 305.

The main aspiration of this book is to achieve the greatest use and effectiveness of the stability concept for international energy investments. In order to achieve such stability, the recommendation of this study is that the legitimate expectations principle should be employed as the main investment protection tool when a dispute arises on account of unilateral host state alterations. John Bowman discussed the importance of dispute resolution planning in a 2001 article,[54] and this book, starting from this point, attempts to present a significant argument for investors once a dispute arises. It is important for an investor to know beforehand upon which substantive foundations it might build its arguments.

As indicated by several authors, stability provisions are not effective in preventing unilateral modification by host states.[55] However, even if they are inefficient at curtailing host states' unilateral actions, they have been considered useful during the dispute resolution process.[56] In this book, the stability provisions are considered an effective dispute resolution tool, and it will be shown that they are indeed effective when utilised in conjunction with the legitimate expectations principle in investment treaty arbitration.

IV. Methodology and Structure of the Book

This book will mainly involve the doctrinal analysis method in order to discuss the issue and accomplish its objectives. As Jain explains:

> [W]hat distinguishes law from other social sciences … is its normative character.
> This fact along with the fact that stability and certainty of law are desirable goals and
> social values to be pursued make doctrinal research to be of primary concern to a legal
> researcher.[57]

Doctrinal research aims to 'clarify ambiguities within rules, place them in a logical and coherent structure and describe their relationship to other rules'.[58]

This book is an attempt to analyse the stability concept in international energy investments through the lens of the legitimate expectations principle under international investment law. Stabilisation provisions found under different legal

---

[54] J Bowman, 'Dispute Resolution Planning for the Oil and Gas Industry' (2001) 16(2) *ICSID Review – Foreign Investment Law Journal* 332.

[55] JV de Macedo, 'From Tradition to Modernity: Not Necessarily an Evolution – The Case of Stabilisation and Renegotiation Clauses' (2011) 9(1) *Oil, Gas & Energy Law* 1, 4; G Joffé et al, 'Expropriation of Oil and Gas Investments: Historical, Legal and Economic Perspectives in a New Age of Resource Nationalism' (2009) 2(1) *Journal of World Energy Law & Business* 3, 22; HR Al Khalifa, 'Negotiating and Arbitrating against Government Entities' (2003) 19(5) *Construction Law Journal* 258, 264–65.

[56] Erkan, *Stability*, 141; RD Bishop, SD Dimitroff and CS Miles, 'Strategic Options Available When Catastrophe Strikes the Major International Energy Project' (2001) 36(4) *Texas International Law Journal* 635, 642.

[57] SN Jain, 'Doctrinal and Non-doctrinal Legal Research' (1975) 17(4) *Journal of the Indian Law Institute* 516, 516.

[58] P Chynoweth, 'Legal Research' in A Knight and L Ruddock (eds), *Advanced Research Methods in the Built Environment* (Wiley-Blackwell, 2008) 29.

sources in various forms and the stability requirement inherent to investment treaties will be analysed in conjunction with the legitimate expectations principle.

The stability concept is addressed in two particular ways: first, as a more general and abstract issue, and second, as a substantial stability provision that is part of a contract or legislation. The legitimate expectations principle, on the other hand, is evaluated through its application under the FET standard. The normative content of the FET standard will be analysed prior to the legitimate expectations principle in order to show the origins of the principle.

When conducting this analysis, there are several primary and secondary sources to be evaluated. In explaining the stability provisions, clauses under international investment agreements, legal stability agreements and domestic legislation will be referenced. In the second phase, while discussing the legitimate expectations principle, investment arbitration decisions will be at the forefront of the analysis. The main reason for conducting this analysis through arbitral decisions is that international investment law and its related principles mainly progress through arbitral cases.[59] Nevertheless, the FET standards of various international investment agreements (bilateral and multilateral investment treaties (BITs and MITs)) will also be employed in the analysis.

Alongside these primary sources, this book will refer to such academic secondary sources as books, journal articles, institutional reports, PhD theses, working papers and some online investment arbitration databases.

The case analyses will be limited to published documents or comments on the ICSID website,[60] and the italaw[61] and Investment Arbitration Reporter[62] databases.

This book consists of seven chapters, including this introductory chapter, which presents the background issues, the justification and scope of the research, and the methodology adopted.

The book is designed to analyse the two concepts separately under successive chapters, and then to combine them in chapter six in order to reveal the nexus between them and to understand the scope of protection and stability provided to the investment.

Since the focus of this book is on international energy investments, it is important first to define what an investment under international investment law is. Therefore, chapter two starts with a look at the investment concept under the ECT and the ICSID Convention, since these are the main documents upon which investment arbitral tribunals rely when deciding whether a transaction should be considered an investment. The approaches taken by the ECT and numerous other

---

[59] F Grisel, 'The Sources of Foreign Investment Law' in Z Douglas, J Pauwelyn and JE Vinuales (eds), *The Foundations of International Investment Law: Bringing Theory into Practice* (Oxford University Press, 2014) 225–33; TW Waelde, 'International Investment Law: An Overview of Key Concepts and Methodology' (2007) 4(4) *Transnational Dispute Management* 1, 4.

[60] https://icsid.worldbank.org/en/Pages/cases/AdvancedSearch.aspx.

[61] www.italaw.com.

[62] www.iareporter.com.

BITs towards the definition of investment are similar, and since it is directly related to energy investments, the ECT has been chosen as reflective of all BITs. Further, the ECT's direct reference to the stability under its objectives will be discussed in chapter six.

This discussion will be followed by an analysis of the main features of international energy investments, which lead to a heightened requirement for stability as a result of the high political risk prevalent in the sector. This political risk, as one of the most significant characteristics of energy investments, will be analysed in chapter two, and will link that chapter to the next one.

Chapter three is devoted to the stability concept. After discussing the stability concept in general, the historical roots of stability provisions, the most common types found in practice and several surrounding discussions, such as validity and internationalisation, will be analysed under this chapter. The main objective of the chapter is to present a holistic understanding of the stability concept in international energy investments. The chapter should enable the reader to understand the mode of operation of stability provisions under different legal sources.

Chapter four is the first step in explaining the legitimate expectations principle. This chapter is required in order to show from where the principle has been adopted by arbitral tribunals. Some authors argue that the legitimate expectations principle does not belong to international investment law and therefore must be abandoned;[63] however, the argument expounded in this chapter will demonstrate otherwise, and will highlight why its application by arbitral tribunals is totally justified. The legitimate expectations principle is applied under the FET standard in almost all cases. It is therefore necessary to touch upon the FET standard briefly and to reveal the relationship between the principle and the FET standard. The chapter starts with an analysis of the FET standard, and then continues on to the legitimate expectations principle as the most important component of it. This chapter will provide an explanation of the roots of this principle, both under domestic laws and international investment law.

Chapter five is an analysis of the current contours of the legitimate expectations principle under investment treaty law, and it provides an in-depth understanding of the principle. As already stated, the scope of the principle is not clearly defined, and requires more elaboration. This chapter will present the sources that could create legitimate expectations for investors. While there are two main views regarding the extent of these sources, the argument put forward in the chapter is that the broader application of the principle should prevail in order to satisfy the stability needs of international energy investors. The analyses in the chapter underpin the following chapter's analytical discussions.

Chapter six combines the two central concepts of this book – stability and legitimate expectations – in order to unveil the interaction between them in

---

[63] Campbell, 'House of Cards'.

providing protection to investments. In this chapter, two possible ways in which these concepts interact are identified, and are conceptualised under the headings 'legitimate expectations from stability' and 'legitimate expectations to stability'. It is demonstrated how already existing stability provisions create legitimate expectations worthy of protection under the treaty frameworks. In addition to this, the chapter also features an examination of the status of legitimate expectations when there is no explicit stability undertaking by host states.

Chapter seven concludes the book with a summary of the key findings, and several recommendations for international energy investors and arbitral tribunals are presented.

2

International Energy Investments, the Risks and the Protection Methods

I. Introduction

The need for the protection of an international energy investment is acute, for several associated reasons. The vulnerability of the investors increases after the largest part of the investment is sunk, which makes the investment open to unilateral interventions by the associated host state. Hence, investors need to protect their investments in various ways.

In order for an energy investor to rely on investment treaty protection in the event of a dispute, it must satisfy the requirements of that particular treaty. Its investment must qualify as such within the scope of that treaty. If an energy investor wishes to rely on the legitimate expectations principle in a dispute, as will be discussed in the following chapters, it must be able to show that it is an investor and that the investment fulfils the criteria set forth under the relevant treaty. Therefore, this chapter examines the criteria through which one can assess what qualifies as an investment under investment treaty law. This chapter will show that the main features of international energy investments mostly satisfy the appropriate requirements to be regarded as investments and therefore should be subject to investment treaty protection.

This chapter will review international energy investments, the risks associated with them – especially political risk – the ways in which these risks can be mitigated and the protection provided against them. The term 'energy investment' will be employed in its broadest sense, in that it will include any type of transaction in the energy sector that could be regarded as an investment under the relevant treaty. Since the main focus of the book is unilateral host state alterations and the treaty protection provided against them under the legitimate expectations principle, the slight distinctions between the various types of energy investments essentially become insignificant. However, the upstream petroleum industry might have a heavier influence on the narrative by virtue of its close historical relevance to the concepts of political risk and stability. Despite this, several renewable energy disputes will also be analysed in the following chapters. It should thus be noted that energy investment does not refer exclusively to the petroleum industry in this book.

The structure of this chapter is as follows: it will start by defining the notion of investment under various international instruments in order to grasp the nature of international investments. It will then discuss different energy investment types and the main characteristics of an international energy investment, and attempt to show whether transactions in this sector can be deemed to be investments with respect to these same international instruments.

Since one of the most significant characteristics of an international energy investment is the risks inherent in the investment project, the study will continue with a discussion of the associated risks, in particular with political risk, which is the most prominent type in this sector. Investors may find several protection instruments in various legal sources, such as domestic legislation, international investment agreements and international investment contracts. Political risk insurance is another method employed by investors to help allocate this risk. This chapter will touch briefly upon those protection methods and thus set the scene for their detailed analysis in the following chapters.

II. Definition of Investment

Even though one might assume that the meaning of the term 'investment' is clear, defining this term actually constitutes one of the most fundamental issues of international investment law. The notion might mean different things to a lawyer, an economist or an entrepreneur.[1] Indeed, the differences between the definitions of the notion of investment may affect the scope of the protection granted to a particular asset or transaction.[2] A transaction considered an investment by an economist may not have the necessary requirements to be considered an investment under a contract or a treaty. Thus, we need to define what 'investment' means in the context of international investment law in order to determine the boundaries of the protection that it acquires.

Salacuse defines an investment as 'the commitment of resources by a physical or legal person to a specific purpose in order to earn a profit or to gain a return'.[3] This is one of the most basic and general definitions of the term, but when it comes to the international legal arena, the meaning and the effects might change as stated above.

There has been an obvious evolution of the definition of investment under international law over time.[4] Initially, it was only restricted to foreign direct

---

[1] JW Salacuse, *The Three Laws of International Investment: National, Contractual, and International Frameworks for Foreign Capital* (Oxford University Press, 2013) 3.
[2] ibid.
[3] JW Salacuse, *The Law of Investment Treaties* (Oxford University Press, 2015) 26.
[4] For a detailed historical perspective, see ME Hiscock, 'The Emerging Legal Concept of Investment' (2009) 27(3) *Penn State International Law Review* 765.

investments with regard to the protection of their physical properties and the tangible assets of the foreigner.[5] Gradually, the meaning of the term expanded to cover intangible assets (mainly associated with contractual rights), shares in companies, intellectual property rights and administrative rights (eg environmental licences, planning permission).[6]

Sornarajah defines a foreign investment as 'the transfer of tangible or intangible assets from one country to another for the purpose of their use in that country to generate' wealth under the total or partial control of the owner of the assets'. In general, definitions of foreign investment include three basic elements: a capital-exporting country, a foreign investor and a capital-importing country.[8]

Since this study is interested in international energy investments, the concept of investment will be scrutinised under the international investment law regime with appropriate definitions given accordingly. The different international organisations and different bilateral or multilateral treaties (BITs or MITs) and conventions have various definitions of investment. Some of these will be reviewed in the following sections.

The Energy Charter Treaty (ECT) is of particular significance as the approach it takes is similar to those of the majority of BITs and is directly relevant to energy investments. Therefore, the ECT can be consulted as reflecting the approach taken by BITs on the definition of investment in general, and as an energy-specific treaty in particular.

A. Investment under the Energy Charter Treaty

The ECT, as one of the most important multilateral treaties in terms of promoting and protecting investments, provides a broad definition of the term 'investment'. According to the first paragraph of Article 1(6):

> 'Investment' means every kind of asset, owned or controlled directly or indirectly by an Investor and includes:
>
> (a) tangible and intangible, and movable and immovable, property, and any property rights such as leases, mortgages, liens, and pledges;
> (b) a company or business enterprise, or shares, stock, or other forms of equity participation in a company or business enterprise, and bonds and other debt of a company or business enterprise;
> (c) claims to money and claims to performance pursuant to contract having an economic value and associated with an Investment;
> (d) Intellectual Property;

---

[5] M Sornarajah, *The International Law on Foreign Investment* (Cambridge University Press, 2010) 11.
[6] ibid 11–16.
[7] ibid 8.
[8] F Alkahtani, 'Legal Protection of Foreign Direct Investment in Saudi Arabia' (PhD Thesis, Newcastle University, 2010), 5.

(e)   Returns;
(f)   any right conferred by law or contract or by virtue of any licences and permits
      granted pursuant to law to undertake any Economic Activity in the Energy
      Sector ...[9]

This is a typical broad, asset-based definition of investment that defines the notion simply as every kind of asset; it further provides non-exhaustive examples of the kinds of assets covered.[10] According to the ECT, this investment must be associated with an economic activity in the energy sector. An economic activity can be related to exploration, extraction, refining, production, storage, land transport, transmission, distribution, trade, marketing or sale of energy materials and products according to Article 1(5). The approach that the ECT adopts in defining an investment is similar to that found in the majority of BITs, which extends the coverage to every kind of asset and hence gives the definition a rather broad scope.[11]

The second paragraph of Article 1(6) indicates that when a change occurs in the form of an investment, that does not affect its protection as an investment.[12] Even if changes to the legal, political or economic conditions of a host state alter the original form of investment, the assets will nevertheless sustain the required protection under the Treaty in their initial forms as investments.[13]

The *Petrobart v Kyrgyzstan* Tribunal assessed an ECT-based claim and discussed whether an investment existed in that case.[14] Since the ECT's definition of investment is relatively broad, it does not produce the kind of ambiguity that the International Centre for Settlement of Investment Disputes (ICSID) Convention does. The Tribunal decided that the contract for the sale of the gas condensate was an investment pursuant to Article 1(6)(f) of the ECT, which states that: 'any right conferred by law or contract or by virtue of any licences and permits granted pursuant to law to undertake any Economic Activity in the Energy Sector'.[15] *Plama v Bulgaria* was another ECT-based case in which the broad nature of the meaning of investment was underlined by stating that the list in Article 1(6) includes 'a broad, non-exhaustive list of different kinds of assets encompassing virtually any right, property or interest in money or money's worth'.[16]

---

[9] Energy Charter Treaty, Art 1(6).

[10] M Malik, 'Definition of Investment in International Investment Agreements' (International Institute for Sustainable Development, 2009) www.iisd.org/publications/definition-investment-international-investment-agreements.

[11] E Gaillard, 'Investments and Investors Covered by the Energy Charter Treaty' in C Ribeiro (ed), *Investment Arbitration and the Energy Charter Treaty* (JurisNet, 2006) 59; A van Aaken, 'Perils of Success? The Case of International Investment Protection' (2008) 9(1) *European Business Organization Law Review* 1, 6; R Dolzer and C Schreuer, *Principles of International Investment Law* (Oxford University Press, 2012) 63.

[12] Energy Charter Treaty, Art 1(6).

[13] Gaillard, 'Investments and Investors', 63.

[14] *Petrobart Limited v The Kyrgyz Republic*, Award, SCC Case No 126/2003, 29 March 2005.

[15] ibid para 72.

[16] *Plama Consortium Limited v Republic of Bulgaria*, Decision on Jurisdiction, ICSID Case No ARB/03/24, 8 February 2005, para 125.

B. Investment under the ICSID Convention

The ICSID was established by the World Bank in 1966 through the ICSID Convention. According to Article 1(2) of the ICSID Convention, the aim of the Centre is 'to provide facilities for conciliation and arbitration of investment disputes between Contracting States and nationals of other Contracting States in accordance with the provisions of this Convention'.[17]

Although the sole focus of the ICSID Convention is investment disputes, as mentioned in Article 25,[18] it does not itself provide a definition of the term 'investment'.[19] The issue of whether to propose a definition within the Convention or otherwise was comprehensively discussed during the drafting period.[20] The drafters decided not to include a strict definition by virtue of the absence of a consensus on the definition of the notion of investment between the representatives, as well as the fact that not proposing a definition might be of help when attempting to accommodate new forms of investments in the future.[21]

Since the respondent states challenged the jurisdiction of ICSID Tribunals based on the argument that the claimant (investor) did not have a valid 'investment' under the ICSID Convention, Tribunals started to interpret this notion in order to decide whether they had a jurisdiction in any given dispute.[22] This phase has not yet been concluded, and the discussion over the definition of investment still continues before both ICSID Tribunals and in the literature.[23] As one can see from their more recent awards,[24] the Tribunals still appraise the notion of

[17] International Centre for the Settlement of Investment Disputes Convention, Art 1(2), 14 October 1966 (hereinafter ICSID Convention).

[18] ICSID Convention, Art 25(1): 'The jurisdiction of the Centre shall extend to any legal dispute arising directly out of an investment, between a Contracting State (or any constituent subdivision or agency of a Contracting State designated to the Centre by that State) and a national of another Contracting State ...'

[19] Y Caliskan, 'ICSID Jurisdiction: Whose Dictionary Will Be Used for the Definition of "Investment" and the "Scope of Consent"' in C Sural and E Omeroglu (eds), *Foreign Investment Law* (Seckin, 2016) 102.

[20] WB Hamida, 'Two Nebulous ICSID Features: The Notion of Investment and the Scope of Annulment Control: Ad Hoc Committee's Decision in Patrick Mitchell v Democratic Republic of Congo' (2007) 24(3) *Journal of International Arbitration* 287, 288.

[21] ibid 289; F Yala, 'The Notion of 'Investment' in ICSID Case Law: a Drifting Jurisdictional Requirement? Some "Un-Conventional" Thoughts on Salini, SGS & Mihaly' (2004) 1(4) *Transnational Dispute Management* 1, 1; N Rubins, 'The Notion of "Investment" in International Investment Arbitration' in N Horn (ed), *Arbitrating Foreign Investment Disputes: Procedural and Substantive Legal Aspects* (Kluwer Law International, 2004) 287.

[22] B Legum and C Mouawad, 'The Meaning of "Investment" in the ICSID Convention' in PHF Bekker, R Dolzer and M Waibel (eds), *Making Transnational Law Work in the Global Economy: Essays in Honour of Detlev Vagts* (Cambridge University Press, 2010) 329.

[23] Caliskan, 'ICSID Jurisdiction', 103.

[24] *Vestey Group Ltd v Bolivarian Republic of Venezuela*, Award, ICSID Case No ARB/06/4, 15 April 2016; *İçkale İnşaat Limited Şirketi v Turkmenistan*, Award, ICSID Case No ARB/10/24, 8 March 2016; *Tenaris SA and Talta – Trading E Marketing Sociedade Unipessoal Lda v Bolivarian Republic of Venezuela*, Award, ICSID Case No ARB/11/26, 29 January 2016; *Renée Rose Levy and Gremcitel SA v Republic of Peru*, Award, ICSID Case No ARB/11/17, 9 January 2015; *Mr Hassan Awdi, Enterprise Business Consultants, Inc. and Alfa El Corporation v Romania*, Award, ICSID Case No ARB/10/13, 2 March 2015.

investment in order to determine their jurisdictions. Ongoing debates on invest-
ment do not for the most part originate from the definitions provided in BITs or
MITs, but rather arise as a result of the lack of any definition of this term in the
ICSID Convention.[25]

This attempt by ICSID Tribunals to define 'investment' has resulted in two
significant approaches, namely *the subjective theory* and *the objective theory*.[26]

(i) The Subjective Theory

This theory is also referred to as the 'consensual approach'[27] or the 'party-defined
approach',[28] which suggests that the notion of investment should be defined by
the consent of the parties to ICSID arbitration.[29] The parties determine whether
to characterise a transaction as an investment within the purposes expressed in
Article 25.[30] According to this view, whereas the ICSID Convention does not
provide a definition of investment, this gap might be filled according to the parties'
intentions.[31] This approach finds its roots in one of the passages of a much-cited
report by the Executive Directors on the ICSID Convention, which states:

> No attempt was made to define the term 'investment' given the essential requirement
> of consent by the parties, and the mechanism through which Contracting Parties can
> make known in advance, if they so desire, the classes of disputes which they would or
> would not consider submitting to the Centre (Article 25(4)).[32]

An example of this view was presented by the *CMS v Argentine* Annulment
Committee as: 'Article 25 of the ICSID Convention did not attempt to define
"investment". Instead this task was left largely to the terms of bilateral investment
treaties or other instruments on which jurisdiction is based.'[33] The *Azurix Corp
v Argentine* Tribunal held the same view in its decision on jurisdiction, finding

---

[25] Dolzer and Schreuer, *Principles*, 65.

[26] This characterisation is borrowed from Hamida, 'Two Nebulous ICSID Features'; For another
article using the same characterisation, see M Sattorova, 'Defining Investment under the ICSID
Convention and BITs: Of Ordinary Meaning, Telos, and Beyond' (2012) 2(2) *Asian Journal of Inter-
national Law* 267. For different characterisations, see E Gaillard, 'Identify or Define? Reflections on
the Evolution of the Concept of Investment in ICSID Practice' in C Binder et al (eds), *International
Investment Law for the 21st Century: Essays in Honour of Christoph Schreuer* (Oxford University
Press, 2009); B Demirkol, 'The Notion of "Investment" in International Investment Law' (2015) 1(1)
Turkish Commercial Law Review 41; M Dekastros, 'Portfolio Investment: Reconceptualising the Notion
of Investment under the ICSID Convention' (2013) 14(2) *Journal of World Investment & Trade* 286;
P Vargiu, 'Beyond Hallmarks and Formal Requirements: A Jurisprudence Constante on the Notion of
Investment in the ICSID Convention' (2009) 10(5) *Journal of World Investment & Trade* 753.

[27] Demirkol, 'The Notion of Investment', 43; Dekastros, 'Portfolio Investment', 294.

[28] Dolzer and Schreuer, *Principles*, 74.

[29] Hamida, 'Two Nebulous ICSID Features', 289; Rubins, 'The Notion of Investment', 291.

[30] D Krishan, 'A Notion of ICSID Investment' (2009) 6(1) *Transnational Dispute Management* 1, 5.

[31] Demirkol, 'The Notion of Investment', 43.

[32] Report of the Executive Directors on the Convention on the Settlement of Investment Disputes
between States and Nationals of Other States, 18 March 1965, para 27.

[33] *CMS Gas Transmission Company v Argentine Republic*, Decision of the ad hoc Committee on the
Application for Annulment of the Argentine Republic, ICSID Case No ARB/01/8, 25 September 2007,
para 71.

that a concession contract qualifies as an investment under the concerned BIT; further, it held that since the concession agreement itself refers repeatedly to investments, this renders the company in question an investment.[34]

Under this theory, the terms of the instrument (treaty, contract, etc) that consented to ICSID jurisdiction will be the determining factors when scrutinising whether an investment is existent within the meaning of Article 25(1) of the ICSID Convention.[35] The notion of investment does not have an autonomous, self-standing meaning here; rather, it is dependent on an instrument that bears the consent of the parties.[36] So, the meaning and scope of this notion may vary from case to case and therefore the arbitrators must determine whether the relevant definition of investment captures the issue at hand as well.[37]

Although not strictly the case, the *Biwater v Tanzania* Tribunal also obliquely supports this view by stating that:

> If very substantial numbers of BITs across the world express the definition of 'investment' more broadly than the Salini Test, and if this constitutes any type of international consensus, it is difficult to see why the ICSID Convention ought to be read more narrowly.[38]

The Tribunal rejected the respondent's argument that an autonomous and objective definition of investment must be applied to determine whether an investment actually exists. The Tribunal concluded that the definition should be more flexible and pragmatic by considering the instrument that included the consent to ICSID jurisdiction in conjunction with the objective criteria.[39]

The majority of the ad hoc committee of the *Malaysian Historical Salvors v Malaysia* case also followed the same line of reasoning offered by the *Biwater v Tanzania* Tribunal and took the definition of investment into account in the applicable BIT.[40] It stated that:

> While this Committee's majority has every respect for the authors of the *Salini v Morocco* Award and those that have followed it, such as the Award in *Joy Mining v Egypt*, and for commentators who have adopted a like stance – and, it need hardly add, for its distinguished co-arbitrator who attaches an acute Dissent to this Decision – it gives precedence to awards and analyses that are consistent with its approach, which it finds consonant with the intentions of the Parties to the ICSID Convention.[41]

---

[34] *Azurix Corp v The Argentine Republic*, Decision on Jurisdiction, ICSID Case No ARB/01/12, 8 December 2003, para 62.

[35] Legum and Mouawad, 'The Meaning of Investment', 331.

[36] ibid.

[37] Rubins, 'The Notion of Investment', 291.

[38] *Biwater Gauff (Tanzania) Ltd v United Republic of Tanzania*, Award, ICSID Case No ARB/05/22, 24 July 2008, para 314.

[39] ibid para 316.

[40] *Malaysian Historical Salvors SDN BHD v The Government of Malaysia*, Decision on the Application for Annulment, ICSID Case No ARB/05/10, 16 April 2009, paras 58–61.

[41] ibid para 78.

This approach has been criticised by some authors for providing extended power to instruments other than the ICSID Convention in order to define what may qualify as an investment. Yala argues:

> Whatever the case may be, if the liberal trend promoting an extension of ICSID jurisdiction to any kind of economic operation, even those without any connection to 'authentic' investment, continues to grow, ICSID may well become just another arbitration institution, competing with a range of others (ICC, LCIA, AISCC, etc). In this case, the important renouncements of sovereignty that Contracting States accepted when signing the Washington Convention (applicability of international law – article 42, recourse against awards limited to an ad hoc committee, etc) could be jeopardized, and lose their *raison d'être*.[42]

Indeed, it was further argued by Demirkol that if the definition of investment is left purely to the parties' consensus, 'investment' might lose its role as a jurisdictional condition under Article 25(1) of the ICSID Convention altogether.[43]

However, these objections are not related to the practical implications or harms inherent to this approach, which are mostly, though somewhat ambiguously, associated with the ICSID Convention's future. It is not clear why some states should not be able to agree on the definition of investment and consider certain types of assets to constitute investments for the purposes of ICSID jurisdiction.[44] Parties' consent that does not impair the express wording or intent of the Convention should be recognised by the tribunals.[45]

A strong defence of this approach is presented by Mortenson.[46] In his article, he proposes three arguments supporting the approach of individual states deciding the meaning of investment rather than arbitral tribunals.[47] First, he argues that accepting the interpretations of the states in this issue provides them with a policy flexibility with which they can offer ICSID protection to economic assets or transactions that fall short of satisfying the conditions of the objective theory, and further gives them the opportunity to tailor their investment incentive packages according to changing circumstances.[48]

Secondly, he argues that the states have superior expertise or political legitimacy in designating the margins of a legal norm than arbitral tribunals.[49] He bases this argument on the ICSID Convention's underlying purpose, namely that

---

[42] Yala, 'The Notion of Investment', 18–19. The same concerns were raised by the tribunal in *Joy Mining Machinery Limited v Arab Republic of Egypt*, Award on Jurisdiction, ICSID Case No ARB/03/11, 6 August 2004, para 58.

[43] Demirkol, 'The Notion of Investment', 44.

[44] Legum and Mouawad, 'The Meaning of Investment', 353.

[45] Krishan, 'ICSID Investment', 11.

[46] JD Mortenson, 'The Meaning of "Investment": ICSID's Travaux and the Domain of International Investment Law' (2010) 51(1) *Harvard International Law Journal* 257.

[47] ibid 301.

[48] ibid 302. This view is also supported by S Manciaux, 'The Notion of Investment: New Controversies' (2008) 9(6) *Journal of World Investment & Trade* 443, 447.

[49] Mortenson, 'The Meaning of Investment', 304.

of promoting the economic development of host states by increasing the flow of foreign investment, and concludes that states have better competence than the arbitral tribunals to assess the relationship between an economic activity and their economic developments.[50]

Lastly, deferring to a state-based interpretation of investment protects vulnerable interests by hindering states' ability to escape from or otherwise evade their commitments (in treaties or other legal instruments) by relying on the narrower interpretation of investment in litigation.[51] Accordingly, the tribunals treat states as the competent parties who can make binding commitments in accordance with their own interpretations while determining whether a transaction or asset constitutes an investment.[52]

Of course, this consensual approach does not grant the parties unlimited freedom to accept anything that they may wish to as an investment. The drafting history of the Convention clearly demonstrates that ordinary commercial transactions cannot be regarded as investments, any contrasting consensus between the parties notwithstanding.[53] In the hypothetical case where an investment treaty defines the associated investment as an asset and lists a metro ticket as an example of such, the ICSID Tribunal would have to decline jurisdiction over the case due to the conflict in the definitions between the treaty and the ICSID Convention.[54] The tribunals should have the screening role in this regard, and could eliminate anything expressly inconsistent with the Convention, even in the face of consent between the parties.[55]

(ii) The Objective Theory

This theory suggests that there is an autonomous and objective definition of investment for the purposes of Article 25(1) of the ICSID Convention,[56] which is also commonly referred to as the 'self-contained approach'.[57] Some tribunals that follow this theory have adopted a meaning of the term 'investment' that is narrower than the ones stipulated in many BITs.[58]

According to this theory, the term has a self-standing meaning that sets the outer limits of Article 25(1), and any transaction that falls out of the scope of this

---

[50] ibid 305.
[51] ibid 306.
[52] ibid.
[53] C Schreuer et al, *The ICSID Convention: A Commentary* (Cambridge University Press, 2009) 117.
[54] Z Douglas, *The International Law of Investment Claims* (Cambridge University Press, 2009) 165.
[55] Mortenson, 'The Meaning of Investment', 317.
[56] Demirkol, 'The Notion of Investment', 45; Y Caliskan, 'Dispute Settlement in International Investment Law' in Y Aksar (ed), *International Economic Law through Dispute Settlement Mechanisms* (Martinus Nijhoff Publishers, 2011) 138; Krishan, 'ICSID Investment' 5; Hamida, 'Two Nebulous ICSID Features' 290.
[57] Dolzer and Schreuer, *Principles*, 74.
[58] KJ Vandevelde, *Bilateral Investment Treaties: History, Policy, and Interpretation* (Oxford University Press, 2010) 134.

definition should not be considered an investment within the context of ICSID jurisdiction, regardless of the parties' agreements or intentions.[59] It is argued that defining the notion of investment is necessary in order to avert the incoherence inherent to ICSID jurisdiction and thus to provide legal security for foreign investors and capital-importing states.[60]

This approach was first introduced by Schreuer as 'characteristics of investment'.[61] Schreuer's characterisation was followed by the *Fedax v Venezuela* Tribunal, which was the first case before the ICSID Tribunals in which their jurisdiction was objected to, as based on the argument that the transaction in question did not bear the requirements of an investment.[62] However, the most notable case in this regard was *Salini v Morocco*, in which the Tribunal presented a test to identify an investment.[63]

In identifying the features of an investment, Schreuer proposes five elements: (1) a certain *duration*; (2) a certain regularity of *profit or return*; (3) the assumption of *risk*; (4) a substantial *commitment*; (5) and significance for the host state's *development*.[64] He also adds that these are not jurisdictional requirements, but are rather purely the typical characteristics of investments under the ICSID Convention.[65] Even if Schreuer states that these are not constitutive elements, some ICSID Tribunals and scholars have considered them otherwise. However, the absence of any of these elements does not in itself constitute evidence as to the lack of qualification as an investment; on the contrary, these elements are generally intertwined and, as such, must be analysed together to determine whether a transaction or asset constitutes an investment.[66]

As mentioned above, the *Salini* Tribunal's approach became a landmark in this debate and was followed by many other tribunals. This approach is generally referred to as the 'Salini Test'. The *Salini* Tribunal identified four elements indicative of an investment, and stated them as follows:

> The doctrine generally considers that investment infers: contributions, a certain duration of performance of the contract and a participation in the risks of the transaction (cf. Commentary by E. Gaillard, cited above, p. 292). In reading the Convention's

---

[59] Krishan, 'ICSID Investment', 6.

[60] Manciaux, 'The Notion of Investment', 448.

[61] C Schreuer, 'Commentary on the ICSID Convention' (1996) 11(2) *ICSID Review – Foreign Investment Law Journal* 318, 371.

[62] *Fedax NV v The Republic of Venezuela*, Decision of the Tribunal on Objections to Jurisdiction, ICSID Case No ARB/96/3, 11 July 1997.

[63] *Salini Costruttori SpA and Italstrade SpA v Kingdom of Morocco*, Decision on Jurisdiction, ICSID Case No ARB/00/4, 23 July 2001.

[64] Schreuer, 'Commentary', 372. These characteristics will not be examined in depth in this study. For a detailed discussion, see Yala, 'The Notion of Investment'; Hamida, 'Two Nebulous ICSID Features'; A Grabowski, 'The Definition of Investment under the ICSID Convention: A Defense of Salini' (2014) 15(1) *Chicago Journal of International Law* 287; Gaillard, 'Identify or Define?'; Krishan, 'ICSID Investment'.

[65] Schreuer, 'Commentary', 373; Schreuer et al, *A Commentary*, 128.

[66] M Waibel, 'Opening Pandora's Box: Sovereign Bonds in International Arbitration' (2007) 101(4) *The American Journal of International Law* 711, 723.

preamble, one may add the contribution to the economic development of the host State of the investment as an additional condition.[67]

So, the Salini Test is composed of four prongs: contribution (commitment), duration, risk and contribution to the economic development of the host state.

With this, the *Salini* Tribunal rendered Schreuer's descriptive characteristics into legally binding conditions and built its decision accordingly.[68] There is no precedence in ICSID jurisdiction, yet subsequent tribunals took the Salini Test into account before rendering their own decisions.[69] While some of them strictly applied the same test,[70] others broadened or narrowed its scope, adding new features or excluding certain existent ones.[71]

For instance, the *Phoenix v Czech Republic* Tribunal added two more features – legality and good faith (bona fide) – to the Salini Test, and stated:

> To summarize all the requirements for an investment to benefit from the international protection of ICSID, the Tribunal considers that the following six elements have to be taken into account:
>
> 1. a contribution in money or other assets;
> 2. a certain duration;
> 3. an element of risk;
> 4. an operation made in order to develop an economic activity in the host State;
> 5. assets invested in accordance with the laws of the host State;
> 6. assets invested bona fide.[72]

In contrast, the *Saba Fakes v Turkey* Tribunal removed the necessity of any contribution to the host state's economic development and stated that only the first three criteria (contribution, duration, risk) are necessary and sufficient to define an investment.[73] The *Quiborax v Bolivia* Tribunal also rejected the fourth prong on

---

[67] *Salini v Morocco*, Decision on Jurisdiction, para 52.

[68] Gaillard, 'Identify or Define?', 404.

[69] M Hwang and J Fong Lee Cheng, 'Definition of "Investment" – A Voice from the Eye of the Storm' (2011) 1(1) *Asian Journal of International Law* 99, 101.

[70] See, eg *Jan de Nul NV and Dredging International NV v Arab Republic of Egypt*, Decision on Jurisdiction, ICSID Case No ARB/04/13, 16 June 2006; *Bayindir Insaat Turizm Ticaret Ve Sanayi AS v Islamic Republic of Pakistan*, Decision on Jurisdiction, ICSID Case No ARB/03/29, 14 November 2005; *Malaysian Historical Salvors SDN BHD v The Government of Malaysia*, Award on Jurisdiction, ICSID Case No ARB/05/10, 17 May 2007; *Saipem SpA v The People's Republic of Bangladesh*, Decision on Jurisdiction and Recommendation on Provisional Matters, ICSID Case No ARB/05/07, 21 March 2007; *Mamidoil Jetoil Greek Petroleum Products Societe SA v Republic of Albania*, Award, ICSID Case No ARB/11/24, 30 March 2015.

[71] See, eg *LESI SpA and Astaldi SpA v Republic of Algeria*, Decision on Jurisdiction, ICSID Case No ARB/05/3, 12 July 2006 cited in Hamida, 'Two Nebulous ICSID Features', 291; *Consortium RFCC v Kingdom of Morocco*, Decision on Jurisdiction, ICSID Case No ARB/00/6, 16 July 2001 cited in ibid; *Joy Mining v Egypt; Nova Scotia Power Incorporated v Bolivarian Republic of Venezuela*, Excerpts of the Award, ICSID Case No ARB (AF)/11/1, 30 April 2014.

[72] *Phoenix Action, Ltd v The Czech Republic*, Award, ICSID Case No ARB/06/5, 15 April 2009, para 114.

[73] *Saba Fakes v Republic of Turkey*, Award, ICSID Case No ARB/07/20, 14 July 2010, para 110.

the basis that economic development of the host state is merely a consequence of an investment, not a constitutive element of it.[74]

The *Nova Scotia v Bolivia* Tribunal followed a modified version of the Salini Test, expressly rejecting the subjective approach by stating:

> The Tribunal is of the view that in examining whether or not an investment is present, the definition of 'investment' in the BIT cannot be considered self-sufficient ... In ascertaining the ordinary meaning of 'investment', the Tribunal must do more than simply look to the list of examples offered in Article I(f) of the BIT.[75]

The Tribunal opted to follow the objective theory by arguing that the term 'investment' bears an ordinary meaning with inherent features, and that it must take these features into account when deciding whether an investment actually exists.[76] With a slight divergence from the Salini Test, the *Nova Scotia v Bolivia* Tribunal considered that an investment requires contribution, duration and risk as its defining features.[77]

Although there are extensive discussions and significant differences in both the literature and within arbitral jurisprudence, such as how to define conclusive features of an investment, whether to include contribution to the economic development of the host state or good faith as essential features or how to assess the contribution, there is nevertheless consensus among these same parties as to the necessity of an objective definition of investment.

The Salini Test and the objective theory have been criticised for representing an outdated view of investment and for not taking different forms of investment other than direct investment into account.[78] Also, this approach might create problems where an asset is considered an investment under a treaty which provides only for ICSID arbitration as the dispute settlement forum, but does not fulfil the criteria that the objective theory suggests.[79] In such a case, an investor would have a valid investment under the subject treaty, but would lack a forum before which it can bring a claim in the event of a breach.[80]

Another criticism of this approach is that by deducing a different definition of investment from the ICSID Convention than the BITs that the state parties agreed upon, some commentators seem to argue that BITs and the ICSID Convention have separate or opposing objectives.[81] However, the author argues that these two instruments pursue the same objective, namely that of protecting investments, and thus should not be interpreted as though they have contradictory aims.[82]

---

[74] *Quiborax SA, Non Metallic Minerals SA, and Allan Fosk Kaplun v Plurinational State of Bolivia*, Decision on Jurisdiction, ICSID Case No ARB/06/2, 27 September 2012, para 222.
[75] *Nova Scotia v Bolivia*, Award, para 77.
[76] ibid para 81.
[77] ibid para 84.
[78] Krishan, 'ICSID Investment', 12.
[79] Legum and Mouawad, 'The Meaning of Investment', 332.
[80] ibid.
[81] Sattorova, 'Defining Investment', 272.
[82] ibid.

In addition to these, the requirement set by the economic development criterion has been challenged on the basis that an investment does not have to carry some guarantee of success in order to receive treaty protection.[83] It is not always possible to measure the scope of the economic development or, indeed, its success.[84]

In *Biwater v Tanzania*, the Tribunal criticised the Salini Test by stating:

> Further, the Salini Test itself is problematic if, as some tribunals have found, the 'typical characteristics' of an investment as identified in that decision are elevated into a fixed and inflexible test, and if transactions are to be presumed excluded from the ICSID Convention unless each of the five criteria are satisfied. This risks the arbitrary exclusion of certain types of transaction from the scope of the Convention. It also leads to a definition that may contradict individual agreements (as here), as well as a developing consensus in parts of the world as to the meaning of 'investment' (as expressed, eg in bilateral investment treaties) …[85]

(iii) Discussion

It is obvious that retaining the objective theory offers a more predictable legal environment to the parties and thus enhances the associated legal security because this theory openly specifies the criteria which constitute an investment. If this test continues to be applied by the tribunals, the parties should be able to predict the likely outcome of a tribunal. Having a clear and uniform approach would prevent inconsistent interpretations and provide a common framework regarding the investment concept.[86]

On the other hand, investment is not a stable phenomenon. Rather, it is a fluid concept that cannot be fixed about a specific definition.[87] Were a strict definition and the same requirements to be applied in every case, this would clearly lack the flexibility required to meet the demands of today's international economic order. This is why subjective theory might work better under some circumstances. The parties should be regarded as competent to judge whether something constitutes an investment. As already mentioned, there will be some thresholds that cannot be ignored, and the tribunals must thus play a supervisory role to prevent anything expressly absurd from being deemed an investment.[88]

To build a more comprehensive ICSID jurisdiction, it is necessary to take both approaches into consideration when deciding whether an investment exists.[89] Instead of applying the same objective criteria to every single case, tribunals should adopt a holistic approach to each case and attempt to understand the inherent meaning of investment in any particular dispute; resorting to a fixed,

---

[83] Vandevelde, *Bilateral Investment Treaties*, 134.
[84] ibid.
[85] *Biwater Gauff v Tanzania*, Award, para 314.
[86] Hwang and Fong Lee Cheng, 'Definition of Investment', 113.
[87] Krishan, 'ICSID Investment', 9.
[88] Mortenson, 'The Meaning of Investment', 318.
[89] Caliskan, 'ICSID Jurisdiction', 106.

trict definition of the notion of investment might otherwise impair the ICSID Convention's intent in not providing a definition for this term. The best approach to dealing with this issue would be to take the flexible combinations of the two theories into account and to not apply the same strict criteria in every case.[90]

III. International Energy Investments: What is Special about them?

A. Energy Investment Types

When one looks at reports and studies about the energy investments conducted by certain international organisations, the first thing one is struck by is the width of the energy sector. It is one of the biggest industries – if not the biggest – in the world and its nature brings along a need for continuing investments. What should be understood when one refers to 'energy investments' therefore includes a wide spectrum of subjects. The World Energy Investment Report by the International Energy Agency categorises the energy investment sectors as: upstream oil and gas; mid/downstream oil and gas; coal supply; renewable power; fossil fuel power; nuclear power; electricity networks; efficiency; and renewable for transport/heat.[91] The ECT also identifies the activities that might be undertaken within these sectors and would be considered as investment and that is a comprehensive approach as well.[92]

The majority of scholarly publications related to international energy investments or energy investment arbitration mainly deal with investments connected to oil, gas and renewable energy. This is understandable because the energy-related cases that go before arbitral tribunals are predominantly from these subsectors. However, what should be borne in mind is that a change in the international energy investment arena also transforms the dispute types, and this is eventually reflected in the literature.

If one looks at Waelde's article entitled 'International Energy Investment' from 1996,[93] it can be seen that he refers only to oil and gas investments and the legal issues surrounding these investments. However, today, one can hardly find a publication which deals with international energy investment that does not mention renewable energy investments. As will be discussed later in this book, there are many recently concluded and still ongoing renewable energy investment cases before several arbitral institutions.

---

[90] Dolzer and Schreuer, *Principles*, 76.
[91] IEA, 'World Energy Investment 2020' (International Energy Agency, 2020) www.iea.org/reports/world-energy-investment-2020.
[92] This was discussed in s IIA above.
[93] TW Waelde, 'International Energy Investment' (1996) 17 *Energy Law Journal* 191.

It is therefore important to be aware of this wide range of energy-related subsectors and the increasing number of international investments happening in them. We might be talking about another type of energy investment two decades from now. However, as discussed in the following sections and chapters, this change in energy investment types does not necessarily alter the content or the crux of the investment law that applies to the disputes emerging from them. Even though the focal point of arguments and the protection standards employed in the dispute resolution phase may shift from one place to another, they still remain within the boundaries of international investment law.

B. Main Characteristics

Although there have been several attempts to define the terms 'energy' and 'energy investment' within the context of law, these mostly fall short due to the complexity inherent to the term 'energy' itself.[94] While 'energy law' is considered an academic discipline in its own right by some scholars,[95] international energy investment law is actually not strictly distinct from general international investment rules. There is a common history between the international energy sector and international investment law in many ways.[96] According to Schill, energy investment law is *pars pro toto* of foreign investment law and the findings pertaining to this sector can also be applied to general foreign investment law.[97] Thus, it can be stated that energy investment law is an integral part of international investment law, although it also possesses some further specificities.[98]

As such, international energy investments are not substantially different from other types of international investments in general. In fact, it is possible to refer to these investments as international investments in the energy sector.[99] The general rules and standards on investment protection are also applicable to those international investments in the energy sector.[100]

---

[94] O Varis, 'Redefining Energy in the Post-Pandemic Era' (2020) 1(2) *Global Energy Law and Sustainability* 164.

[95] K Talus and RJ Heffron, 'What is "International Energy Law" or "Energy Law"?' (2018) 16(3) *Oil, Gas & Energy Law* 1; RJ Heffron et al, 'A Review of Energy Law Education in the UK' (2016) 9(5) *Journal of World Energy Law & Business* 346; A Bradbrook, 'Energy Law as an Academic Discipline' (1996) 14(2) *Journal of Energy and Natural Resources Law* 193.

[96] PM Blyschak, 'Arbitrating Overseas Oil and Gas Disputes: Breaches of Contract versus Breaches of Treaty' (2010) 27(6) *Journal of International Arbitration* 579, 585.

[97] SW Schill, 'Foreign Investment in the Energy Sector: Lessons for International Investment Law' in E de Brabandere and T Gazzini (eds), *Foreign Investment in the Energy Sector: Balancing Private and Public Interests* (Brill Nijhoff, 2014) 260.

[98] ibid 261.

[99] O Varis, 'International Energy Investments: Tracking the Legal Concept' (2014) 2(1) *Groningen Journal of International Law* 81, 90.

[100] K Talus, 'Internationalization of Energy Law' in K Talus (ed), *Research Handbook on International Energy Law* (Edward Elgar Publishing, 2014) 5.

As of 2020, 24 per cent of all cases registered under the ICSID Convention pertained to the oil, gas and mining sectors, with an additional 17 per cent pertaining to electric power and other energy sector branches.[101] Even this statistic only shows the significant position of international energy investments within the scope of international investment. It is also possible to see from these cases how diverse the energy industry is.

While international energy investments have a number of characteristics that are similar to other types of investment, they also have some distinctive characteristics. Erkan claimed that 'energy investments are themselves unique transactions between investors and host states'.[102]

Investments in the energy sector are generally on a large scale, of long duration, capital-intensive and requiring high technology.[103] If we consider the petroleum industry, the exploration phase of these investments alone may take up to 10 years to complete and cost billions of dollars even before determining whether the exploration is successful.[104] The long duration of this type of investment brings a change in operating conditions and in the political environment of the host state.[105] These investments also bear considerable risks (geological, commercial and political),[106] and can easily be affected – extensively – by political change.[107] The energy resources are also deemed to be strategically important,[108] and this fact alone can increase the chances of such investments being interfered with by the host state.

Some of the above-mentioned risks are common to all types of international investments, but some are particularly relevant to the energy industry.[109] In particular, this strategic feature of an investment is more apparent in the energy sector and thus makes investments in this area both distinctive and vulnerable. The political risk that an energy investment may face is also increased by the long duration of the investment.[110]

---

[101] ICSID, 'The ICSID Caseload – Statistics' (2020) 2020-2 https://icsid.worldbank.org/sites/default/files/publications/The%20ICSID%20Caseload%20Statistics%20%282020-2%20Edition%29%20ENG.pdf.

[102] M Erkan, *International Energy Investment Law: Stability through Contractual Clauses* (Kluwer Law International, 2011) 27.

[103] UNCTAD, 'World Investment Report: Transnational Corporations, Extractive Industries and Development' (United Nations, 2007) 91; PD Cameron, *International Energy Investment Law: The Pursuit of Stability* (Oxford University Press, 2010) 24; PD Cameron and A Kolo, 'What Is Energy Investment Law and Why Does It Matter?' (2012) EI Source Book Working Paper.

[104] UNCTAD, 'World Investment Report 2007', 92; JV de Macedo, 'From Tradition to Modernity: Not Necessarily an Evolution – The Case of Stabilisation and Renegotiation Clauses' (2011) 9(1) *Oil, Gas & Energy Law* 1, 1.

[105] A Al Faruque, 'The Rationale and Instrumentalities for Stability in Long-Term State Contracts' (2006) 7(1) *Journal of World Investment & Trade* 85, 88.

[106] TW Waelde and G Ndi, 'Stabilizing International Investment Commitments: International Law versus Contract Interpretation' (1996) 31 *Texas International Law Journal* 215, 220.

[107] UNCTAD, 'World Investment Report 2007', 83.

[108] ibid 92.

[109] Erkan, *Stability*, 26.

[110] ibid 28.

Market price volatility is another specific and highly important aspect of the energy industry. In particular, the volatility in the oil market can have a considerable effect on investors (affecting planning, definitions of commerciality, etc) and makes managing the associated risks difficult.[111]

Consequently, the main characteristics of energy investments can be summarised as follows:

- Large-scale
- Long duration
- Capital-intensive
- High risk inherent
- Strategically and politically important
- Volatile price

C. Do the Undertakings in the Energy Sector Qualify as Investments?

After having reviewed the main characteristics of energy investments, we can test them against the definitions of investment provided in the previous section in order to test whether these undertakings can be acknowledged as investments within the meaning of the above-mentioned international law instruments.

Under the ECT, any kind of asset that is associated with an economic activity in the energy sector is considered an investment, as previously mentioned. Hence, it is safe to say that the majority of undertakings in the energy sector would qualify as investments within the scope of the ECT if they satisfy the other required criteria too.

Since the subjective theory of ICSID jurisdiction prioritises the consensus of the parties when determining whether an undertaking is an investment, the same is applied to the energy sector. Each case should be reviewed in its own right with respect to the document (treaty, contract, law, etc) upon which the consensus was built in order to determine whether an investment exists.

When it comes to the objective theory, the main characteristics of energy investments and the requirements of an investment under this theory resemble each other. A parallel can be drawn between the four criteria of the famous Salini Test and the main characteristics of international energy investments (Table 1).

---

[111] Lovells International Law Firm and Association of Corporate Counsel, 'Sino-Foreign Oil and Gas Industry: Legal Risk Comparative Analysis' (2005) 6.

Table 1 The Salini Test and the Characteristics of Energy Investments

The Salini Test Requirements	Characteristics of Energy Investments
A contribution in money or other assets	Large-scale, capital-intensive
A certain duration of performance	Long duration
Participation in the risks	High risk inherent (geological, commercial, political)
Contribution to the economic development of the host state	Strategically important for host states

As Table 1 shows, the main characteristics of international energy investments fulfil the requirements set forth by the objective theory approach, namely the Salini Test. It is not possible to say whether all the projects in the energy sector would qualify as investments, but we can say that the ones that adhere to the general main characteristics stated above would be considered to be investments according to the objective theory.

IV. Risks in Energy Investments

As stated in the previous section, one of the main characteristics of international energy investments is the high risk inherent to those projects which are undertaken by the investors in return for a high profit.[112] The risk element is also an important determinant to the arbitral tribunals when deciding whether an investment exists. Every kind of investment has some element of risk, and indeed investors should expect to encounter a number of risks over the course of their investments.[113]

Even though there is no unique definition of 'risk', it is generally defined as the probability of an event which might have an adverse outcome once it materialises.[114] Actualisation of a risk is perceived as a major threat to investments.[115] A distinction between risk and uncertainty is also made by scholars; while risks are measurable probabilities and risk implies the capability to calculate probabilities and to provide protection against the associated future adverse effects, uncertainty deals with a subjective potentiality of a loss and refers to future events whose nature and probability are impossible to predict.[116]

---

[112] de Macedo, 'From Tradition to Modernity', 1.
[113] Erkan, *Stability*, 21.
[114] T Aven and O Renn, 'On Risk Defined as an Event Where the Outcome is Uncertain' (2009) 12(1) *Journal of Risk Research* 1, 1–2.
[115] Al Faruque, 'Stability in Long-Term State Contracts', 89.
[116] HL Lax, *Political Risk in the International Oil and Gas Industry* (International Human Resources Development Corporation, 1983) 8; Al Faruque, 'Stability in Long-Term State Contracts' 89.

The risks that an investment might face can be: 'commercial risk (price volatility), financial risk (interest rate volatility), geological risk (no economically viable deposit identified), technical risk (failure of the installations to function as envisaged), managerial risk, or natural risk (natural disasters)',[117] as well as market risks, operational risks, physical and logistical risks,[118] social and environmental risks.[119] Most of these risks are common to the vast majority of sectors (as well as the energy sector itself), some of which cannot be managed by contractual mechanisms and are beyond the parties' control.[120]

There is one other type of risk which is not independent of the parties and that can be addressed by contractual or indeed other legal means: political risk.[121] Political risks are more common and acute in international energy investments due to their specific characteristics.[122] Since the host states are typically the owners of these resources and their development and use are perceived as economically and strategically significant by them, energy investments carry a particular sensitivity.[123] In addition to its strategic importance, maintaining the flow of energy at a reasonable price for public use has always been a significant state policy objective.[124] This sensitivity frequently takes the form of political risks for investors.

In summary, the risks in the energy sector are:

- Commercial risk

- Financial risk

- Technical risk

- Managerial risk

- Market risk

---

[117] Waelde and Ndi, 'Stabilizing International Investment Commitments' 221; TW Waelde, 'Investment Arbitration under the Energy Charter Treaty – From Dispute Settlement to Treaty Implementation' (1996) 12(4) *Arbitration International* 429, 431.

[118] A Xenofontos, 'Managing Investor–State Disputes in Upstream Oil and Gas Industry: IOCs' Perspective' (2018) 4 *Oil, Gas & Energy Law* 1, 1; SF Halabi, 'Efficient Contracting between Foreign Investors and Host States: Evidence from Stabilized Clauses' (2011) 31(2) *Northwestern Journal of International Law & Business* 261, 267; RA James and JG Mauel, 'An Integrated Approach to International Energy Investment Protection' (LexisNexis Matthew Bender, 2007) 5.

[119] R Supapa, 'The Protection of Upstream Energy Contracts under Investment Treaty Arbitration: A Study of the Interaction between Contract and Treaty Instruments' (PhD Thesis, University of Aberdeen, 2014), 53.

[120] Waelde and Ndi, 'Stabilizing International Investment Commitments', 221; Al Faruque, 'Stability in Long-Term State Contracts', 90.

[121] MTB Coale, 'Stabilization Clauses in International Petroleum Transactions' (2001) 30(2) *Denver Journal of International Law & Policy* 217, 220; Waelde and Ndi, 'Stabilizing International Investment Commitments' 221; JO Voss, *Impact of Investment Treaties on Contracts between Host States and Foreign Investors* (Martinus Nijhoff Publishers, 2010) 16.

[122] Erkan, *Stability*, 21; C Hajzler, 'Resource-Based FDI and Expropriation in Developing Economies' (University of Otago, 2010) 2; RW Click and RJ Weiner, 'Resource Nationalism Meets the Market: Political Risk and the Value of Petroleum Reserves' (2010) 41 *Journal of International Business Studies* 783, 785.

[123] Cameron, *International Energy Investment Law*, 3.

[124] Schill, 'Foreign Investment in the Energy Sector', 263.

- Operational risk
- Geological risk
- Natural risk
- Logistical risk
- Political risk

V. Political Risks

A. Defining the Political Risk

Political risk is considered to be one of the top five challenges that the energy industry faces.[125] Even though there have been various definitions put forward by a number of scholars[126] and institutions, as yet there has been no consensus among them as to the meaning of political risk.[127] International organisations, the insurance industry, economists or legal scholars have different approaches to defining and classifying political risk. In order to grasp this concept, a review of some of its definitions would be helpful.

According to the World Bank report, political risk

> is the probability of disruption of the operations of companies by political forces and events, whether they occur in host countries or result from changes in the international

---

[125] A Van de Putte, DF Gates and AK Holder, 'Political Risk Insurance as an Instrument to Reduce Oil and Gas Investment Risk and Manage Investment Returns' (2012) 5(4) *Journal of World Energy Law & Business* 284, 284.

[126] For a detailed discussion, see E Eljuri and Y Abul-Failat, 'Political Risk Management in Natural Resources Projects in the MENA and the Latin American Regions' (2018) 16(3) *Oil, Gas & Energy Law* 1; C Dupont, T Schultz and M Angin, 'Political Risk and Investment Arbitration: An Empirical Study' (2016) 7(1) *Journal of International Dispute Settlement* 136; F Solimene, 'Political Risk in the Oil and Gas Industry and Legal Tools for Mitigation' (2014) (2) *International Energy Law Review* 81; JW Yackee, 'Political Risk and International Investment Law' (2014) 24 *Duke Journal of Comparative & International Law* 477; E Mohajeri, 'Overview of Political and Regulatory Risks in International Energy Investment' (2013) 11(2) *Oil, Gas & Energy Law* 1; O Osasu, 'Legitimate Expectations and Political Risk: Lessons from Investment Arbitration for Energy Investors' (2013) 6 *International Energy Law Review* 249; CE Sottilotta, 'Political Risk: Concepts, Definitions, Challenges' (LUISS School of Government, 2013); D Restrepo, R Correia and J Poblacion, 'Political Risk and Corporate Investment Decisions' (Universidad Carlos III de Madrid, 2012); N Jensen, 'Political Risk, Democratic Institutions, and Foreign Direct Investment' (2008) 70(4) *Journal of Politics* 1040; AJ Boulos, 'Assessing Political Risk: A Supplement to the IPAA International Primer' (2003) www.ipaa.org/wp-content/uploads/2017/01/PoliticalRisk.pdf; Waelde and Ndi, 'Stabilizing International Investment Commitments'; PE Comeaux and NS Kinsella, 'Reducing Political Risk in Developing Countries: Bilateral Investment Treaties, Stabilization Clauses, and MIGA & OPIC Investment Insurance' (1994) 15(1) *New York Law School Journal of International and Comparative Law* 1; M Fitzpatrick, 'The Definition and Assessment of Political Risk in International Business: A Review of the Literature' (1983) 8(2) *Academy of Management Review* 249; SJ Kobrin, 'Political Risk: A Review and Reconsideration' (Alfred P Sloan School of Management, 1978) Working Paper 998-78 http://dspace.mit.edu/bitstream/handle/1721.1/48801/politicalriskrev00kobr.pdf?s.

[127] Yackee, 'Political Risk', 481.

environment. In host countries, political risk is largely determined by uncertainty over the actions not only of governments and political institutions, but also of minority groups and separatist movements.[128]

While this approach includes changes in the international environment in its definition, the insurance industry utilises a narrower definition which only takes into account any changes in the host countries.[129]

Another international organisation, the IMF, defines political risk as:

> The risk of nonpayment on an export contract or project due to action taken by the importer's host government. Such action may include intervention to prevent transfer of payments, cancellation of a license, or events such as war, civil strife, revolution and other disturbances that prevent the exporter from performing under the supply contract or the buyer from making payment. Sometimes physical disasters such as cyclones, floods, and earthquakes come under this heading.[130]

What is salient in this definition is that it also acknowledges certain geographical incidents, such as earthquakes and floods, as themselves constituting political risks. It is not possible to directly relate natural disasters (natural risks) with political risk, but this definition might be ascribing this indirectly in the sense of a government not taking the necessary measures to prevent those disasters from adversely affecting an investment.[131] The IMF's definition is also broad, covering a wide range of issues, as indeed does the World Bank's.

Restrepo et al suggest a comprehensive as well as somewhat ambiguous definition in the following form: 'Political risk represents the risk associated with the effect that actions of agents pursuing political objectives may have on the value of the assets of agents pursuing economic objectives.'[132] This is a comprehensive definition because it highlights all the potential parties to a political risk and does not limit them. On one side, there is the party that stimulates the risk by virtue of a political aim, whilst on the other, there is the party that pursues an economic interest and is being affected by such risks. The ambiguity stems from the point that this definition does not differentiate between the positive and negative effects of these actions. The authors argue that there is a potential upside to political risk, and that the effect may not always be negative; thus, the definition they propose follows a neutral path.[133] For the purposes of this study, the scope of political risk will be limited to its detrimental effects only.

---

[128] MIGA, 'World Investment and Political Risk 2011' (World Bank, 2011) 21.
[129] MIGA, 'World Investment and Political Risk 2009' (World Bank, 2009) 28.
[130] IMF, 'External Debt Statistics: Guide for Compilers and Users-Appendix 3' (International Monetary Fund, 2003) www.imf.org/external/pubs/ft/eds/Eng/Guide/file6.pdf.
[131] Erkan, *Stability*, 23.
[132] Restrepo et al, 'Political Risk', 4.
[133] ibid 3.

Boulos applies this issue to the oil and gas industry, and defines political risk as the possibility of expropriation, nationalisation or introduction of unilateral changes to the detriment of the oil company by the host state in any oil and gas investment.[134] What distinguishes political risks from other types of risk is that they are mostly caused by unilateral actions of the host state, unlike the other types mentioned above.[135]

While Comeaux and Kinsella defined political risk as the risk of confiscation of the investor's property rights, either fully or partially, by the host state,[136] they utilised a more specific definition from a legal perspective in an earlier work. According to this, a political risk is

> the risk that the laws of a country will unexpectedly change to the investor's detriment after the investor has invested capital in the country, thereby reducing the value of the individual's investment. Put simply, political risk is the risk of government intervention.[137]

This last approach is the one that will be followed throughout this book. Political risk, within the scope of this book, refers to the risks that stem from unilateral regulatory changes as enacted by host states.[138] This narrower definition, merely confined to the regulatory risks, will be employed by this study. The stability concept and the legitimate expectations principle are both utilised by investors against these regulatory risks.

The source of a political risk lies not in the type of the political system in operation (be it capitalist, socialist, democracy or monarchy) in the host state, but, rather, is located in changes in political and socio-economic conditions.[139] This type of risk is not limited to underdeveloped or developing states; it is also possible to witness changes that adversely affect investors in developed countries such as the UK, France, Canada or the USA.[140] The latest investment disputes concerning renewable energy in Spain, the Czech Republic and Italy also demonstrate this stance.[141] Indeed, the autocratic regimes that are frequently perceived as riskier might, in fact, be less risky than some democratic regimes in terms of the realisation of a political risk.[142]

---

[134] Boulos, 'Assessing Political Risk', 3.

[135] Mohajeri, 'Political and Regulatory Risks', 3.

[136] PE Comeaux and NS Kinsella, *Protecting Foreign Investment under International Law: Legal Aspects of Political Risk* (Oceana Publications, 1997) 1.

[137] Comeaux and Kinsella, 'Reducing Political Risk', 4.

[138] G Bellantuono, 'The Misguided Quest for Regulatory Stability in the Renewable Energy Sector' (2017) 10(4) *Journal of World Energy Law & Business* 274, 275.

[139] A Berlin and AI Berlin, 'Managing Political Risk in the Oil and Gas Industries' (2004) 1(1) *Transnational Dispute Management* 1, 3.

[140] ibid; MH Masood, 'International Arbitration of Petroleum Disputes' (PhD Thesis, University of Aberdeen, 2004), 29.

[141] See ch 6.

[142] Restrepo et al, 'Political Risk', 3.

B. Types and Classification of Political Risk

Political risk can either be a one-time event or it can result from an evolving political process.[143]

According to a survey, the political risks that are of most concern to foreign investors are regulatory changes, civil disturbance, non-honouring of sovereign guarantees, transfer and convertibility restrictions, expropriation, breach of contract, war and terrorism.[144] As stated by Waelde in 1996, while nationalisation, forced renegotiation and barriers to repatriation of capital and earnings are the most significant political risks in energy investments, there are also others, such as breach of licence rights, difficulties of access to export pipelines and insecurity of title.[145]

It is possible to see that the main perceptions of political risk have not changed for the last two decades, and indeed are still considered major concerns by investors.[146] This is also proven by Erkan's survey, in which he finds that the most important political risks are indirect expropriation, unilateral change of contractual terms and nationalisation.[147]

Analysing the three most common strands in the literature, Dupont et al categorise political risks as being of three main types: those resulting from poor governance (lack of rule of law, lack of transparency and lack of individual rights); severe economic conditions; and economic nationalism (including resource nationalism).[148] These three different types do not generally exist separately; rather, they emerge in various combinations.[149] According to Dupont et al's empirical findings, bad governance and economic nationalism are frequently associated with arbitration claims in the oil and gas sector.[150]

From an insurance perspective, Williams divides the political risk that a foreign investor may face into three categories: the risk of occurrence of political violence; the risk that the host state will take deliberate, unilateral measures which interfere with the investors' rights; and the risk of restriction on the conversion of local currency into foreign exchange.[151]

---

[143] ibid 2.

[144] MIGA, 'World Investment and Political Risk 2010' (World Bank, 2010) 9.

[145] Waelde, 'Investment Arbitration under the ECT', 431.

[146] There are also some new forms of conduct that are considered modern political risks, including, but not limited to, corruption, bureaucratic delay and lack of confidentiality. For details, see TW Waelde, 'The Role of Arbitration in the Globalisation of Energy Markets: Perspective in the Year 2000' (2008) 6(3) *Oil, Gas & Energy Law* 1, 9; A Al Faruque, 'Stability in Petroleum Contracts: Rhetoric and Reality' (PhD Thesis, University of Dundee, 2005), 61.

[147] Erkan, *Stability*, 51.

[148] C Dupont et al, 'Types of Political Risk Leading to Investment Arbitrations in the Oil and Gas Sector' (2015) 8(4) *Journal of World Energy Law & Business* 337, 342.

[149] ibid.

[150] ibid 354.

[151] SL Williams, 'Political and Other Risk Insurance: OPIC, MIGA, EXIMBANK and Other Providers' (1993) 5(1) *Pace International Law Review* 59, 64.

C. Political Risk and the Energy Industry

As mentioned above, the energy industry, as a high-profile and often controversial[152] sector in host states, has a greater potential to face political risks than any other industry. This vulnerability stems from the distinctive characteristics inherent to energy investments.[153] The realisation of political risks might directly or indirectly affect the pursuit of earnings by an energy company.[154]

The role of geopolitics in the energy industry and the extensive participation of the host government in energy projects can be considered the main factors contributing to the political risk in the energy sector.[155] A high percentage of the world's proven oil resources are located in states which have experienced, or are currently experiencing, wars, embargoes or civil unrest and that have a history of political and social instability.[156]

Also, the economic survival and societal legitimacy of many resource-rich countries are highly dependent on the revenues derived from the energy industry.[157] Since the rent from these resources affects almost everything from salaries and education to the general well-being of the citizens[158] of a host state, these countries attempt to increase their participation in these projects in every manner possible. This dependency and the wish of host states for the projects to come under their control make resource-rich host states more fertile places for political risk.[159]

While this is certainly the case for the petroleum industry, other branches of the energy sector bear similar problems. As will be seen in the following chapters,[160] renewable energy investments might also face certain regulatory changes because of the fact that the pricing of their products has a direct effect on their consumers, which in turn might eventually affect the governments involved. Despite their

---

[152] Berlin and Berlin, 'Managing Political Risk', 2.

[153] These were reviewed in s IIIA.

[154] MK Kachikwu, 'The Changing Face of Political Risk in the Energy Industry' in J Werner and AH Ali (eds), *A Liber Amicorum: Thomas Wälde – Law Beyond Conventional Thought* (CMP Publishing, 2009) 88.

[155] Mohajeri, 'Political and Regulatory Risks', 4.

[156] GK Foster, 'Managing Expropriation Risks in the Energy Sector: Steps for Foreign Investors to Minimise Their Exposure and Maximise Prospects for Recovery When Takings Occur' (2005) 23(1) *Journal of Energy and Natural Resources Law* 36, 37; Mohajeri, 'Political and Regulatory Risks', 4; Berlin and Berlin, 'Managing Political Risk', 2.

[157] JD Wilson, 'Understanding Resource Nationalism: Economic Dynamics and Political Institutions' (2015) 21(4) *Contemporary Politics* 399, 406; Click and Weiner, 'Resource Nationalism Meets the Market', 4.

[158] JL Valera, 'Political Risks for International Oil Companies Investing in Latin America' (2006) 4(1) *Oil, Gas & Energy Law* 1, 6.

[159] NM Jensen and NP Johnston, 'Political Risk, Reputation, and the Resource Curse' (2011) 44(6) *Comparative Political Studies* 662, 662.

[160] See ch 6.

differences, renewable and conventional energy investments are susceptible to similar kinds of risk.[161]

Since energy products, be they oil, gas or electricity, are widely consumed by the people of the host states, both the pricing and the economics of the projects affect voter behaviour.[162] At certain times, politicians may interfere with foreign investments in order to increase their public support.[163] Also, newly elected governments might want to alter previously signed contracts that they allege were subject to corruption.[164]

All of these factors have an important effect in increasing political risk, especially in the energy sector. The long-term and capital-intensive characteristics of energy investments give way to unilateral government interventions. The obsolescing bargain method is one means by which host states can put such interferences into practice in the energy sector.

(i) *The Obsolescing Bargain*

One of the consequences of a long-term, capital-intensive investment is its exposure to the obsolescing bargain, a concept which was first developed by Raymond Vernon.[165] Investors having the technological means and necessary financial sources in order to develop the resources of a host state which itself lacks the appropriate know-how and capital are in a powerful position at the beginning of the relationship.[166] However, this bargaining power will start to shift in favour of the host state once the majority of the investment costs have been sunk.[167] This is particularly the case if the profit derived from the investment proves to be much greater than initially anticipated, and the government's benefit-to-cost ratio changes swiftly.[168]

Cameron analyses this phenomenon as follows:

> After the bulk of the investment has been made, the allocation of risks shifts rapidly from the capital-hungry host state to the investor. Negotiating leverage shifts during the

---

[161] T Restrepo, 'Modification of Renewable Energy Support Schemes under the Energy Charter Treaty: Eiser and Charanne in the Context of Climate Change' (2017) 8(1) *Goettingen Journal of International Law* 101, 103.

[162] Valera, 'Political Risk', 5.

[163] James and Mauel, 'An Integrated Approach to International Energy Investment Protection', 8; TW Waelde, 'Renegotiating Acquired Rights in the Oil and Gas Industries: Industry and Political Cycles Meet the Rule of Law' (2008) 1(1) *Journal of World Energy Law & Business* 55, 72.

[164] Sornarajah, *The International Law on Foreign Investment*, 75.

[165] R Vernon, 'Long-Run Trends in Concession Contracts' (1967) 61 *Proceedings of the American Society of International Law* 81; R Vernon, *Sovereignty at Bay: The Multinational Spread of US Enterprises* (Longman, 1971) 46.

[166] Al Faruque, 'Stability in Long-Term State Contracts', 89; Wilson, 'Understanding Resource Nationalism', 402.

[167] SM Jasimuddin and AFM Maniruzzaman, 'Resource Nationalism Specter Hovers Over the Oil Industry: The Transnational Corporate Strategy to Tackle Resource Nationalism Risks' (2016) 32(2) *Journal of Applied Business Research* 387, 389.

[168] L Eden, S Lenway and DA Schuler, 'From the Obsolescing Bargain to the Political Bargaining Model' (Bush School of Government & Public Service, 2004) 5.

project life cycle: the investors require a long period to achieve their expected return while, once the investment is made, the host state has what it requires. For a variety of reasons, the host state may then conclude that the original bargain is obsolete and force a revision of its terms.[169]

This concept is also referred to as the 'hostage effect of sunk investment'.[170] Since the investor cannot leave the country due to its heavy commitments, both in fiscal and technological terms, eventually it effectively becomes hostage to the host state.

Realisation of the risk of the obsolescing bargain hinges upon the investor's fixed assets, which means that the sectors that require fixed real assets that cannot be easily moved out of the host state (ie are immobile) are more susceptible to the obsolescing bargain.[171] This is one of the reasons why the energy industry is so vulnerable in this regard. As aptly clarified by Rubins and Kinsella:

> Where a project is long-term with heavy capital investment (sunk costs) at the start, and uses assets that are not easily sold or converted to other purposes, the government has a great deal of leverage over the foreign investor, who cannot credibly threaten to abandon his investment plans if conditions deteriorate. This imbalance creates an almost irresistible temptation for local officials to extract short-term political advantage by shifting foreign investment profits to constituents either within the government or the public at large.[172]

One of the driving forces behind the change in the host state's attitude towards investors and the twin factor of the obsolescing bargain, as Clement-Davies argues,[173] is *the price cycle*. According to this concept, when there is a dramatic rise in the international price which provides the investor with windfall profits, the host state tends to seize a part of that gain by introducing new measures.[174] This is another element that motivates the host state's interference with the investment, alongside the shift in bargaining power. A dramatic rise in price helps the host state to introduce the obsolescing bargain model. These twin sources of political risk recur in a cyclical manner. This cyclical development generates periodic instability for investors.[175]

While rising oil or gas prices might act as incentives for host states to take a larger share of the profits by changing the legal and financial conditions of the investment, this cyclical interference is not exclusive to the extractives sector; for instance, Spain, the Czech Republic and Italy have taken similar actions in the

---

[169] Cameron, *International Energy Investment Law*, 5.

[170] Eden et al, 'Obsolescing Bargain', 5; Waelde and Ndi, 'Stabilizing International Investment Commitments', 225.

[171] Yackee, 'Political Risk', 485; S Bauerle Danzman, 'Contracting with Whom? The Differential Effects of Investment Treaties on FDI' (2016) 42(3) *International Interactions* 452, 454.

[172] N Rubins and NS Kinsella, *International Investment, Political Risk and Dispute Resolution: A Practitioner's Guide* (Oceana Publications, 2005) 3.

[173] C Clement-Davies, 'Contractual Stability in the Energy Sector: Reconciling the Needs of States and Investors' (2014) (2) *International Energy Law Review* 47, 1.

[174] Cameron, *International Energy Investment Law*, 5.

[175] ibid.

renewables sector. After large investments were made to develop solar energy in these states, the relevant governments altered the conditions based on the argument that since the production costs of the investors had decreased, they were receiving unreasonably high profits to the detriment of their consumers.[176] In such cases, the renewable energy investor also has fixed assets in the host state; and since it cannot dismantle its power plants and leave the country, it inevitably falls into the obsolescing bargain trap.

The vagueness and instability created by these political risks and the consequential developments incentivise investors to protect their investments. Therefore, various legal methods have been created in order to provide protection to these investments.

VI. Sources of Investment Protection against Political Risks

A. The Need for Protection

Protection of investment essentially amounts to compensation following unilateral acts by host states (government or agencies) that damage investments, but also includes the damages caused by third parties where the host state is responsible for the protection.[177]

If we trace the causes of investment disputes back, we find the need for the protection of investment. Sornarajah lists the potential causes of an investment dispute as follows: taking of land and tangible properties; interference with contractual rights; interference with intangible rights; changes of circumstances; administrative interference with the investment; environmental grounds for interference; violations of human rights; disputes arising from internationally protected areas; and allegations of contract formation through bribery.[178] If we take all of these sources of an investment dispute and the long-term characteristics of energy investments into account, it becomes clear that investors are vulnerable to potential interferences and that they have to have some form of protection mechanism in place in order to be able to maintain their investments, defend them or at least leave the host state unharmed.

The reasons for adopting an investment protection method are threefold. In the best-case scenario, the main idea would be to prevent any detrimental effect

---

[176] Restrepo, 'Renewable Energy', 104.

[177] N Horn, 'Arbitration and the Protection of Foreign Investment: Concepts and Means' in N Horn (ed), *Arbitrating Foreign Investment Disputes: Procedural and Substantive Legal Aspects* (Kluwer Law International, 2004) 7.

[178] M Sornarajah, *The Settlement of Foreign Investment Disputes* (Kluwer Law International, 2000) 61–77.

to the investment and maintain the investment relationship in its original form. By using protection methods, investors bargain for a stable and unproblematic investment relationship. If this is not possible, the second phase is to resolve any disputes that arise by appropriate legal means. These methods can be used to protect investors' rights in the event of a dispute. The worst-case scenario would be to finalise operations in the host state and leave there without exposure to undue damages. Various investment protection instruments have been developed to address these scenarios.

B. Domestic Legislation

Investment protection provisions can be found under national legislation. Host states in need of foreign investment endeavour to encourage investors to invest in their countries by offering them broad incentives and enhanced freedom.[179] In this regard, the investment environment is equipped with the necessary national legal framework to attract investments.[180] While these incentives may include certain fiscal guarantees, they also may take the form of legal protection of the investment against the political risks it may encounter.[181] This legal protection may be ensured by general investment codes and sector-specific legislation and policies.[182]

A considerable amount of national legislation contains provisions that assure minimum protective standards and offers investment protection in the energy sector that covers expropriation, non-discrimination and access to international arbitration.[183] There are also various forms of domestic legislation which provide for contractual stability between the investors and the host states.[184] Host states may also protect investments through constitutional provisions.[185]

While it is possible for the investors to rely on this domestic legal protection, there are nevertheless drawbacks to this system. The concern here is that the domestic judiciary system might overlook the main legal principles of fairness and justice, and act with prejudice in the event of a dispute in order to favour its government, ie the host state.[186] For this reason, foreign investors do not often

---

[179] Salacuse, *Three Laws*, 36.
[180] ibid.
[181] K Tienhaara, 'Unilateral Commitments to Investment Protection: Does the Promise of Stability Restrict Environmental Policy Development?' (2006) 17(1) *Yearbook of International Environmental Law* 139, 142.
[182] ibid 87; AFM Maniruzzaman, 'The Issue of Resource Nationalism: Risk Engineering and Dispute Management in the Oil and Gas Industry' (2009) 5(1) *Texas Journal of Oil, Gas, And Energy Law* 79.
[183] Tienhaara, 'Unilateral Commitments', 143; Horn, 'Protection of Foreign Investment', 12.
[184] AFM Maniruzzaman, 'National Laws Providing for Stability of International Investment Contracts: A Comparative Perspective' (2007) 8(2) *Journal of World Investment & Trade* 233.
[185] Al Faruque, 'Rhetoric and Reality', 45.
[186] JJ Norton, 'An "Environmental" Approach to FDI and Effective Dispute Resolution: The Exhortations of the Monterrey Consensus' in N Horn (ed), *Arbitrating Foreign Investment Disputes: Procedural and Substantive Legal Aspects* (Kluwer Law International, 2004) 103.

have recourse to domestic courts.[187] Also, based upon the sovereignty principle, governments have the right to alter their legislation any time after an investment is made by exercising their sovereign power.[188] Thus, protection via domestic legislation might not always be convenient for investments from a practical perspective.

There might be various provisions in domestic legislation that allow for protection of investments, but this study will only appraise national legislation with respect to the stability provisions so provided.

C. International Investment Agreements

International investment agreements (IIAs) comprise BITs, MITs and free trade agreements (FTAs).[189] BITs and MITs, the legal instruments that are concluded between two or more states, are specifically aimed at promoting investment and providing legal protection to foreign investments, and political risks may be mitigated through them to a considerable extent.[190] BITs and MITs have emerged to avoid uncertainties and enhance the legal certainty in investment protection under international law.[191] These instruments help protect investments because their breach would constitute a violation of a treaty with the home state as well as a violation of customary international law, a situation that renders the host state more reluctant to commit or allow breaches.[192] FTAs are also signed between states, but they are generally concerned with wider economic subject matter and focus on investment protection as part of this.[193]

As of March 2021, there are 3321 BITs or treaties with investment provisions worldwide (not all of them in force) according to the United Nations Conference on Trade and Development (UNCTAD).[194] This figure illustrates the extent of this international regime, and one of the principal reasons that states join the regime is to provide protection for their investments in the contracting host states.[195] BITs can be deemed the most significant source of modern international investment law, and indeed some countries (Germany, China, etc) have concluded more than 100 BITs with other countries.[196]

---

[187] Bauerle Danzman, 'Contracting with Whom?', 455.

[188] Sornarajah, *The Settlement of Foreign Investment Disputes*, 87; Salacuse, *Three Laws*, 355.

[189] Cameron, *International Energy Investment Law*, 146. For a history of International Investment Agreements, see KJ Vandevelde, 'A Brief History of International Investment Agreements' (2005) 12(1) *UC Davis Journal of International Law & Policy* 157.

[190] Bauerle Danzman, 'Contracting with Whom?', 456; Comeaux and Kinsella, 'Reducing Political Risk', 5.

[191] Al Faruque, 'Stability in Long-Term State Contracts', 109; L Vanhonnaeker, 'Promoting Successful and Sustainable Foreign Direct Investment through Political Risk Mitigation Strategies' (2016) 1(2) *The Chinese Journal of Global Governance* 133, 138.

[192] Comeaux and Kinsella, *Legal Aspects of Political Risk*, 100.

[193] Cameron, *International Energy Investment Law*, 146.

[194] Of which 2659 are in force. For detailed statistics, see https://investmentpolicy.unctad.org/international-investment-agreements.

[195] Cameron, *International Energy Investment Law*, 147.

[196] Dolzer and Schreuer, *Principles*, 13.

The substantive provisions of the majority of IIAs are very similar and include: protection against expropriation (direct or indirect); guarantees against arbitrary and discriminatory treatment; the requirement of fair and equitable treatment of the investor; national and most favoured nation treatment; full protection and security; and a general provision about the assurance given by the contracting state to honour its obligations to the investor (referred to as the 'umbrella clause'). These substantive standards are strengthened by the availability of investor–state or state–state dispute resolution provisions.[197] While these standards are all autonomous provisions and nominally separate from each other, it should be noted that they may interrelate to some extent.[198]

This study focuses on just one of the standards – the fair and equitable treatment standard – which has a close relationship with the concept of stability.

D. Political Risk Insurance

Political risk insurance (PRI) is another tool used by international energy investors for political risk mitigation.[199] Purchasing PRI is one of the easiest ways in which an investor can mitigate its exposure to political risk. In essence, it is not much different from regular business risk insurance.[200] Traditionally, PRI mainly covers similar risks to those addressed in BITs, such as direct and indirect expropriation, breach of contract, political violence and currency inconvertibility risks.[201]

There are several available investment insurance sources in the PRI market: they might be from a state-sponsored insurance agency, such as the US Overseas Private Investment Corporation (OPIC); a multilateral agency, such as the Multilateral Investment Guarantee Agency (MIGA) under the World Bank; the export credit agencies of the states; or private insurance companies, such as Lloyd's of London, American International Group, Chubb and Zurich Emerging Markets Solutions.[202]

PRI is significant not just in terms of protecting investments against potential damage, but also because lenders often require insurance as a prerequisite

---

[197] Cameron and Kolo, 'What Is Energy Investment Law?', 5; Dolzer and Schreuer, *Principles*, 13; Caliskan, 'Dispute Settlement in International Investment Law', 126; van Aaken, 'Perils of Success', 6–7.

[198] C Schreuer, 'Introduction: Interrelationship of Standards' in A Reinisch (ed), *Standards of Investment Protection* (Oxford University Press, 2008) 3.

[199] Maniruzzaman, 'Issue of Resource Nationalism', 99.

[200] Comeaux and Kinsella, *Legal Aspects of Political Risk*, 151.

[201] FG Sourgens, 'Keep the Faith: Investment Protection Following the Denunciation of International Investment Agreements' (2012) 11 *Santa Clara Journal of International Law* 335, 351; Comeaux and Kinsella, *Legal Aspects of Political Risk*, 151; Maniruzzaman, 'Issue of Resource Nationalism', 99; Dolzer and Schreuer, *Principles*, 230.

[202] G Joffé et al, 'Expropriation of Oil and Gas Investments: Historical, Legal and Economic Perspectives in a New Age of Resource Nationalism' (2009) 2(1) *Journal of World Energy Law & Business* 3, 12; Maniruzzaman, 'Issue of Resource Nationalism', 99; Comeaux and Kinsella, *Legal Aspects of Political Risk*, 151; Foster, 'Managing Expropriation Risks', 50.

for financing an investment in a developing state.[203] PRI can also be utilised as a check-up tool to assess the vulnerability of an investment against political risk. If it is not possible to find an insurer prepared to cover the investment, this means that either the risk of expropriation in the host state is inadmissibly high or the structure of the investment itself is vulnerable to political risk.[204] Even if the PRI protects the investor against these risks, it cannot rescue a bad project or render a poorly written contract into a good one.[205]

E. Investor–State Contracts

Domestic legislation of host states and the IIAs discussed above may not always be sufficient to address the specific conditions of an investment;[206] this is true in the case of international energy investments. It is believed that investment contracts insulate the investment from unilateral, detrimental acts of host states to a greater extent than domestic legislation.[207] Thus, the parties may be in need of an additional tool which can cover any necessary aspects that are not covered by other legal instruments. Investor–state contracts, which are also referred to as international investment contracts or state contracts, are legal instruments formed by law which attempt to provide investments with the required protection and create legally enforceable obligations.[208] An international investment contract, in essence, is different to a domestic contract because it contains provisions for the transfer of items between two states and has a legal relationship with each.[209]

These contracts have several benefits with regard to investment protection. The investment contracts concluded by investors and host states may be of help in reducing the associated political risks since the parties have the chance to ponder any potential areas of dispute beforehand.[210] Further, by internationalising[211]

---

[203] Foster, 'Managing Expropriation Risks', 50.

[204] ibid.

[205] A Kolo, 'Managing Political Risk in Transnational Investment Contracts' (CEPMLP, University of Dundee Working Paper, 1994) 16 https://dundee.primo.exlibrisgroup.com/discovery/fulldisplay?docid= alma990001397550302991&context=L&vid=44DUN_INST:dun&lang=en&search_scope=MyInst_ and_CI&adaptor=Local%20Search%20Engine&tab=Everything&query=any,contains,abba%20 kolo.

[206] Dolzer and Schreuer, *Principles*, 79.

[207] Waelde and Ndi, 'Stabilizing International Investment Commitments', 234.

[208] Salacuse, *Three Laws*, 159.

[209] Sornarajah, *The Settlement of Foreign Investment Disputes*, 26.

[210] Comeaux and Kinsella, *Legal Aspects of Political Risk*, 133.

[211] Internationalising a contract means: 'The removal of the foreign investment transaction from the sphere of the host state's law and its subjection to an immutable, supranational system is seen as essential for the protection of foreign investment under the theory of internationalisation. The contract acquires stability when it is removed from the legislative control of the state authority and its other sovereign powers. This neutralisation of the power of the state to change the contract is seen as essential to the stability of the foreign investment contract.' For this and detailed analysis of this subject, see Sornarajah, *The International Law on Foreign Investment*, 289–99.

the agreement, the contract may render the investment relationship subject to international law, thus imposing certain responsibilities and obligations on the host state under international law and thereby providing a wider sphere of protection to the investor.[212]

Investment contracts are mostly the result of negotiations between investors and host states, based on their respective bargaining powers.[213] This characteristic makes the investment contract more specific than other sources of protection. The investor has the opportunity to negotiate the extent of the protection provided, unlike with domestic legislation or IIAs, where only the will of the governing authorities of the states are of importance in terms of defining the content, and not the will of investors.[214] Furthermore, the parties are free to decide which law will regulate their relations in their investment contract; they can choose the host state's law, a third country's law, international law or the general principles of law as the governing law.[215]

One of the most important functions of an investment contract is its utilisation as a risk allocation tool.[216] The contracting parties may decide whether either will bear particular risks or whether these risks will be transferred to a third-party insurer.[217] Hence, the investors might be able to protect themselves from political risk by inserting appropriate protective clauses into the investment contract by means of negotiation or by simply shifting the risk to a political insurance scheme.

There are several contractual clauses that an investor may rely on as a means by which to manage political risks and protect the investment, such as an arbitration clause, a choice of law clause, a stabilisation clause, a damages clause, no requirement to exhaust local remedies, a waiver of sovereign immunity, a conversion of currency clause, an interest rate clause or a *force majeure* clause.[218] However, this study will focus solely on the stabilisation clause inserted in an investment contract in order to strengthen the protection provided to the investment.

VII. Conclusion

In order to understand international energy investments and their protection methods, one must start with a definition of the notion of investment. There are several international documents and scholarly writings that provide just such

---

[212] Comeaux and Kinsella, *Legal Aspects of Political Risk*, 133.
[213] P Bernardini, 'Investment Protection under Bilateral Investment Treaties and Investment Contracts' (2001) 2(2) *Journal of World Investment & Trade* 235, 240.
[214] Salacuse, *Three Laws*, 159.
[215] A Kolo, 'State Regulation of Foreign Property Rights: Between Legitimate Regulation and Nationalisation – An Analysis of Current International Economic Law in Light of the Jurisprudence of the Iran–United States Claims Tribunal' (2004) 1(4) *Transnational Dispute Management* 1, 33.
[216] Salacuse, *Three Laws*, 167.
[217] ibid.
[218] Comeaux and Kinsella, *Legal Aspects of Political Risk*, 134–48.

a definition. While the majority of BITs and, indeed, some MITs hold similar asset-based, wide approaches to the term, the ICSID Convention takes a different approach. There are two prominent schools among ICSID Tribunals with regard to the meaning of investment: the ones that place emphasis on the consent of the parties constitute the subjective theory, and those who assert that there is a self-standing meaning of the notion of investment constitute the objective theory. Both theories have various flaws, and hence the tribunals should take both views into account in a flexible manner and should not strictly adhere to just one approach and apply the same in every case.

Taking the main characteristics of international energy investments (long-term, capital-intensive, high risk inherent, strategic for the host state) and the requirements set by ECT, BITs and ICSID into account in order to identify some given transaction as an investment, it could be concluded that the majority of transactions in this sector can be regarded as such.

One of the main characteristics of an international energy investment is the high risk inherent to these projects. There are various risks that an energy investment may face during the lifespan of the project. Political risk is one of the most important risks that an investment might encounter. Since a host state has to be involved to entail political risk, it is likely that a unilateral act on the part of the host state might reduce the value of the investment to a considerable, if not critical, extent.

This chapter has briefly reviewed some of the mechanisms that provide protection for investments against just such political risks. Domestic legislation, international law (by means of IIAs) and investment contracts are the legal sources through which the provisions that offer such protection can be found. Political risk insurance is another means of allocating risk by simply shifting it from the investor to the insurer. There are various clauses in these tools which provide protection for the investment, but the focus of this study will be on those that provide protection by utilising stability mechanisms.

This chapter has set the scene for the following chapters by giving a detailed definition of the term investment, providing the main characteristics of an international energy investment, reviewing the risks that an investment might face during its lifespan, examining political risk as the most prominent form of risk in the energy industry and demonstrating the ways in which political risk can be mitigated.

3

Stability in International Energy Investments

I. Introduction

The previous chapter briefly examined the commonly available mechanisms used to protect international energy investments. One of the protection tools mentioned in that chapter was the stability guarantee. This chapter analyses the stability concept in general and the various kinds of stability guarantee in particular, and further provides a brief overview of the history of stability provisions. This is followed by the definition and the types of stability provisions found in practice. There is a discrepancy in the terminology used in defining types of stability provisions, and this problem will also be mentioned.

A widely discussed issue regarding stability provisions is the validity aspect of these guarantees. There are two facets to this issue, the first being the theoretical discussion in the literature with respect to the permanent sovereignty over natural resources principle and the other being the practical aspect that we witness by means of arbitral jurisprudence. It can be said that there is almost a consensus on the legal validity of these provisions. Both the literature and arbitral jurisprudence aspects of the validity discussion will be analysed in this chapter.

The next section reviews the sources of stability guarantees. An international energy investor may rely on legal provisions from various sources to provide protection for their investments. These sources can be international investment contracts, domestic legal frameworks of the host states or international investment agreements. After this, the changing role of stability provisions will be discussed. Once, they were only perceived as protection tools against nationalisations or expropriations; today, however, they are considered an important aspect of investment treaty protection.

A stability provision can be found under an investment contract, within a legal stability agreement, or it can be offered through the legislation of the host states. In addition, some substantive standards of treaties might be utilised so as to provide stability to the investment environment. Each of these sources will have different effects on the scope of the protection provided to the investment. In order to set the scene for the analysis in the following chapters, this chapter will conclude with this issue.

II. The Stability Concept in General

The ordinary meaning of the term 'stable' is defined in the following ways by the *Oxford Dictionary of English*:

- not likely to give way or overturn; firmly fixed.
- not likely to change or fail; firmly established.[1]

Although its ordinary definition can be easily construed, the term itself would not have the same meaning for a computer scientist, an economist, a sportsman or, indeed, an investment lawyer. The type of stability that this book is interested in is the stability in the legal and regulatory environment of a host state. Legal stability is considered a fundamental element of the rule of law principle.[2]

Legal or regulatory stability as a technical term under international investment law might be understood as keeping the legal conditions surrounding an investment stable throughout the duration of the investment. This legal environment consists of contractual or semi-contractual arrangements, unilateral host state guarantees or the host state's general legal framework at the time of the investment.[3]

Regulatory stability is considered important by international energy investors since the commercial viability of such projects is highly contingent upon the stability of the regulatory framework.[4] Unanticipated regulatory changes by host states might considerably hinder the expected profits.[5] The stability concept does not imply a one-way benefit only; rather, it is also advantageous to the host states because stability helps to attract foreign investors.[6] Stability has great benefits to both parties of an investment relationship.[7]

While the obligation to maintain the regulatory stability surrounding the investment might stem from substantive provisions under investment contracts or domestic laws, it might equally arise from international investment treaties. The *Occidental v Ecuador* Tribunal also emphasised this condition under international

---

[1] *Oxford Dictionary of English*, 3rd edn (Oxford University Press, 2010) sv 'Stable'.

[2] SA Lindquist and FC Cross, 'Stability, Predictability and the Rule of Law: Stare Decisis as Reciprocity Norm' (University of Texas School of Law, Conference on Measuring the Rule of Law, 2010) 1.

[3] M Hirsch, 'Between Fair and Equitable Treatment and Stabilization Clause: Stable Legal Environment and Regulatory Change in International Investment Law' (2011) 12(6) *Journal of World Investment & Trade* 783, 784.

[4] F Costamagna, 'Protecting Foreign Investments in Public Services: Regulatory Stability at Any Cost?' (2017) 17(3) *Global Jurist* 1, 1; L Cotula, 'Reconciling Regulatory Stability and Evolution of Environmental Standards in Investment Contracts: Towards a Rethink of Stabilization Clauses' (2008) 1(2) *Journal of World Energy Law & Business* 158, 158.

[5] Hirsch, 'FET and Stabilization', 783.

[6] G Bellantuono, 'The Misguided Quest for Regulatory Stability in the Renewable Energy Sector' (2017) 10(4) *Journal of World Energy Law & Business* 274, 274; G Verhoosel, 'Foreign Direct Investment and Legal Constraints on Domestic Environmental Policies: Striking a Reasonable Balance between Stability and Change' (1997) 29(4) *Law and Policy in International Business* 451, 453.

[7] C Partasides and L Martinez, 'Of Taxes and Stabilisation' in JW Rowley, RD Bishop and G Kaiser (eds), *The Guide to Energy Arbitrations* (Global Arbitration Review, 2017) 60.

investment law by stating that 'there is certainly an obligation not to alter the legal and business environment in which the investment has been made'.[8]

The term 'stability' has, generally speaking, been used in the sense of contractual stabilisation clauses in international energy investments. The main underlying cause of this understanding is related to the historical development of the stability concept. Those provisions were first employed under investment contracts as a protection tool, as will be seen below. However, in its contemporary understanding, the stability concept comprises a wide range of protection mechanisms. Alongside the contractual or legislative stability provisions, the stability concept has also extended its reach by means of international investment agreements.[9]

In short, this book approaches the stability concept in a holistic manner, and considers all facets of it. Whereas this chapter will consider the stability provisions found under contracts and domestic laws, which will be analysed in depth, the following chapters will also discuss the stability requirement in the absence of explicit provisions with reference to the FET standard and the legitimate expectations principle.

III. Stability Provisions Defined

A. History of Stability Provisions

It is possible to trace the stability provisions back to the period between the two world wars.[10] Sir Gerald Fitzmaurice, in his separate opinion in the *Kuwait v Aminoil* case award, stated:

> But between the two Wars things began to change. Particularly in Latin-America, there were increasing cases in which the local government, having granted a concession to a foreign corporate entity for the construction and running of railways, tramways etc, or to extract and process mineral products, would wait until the undertaking had got past its 'teething' troubles and had become a 'going concern', and would then step in and take it over. The appellation of 'nationalisation' was not then much in vogue, but the effect was the same, namely that the State compulsorily acquired the undertaking, either itself to operate it, or to hand it over to a corporation of local nationality.
>
> It was specifically in the light of those occurrences that stabilization clauses began to be introduced into concessionary contracts, particularly by American Companies in view of their Latin-American experiences, and for the express purpose of ensuring that

---

[8] *Occidental Exploration and Production Company v The Republic of Ecuador*, Final Award, LCIA Case No UN3467, 1 July 2004, para 191.

[9] PD Cameron, *International Energy Investment Law: The Pursuit of Stability* (Oxford University Press, 2010) 145–78.

[10] PD Cameron, 'Stabilisation in Investment Contracts and Changes of Rules in Host Countries: Tools for Oil & Gas Investors' (AIPN, 2006) www.international-arbitration-attorney.com/wp-content/uploads/arbitrationlaw4-Stabilisation-Paper.pdf.

Concessions would run their full term, except where the case was one for which the concession itself gave a right of earlier termination.[11]

Although the first arbitration case to include a stabilisation clause was *Lena Goldfields Ltd v USSR* in 1930,[12] the first known case that concerned upstream international petroleum investment relationship and included a review of the stabilisation clause was the case of *Sapphire International Petroleum Ltd v National Iranian Oil Company*.[13] This case was about an oil concession agreement signed in 1958 whose stabilisation clause stated:

> [N]o general or statutory enactment, no administrative measure or decree of any kind, made either by the government or by any governmental authority in Iran (central or local), including NIOC, can cancel the agreement or affect or change its provisions, or prevent or hinder its performance. No cancellation, amendment or modification can take place except with the agreement of the two parties.[14]

Just before World War II, nearly all of the world's petroleum production was derived from a small number of major oil companies collectively known as the 'Seven Sisters'.[15] Until the 1960s, and unlike today, the participation of host states in petroleum operations was limited due to the lack of knowledge of the host states; hence, investor precedence prevailed at the negotiations table and it was at this time that stabilisation clauses began to emerge.[16] Today, as will be shown in this chapter, one can witness stability provisions in several legal forms in practice; originally, however, there were only contractual stabilisation clauses. International contractual practice has affected the national laws and treaty application in this regard.

According to Cameron, the major driving force behind the design of stabilisation clauses is the foreign investor's need for a mechanism that protects against the cyclical resurrection of unilateral host state actions as a consequence of the obsolescing bargain and price cycle.[17] Hence, it can be argued that these clauses were born as a result of unilateral host state actions and started to be widely used because international investors had the upper hand in negotiations around the 1960s. The political risks that the energy investors had been facing paved the way for the creation of such clauses.

[11] *The Government of the State of Kuwait v the American Independent Oil Company (Aminoil)*, Separate Opinion of Gerald Fitzmaurice, 24 March 1982, fn 7, 1052.
[12] Cameron, *International Energy Investment Law*, 107.
[13] FV Garcia-Amador, 'State Responsibility in Case of Stabilization Clauses' (1993) 2 *Journal of Transnational Law and Policy* 23, 38.
[14] *Sapphire International Petroleums Limited v National Iranian Oil Company*, Award, 15 March 1963, cited in MTB Coale, 'Stabilization Clauses in International Petroleum Transactions' (2001) 30(2) *Denver Journal of International Law & Policy* 217, 228.
[15] AJ Boulos, 'Assessing Political Risk: A Supplement to the IPAA International Primer' (2003) www.ipaa.org/wp-content/uploads/2017/01/PoliticalRisk.pdf.
[16] TW Waelde and G Ndi, 'Stabilizing International Investment Commitments: International Law versus Contract Interpretation' (1996) 31 *Texas International Law Journal* 215, 222.
[17] Cameron, *International Energy Investment Law*, 5.

During the last few decades, we have witnessed several phases regarding interest in the use of stabilisation provisions. In the first phase, the aim of these provisions was to reinforce the contract against expropriations and nationalisations.[18] After these provisions had started to be incorporated into contracts, a decline in their use – although the academic discussion was still alive – was seen in the late 1970s, and it was anticipated that host states would no longer include them in their contracts due to emerging international concepts such as permanent sovereignty over natural resources and the new international economic order.[19]

However, it did not take long for the deficiencies in these predictions come to light and, starting from the mid-1980s, stabilisation clauses took to the stage again.[20] One of the reasons for this unanticipated comeback was the increasing number of national oil companies (NOCs), because foreign investors started to deal with the NOCs instead of the host states themselves, easing the negotiation and granting processes relating to these clauses.[21] Besides, dramatically falling mineral prices during the 1980s affected the incomes of the many resource-rich developing states, which were thus obliged to embrace new fiscal policies designated by certain international organisations (eg World Bank), which included stability provisions too.[22]

The discussion over stabilisation clauses remained alive due to the volatile oil prices along with the unilateral changes to the contractual relationship implemented by the host states and growing numbers of resource nationalisations.[23] The last phase of the renewed interest in stabilisation clauses started in the early 2000s. Unlike its predecessors, this phase entailed a more complicated and evolved framework by virtue of unilateral host state actions that commenced shortly after 2000 – the Millennium Wave, as Cameron calls it.[24] These modern types of stability provisions were utilised to protect investors from the negative effects of host states' actions, even if they could not be deemed as expropriation or nationalisation, by transferring nearly all of the associated political risks to the host states themselves.[25]

Stabilisation clauses have thus been around for more than 80 years. Even if there were some periods in which the interest in these clauses decreased, stability

---

[18] Cameron, 'Stabilisation in Investment Contracts', 15. Fitzmaurice, *Kuwait and the American Independent Oil Company (Aminoil)*, 1052.

[19] Waelde and Ndi, 'Stabilizing International Investment Commitments', 217.

[20] S Frank, 'Stabilisation Clauses and Foreign Direct Investment: Presumptions versus Realities' (2015) 16(1) *Journal of World Investment & Trade* 88, 92.

[21] Cameron, 'Stabilisation in Investment Contracts', 17.

[22] Frank, 'Presumptions v Realities', 92.

[23] JN Emeka, 'Anchoring Stabilization Clauses in International Petroleum Contracts' (2008) 42(4) *International Lawyer* 1317, 1319.

[24] PD Cameron, 'Stability of Contract in the International Energy Industry' (2009) 27(3) *Journal of Energy and Natural Resources Law* 305, 307.

[25] S Frank, 'Stabilisation Clauses and Sustainable Development in Developing Countries' (PhD Thesis, University of Nottingham, 2014), 13.

provisions have always come back, albeit in different, modified forms. The current decade represents an important phase for stability provisions since we are experiencing a period of relatively low oil prices and new developments in the area of renewable energy.

Low oil prices affect the decisions of international energy investors to invest in upstream petroleum operations and they become more selective. Low-price periods reduce the bargaining power of host states, and it is always compelling for host states to lure investment in these low-price cycles, which is why they tend to offer investment guarantees to investors.[26] Since one of the widely used guarantees is a stability provision, it would not be surprising to witness the inclusion of these clauses in investment contracts or in the local laws of the host states during these low-price periods.

B. Definition and the Objectives of Stability Provisions

Foreign investors frequently come across many types of risks which are noncommercial in nature, such as political, legislative, fiscal and regulatory risks.[27] Some of the risks can be found in all types of investments, but political risks in particular are associated with international energy investments, as discussed in the previous chapter, because, as indicated there, international energy investments have specific characteristics, with their long durations and capital-intensive profiles.[28] The long terms of this type of investment render them vulnerable to external impacts that were not possible to anticipate at the time the contract was concluded.[29] Thus, international energy investors always tend to pursue a more stable contractual relationship between themselves and the host states by placing their emphasis on the legal framework that was available at the time they invested in the host state.[30] A stabilisation provision aims to insulate the contract/investment from a variety of issues, ie taxation, environmental and other kinds of regulations, and avert the destruction of the relationship before it expires.[31]

When it comes to the term 'stabilisation clause', it is possible to find numerous definitions of such in the literature. One of the earliest definitions was delivered

---

[26] TW Waelde, 'Renegotiating Acquired Rights in the Oil and Gas Industries: Industry and Political Cycles Meet the Rule of Law' (2008) 1(1) *Journal of World Energy Law & Business* 55, 71–72.

[27] AFM Maniruzzaman, 'Drafting Stabilization Clauses in International Energy Contracts: Some Pitfalls for the Unwary' (2007) 2 *International Energy Law & Taxation Review* 23, 23.

[28] Cameron, 'Stabilisation in Investment Contracts', 12.

[29] KP Berger, 'Renegotiation and Adaption of International Investment Contracts: The Role of Contract Drafters and Arbitrators' (2003) 36 *Vanderbilt Journal of Transnational Law* 1347, 1348.

[30] A Al Faruque, 'Typologies, Efficacy and Political Economy of Stabilisation Clauses: A Critical Appraisal' (2007) 5(4) *Oil, Gas & Energy Law* 1, 2.

[31] M Sornarajah, *The International Law on Foreign Investment* (Cambridge University Press, 2010) 282; Verhoosel, 'Legal Constraints', 455.

by an arbitral tribunal in the *Amoco International Finance Corporation v Iran* case as:

> [C]ontract language which freezes the provisions of a national system of law chosen as the law of the contract as of the date of the contract, in order to prevent the application to the contract of any future alterations of this system.[32]

Shemberg defines these clauses as the provisions found in contracts between investors and host states that concern the alterations of the laws of these host states over the lifespan of the contract.[33] This is actually one of the more ambiguous definitions of this term, and some parts remain unclear. According to Hirsch, the main aim of these clauses is to render new laws or regulatory alterations inapplicable to the investment contract or, if they are applicable, to make sure that the investor is remunerated for the burden that it took in order to comply with the changes.[34] In addition to this, Comeaux and Kinsella state that 'by agreeing to a stabilization clause, a state alienates its right to unilaterally change the regime and rights relied upon by, and promised to, the investor'.[35] Allison, on the other hand, defines this clause as a provision agreed by both the investor and the host state which states that there will not be any unilateral modifications of the investment contract.[36] The main element of a stability provision is to negate the host state's right to affect investors' rights by simply modifying its municipal laws.[37]

A more detailed and comprehensive definition will be employed in this book. Cameron and Montembault hold similar views on the definition of stabilisation clauses. According to them, it is a tool that comprises contractual or any other type of instruments that intend to keep the contract insulated from the adverse effects of economic and legal changes that occur after the conclusion of the contract for the entirety of its duration.[38]

---

[32] *Amoco International Finance v Iran*, 15 Iran-US CTR 189, 239, cited in RD Bishop, 'International Arbitration of Petroleum Disputes: The Development of a Lex Petrolea' (1998) 23 *Yearbook Commercial Arbitration* 1131, 1158.

[33] A Shemberg, 'Stabilization Clauses and Human Rights: A Research Project Conducted for IFC and the United Nations Special Representative to the Secretary General on Business and Human Rights' (2009) www.ifc.org/wps/wcm/connect/0883d81a-e00a-4551-b2b9-46641e5a9bba/Stabilization%2BPaper.pdf?MOD=AJPERES&CACHEID=ROOTWORKSPACE-0883d81a-e00a-4551-b2b9-46641e5a9bba-jqeww2e.

[34] Hirsch, 'FET and Stabilization', 787.

[35] PE Comeaux and NS Kinsella, 'Reducing Political Risk in Developing Countries: Bilateral Investment Treaties, Stabilization Clauses, and MIGA & OPIC Investment Insurance' (1994) 15(1) *New York Law School Journal of International and Comparative Law* 1, 23.

[36] RC Allison, *Protecting against the Expropriation Risk in Investing Abroad* (Matthew Bender, 1988) 2–18.

[37] PE Comeaux and NS Kinsella, *Protecting Foreign Investment under International Law: Legal Aspects of Political Risk* (Oceana Publications, 1997) 139.

[38] B Montembault, 'The Stabilisation of State Contracts Using the Example of Oil Contracts. A Return of the Gods of Olympia?' (2003) 6 *International Business Law Journal* 593, 596; Cameron, *International Energy Investment Law*, 69.

The source of the stability provision can be contracts, national legislation or treaties.[39] Even if the scholarly discussion on definitions of the term mainly focus on contractual stability provisions, we can use the same definitions for the stability provisions found in national legislation as well, since the objectives of both provisions are the same. The main objectives of stability provisions are mostly indicated to be protection against political risk and promotion of foreign investment.[40]

The most overt purpose of a stability provision is its application as a barrier against political risks, since it is specifically designed to manage them.[41] Its role as a mechanism to protect the investment from the adverse effects of political risks has not been contested to any real extent in the literature and, indeed, the majority of definitions focus on this aspect. It is accepted as a tool that aims to achieve this result. Whether it is effective or not in practice is another matter entirely.

However, there have been various views on its role of promoting foreign investment. Some scholars argue that stability provisions have been used by host states as a tool to attract the foreign investment that they are in need of.[42] Waelde argues that the practice of freezing clauses may be interpreted as a result of the weaker bargaining positions of the host states, which are 'trying to attract investment at all costs'.[43] Host states might at times find a contractual stabilisation clause to be preferable to negotiating investment treaties when trying to lure investments.[44] Also, a host state that wants to compete with its neighbours might offer stabilisation clauses if its neighbours are already offering them.[45]

On the other hand, some argue that this view of developing states competing for foreign investment, and thus offering stability provisions, is merely rhetoric in the literature without any realistic reasoning.[46] Indeed, this view is also supported by Cameron to an extent. He states that there are many host states which do not

---

[39] There is not a direct stability provision under treaties in the sense that is used under contracts or national laws, rather some of the standards can be used to provide stability to the investment relationship. This issue will be discussed under s IV.

[40] J Gjuzi, *Stabilization Clauses in International Investment Law: A Sustainable Development Approach* (Springer, 2018) 22–33; A Umirdinov, 'The End of Hibernation of Stabilization Clause in Investment Arbitration: Reassessing Its Contribution to Sustainable Development' (2015) 43 *Denver Journal of International Law & Policy* 455, 456; Al Faruque, 'Typologies, Efficacy and Political Economy', 10–14.

[41] Gjuzi, *Stabilization*, 81; K Gehne and R Brillo, 'Stabilization Clauses in International Investment Law: Beyond Balancing and Fair and Equitable Treatment' (NCCR Trade Regulation, 2014) 4; Waelde and Ndi, 'Stabilizing International Investment Commitments', 221.

[42] Umirdinov, 'End of Hibernation', 456; Gehne and Brillo, 'Stabilization Clauses', 28; R Dolzer and C Schreuer, *Principles of International Investment Law* (Oxford University Press, 2012) 82; Al Faruque, 'Typologies, Efficacy and Political Economy', 14; Comeaux and Kinsella, 'Reducing Political Risk', 31–32; E Paasivirta, 'Internationalization and Stabilization of Contracts versus State Sovereignty' (1989) 60(1) *British Yearbook of International Law* 315, 325; CT Curtis, 'The Legal Security of Economic Development Agreements' (1988) 29(2) *Harvard International Law Journal* 317, 319–21.

[43] TW Waelde, 'Negotiating for Dispute Settlement in Transnational Mineral Contracts: Current Practice, Trends, and an Evaluation from the Host Country's Perspective' (1977) 7 *Denver Journal of International Law & Policy* 33, 69.

[44] Dolzer and Schreuer, *Principles*, 83.

[45] PD Cameron, 'Stabilization and the Impact of Changing Patterns of Energy Investment' (2017) 10(5) *Journal of World Energy Law & Business* 389, 393.

[46] Frank, 'Presumptions v Realities', 52.

offer these clauses and yet have no problem attracting foreign investment, so the stability provision does not seem a mandatory requirement in that sense.[47]

Furthermore, Frank asserts that there is no proven correlation between stability provisions offered by the host states and the foreign investment attracted into that state, even though such provisions are recommended by some international organisations.[48] According to this view, these provisions are viewed simply as rent-seeking behaviour on the part of the investors, and their lawyers will get a stability provision incorporated into the contract if they can as it increases the profit margin without the need for any additional reasoning.[49]

That said, it should be noted that an international energy investment process is not simply a yes or no question. Rather, it includes various complex stages, such as economical calculations and risk assessment aspects. The presence of stability provisions might not be an indicative factor when all the other elements of the investment evaluation prove that the investment would be profitable, but stability provisions may play a determinant role as an incentive tool when the assessment results are not crystal clear on the investor's side.

C. Types of Stability Provisions and Discrepancy in Terminology in the Literature

One of the issues that one faces in the literature is the discrepancy in the denomination of stabilisation provisions. Different authors give different names to the exact same legal provisions, which causes complexity and confusion when attempting a rigorous analysis. One of the reasons for this problem is that, in practice, these clauses are designed and drafted to provide stability to the investment relationship in various flexible ways, not in strict forms.[50] The investment contract negotiators of international investors – generally their lawyers – produce tailor-made contractual provisions that best suit their needs. Therefore, one ends up with various approaches to the exact same condition. Moreover, the scholars interpret these provisions by virtue of their own perceptions and understandings of the issue and their own legal backgrounds.

Whereas Alexander groups stabilisation clauses under eight different headings and regards freezing clauses as classic types and the rest as modern types,[51]

---

[47] Cameron, 'Stabilisation in Investment Contracts', 12–13.

[48] Frank, 'Presumptions v Realities', 115.

[49] H Mann, 'Stabilization in Investment Contracts: Rethinking the Context, Reformulating the Result' (*Investment Treaty News*, 2011) www.iisd.org/itn/2011/10/07/stabilization-in-investment-contracts-rethinking-the-context-reformulating-the-result/; R Howse, 'Freezing Government Policy: Stabilization Clauses in Investment Contracts' (*Investment Treaty News*, 2011) www.iisd.org/itn/2011/04/04/freezing-government-policy-stabilization-clauses-in-investment-contracts-2/.

[50] Frank, 'Presumptions v Realities', 90.

[51] These are: freezing, specified economic balancing, non-specified economic balancing, negotiated economic balancing, government pays-without limitation, government pays-with limitation,

Bernardini argues that the freezing clause type is the prevailing stability provision and that it is different to adaptation/renegotiation clauses.[52] In a similar vein, while Erkan acknowledges that there are various types of stabilisation clauses, he argues that stabilisation and renegotiation (equilibrium) clauses are rival contractual mechanisms.[53] However, the prevailing opinion in the contemporary literature, including works by Cameron, Alexander, Maniruzzaman, Shemberg and Cotula, is that economic balancing (adaptation) clauses are a part of stabilisation clauses.[54]

Likewise, hybrid clauses also create a certain ambiguity in the literature. While Faruque argues that this is another name for economic stabilisation clauses,[55] other scholars characterise hybrid clauses as a sub-type of stabilisation clauses.[56]

As is also seen from this discussion, the very same contractual practice can be called by different names in the literature, such as adaptation, renegotiation, economic balancing or equilibrium clauses. This book will attempt to adopt a broad meaning of the term 'stabilisation clause' and will not restrict it to just the freezing types.

This book groups stabilisation clauses under five different categories: freezing, intangibility, economic balancing, allocation of burden and hybrid. Indeed, some contemporary authors share similar views regarding these categories, as will be seen below. However, in some articles published before 2000 it is possible to note that, in particular, intangibility clauses were not considered stabilisation clauses.[57] Yet, in numerous articles, these are considered stabilisation clauses, and sometimes as parts of freezing clauses as well.[58]

---

government indemnifies-without limitation, government indemnifies-with limitation. For detailed definitions, see F Alexander, 'Comment on Articles on Stabilization by Piero Bernardini, Lorenzo Cotula and AFM Maniruzzaman' (2009) 2(3) *Journal of World Energy Law & Business* 243.

[52] P Bernardini, 'Stabilization and Adaptation in Oil and Gas Investments' (2008) 1(1) *Journal of World Energy Law & Business* 98, 98–101.

[53] M Erkan, *International Energy Investment Law: Stability through Contractual Clauses* (Kluwer Law International, 2011) 196.

[54] Cameron, 'Stabilisation in Investment Contracts', 31; AFM Maniruzzaman, 'The Pursuit of Stability in International Energy Investment Contracts: A Critical Appraisal of the Emerging Trends' (2008) 1(2) *Journal of World Energy Law & Business* 121, 126; Shemberg, 'Stabilization Clauses', 7; Cotula, 'Reconciling Regulatory Stability', 161.

[55] Al Faruque, 'Typologies, Efficacy and Political Economy', 9; the same approach can also be found in K Tienhaara, 'Unilateral Commitments to Investment Protection: Does the Promise of Stability Restrict Environmental Policy Development?' (2006) 17(1) *Yearbook of International Environmental Law* 139, 150.

[56] Shemberg, 'Stabilization Clauses', 26; M Mansour and C Nakhle, 'Fiscal Stabilization in Oil and Gas Contracts: Evidence and Implications' (Oxford Institute for Energy Studies, 2016) www.oxfordenergy.org/publications/fiscal-stabilization-in-oil-and-gas-contracts-evidence-and-implications/; SF Halabi, 'Efficient Contracting between Foreign Investors and Host States: Evidence from Stabilized Clauses' (2011) 31(2) *Northwestern Journal of International Law & Business* 261, 293.

[57] Paasivirta, 'Internationalization and Stabilization', 323; Garcia-Amador, 'State Responsibility', 23.

[58] L Mistelis, 'Contractual Mechanisms for Stability in Energy Contracts' in M Scherer (ed), *International Arbitration in the Energy Sector* (Oxford University Press, 2018) 156; Partasides and Martinez, 'Stabilisation', 63; P Pusceddu, 'Contractual Stability in the Oil and Gas Industry: Stabilization, Renegotiation and Unilateral State's Undertakings' (2014) (2) *International Energy Law Review* 58, 59; Gehne and Brillo, 'Stabilization Clauses'; Cameron, *International Energy Investment Law*, 28; Cotula, 'Reconciling Regulatory Stability', 160; Coale, 'Stabilization Clauses', 223; W Peter, 'Stabilization Clauses in State Contracts' (1998) (8) *International Business Law Journal* 875, 875.

These five categories could also be reviewed under two common strands: traditional clauses and contemporary clauses. The clauses that aim to prevent a change, partially or totally, to the legal framework of the investment might be considered traditional, whereas those in which a change in the circumstances and the balancing act that follows the modification have already been stipulated might be seen as contemporary.

(i) Freezing Clauses

One of the oldest forms of stabilisation provisions is the freezing clause, and this is generally referred to as the classic or traditional approach. This clause is also named the stabilisation clause *sensu stricto* in the literature.[59] In a nutshell, it prevents the host states from altering their laws or putting new legislation in place after the conclusion of the contract that is inapplicable to that particular investment contract.[60] These clauses have the aim of freezing the applicable law, the fiscal regime and the surrounding investment circumstances at the time the contract was concluded, thereby leaving the contract outside of the scope of application of new legislation.[61] In other words, they try to set a limit to the legislative competence of the host state.[62]

Cameron describes this clause as 'handcuffing' the host state and incapacitating it with regard to performing its sovereign rights and altering its laws as it desires.[63] According to Shemberg, freezing clauses have been used in the last two decades in numerous parts of the world, including sub-Saharan Africa, the Middle East, North Africa, Latin America, the Caribbean, Eastern Europe, Southern Europe, Central Asia, South Asia, East Asia and the Pacific.[64] This data tells us that although this type of stabilisation clause is considered 'classic' or 'traditional', it is still being used in contemporary contractual practice. Even though full-freezing forms are not common today, limited-freezing forms can still be found in modern contracts of numerous host states.[65]

Alongside the contractual practice, some authors have also asserted that this type was considered the most effective stabilisation method used by international lawyers.[66] However, the prevailing view in the literature and in legal practice

---

[59] Coale, 'Stabilization Clauses', 223; Gjuzi, *Stabilization*, 38.

[60] Cameron, *International Energy Investment Law*, 70; Shemberg, 'Stabilization Clauses', 5.

[61] Waelde and Ndi, 'Stabilizing International Investment Commitments', 260; Curtis, 'Legal Security', 346; Montembault, 'State Contracts', 596.

[62] TAQ Al Emadi, 'Stabilization Clauses in International Joint Venture Agreements' (2010) (3) *International Energy Law Review* 54, 55.

[63] Cameron, *International Energy Investment Law*, 70.

[64] Shemberg, 'Stabilization Clauses', 20–21.

[65] Cameron, *International Energy Investment Law*, 71.

[66] AS El-Kosheri, 'Settling Disputes in the Energy Sector: The Particularity of the Conflict Avoidance Methods Pertaining to Petroleum Agreements' (1996) 11(2) *ICSID Review – Foreign Investment Law Journal* 272, 277.

regarding the efficiency of stabilisation clauses today contradicts this statement. It is possible to see from the literature and contractual practice that there is a shift from pure freezing clauses towards more contemporary stabilisation clauses.[67]

A comprehensive example of the freezing clause can be found in the Tunisian Model Production Sharing Contract:

> The Contractor shall be subject to the provisions of this Contract as well as to all laws and regulations duly enacted by the Granting Authority and which are not incompatible or conflicting with the Convention and/or this Agreement. It is also agreed that no new regulations, modifications or interpretation which could be conflicting or incompatible with the provisions of this Agreement and/or the Convention shall be applicable.[68]

As can be seen, this clause prevents the host state from changing its legislation or applying changes to the contract, and even prohibits subsequent alteration of the interpretation of the existent legislation. This is a strict type of freezing clause and leaves no room for the host state to apply changes to the contracting party. This is sometimes referred to as a full-freezing clause, which aims to freeze all laws.[69]

When a freezing clause focuses only on certain laws, such as tax law or labour law, and intends to insulate the investor from the changes of those specific laws, then this type is considered a limited-freezing clause.[70] An example of this form is:

> The … Laws and Decrees which may in the future impose higher rates or more progressive rates of [tax] or would otherwise impose a greater … tax liability than that anticipated under Section … of the Upstream Project Agreement shall not apply to the Company.[71]

(ii) Intangibility Clauses

An intangibility clause, sometimes referred to as *inviolability*, aims to prevent host states from unilaterally altering the terms of the contract or abrogating the contract by exercising their sovereign powers.[72] As mentioned above, a freezing clause provides that the host state may not change the law applicable to the contract through the use of its legislative power. An intangibility clause, on the other hand, freezes the contract provisions, not the law itself.[73] This is a measure against the host state's administrative threat.[74] An intangibility clause, like a freezing clause, is also considered an early form of stabilisation clause, which means that they were

---

[67] Even if there is a trend of praising contemporary stabilisation clauses in the literature, this book will dispute this premise with respect to the legitimate expectations principle in ch 6.

[68] Tunisia Model Production Sharing Contract (1989), Art 24.1, cited in Cameron, *International Energy Investment Law*, 71.

[69] Shemberg, 'Stabilization Clauses', 6.

[70] Al Faruque, 'Typologies, Efficacy and Political Economy', 4.

[71] Shemberg, 'Stabilization Clauses', 6.

[72] Coale, 'Stabilization Clauses', 223; Garcia-Amador, 'State Responsibility', 23; Curtis, 'Legal Security', 346.

[73] Cameron, *International Energy Investment Law*, 74.

[74] Montembault, 'State Contracts', 599.

widely used during an era in which the international investors had the bargaining power and upper hand in contract negotiations.[75] That is to say, Cameron's handcuffing metaphor for freezing clauses mentioned above also applies here in the sense of the intangibility clause's aim to restrict the host state's capability to alter the contract.

An example of this clause can be found in the concession contract between Liamco and Libya:

> (1) The Government of Libya, the Commission and the appropriate provincial authorities will take all steps necessary to ensure that the Company enjoys all the rights conferred by this Concession. The contractual rights expressly created by this Concession shall not be altered except by mutual consent of the parties.[76]

This type of clause generally entails the mutual consent of both parties to change the provisions of the contract. The requirement of the consent provides the parties with a chance to discuss the future of the contract and prevent any potential deteriorations in the contractual relationship.[77]

The Model Production Sharing Agreement of Tanzania, which is a contemporary contract, also includes a brief intangibility clause: '(a) This Agreement shall not be amended or modified in any respect except by the mutual consent in writing of the parties hereto.'[78]

Some contracts use both freezing and intangibility clauses together. An example of this type of provision is available in the agreement between the Sultan of Oman and the Sun Group:

> 22.1 The Sultan shall not annul this Agreement by general or special legislation or by administrative measures or by any other act [except in the event of default by the other party].
>
> 22.2 The mutual written consent of the Sultan and the Sun Group shall be required to annul, amend or modify the provisions of this Agreement.
>
> 22.3 The Sultan agrees that no discriminatory laws or decrees affecting the Sun Group or its operations will be enacted.[79]

(iii) Economic Balancing Clauses

Since it is not possible for classic stabilisation clauses to fully hinder the sovereign powers of the host states, a new technique was accordingly developed to maintain

---

[75] Al Emadi, 'Stabilization Clauses', 55.

[76] *LIAMCO v Libya*, 62 ILR 140, 170 (1980), cited in Comeaux and Kinsella, 'Reducing Political Risk', 24.

[77] Cameron, *International Energy Investment Law*, 74.

[78] Model Production Sharing Agreement of Tanzania (2013), Art 35 www.wgei.org/wp-content/uploads/2015/10/Tanzania-Model-Production-Sharing-Agreement-2013.pdf.

[79] The Petroleum Agreement of 4 February 1973 between the Sultan of Oman and the Sun Group, cited in Paasivirta, 'Internationalization and Stabilization', 324.

the economic balance of the contract.[80] Economic balancing clauses, frequently referred to as *economic equilibrium* or *rebalancing clauses*, are considered 'modern' forms of stabilisation clauses.[81] Although they are called such, this does not mean that they are new in practice; rather, it is possible to come across these clauses in contracts that were concluded more than two decades ago,[82] and scholarly works were likewise mentioning them around the same time.[83]

These clauses suggest that when host states alter the conditions of the contractual relationship in a way that damages the economic benefits of the investor, then an economic balancing or restoring should take place.[84] While freezing and intangibility clauses try to prevent or negate the effects of host states exercising their sovereign rights, economic balancing clauses do not make the same attempt, but, rather, stipulate a counterbalance for changes made by the host states and suggest the maintenance of the economic equilibrium of the contract, as of its effective date, for the duration of its lifespan.[85] Economic balancing clauses deal with changes after they occur (ex post); however, classic types intend to avert them before they take place (ex ante).[86]

Economic equilibrium was defined in the Baku–Tbilisi–Ceyhan Host Government Agreements as:

> Economic Equilibrium means the economic value to the Project Participants of the relative balance established under the Project Agreements at the applicable date between the rights, interests, exemptions, privileges, protections and other similar benefits provided or granted to such Person and the concomitant burdens, costs, obligations, restrictions, conditions and limitations agreed to be borne by such Person.[87]

In practice, different types of economic balancing clauses are developed for different situations. For the purpose of this book, they will be collected under three different headings: specified economic balancing; non-specified economic balancing; and negotiated economic balancing.[88]

The specified economic balancing clause is referred to as stipulated economic balancing by some authors.[89] According to this type of provision, the parties have already agreed on how to provide the balancing if the host state's unilateral action takes place and affects the investor's economic position as prevailed on the

---

[80] Maniruzzaman, 'The Pursuit of Stability', 126.

[81] Gehne and Brillo, 'Stabilization Clauses', 3; Verhoosel, 'Legal Constraints', 455.

[82] Alexander, 'Comment on Articles on Stabilization', 246.

[83] GR Delaume, 'The Proper Law of State Contracts Revisited' (1997) 12(1) *ICSID Review – Foreign Investment Law Journal* 1, 23–27.

[84] Cameron, *International Energy Investment Law*, 75.

[85] Maniruzzaman, 'The Pursuit of Stability', 126.

[86] Al Faruque, 'Typologies, Efficacy and Political Economy'.

[87] Host Government Agreement between and among the Government of the Republic of Turkey and The MEP Participants, Appendix 1 www.bp.com/content/dam/bp/country-sites/en_az/azerbaijan/home/pdfs/legalagreements/gov-agreements/btc_eng_agmt3_agmt3.pdf.

[88] Alexander, 'Comment on Articles on Stabilization', 246.

[89] Gehne and Brillo, 'Stabilization Clauses'; Maniruzzaman, 'The Pursuit of Stability', 127.

effective date of the contract.[90] This might be done as an automatic amendment by, for example, stipulating a readjustment criterion for profit petroleum split when the contract is a production sharing contract (PSC).[91] An example of this type can be found in a PSC between Burlington and Ecuador:

> Modification to the tax system: In the event of a modification to the tax system or the creation or elimination of new taxes not foreseen in this Contract, which have an impact on the economics of this Contract, a correction factor will be included in the production sharing percentages to absorb the impact of the increase or decrease in the tax.[92]

Another good example of this type was available in an earlier model PSC from Pakistan:

> (b) Where any agency or authority of the Government imposes any tax, cess, fee, duty, levy, or other ancillary payment in addition to the guaranteed payments in Article 31.1(a) as required by the laws of Pakistan other than those concerning health, safety and environmental and related matters of public interest, Government Holdings shall consult with Contractor on appropriate measures in order to compensate Contractor for such unfavourable impacts caused by such amendments. After having quantified the unfavourable impacts, the Government Holdings share of Profit Oil and Profit Gas shall be adjusted in such a manner that the overall fiscal balance is maintained.[93]

Frequently adopted methods of specified balancing in practice include tax rebates, monetary compensation, amended tariffs, adjustment of the profit petroleum share and extension of the concession.[94]

A non-specified economic balancing clause also proposes an automatic adjustment following a unilateral act of the host state which upsets the economic balance of the contract, but does not specify how to achieve this balance or what the amendment should be.[95] It also does not provide that there must be a mutual agreement on the concerned amendment as a result of negotiations between contracting parties.[96] A detailed example of this provision can be seen in the Shah Deniz PSC:

> The rights and interests accruing to Contractor (or its assignees) under this Agreement and its Sub-contractors under this Agreement shall not be amended, modified or reduced without the prior consent of Contractor. In the event that any Governmental Authority invokes any present or future law, treaty, intergovernmental agreement, decree or administrative order which contravenes the provisions of this Agreement or adversely or positively affects the rights or interests of Contractor

---

[90] Gjuzi, *Stabilization*, 46; Alexander, 'Comment on Articles on Stabilization', 244.

[91] Maniruzzaman, 'The Pursuit of Stability', 127.

[92] *Burlington Resources Inc v Republic of Ecuador*, Decision on Jurisdiction, ICSID Case No ARB/08/5, 2 June 2010, para 24.

[93] Model Offshore Production Sharing Agreement of Pakistan, Art 31.1, cited in AFM Maniruzzaman, 'International Energy Contracts and Cross-Border Pipeline Projects: Stabilization, Renegotiation and Economic Balancing in Changed Circumstances – Some Recent Trends' (2006) 4(4) *Oil, Gas & Energy Law* 1, 4.

[94] Frank, 'Stabilisation Clauses', 23.

[95] Gjuzi, *Stabilization*, 47; Alexander, 'Comment on Articles on Stabilization', 244.

[96] Maniruzzaman, 'The Pursuit of Stability', 127.

hereunder, including, but not limited to, any changes in tax legislation, regulations, or administrative practice, or jurisdictional changes pertaining to the Contract Area, the terms of this Agreement shall be adjusted to re-establish the economic equilibrium of the Parties, and if the rights or interests of Contractor have been adversely affected, then SOCAR shall indemnify Contractor (and its assignees) for any disbenefit, deterioration in economic circumstances, loss or damages that ensue therefrom. SOCAR shall within the full limits of its authority use its reasonable lawful endeavours to ensure that the appropriate Governmental Authorities will take appropriate measures to resolve promptly in accordance with the foregoing principles any conflict or anomaly between any such treaty, intergovernmental agreement, law, decree or administrative order and this Agreement.[97]

As can be seen from the provision, it provides in detail for the possibilities as to how the economic balance of the contract can be affected. It also provides that in such an event, the contract shall be adjusted to maintain the economic balance, but does not specify a method to restore the balance. Even if it stipulates an adjustment, it is ambiguous about how to achieve this. This provision also combines an economic balancing clause with a freezing clause by saying that the rights and interests of the contractor cannot be amended.[98]

Unlike the first two forms of economic balancing clause, mentioned above, the last form includes a negotiation phase. In this type of balancing mechanism, parties are expressly obliged to enter a negotiating process in order to specify the methods to be applied with the aim of restoring the original economic balance of the contract.[99] If the parties fail to reach an agreement in these negotiations, a specific adjustment mechanism or the general dispute settlement method of the contract can be introduced to restore the balance.[100] An example of this form is existent in the model PSC of India:

> If any change in or to any Indian law, rule or regulation dealing with income tax or other corporate tax, export/import tax, excise, customs duty or any other levies, duties or taxes imposed on Petroleum or dependent upon the value of Petroleum results in a material change to the expected economic benefits accruing to any of the Parties after the date of execution of the Contract, the Parties shall consult promptly in good faith to make necessary revisions and adjustments to the Contract in order to maintain such expected economic benefits to each of the Parties, provided, however, that the expected economic benefits to the Parties shall not be reduced as a result of the operation of this Article.[101]

As can be seen, this provision is limited to changes in levies, duties or taxes. There are also other factors that might be to the detriment of the investor's financial

---

[97] Agreement on the Exploration, Development and Production Sharing for the Shah Deniz Prospective Area in the Azerbaijan Sector of the Caspian Sea, Art 23(2) www.bp.com/content/dam/bp/country-sites/en_az/azerbaijan/home/pdfs/legalagreements/psas/sd-psa.pdf.

[98] See s IIIC(v) for more details.

[99] Cameron, *International Energy Investment Law*, 75.

[100] Waelde and Ndi, 'Stabilizing International Investment Commitments', 265.

[101] Model Production Sharing Contract of India, 2005, Art 17.10 http://petroleum.nic.in/sites/default/files/MPSC%20NELP-V.pdf.

position. A provision that encompasses all the changes that might affect the economic balance of the contract can be found in the model PSC of Qatar:

> Whereas the financial position of the Contractor has been based, under the Agreement, on the laws and regulations in force at the Effective Date, it is agreed that, if any future law, decree or regulation affects Contractor's financial position, and in particular if the customs duties exceed … percent during the term of the Agreement, both Parties shall enter into negotiations, in good faith, in order to reach an equitable solution that maintains the economic equilibrium of this Agreement. Failing to reach agreement on such equitable solution, the matter may be referred by either Party to arbitration pursuant to Article 31.[102]

There are some features common to all negotiated economic balancing clauses, such as a triggering event (what causes the need for balancing), the objective of the balancing process (to restore the economic balance), a procedure for a negotiation phase (request, meeting, decision) and a course of action when negotiations fail.[103] However, it is also noteworthy that the triggering event is not specifically stated in the majority of contracts.[104] Some terms, such as 'adversely affected', 'significantly affect' or 'materially affect', are used in order to define the intensity of the triggering event.[105] This means that a need to restore the economic balance of the contract emerges when the contract is affected significantly or materially. These terms are also generally not defined in the contract but are left to the parties to decide or, in the event of a dispute, to the arbitrator.

The triggering events that affect the economic balance of the contractual relationship might include, inter alia, a change in the tax rate, a requirement for the investor to purchase 80 per cent of its goods and services from local companies (local content) or a requirement for the company to allocate funds to social spending, such as building schools and hospitals.[106]

While some of the balancing clauses only consider the interests of the investors, there are those that protect the interests of *any* parties involved.[107] According to these clauses, when the balance of the contract deteriorates on the host state side, the host state can also ask for an adjustment. This is also a distinguishing feature of modern stabilisation clauses. As mentioned above, during the early phases of stabilisation clauses, they were meant to protect investors from the adverse effects of host states' unilateral acts. They were introduced into international energy investment contracts while investors still held the balance of any bargaining power.

---

[102] Model Exploration and Production Sharing Agreement of 1994 of Qatar, Art 34.12; Barrows, Basic Oil Laws and Concession Contracts, Middle East, Supplement 124, 1 (1995), cited in P Bernardini, 'The Renegotiation of the Investment Contract' (1998) 13(2) *ICSID Review – Foreign Investment Law Journal* 411, 416.

[103] Cameron, *International Energy Investment Law*, 76; Bernardini, 'Stabilization and Adaptation', 103.

[104] Maniruzzaman, 'The Pursuit of Stability', 129.

[105] ibid.

[106] PD Cameron, 'Reflections on Sovereignty over Natural Resources and the Enforcement of Stabilization Clauses' in KP Sauvant (ed), *Yearbook on International Investment Law & Policy 2011–2012* (Oxford University Press, 2013) 324.

[107] Maniruzzaman, 'The Pursuit of Stability', 128.

It can be argued that one of the reasons for the shift from classic stabilisation clauses towards modern ones lies in this context. It can be said that with the effects of globalisation, host states are becoming more 'equal' in contract negotiations than they were before because they can easily acccess sample or model investment contracts and their stabilisation provisions and adapt them to their own needs without too much difficulty. As a result of this, stabilisation clauses included in modern contracts are more prone to reciprocal protection and adjustments.

However, this practice of protecting the interests of both parties is still rare, especially in the extractive industry, and the majority of the stabilisation clauses that we can see in arbitral cases are only intended to insulate the investors from those changes that might affect the contractual relationship.[108]

(iv) Allocation of Burden Clauses

Since the classic types of stabilisation clauses generate discussions regarding the sovereignty of host states, contractual practice has shifted towards new types of clauses – 'modern types', as they are called in the literature.[109] Allocation clauses are one of these modern types, the other being economic balancing clauses.

It is possible to find these clauses in a variety of forms, but generally they require the national oil companies (NOCs) that are contracting with the foreign investors to shoulder the burden of the host states' unilateral changes.[110] The reason underlying this approach is that these modern types of clauses pursue stability without the need for clashing with the sovereignty of the host states.[111] These are different from economic balancing clauses because there is no requirement for balancing; they only stipulate a transfer of any additional burden, emergent after the host states' alteration, from investors to NOCs and there is no change made to the contract.[112]

It is possible to see an example of this type of clause in the 2002 model production sharing agreement (PSA) of Qatar:

> The Government shall assume, pay and discharge or cause to be discharged on behalf of Contractor all Qatar income tax of the Contractor (including for greater certainty, Qatar income tax payable on payments made on behalf of Contractor pursuant to this Article 22.5). Qatar Petroleum, acting on behalf of the Government shall perform these duties.[113]

Since there is no need for contract amendment in the instance of any unilateral alteration by the host state that affects the economic balance of the contract and

---

[108] Frank, 'Stabilisation Clauses', 27.

[109] Waelde and Ndi, 'Stabilizing International Investment Commitments', 266.

[110] ibid; Cameron, *International Energy Investment Law*, 80.

[111] Erkan, *Stability*, 107.

[112] Cameron, *International Energy Investment Law*, 80.

[113] Qatar Model Development and Production Sharing Agreement (2002) between the Government of Qatar and Contractor (North Field), cited in Cameron, 'Reflections on Sovereignty', 329.

no discussion of the host state's sovereign authority, this type of stabilisation clause can be deemed to have a beneficial form.[114] These clauses do not tie the hands of the host state, thus allowing it to make changes.[115]

(v) Hybrid Clauses

The last form of stabilisation clauses is hybrid clauses, which include features of both freezing and economic balancing clauses.[116] So, a freezing clause in the classic meaning becomes a hybrid clause when it provides that in the event of an alteration in any laws affecting investor's economic position, the economic balance shall be readjusted accordingly.[117]

In hybrid clauses, the investors are not automatically exempted from amendments made by the host states, as in economic balancing clauses.[118] Shemberg presents an example of this clause in her research:

> Based upon Article … above, if any existing Laws of … or any other applicable or existing law of any other Government, is changed or repealed, or if new laws are introduced, or if there occurs a rise in the tax rate or the introduction of a new tax, which bears unfavourably on the financial status of the Joint Venture or the Parties, then the Parties will apply all efforts that are necessary to completely or partially release the Joint Venture or the Parties from the above-mentioned changes, or the Parties will undertake all other necessary steps to alleviate the unfavourable impact of these changes.[119]

While hybrid clauses in this book are considered to be combinations of freezing and economic balancing clauses, it should be noted that there are other possible combinations as well. None of the forms of stabilisation clauses are exclusive.[120] So, for example, intangibility and freezing clauses are used together in some stability provisions.[121]

D. Validity Aspect of Stability Provisions

(i) Validity Discussion

The validity of stabilisation clauses under international law has long been discussed by commentators and by arbitral tribunals. Even if the practical use and benefits

---

[114] ibid 331.
[115] PD Cameron, 'Investment Cycles and the Rule of Law in the International Oil and Gas Industry: Some Reflections on Changing Investor–State Relationships' (2016) 38(3) *Houston Journal of International Law* 755, 788.
[116] Shemberg, 'Stabilization Clauses', vii.
[117] ibid x.
[118] ibid 8.
[119] ibid.
[120] Cameron, *International Energy Investment Law*, 81.
[121] Erkan, *Stability*, 106.

of stabilisation clauses remain vague and controversial, there is almost a consensus in the literature and arbitral jurisprudence about the validity of such clauses. Since these clauses are considered valid by the vast majority of contemporary literature and arbitral tribunals, this book will not start a discussion of this issue from its roots; rather, it will provide a glimpse of the available discussions and analyse the challenges and arguments brought forward against the validity of these clauses.

The first aspect of the validity discussion originates from the permanent sovereignty over natural resources principle of international law. While discussing the validity of such clauses, this principle is used as the major argument against them. Hence, this book will start by analysing the principle and will then continue with some arbitral awards which discuss the validity of stabilisation clauses.

(ii) Permanent Sovereignty over Natural Resources

According to some authors, stabilisation clauses are invalid under international law.[122] The main argument that they propound is that these clauses hamper host states' sovereignty over their natural resources.[123] In order to assess this argument, we first need to look at the subject principle. The concept of permanent sovereignty means that natural resources must be used and controlled by the states in which they are located and its main aim is thus to maintain national control over natural resources.[124]

The permanent sovereignty over natural resources principle is based on the self-determination principle and evolved through several resolutions of the General Assembly of the United Nations.[125] One of the most widely supported resolutions was adopted in 1962 (entitled 'Permanent Sovereignty over Natural Resources') and states that: 'the right of peoples and nations to permanent sovereignty over their natural wealth and resources must be exercised in the interest of their national development'.[126] Another article of the same resolution states:

> Foreign investment agreements freely entered into by or between sovereign States shall be observed in good faith; States and international organizations shall strictly and conscientiously respect the sovereignty of peoples and nations over their natural wealth and resources in accordance with the Charter and the principles set forth in the present resolution.[127]

---

[122] TJ Pate, 'Evaluating Stabilization Clauses in Venezuela's Strategic Association Agreements for Heavy-Crude Extraction in the Orinoco Belt: The Return of a Forgotten Contractual Risk Reduction Mechanism for the Petroleum Industry' (2009) 40(2) *University of Miami Inter-American Law Review* 347, 351.

[123] M Sornarajah, 'The Myth of International Contract Law' (1981) 15(3) *Journal of World Trade* 187, 187.

[124] Paasivirta, 'Internationalization and Stabilization', 341–45.

[125] TB Hansen, 'The Legal Effect Given Stabilization Clauses in Economic Development Agreements' (1987) 28 *Virginia Journal of International Law* 1015, 1025.

[126] GA Res 1803, 17 UN GAOR Suppl (No 17), 15, UN Doc A/5217, Art 1(1) (1962) (hereinafter Resolution 1803), cited in ibid 1026.

[127] Resolution 1803, Art 8.

Considering UN Resolution 1803 and its subsequent resolutions, it is possible to say that this principle is considered a principle of international law.[128] However, the recognition of this principle within international law does not grant it the status of *jus cogens* as some have argued.[129] According to this argument, the permanent sovereignty over natural resources principle constitutes a *jus cogens*, which means a right that states cannot waive and an overriding principle of international law from which no derogation is acceptable.[130]

From this point of view, critics argue that the host states cannot waive or alienate their inalienable right to natural resources by contractual clauses, and thus a stabilisation clause which aims to derogate the host state's legislative power in this regard is null, void and unenforceable.[131] This led some host states to think that since their right to exploit their natural resources is permanent, a commitment made to private parties cannot derogate it.[132] That is to say, host states can exercise their sovereign powers to end contracts without having to pay compensation.[133] However, according to Hansen, claiming that this principle has embraced the *jus cogens* status is an overstatement of the principle.[134]

Sornarajah states that:

> The state, in theory, must act in the public good as it perceives it to be at any given time. It may not be possible, as a matter of constitutional theory, for a state to bind itself by a contract made with a private party, particularly a foreign party, to fetter its legislative power. It is trite law that a legislature is not bound by its own legislation and has the power to change it. That being so, a provision in a contract cannot bind the state. As a matter of constitutional theory, a stabilisation clause may not be able to achieve what it sets out to do.[135]

This view is shared by Chowdhury, who claims that it is inconsistent with the state sovereignty principle to accept that a government can bind the state continually by contractual guarantees given to foreigners.[136]

While some commentators argue that stabilisation clauses are invalid due to the argument explained above, others emphasise the sanctity of contracts (*pacta sunt servanda*) principle and claim that if it is possible for a state to bind itself with

---

[128] Erkan, *Stability*, 120.
[129] A Al Faruque, 'Validity and Efficacy of Stabilisation Clauses: Legal Protection vs. Functional Value' (2006) 23(4) *Journal of International Arbitration* 317, 323.
[130] Waelde and Ndi, 'Stabilizing International Investment Commitments', 244; J Crawford, *Brownlie's Principles of Public International Law* (Oxford University Press, 2012) 594.
[131] E Oshionebo, 'Stabilization Clauses in Natural Resource Extraction Contracts: Legal, Economic and Social Implications for Developing Countries' (2010) 10 *Asper Review of International Business and Trade Law* 1, 9.
[132] Bernardini, 'Stabilization and Adaptation', 101.
[133] Sornarajah, 'The Myth', 217.
[134] Hansen, 'The Legal Effect', 1027.
[135] Sornarajah, *The International Law on Foreign Investment*, 282.
[136] SR Chowdhury, 'Permanent Sovereignty and Its Impact on Stabilization Clauses, Standards of Compensation and Patterns of Development Co-operation' in K Hossain and SR Chowdhury (eds), *Permanent Sovereignty Over Natural Resources in International Law* (Frances Pinter, 1984) 53.

another state by a treaty and restrict the use of its prerogatives, it should also be possible for that state to bind itself with a contract.[137] Moreover, it is not legally or morally justifiable for a state to avoid its responsibilities after it commits itself in this manner.[138] Also, sovereignty does not embrace anything that prevents states from exercising their duties under a contract.[139] Indeed, it is an exercise of the very same sovereign authority by the host state to provide guarantees for protection of foreign investors, not a derogation of sovereign power.[140]

In fact, those who claim that stabilisation clauses are invalid do not implicitly recognise the sovereign authority of host states. If sovereignty includes the right to act freely and undertake contractual liabilities, arguing that a contractual clause that a host state entered into of its own free will is invalid amounts to a repudiation of the state's sovereign authority.

The view of the International Law Association is the same regarding this matter; it acknowledges that 'permanent sovereignty over natural resources, economic activities, and wealth is inalienable', and also states that 'a State may, however, accept obligations with regard to the exercise of such sovereignty, by treaty or by contract, freely entered into'.[141]

There is no obstacle to a host state undertaking obligations through stabilisation clauses provided that constitutional and legislative necessities are met.[142]

The permanent sovereignty over natural resources principle may be used by some host states as an exit door to challenge their former commitments under the shelter of this principle when they find it lucrative or expedient to do so.[143] A significant point that should be addressed here is that although a stabilisation clause is deemed valid under international law, this does not restrict the host states from intervening in that contract clause by altering its conditions.[144] The principle of permanent sovereignty over natural resources finds its meaning in this situation. If a host state decides to amend the contract, nothing can prevent it from doing so.[145] Judge Jimenez de Arechaga also indicates 'that the territorial state can never lose its legal capacity to change the destination or the method of exploitation

[137] Tienhaara, 'Unilateral Commitments', 155; Paasivirta, 'Internationalization and Stabilization', 329.
[138] LT Kissam and EK Leach, 'Sovereign Expropriation of Property and Abrogation of Concession Contracts' (1959) 28(2) *Fordham Law Review* 177, 204.
[139] ibid.
[140] Hansen, 'The Legal Effect', 1031; Chowdhury, 'Permanent Sovereignty and its Impact on Stabilization Clauses', 47.
[141] Declaration on the Progressive Development of Principles of Public International Law Relating to a New International Economic Order, in International Law Association Report of the Sixty-Second Conference held at Seoul 2, 6–7 (1987), cited in Garcia-Amador, 'State Responsibility', 36.
[142] Peter, 'Stabilization Clauses', 882.
[143] JV de Macedo, 'From Tradition to Modernity: Not Necessarily an Evolution – The Case of Stabilisation and Renegotiation Clauses' (2011) 9(1) *Oil, Gas & Energy Law* 1, 3.
[144] Verhoosel, 'Legal Constraints', 456; Allison, *Protecting Against the Expropriation*, 2–21.
[145] HT Mato, 'The Role of Stability and Renegotiation in Transnational Petroleum Agreements' (2012) 5(1) *Journal of Politics and Law* 33, 34; Verhoosel, 'Legal Constraints', 456.

of those resources whatever arrangements have been made for its exploitation and administration.[146]

If host states believe that stabilisation clauses deteriorate their economic or political positions in any manner, the solution should be to reassess the necessity of the inclusion of such clauses in their contracts when they negotiate with foreign investors. Asserting their invalidity after freely negotiating with the investors and accepting stabilisation clauses has no meaning. Host states must scrutinise these clauses in depth and decide whether there is an actual need and benefit to use them before they enter into the associated investment contract. As discussed above, after concluding the contract and allowing the foreign investor to start its project, it is pointless to argue the invalidity of stabilisation clauses if they have been included.

Another argument brought forward in defence of the validity of stabilisation clauses is the principle of estoppel. According to this principle, a state should not withdraw a promise that it undertook willingly and upon which the foreign investor has reasonably relied.[147]

(iii) Validity under Arbitral Jurisprudence

Arbitral awards have consistently recognised the validity of stabilisation clauses where they were undermined by unilateral host state actions.[148] Even if the consequences of violation of stabilisation clauses are not clear or different arbitrators have different opinions on it, the validity of such clauses has been upheld by international law in principle.[149]

There are numerous awards that include a discussion of stabilisation clauses, even if the awards were not based exclusively on them. Awards concerning arbitral jurisprudence on stabilisation clauses can be divided into three categories: the first includes awards from the 1970s and 1980s which deal with intangibility/freezing clauses; the second includes arguments based mainly on bilateral investment treaties, not on contracts; and the last includes those contemporary cases that discuss stabilisation clauses extensively.[150] This subsection will cover some of these awards with the intention of showing the position of arbitral jurisprudence.

In the *Saudi Arabia v Aramco* case, it was stated:

> By reason of its very sovereignty within its territorial domain, the State possesses the legal power to grant rights which it forbids itself to withdraw before the end of Concession, with the reservation of Clauses of the Concession Agreement relating to

[146] Jimenez de Arechaga, 'International Law in the Past Third of a Century' (1978) 159 *Recueil des Cours* 297, cited in Chowdhury, 'Permanent Sovereignty and its Impact on Stabilization Clauses', 46.

[147] Al Faruque, 'Validity and Efficacy', 323.

[148] Cameron, 'Reflections on Sovereignty', 337.

[149] Comeaux and Kinsella, 'Reducing Political Risk', 25.

[150] Frank, 'Stabilisation Clauses', 30.

its revocation. Nothing can prevent a State, in the exercise of its sovereignty, from binding itself irrevocably by the provisions of a concession and from granting to the concessionaire irretractable rights. Such rights have the character of acquired rights.[151]

From this award, we can see that the arguments claiming that it is not possible for a state to bind itself with contractual clauses have not been considered valid by arbitral tribunals. On the contrary, the Tribunal considered such action an exercise in the state's sovereignty. Arbitral tribunals have balanced the sovereignty principle and the sanctity of contracts by reasoning that this contractual undertaking means exactly this.[152]

An arbitral award from 1979 (*Agip v Congo*) discusses this issue:

86. These stabilization clauses, freely accepted by the Government, do not affect the principle of its sovereign legislative and regulatory powers, since it retains both in relation to those, whether nationals or foreigners, with whom it has not entered into such obligations, and that, in the present case, changes in the legislative and regulatory arrangements stipulated in the agreement simply cannot be invoked against the other contracting party.[153]

The stabilisation clause was deemed valid and enforceable under international law by this award and was not seen as a derogation from the permanent sovereignty principle.[154]

In *Texaco v Libya*, sole arbitrator Rene-Jean Dupuy dealt with the stabilisation clause as follows:

71. Such a provision, the effect of which is to stabilize the position of the contracting party, does not, in principle, impair the sovereignty of the Libyan State. Not only has the Libyan State freely undertaken commitments but also the fact that this clause stabilizes the petroleum legislation and regulations as of the date of the execution of the agreement does not affect in principle the legislative and regulatory sovereignty of Libya. Libya reserves all its prerogatives to issue laws and regulations in the field of petroleum activities in respect of national or foreign persons with which it has not undertaken such a commitment.[155]

Waelde and Ndi argued that even if these arbitral awards seem to recognise the validity of stabilisation clauses, a small number of awards cast doubt on this conclusion.[156] According to their analysis, two out of three awards in Libyan nationalisation cases concluded that stabilisation clauses cannot avert unilateral

---

[151] *Saudi Arabia v Arabian American Oil Company (Aramco)*, 27 ILR 117 (1958), 168, cited in Cameron, 'Reflections on Sovereignty', 336.

[152] Emeka, 'Stabilization Clauses', 1324.

[153] *AGIP Company v Popular Republic of the Congo*, Award, 30 November 1979; (1982) 21 *International Legal Materials* 726, 735–36.

[154] TW Waelde and G Ndi, 'Fiscal Regime Stability and Issues of State Sovereignty' in J Otto (ed), *Taxation of Mineral Enterprises* (Graham & Trotman, 1995) 81.

[155] *Texaco Overseas Petroleum Company/California Asiatic Oil Company v the Government of the Libyan Arab Republic*, Award, 19 January 1977; (1978) 17 *International Legal Materials* 24.

[156] Waelde and Ndi, 'Fiscal Regime Stability', 82.

alterations on the part of host states, and thus their validity is uncertain.[157] In their words: 'A great deal of uncertainty therefore exists as to the precise status of international norms – as well as the position of arbitrary practice – on the question of the validity of the stabilization clause under international law.'[158] However, a distinction must be made here between the validity and the effectiveness of stabilisation clauses. It might not always be possible for a contractual provision to be effective. However, lack of effectiveness does not render them invalid. Judge Jimenez de Arechaga also discussed this, stating:

> This does not mean that such stabilization clauses have no legal effect and may be considered as unwritten. An anticipated cancellation in violation of a contractual stipulation of such a nature would give rise to a special right to compensation; the amount of the indemnity would have to be much higher than in normal cases since the existence of such a clause constitutes a most pertinent circumstance which must be taken into account in determining the appropriate compensation.[159]

A more recent case from 2008 between Aguaytia and Peru also addresses stabilisation clauses extensively. In that award, the Tribunal stated:

> There is no need here to dwell on the importance for investors, obviously including the Claimant, of the stability guarantees given in the field of taxes, foreign currency, free remittance of profits and capital and exchange rates. Also, the 'stability of the right to non-discrimination' itself is of obvious importance for a foreign investor. It freezes the laws, rules and regulations applicable to it, as they were in existence at the time the Agreement was concluded. This means that no new law may be passed which would state that certain rules regarding non-discrimination would no longer apply to the Claimant. It especially guaranteed the constitutional right to equality before the law …[160]

Another important arbitral award from the same year was *Duke v Peru*. According to this award, the Tribunal not only found the stabilisation clause valid, but also expanded its scope and stated that it covers the changes in its interpretation and application by administrative or judicial bodies as well as amendments to applicable tax law.[161]

The Tribunal stated:

> [T]ax stabilization guarantees that: (a) laws or regulations that form part of the tax regime at the time the LSA is executed will not be amended or modified to the detriment of the investor, (b) a stable interpretation or application that is in place at the time

[157] ibid.

[158] ibid.

[159] Arechaga, 'International Law in the Past Third of a Century', 307, cited in Paasivirta, 'Internationalization and Stabilization', 330.

[160] *Aguaytia Energy LLC v Republic of Peru*, Award, ICSID Case No ARB/06/13, 11 December 2008, para 95.

[161] L Cotula, 'Pushing the Boundaries vs Striking a Balance: The Scope and Interpretation of Stabilization Clauses in Light of the Duke v Peru Award' (2010) 11(1) *Journal of World Investment & Trade* 27, 37.

the LSA is executed will not be changed to the detriment of the investor, and (c) even in the absence of (a) and (b), stabilized laws will not be interpreted or applied in a patently unreasonable or arbitrary manner.[162]

As can be seen from these arbitral awards, there is no doubt as to the validity of stabilisation clauses. While the permanent sovereignty over natural resources principle is accepted by tribunals, this was not considered an obstacle to states freely undertaking contractual obligations. These are just a few of the arbitral awards that have upheld the validity of stabilisation clauses.

E. Effectiveness of Stability Provisions

Even though the validity of stability provisions is well established, the same cannot be said for the effectiveness of such provisions. The main question here is not related to its legal value; rather, the contentious aspect is related to its practical use. It is obvious that the mere existence of a stability provision in any form will not have a hindering effect on a sovereign host state's legislative or regulatory power.[163] A stability provision cannot prevent a host state from unilaterally altering its legal environment.

Joffé et al made the following observation on this issue: 'Stabilisation clauses have rarely been effective since producer governments still enforced changes in contractual terms to reflect their perception of their right to capture additional rent.'[164] So, in achieving what the name of such provisions reflects, 'stability', these provisions fall short. A stabilisation clause is said to have mainly a psychological effect on the host state about not breaching a contract.[165]

The evolution of stability provisions and the shift towards more flexible forms can also be considered a sign of pursuit of a more effective tool to achieve stability.[166] When the investors and their lawyers saw that the early types of stabilisation clauses were not working effectively and achieving what they had aimed for, they embarked on a quest to find alternative methods.

That said, it should be kept in mind that this effectiveness debate is restricted only to the phase prior to any violation of a contract or an investment treaty. Even if these stability provisions may not prevent a host state from taking unilateral steps to damage the investment, and could thus be considered ineffective, they are

---

[162] *Duke Energy International Peru Investments No 1 Ltd v Republic of Peru*, Award, ICSID Case No ARB/03/28, 18 August 2008, para 227.

[163] Al Faruque, 'Validity and Efficacy', 329; E Eljuri and C Trevino, 'Energy Investment Disputes in Latin America: The Pursuit of Stability' (2015) 33(2) *Berkeley Journal of International Law* 306, 340.

[164] G Joffé et al, 'Expropriation of Oil and Gas Investments: Historical, Legal and Economic Perspectives in a New Age of Resource Nationalism' (2009) 2(1) *Journal of World Energy Law & Business* 3, 22.

[165] de Macedo, 'From Tradition to Modernity', 4.

[166] PD Cameron, 'In Search of Investment Stability' in K Talus (ed), *Research Handbook on International Energy Law* (Edward Elgar Publishing, 2014) 138.

still one of the most effective tools in the investment arbitration process. This argument will be expounded in the following chapters.

IV. Sources of Stability Guarantees

The rules applicable to an international investment consist of three legal frameworks, namely the contractual legal framework, the national legal framework and the international legal framework.[167] Thus, the legal atmosphere that surrounds stability guarantees is composed of these legal components. There are various legal sources that an investor or a host state can use to provide a stability guarantee to an investment relationship using one of the above-mentioned types of stability provisions. A stability guarantee might be in the form of a contractual provision, a separate stability agreement, a part of the national legislation of the host state or a treaty standard. In the following subsections, these sources will be identified and analysed.

A. Stability in the Form of a Contractual Clause

This is the most discussed and most widely known/applied source of stability guarantee, both in the literature and in practice. As mentioned in section III, stability provisions were first introduced by international energy investment contracts. Prior to the creation of the investment treaty regime, contracts were the major instruments concerned with the protection of foreign investment, and they were mainly one-sided concessions.[168] The contracts between a sovereign host state and an international investor are often referred to as state contracts or host government contracts.[169] These contracts are not considered to be purely private law instruments, but rather include public law and administrative law features.[170] The most common types of such contracts found in the petroleum industry practice are concession agreements and PSAs.[171]

Contracts are generally preferred by international energy investors over the national legislation of host states.[172] The most important reason underlying that

---

[167] JW Salacuse, *The Three Laws of International Investment: National, Contractual, and International Frameworks for Foreign Capital* (Oxford University Press, 2013) 35.

[168] JO Voss, *Impact of Investment Treaties on Contracts between Host States and Foreign Investors* (Martinus Nijhoff Publishers, 2010) 7.

[169] W Peter, *Arbitration and Renegotiation of International Investment Agreements* (Kluwer Law International, 1995) 46; K Talus, S Looper and S Otillar, 'Lex Petrolea and the Internationalization of Petroleum Agreements: Focus on Host Government Contracts' (2012) 5(3) *Journal of World Energy Law & Business* 181, 183.

[170] Talus, Looper and Otillar, 'Lex Petrolea', 183.

[171] For more details on various types of state contracts, see Voss, *Impact of Investment Treaties*, 15–24.

[172] A Al Faruque, *Petroleum Contracts: Stability and Risk Management in Developing Countries* (Bangladesh Institute of Law and International Affairs, 2011) 57.

preference is the fact that the contractual legal framework of an investment relationship is determined to a large extent by the negotiations of the relevant parties.[173] With that, host states are being pulled down from their sovereign positions to one that is more equal to that of their investors.[174] With the help of the negotiation process, contracts can be designed to cover the specific requirements of an investment[175] and, indeed, the prerogatives of the host state can be contracted away.[176] Yackee also states the same regarding investment contracts: 'Investment contracts are potentially the most effective investment protection instruments available because they allow investors to draft terms tailored to specific investment needs.'[177]

Another reason for the preference of contracts is that the laws of the host state may not be adequate to govern such an investment relationship and therefore a need for a comprehensive governing legal framework arises.[178]

It is argued that by the choice of a contract rather than the local laws of the host state, the investment regime is more protected from unilateral interferences, although it does not completely insulate the investment from interventions.[179] However, contracts are built upon a specific set of legal rules from which the contract takes its force to govern the investment relationship.[180] This body of legal rules might be the laws of the host state which is one of the parties of an investment contract.[181] In such a case, the host state would not be restricted in any way under international law in terms of enacting new laws which might be in breach of the contract[182] since it is not a contract governed by international law.[183] If this is the case, the argument of a contract being more protected is invalid. In order to avoid such a situation and give the contract the required protection and power, a theory called the internationalisation of the investment contract was developed.

(i) Internationalisation of Contracts

As already mentioned, a state contract concluded between a host state and an international investor does not always require the application of international law

---

[173] Salacuse, *Three Laws*, 39.
[174] Waelde and Ndi, 'Stabilizing International Investment Commitments', 234.
[175] Al Faruque, *Petroleum Contracts*, 57.
[176] Peter, *Arbitration and Renegotiation*, 48.
[177] JW Yackee, 'Do We Really Need BITs – Toward a Return to Contract in International Investment Law' (2008) 3(1) *Asian Journal of WTO & International Health Law and Policy* 121, 133. See also Gjuzi, *Stabilization*, 33.
[178] Dolzer and Schreuer, *Principles*, 79.
[179] Waelde and Ndi, 'Stabilizing International Investment Commitments', 234–36.
[180] Salacuse, *Three Laws*, 160.
[181] Curtis, 'Legal Security', 325.
[182] FA Mann, 'The Consequences of an International Wrong in International and National Law' (1977) 48(1) *British Yearbook of International Law* 1, 60; cited in Comeaux and Kinsella, *Legal Aspects of Political Risk*, 28.
[183] Talus, Looper and Otillar, 'Lex Petrolea', 192.

in the event of a dispute. Choosing the law applicable to the contract is considered the most important legal matter for both parties of a contractual relationship.[184] In order to benefit from the protection available under international law, investors tend to subject the contract to international law by inserting a choice of law clause combined with an arbitration clause.[185] While the parties may include a choice of law clause and determine that a law other than the law of the host state be applied when a dispute arises, they may also fail to do so, and therefore the arbitral tribunal should specify the law to be applied in such instances.[186] Internationalisation of the contract theory simply aims to exclude an investment contract from the sphere of national law of the host state and put it under the roof of international law, thereby providing protection to the investor from the host state's unilateral interference.[187]

Mann provided a clarification to the term 'internationalisation of the contract' as follows:

> Although normally the law of a given State will govern the State contract, precisely 30 years ago another possible solution was suggested. It was said that a contract between a State and an alien private person could be 'internationalized' in the sense of being subjected to the only other legal order known to us, namely public international law. This does not mean or was ever intended to mean that the State contract should be considered to be a treaty or should be governed by public international law in the same way as transactions between States. It simply means that by exercising their right to choose the applicable legal system the parties may make public international law the object of their choice.[188]

As can be seen from Mann's explanation, the parties might specify international law as the applicable law to their investment relationship explicitly. However, some arbitral decisions and scholarly writings argue that even in the absence of an explicit submission of the dispute to international law the contract might be deemed internationalised and thus be subject to international law. Several arbitral awards have dealt with this issue, including some which have recognised the stability provisions as evidence of the parties' willingness to submit the dispute to international law.[189]

---

[184] Dolzer and Schreuer, *Principles*, 81.

[185] Waelde and Ndi, 'Stabilizing International Investment Commitments', 241.

[186] Hansen, 'The Legal Effect', 1019.

[187] Voss, *Impact of Investment Treaties*, 26; M Sattorova, 'From Expropriation to Non-expropriatory Standards of Treatment: Towards a Unified Concept of an Investment Treaty Breach' (PhD Thesis, University of Birmingham, 2010) 207–08; Delaume, 'State Contracts', 1; Sornarajah heavily criticises this theory and finds its theoretical foundations weak. For a detailed criticism of this theory, see Sornarajah, *The International Law on Foreign Investment*, 289–99.

[188] FA Mann, *Further Studies in International Law* (Clarendon Press, 1990) 266.

[189] Hansen, 'The Legal Effect', 1020; for early cases that include stability provisions, see Coale, 'Stabilization Clauses'.

One of the most important arbitral decisions on internationalisation of the contract was *Texaco v Libya*, in which the sole arbitrator, Dupuy, noted under paragraph 71 of the Award:

> Thus, the recognition by international law of the right to nationalise is not sufficient ground to empower a state to disregard its commitments, because the same law also recognises the power of a state to commit itself internationally, especially by accepting the inclusion of stabilisation clauses in a contract entered into with a foreign private party.[190]

In addition, under paragraph 73, he continued: 'Thus, in respect of the international law of contracts, a nationalization cannot prevail over an internationalized contract, containing stabilization clauses, entered into between a State and a foreign private company.'[191] In this award, Dupuy indicated three criteria[192] by which to deem a contract as internationalised, and considered the existence of a stability provision to be one of them. Inserting a stability provision into a contract was seen as evidence of the parties' wish to render the contract subject to international law.[193]

According to Paasivirta, the main purpose of internationalisation of a contract is to provide stability to investment relationships by taking them out of the sphere of domestic law.[194] In this, stabilisation clauses play an important role. If they are considered a 'negative choice of law clause', this will leave the national laws of the host state inapplicable to the investment relationship in the event of a dispute.[195] Also, Cameron argues that if a stabilisation clause is existent, the arbitral tribunal might interpret the contract as internationalised.[196] Nevertheless, he adds that there is an ongoing controversy regarding this issue and in order to ensure the internationalisation of a contract, a choice of law clause which specifies international law or another state's national laws as the governing law should be inserted.[197]

On the other hand, some scholars argue that the mere inclusion of a stability provision into a contract does not mean that the contract is internationalised and that therefore local law is inapplicable.[198] According to Sornarajah, the internationalisation theory is based on three early arbitral decisions and several subsequent scholarly writings which are not 'significant sources of law' in the hierarchy of international law norms, so any theory based solely on these should be

---

[190] *Texaco v Libya*, Award, para 71.
[191] ibid para 73.
[192] For a list and detailed analysis of these criteria, see J Cantegreil, 'The Audacity of the Texaco/Calasiatic Award: René-Jean Dupuy and the Internationalization of Foreign Investment Law' (2011) 22(2) *European Journal of International Law* 441.
[193] Sornarajah, *The International Law on Foreign Investment*, 282.
[194] Paasivirta, 'Internationalization and Stabilization', 323.
[195] ibid 327.
[196] Cameron, *International Energy Investment Law*, 68.
[197] ibid.
[198] Al Emadi, 'Stabilization Clauses', 59; Sornarajah, *The International Law on Foreign Investment*, 289–99; Al Faruque, 'Validity and Efficacy', 329.

considered weak.[199] He continues that these arbitral awards should have followed the ordinary conflict of laws rules, which would lead to the application of the law of the host state that had the closest connection to the contract.[200]

However, the arbitrators abstained from following that route, arguing that the laws of those host states were not sophisticated enough to deal with the issues, and instead brought the dispute under international law.[201] Sornarajah rejects this approach and concludes that:

> The theory of internationalisation, though it continues to be advanced in modern writings, can be dismissed as having no merit. No one seriously suggests that agreements made with developed nations are subject to anything other than the law of the state. It would be offensive to the notion of the equality of states to suggest that the same principle does not apply to agreements made with developing countries.[202]

It has also been argued that this theory emerged around the 1950s[203] and therefore fell under the coercive climate of the colonial period,[204] which should not be relevant under contemporary international law.

Further, Fatouros criticised Dupuy's decision in the *Texaco* case mentioned above and asked: 'Would it not be reasonable, however, to require that, for such a serious legal consequence to be brought about, an explicit statement of the intent of the parties should be needed?'[205] Dupuy, indeed, failed to present any reasonable legal basis for his use of the internationalisation theory in that case. El-Kosheri and Riad also heavily criticised the internationalisation theory in general and Dupuy's approach in particular, and considered his decision 'an unnecessary doctrinal argument about negative choice based on the presence in the agreement of a stabilization clause'.[206] They further argued that the existence of a stabilisation clause is itself actually a premise to the future applicability of the domestic legal system because that clause already recognises the domestic law as applicable and attempts to restrict its scope.[207] They finally noted: 'Accordingly, it would be absurd to claim in the name of the stabilization clause a negative choice excluding the domestic legal system per se. Such a proposition renders meaningless the stabilization of an already excluded domestic legal system.'[208]

The issue of whether a stabilisation clause can internationalise an investment contract has been open to debate for some time. The internationalisation theory

---

[199] Sornarajah, *The International Law on Foreign Investment*, 290.
[200] ibid.
[201] ibid 291.
[202] ibid.
[203] AA Fatouros, 'International Law and the Internationalized Contract' (1980) 74 *American Journal of International Law* 134.
[204] Sornarajah, 'The Myth', 190.
[205] Fatouros, 'Internationalized Contract', 135.
[206] AS El-Kosheri and TF Riad, 'The Law Governing a New Generation of Petroleum Agreements: Changes in the Arbitration Process' (1986) 1(2) *ICSID Review – Foreign Investment Law Journal* 257, 276.
[207] ibid 277.
[208] ibid.

has received many criticisms. It does not seem possible for a stabilisation clause to internationalise the contract in the event of an explicit choice of law clause being existent. Even though there are several articles arguing the capability of stability provisions to internationalise the agreement, their foundations are not strong. Also, the arbitral awards and scholarly works that recognise this aspect are all from a certain period of time, which was nearly four to five decades ago. In the contemporary understanding of investment law, this theory does not find many supporters. Therefore, it is important to include in contracts a choice of law clause that makes the applicable law explicit. If the international law is specified as the applicable law in the contract, then the stabilisation clause would have the internationalised effect.

In a nutshell, a stability provision in the form of a contractual clause is attractive to investors because it has a negotiation aspect that allows the investor the possibility to shape the contract in line with their needs in order to obtain a wider protection against a host state's unilateral actions. Although the internationalisation theory found supporters once, it does not seem to be a popular argument in contemporary investment law. Instead of relying on this ambiguous theory, the contract should explicitly specify the applicable law and the stabilisation clause therein, or it should have recourse to the investment treaty protection that is discussed later in this book.

B. Legal Stability Agreements

In pursuit of foreign investment, starting from the 1990s, the Latin American states came up with an innovative form of contractual stability guarantee, which is called a legal stability agreement (LSA).[209] The reasoning behind this innovation was to attract foreign investment and, according to Pereira's study, LSAs have certainly accomplished this aim in the case of Colombia.[210]

Again, the LSA can be considered a contractual form of stability provision; however, in this form, the stability provision is not embedded in the investment contract itself but is concluded as a separate agreement alongside the investment contract. Even though these two are different in form, their objectives are the same: the stability of the investment relationship.[211] LSAs should be seen as an additional incentive to investors since they do not function as a substitute to the already existent investment laws or national laws of the state.[212] They have

---

[209] Cameron, *International Energy Investment Law*, 246; DE Vielleville and BS Vasani, 'Sovereignty over Natural Resources versus Rights under Investment Contracts: Which One Prevails?' (2008) 5(2) *Transnational Dispute Management* 1, 13.

[210] A Pereira, 'Legal Stability Contracts in Colombia: An Appropriate Incentive for Investments?' (2013) 12(2) *Richmond Journal of Global Law and Business* 237, 269.

[211] CA Rodriguez-Yong and KX Martinez-Munoz, 'The Andean Approach to Stabilisation Clauses' (2013) 6(1) *International Journal of Private Law* 67, 71.

[212] Vielleville and Vasani, 'Sovereignty', 14.

the effect of reinforcing these existing rights by providing a type of extended and detailed stability provision.[213]

The Constitutional Court of Colombia defines the LSA in the following manner:

> A legal stability agreement is a contract between the State and a foreign or national investor in which the parties agree that the laws and/or interpretations stated in the agreement will regulate the investment and activities of the investor during the time specified in the contract.[214]

This form of stability guarantee has been adopted by a number of states, including Peru, Chile, Colombia, Ecuador, Venezuela, Papua New Guinea, Bolivia, Timor-Leste, Mongolia and Ghana.[215] While some of these agreements only contain stability provisions related to fiscal aspects, such as taxes and royalties, others aim to stabilise the entire legal framework that an investment is subject to.[216]

The states that offer LSAs view the nature of the agreements differently. While the Colombian Constitutional Court considers them to be administrative contracts, in Peru they are treated as private contracts.[217] Having an administrative or private character plays an important role in determining the governing legal framework that they are subject to. This issue was dealt with in the *Duke v Peru* case, where the Tribunal stated:

> Thus, pursuant to the investment laws of Peru, the main features of LSAs are that (i) the stabilized legal regimes cannot be changed unilaterally by the State, and (ii) the agreements are subject to private or civil law and not administrative law. As private-law contracts, the negotiation, execution, interpretation and enforcement of the provisions set forth in LSAs are subject to the general principles applicable to contracts between private parties under the Peruvian Civil Code. As such, the rights granted by Peru pursuant to an LSA are private contractual rights that are enforceable against the State as if it were a private party.[218]

The process to enter into LSAs often requires authorisation from the state, and in some cases it even requires an additional legislative act to approve the agreement. Vielleville and Vasani thus argue that LSAs enjoy a stronger legal position than regular contractual stabilisation clauses.[219] It is important to realise that, just like

---

[213] Cameron, 'Stability of Contract', 312.

[214] CA Rodriguez-Yong, 'Enhancing Legal Certainty in Colombia: The Role of the Andean Community' (2008) 17(2) *Michigan State University College of Law Journal of International Law* 407, 419.

[215] Cameron, *International Energy Investment Law*, 247; AFM Maniruzzaman, 'National Laws Providing for Stability of International Investment Contracts: A Comparative Perspective' (2007) 8(2) *Journal of World Investment & Trade* 233; Oshionebo, 'Stabilization Clauses in Natural Resource Extraction Contracts', 8; IMF, 'Mongolia: Selected Issues and Statistical Appendix' (International Monetary Fund, 2008) 6.

[216] Tienhaara, 'Unilateral Commitments', 152.

[217] Rodriguez-Yong and Martinez-Munoz, 'The Andean Approach', 76.

[218] *Duke Energy v Peru*, Award, para 44.

[219] Vielleville and Vasani, 'Sovereignty', 14.

any other contractual stability guarantee, these LSAs do not ensure protection of the investor on their own; the law that applies to the investment relationship and the venue of the dispute settlement are important factors in providing comprehensive protection.[220]

Peru was the first state to adopt LSAs in Latin America and is one of the countries that have developed and extended their use the furthest.[221] As of February 2016, there were 960 LSAs concluded in Peru since 1993.[222] The Private Investment Promotion Agency of Peru defines LSAs thus:

> The Legal Stability Agreements are investment instruments promoters, which are implemented through the subscription of agreements with Peruvian Government, which stabilize guarantees for investors or companies receiving, as applicable, for its period of validity. These agreements may only be amended with the consent of both parties.[223]

The sets of rules that are stabilised under the Peruvian LSAs are: the rules of the tax regime; the right to non-discrimination; the right to use the most favourable rate of exchange; the free availability of foreign currency; and the right of free remittance.[224] In Chile, the terms and conditions of the legal, regulatory and policy regimes, as well as some other fiscal aspects, can be stabilised under LSAs.[225]

In Ghana, Article 48 of the Minerals and Mining Act of 2006 grants the minister responsible for mines the power to enter into a stability agreement with any investors. According to this Article:

(1)   The Minister may as a part of a mining lease enter into a stability agreement with the holder of the mining lease, to ensure that the holder of the mining lease will not, for a period not exceeding fifteen years from the date of the agreement,

(a)   be adversely affected by a new enactment, order instrument or other action made under a new enactment or changes to an enactment, order, instrument that existed at the time of the stability agreement, or other action taken under these that have the effect or purport to have the effect of imposing obligations upon the holder or applicant of the mining lease, and

(b)   be adversely affected by subsequent changes to

(i)   the level of and payment of customs or other duties relating to the entry materials, goods, equipment and any other inputs necessary to the mining operations or project,

(ii)   the level of and payment of royalties, taxes, fees and other fiscal imports, and

---

[220] Maniruzzaman, 'National Laws', 238.

[221] Vielleville and Vasani, 'Sovereignty', 14.

[222] Peru Private Investment Promotion Agency www.proyectosapp.pe/RepositorioAPS/1/0/JER/ESTADISTICAS_GRAL_INCENTIVOS_INVERSION/2_2_%20CEJ%20Suscritos%20con%20Inversionistas%20(Bilingue)(1).xls.

[223] Peru Private Investment Promotion Agency www.investinperu.pe/modulos/JER/PlantillaStandard.aspx?are=1&prf=0&jer=5933&sec=17.

[224] Cameron, *International Energy Investment Law*, 248–49; Vielleville and Vasani, 'Sovereignty', 16.

[225] UNCTAD, 'Investment Policy Review of Colombia' (United Nations, 2006) 23.

(iii) laws relating to exchange control, transfer of capital and dividend remittance

(2) A stability agreement entered into under subsection (1) shall be subject to ratification by Parliament.[226]

As can be seen from the Article, ratification by the parliament is required in Ghana and the agreement cannot exceed 15 years. Because the Article is contained in the Minerals and Mining Act, the legal stability agreement does not include every sector, unlike some of the practices in Latin America. While LSAs in Chile and Peru are restricted to a predetermined list of areas, Colombia has adopted a negative list approach, whereby the government is authorised to offer a stability guarantee for any regulation *unless* it is expressly excluded by law.[227] There is also a temporal dimension to LSAs, with durations varying from three years to 20 years in different states, and whereas some of them apply a strict period of time, like Peru, others, such as Colombia and Ecuador, apply a more flexible approach.[228]

As mentioned above, the mere conclusion of an LSA does not guarantee that the host state will not make any changes to its laws. There have been several arbitral cases in which the investors have argued that the host states involved breached the relevant LSA.[229] The most important thing for an investor to consider here is the inclusion of a provision which specifies an international arbitral tribunal as the dispute settlement forum.[230]

C. Stability Based on National Legislation

Offering a stability guarantee to investors through investment laws and domestic legislation (or in some cases through the constitution) is common practice in many developing states.[231]

There are various alternatives for a host state to grant stability on a national legislation basis. The first of these is the inclusion of a law in general legislation, which allows the host state to enter into a legal stability agreement with the investor or offer a contractual stabilisation clause in an investment agreement. The Timor Sea Petroleum Development Act provides under Article 2 that:

1– With respect to any long-term projects (projects that are expected to last over 15 years and the production of which starts after the entry into force of the Timor Sea Treaty), for the carrying on of petroleum activities in the Joint Petroleum Development

---

[226] Ghana Minerals and Mining Act 2006, Act No 703, Art 48.

[227] UNCTAD, 'Colombia', 23.

[228] Rodriguez-Yong and Martinez-Munoz, 'The Andean Approach', 79–80.

[229] For some examples, see Cameron, *International Energy Investment Law*, 252–64.

[230] Maniruzzaman, 'National Laws', 238.

[231] Al Faruque, *Petroleum Contracts*, 52–53; Verhoosel, 'Legal Constraints', 460; Eljuri and Trevino, 'Latin America', 339. For texts of legislative stability provisions in the investment laws of various countries, see JE Neuhaus, 'The Enforceability of Legislative Stabilization Clauses' in DD Caron et al (eds), *Practising Virtue: Inside International Arbitration* (Oxford University Press, 2015).

> Area, the Government is authorised to enter into agreements with contractors to ensure the tax stability of the project, with reference to the laws of the Republic in force on the date of signing of the agreement, in regard to ...[232]

In this type of legislation, the government is allowed to offer a stability guarantee to investors through agreements. Such a guarantee can either be restricted to a specific area or project, as in the above-mentioned law, or it can be applied to all investments on a general basis.[233] This is not a substantive provision that directly grants the stability guarantee to the investors; rather, it is a two-stage process in which the government is first authorised through law to enter into an agreement which contains stability guarantees and then may conclude that agreement with the investor. There is a further action needed by the host state to provide stability.[234]

Another way to offer a legislative stability guarantee to an investor is through substantive provisions in certain acts in the fields of energy, investment, commerce, etc.[235] In this type, the stability guarantee is provided directly by an explicit law in the legislation of the host state without requiring an additional agreement other than the investment itself.[236] An example of this type can be found under the Investment Stability Law of Panama as:

> The law provides for a 10 year stability as of registration of the investment that a legal, tax, customs, municipal and labour rules will remain identical to those in force at the time [of] registration. This equally applies to both foreign and national investments.[237]

This is a classical freezing type of stability provision found in the national legislation of Panama.[238] It freezes certain laws for 10 years and states that they will remain the same throughout that time.

The last type is the one that can be found under the Ghana example quoted above, and indeed other states such as Azerbaijan and Egypt, in which stability is offered through a contract which is subject to ratification by the parliament. The contract itself may be adopted as law by the parliament.[239]

The Egyptian Constitution states expressly in Article 32 that: 'Disposing of State's public properties is prohibited. Granting the right of exploitation of natural resources or public utility concessions shall be by virtue of a law for a period not exceeding thirty (30) years.'[240] According to this, a legislative act is compulsory

---

[232] Law on the Petroleum Development of Timor Sea (Tax Stability), Law No 4/2003 of 1 July, Art 2 http://mj.gov.tl/jornal/lawsTL/RDTL-Law/RDTL-Laws/Law-2003-04.pdf.

[233] Maniruzzaman, 'National Laws', 237.

[234] For some examples to this type, see Gjuzi, *Stabilization*, 34–35.

[235] Cameron, *International Energy Investment Law*, 62.

[236] Some recent examples will be discussed in ch 6.

[237] Investment Stability Law of Panama, Law No 54 of July 22, 1988, cited in Maniruzzaman, 'National Laws', 235.

[238] This can be considered as an example of 'limited freezing clause' mentioned by Shemberg, 'Stabilization Clauses', 6.

[239] Maniruzzaman, 'National Laws', 239; Cameron, *International Energy Investment Law*, 63.

[240] Constitution of the Arab Republic of Egypt, 18 January 2014, Unofficial Translation, Art 32 www.sis.gov.eg/Newvr/Dustor-en001.pdf.

for every concession agreement and this practice of parliament grants the concession agreements the force of law.[241] In the model concession agreement, it is also expressly stated that the agreement will have the force of law.[242] Since these concession agreements also include stabilisation clauses as a safeguard for international investment contracts,[243] the contractual stability guarantee becomes a substantive law at the same time. This method is seen as more protective than the previous one because it 'gives additional sanctity to the individually negotiated contract'.[244] The importance of this type of guarantee becomes more prominent when the contract is concluded between an investor and a host state enterprise.[245]

In the traditional literature on stabilisation guarantees, inserting such a guarantee in a domestic law of a host state is considered ineffective in practice because it is a unilateral assurance given by the host state, and the parliament that enacted this law has the sovereignty and right to undo it in the future.[246] A stability provision in the national legislation cannot be deemed as an explicit and binding stabilisation guarantee[247] and cannot prevent the host state from exercising its sovereign rights[248] as some authors argue.

It is argued that, since the content of the stabilisation guarantee is not specifically directed at an investor, it does not have the same practical value as a contract.[249] However, Cameron argues that a stability guarantee in the national legislation may play the role of reinforcing the investor's claim on legitimate expectations in the event of a dispute.[250] Indeed, unlike in the traditional literature, the recent growing arbitral practice shows that a stability provision under domestic legislation might have a significant effect in terms of creating legitimate expectations that would be protected under the investment treaty framework.[251]

D. Treaty-Based Stability

Investment treaties, also referred to as international investment agreements, comprise bilateral investment treaties (BITs), multilateral investment treaties

---

[241] M Khatchadourian, 'Legal Safeguards in Egypt's Petroleum Concession Agreements' (2008) 22(4) *Arab Law Quarterly* 387, 388–89.
[242] Model Concession Agreement for Petroleum Exploration and Exploitation of the Arab Republic of Egypt, Art 3 https://apexintl.com/wp-content/uploads/2018/04/7-2016-EGPC-Model-Agreement.pdf.
[243] Khatchadourian, 'Legal Safeguards', 389.
[244] Al Faruque, *Petroleum Contracts*, 56.
[245] ibid.
[246] P Daniel and EM Sunley, 'Contractual Assurances of Fiscal Stability' in P Daniel, M Keen and C McPherson (eds), *The Taxation of Petroleum and Minerals: Principles, Problems and Practice* (Routledge, 2010) 406.
[247] Waelde and Ndi, 'Stabilizing International Investment Commitments', 240.
[248] Eljuri and Trevino, 'Latin America', 340.
[249] AA Fatouros, *Government Guarantees to Foreign Investors* (Columbia University Press, 1962) 122.
[250] Cameron, *International Energy Investment Law*, 63. Legitimate expectations will be discussed in the following chapters.
[251] See ch 6.

(MITs) and free trade agreements.[252] The main purpose of these instruments of international law is to protect and promote investment.[253] This protection is provided through the idea that a breach of a treaty would accordingly mean a violation of international law.[254] BITs and MITs were mainly developed to avoid uncertainty in international law with regard to investment protection.[255] They create a set of rules by which the risks are mitigated and a stable investment climate is provided.[256] Sornarajah states: 'It may be claimed that the treaties stabilise pre-existing practices and will contribute to the creation of customary principles in this area in the future.'[257] Vandevelde also stresses the stability function of treaties by stating:

> [A] BIT serves to stabilize the favourable investment climate that exists as a matter of policy in the host state at the time the host state enters into the BIT. The value of a BIT to an investor is thus that it reduces risk.[258]

The primary benefit of a BIT is considered to be the stability of the investment climate it provides.[259] A BIT is aimed at providing protection from non-commercial risks – or, in other words, political risks.[260]

To protect the investment and create a stable investment environment, treaties employ a range of standards. General standards of treatment of international investors may be listed as: fair and equitable treatment, full protection and security, protection from arbitrary and unreasonable measures, expropriation, international minimum treatment, and national and most favoured nation treatment.[261] Even though these are listed separately, in practice and in arbitral jurisprudence they are not considered as totally separate and distinct standards, but are rather deemed as being in close conjunction with each other.[262] An analysis of all these treaty standards is beyond the scope of this book, but the fair and equitable treatment standard will be discussed in depth in subsequent chapters. This choice can be justified through the following quote from Schreuer: 'Practice shows that FET has been applied effectively in a considerable number of cases. In fact, it is currently the most important and successful basis for claims in investor-state arbitrations.'[263] It is true that there is an ever-growing arbitral practice that

---

[252] For a general introduction of investment treaties, See ch 2, s VIC.

[253] JW Salacuse, *The Law of Investment Treaties* (Oxford University Press, 2015) 1.

[254] Comeaux and Kinsella, *Legal Aspects of Political Risk*, 99.

[255] Al Faruque, *Petroleum Contracts*, 59.

[256] ibid; Dolzer and Schreuer, *Principles*, 82.

[257] Sornarajah, *The International Law on Foreign Investment*, 176.

[258] KJ Vandevelde, 'Investment Liberalization and Economic Development: The Role of Bilateral Investment Treaties' (1998) 36(3) *Columbia Journal of Transnational Law* 501, 523.

[259] ibid 525.

[260] SP Subedi, *International Investment Law: Reconciling Policy and Principle* (Hart Publishing, 2012) 87.

[261] Salacuse, *The Law of Investment Treaties*, 228.

[262] C Schreuer, 'Introduction: Interrelationship of Standards' in A Reinisch (ed), *Standards of Investment Protection* (Oxford University Press, 2008) 5.

[263] C Schreuer, PD Friedland and WW Park, 'Selected Standards of Treatment Available under the Energy Charter Treaty' in G Coop and C Ribeiro (eds), *Investment Protection and the Energy Charter Treaty* (JurisNet, 2008) 65.

strengthens the link between the FET standard and the stability guarantee, insofar as some scholars view the FET standard as a new form of stability guarantee based on a treaty.[264] The legitimate expectations principle under the FET standard is in a close relationship with the stability commitments, and subsequent chapters will also discuss this issue.

Treaty-based stability is certainly different to the other forms discussed above. In the other forms, be they contractual or legislative, there is an explicit stability provision where the scope of this provision is often clear. This might be the entire legislation of a host state, or it may apply to only a partial set of legal rules; nevertheless, it is often made explicit to investors which parts are stabilised and under what circumstances an investor might benefit from this guarantee. In treaty protection, however, the standards are broad, and they do not operate in the same way that contractual or legislative stability guarantees operate. It can also be said that substantive standards of treaties play a role in reinforcing the legal value of the other stability provisions[265] rather than substituting them.

Another important aspect of the treaties is that most of them include a dispute resolution clause which allows investors to directly pursue a dispute against the host state through arbitration in the event of a dispute (investor–state arbitration), as well as the possibility for a home state to resort to arbitration against the host state (state–state arbitration).[266]

Other than its classic and formal role as a legal protection tool, the BIT might be utilised as a pressure point and a bargaining chip in negotiations between investors or home states and the host states themselves.[267] What is meant by this is that the investors or home states can remind the host state, which is willing to alter its policy or legal rules, of its obligations under the treaty and the potential consequences of a breach under international law.[268] This is to prevent the host state from altering the legal environment that an investor is subject to. Even though it is not a formal and procedural enforcement of the rights under a BIT, it can be argued that this circumvention has a reinforcing effect with respect to the stability of the investment relationship.

The importance of the stability offered by the treaties ensues in the absence of a stabilisation clause in an investment contract. Arbitral tribunals have made it clear that the FET standard is not a substitute for a contractual stabilisation clause.[269] However, in the absence of such a contractual clause, using the FET standard as the basis for the argument placed before an arbitral tribunal seems one of the best options available to the investor. The following chapter will analyse the FET

---

[264] AP Martin, 'Stability in Contemporary Investment Law: Reconsidering the Role and Shape of Contractual Commitments in Light of Recent Trends' (2013) 10(1) *Manchester Journal of International Economic Law* 38, 58.

[265] Umirdinov, 'End of Hibernation', 480.

[266] Dolzer and Schreuer, *Principles*, 13.

[267] Cameron, *International Energy Investment Law*, 151.

[268] ibid.

[269] Hirsch, 'FET and Stabilization', 802.

standard and the legitimate expectations principle under that standard in depth, and it will reveal the link between stability guarantees and the FET standard.

V. The Changing Role of Stability Provisions

The types of international energy investments and the players at both ends have recently been changing. The entrance of some post-conflict evolving economies into the international investment arena and the incentives they offer bring a new type of energy investor, namely one who has a short-term vision for the investment.[270] Especially in the extractives sector, these investors are mostly focused on a rapid exploration phase and monetising the associated discoveries without being interested in developing the resources.[271]

Alongside these new types of investor and host state in the extractives sector, there are also new developments on the renewable energy front. International energy investments have now shifted from being merely petroleum-oriented to a more inclusive type which considers large-scale wind and solar investments as well.[272] This shift is evident from the great majority of recent arbitral awards in the energy industry where the focus is mostly on renewables. One of the reasons for this shift towards renewables is the growing international consensus regarding the fight against global warming and climate change.[273]

While these changes are happening in the energy industry, the perceived role of stabilisation provisions is also changing. Stability provisions were first used as a preventive tool against nationalisation or expropriation. The intention of investors was to utilise these provisions as an assurance against a potential unilateral host state action. Since these could not prevent the nationalisations, stability clauses were transformed into a more pragmatic and flexible type which would allow adjustments so as to maintain the investment relationship.[274]

At the latest stage, however, stability provisions have attained a new dimension. Even though the motivation behind the host states' stability offer remains essentially the same, the use of the associated stability guarantee has changed. This means that even as the investment-promoting role of stability provisions is still the same for host states, the utilisation of such provisions as an investment protection tool by investors has a new aspect. As Martin notes, 'the role of stabilisation clauses might have significantly evolved over time, from a strong and invasive contract enforcement tool to a more sustainable fairness and equitability indicator'.[275]

---

[270] Cameron, 'Changing Patterns', 389.
[271] ibid 2.
[272] ibid.
[273] JM Tirado, 'Renewable Energy Claims under the Energy Charter Treaty: An Overview' (2015) 12(3) *Transnational Dispute Management* 1, 1.
[274] Cameron, *International Energy Investment Law*, 59.
[275] AP Martin, 'Reviewing Stability Commitments in Investor–State Agreements: Creating Legitimate Expectations for Sustainable Foreign Investment Policies' (PhD Thesis, University of Surrey, 2012).

As this book discusses in the remaining chapters, stability provisions, when analysed through the lens of the legitimate expectations principle, now offer wider protection to investors under investment treaties. Whether the stability guarantee is based on a contract or a domestic law does not make any significant difference with regard to the protection that an investor will receive, as based on the legitimate expectations principle. The only difference would be with regard to the procedure used to identify the existence of legitimate expectations. In its latest incarnation, a stabilisation provision can now be used as an effective protection instrument during the dispute resolution process. This implies that while already existing stability provisions maintain their importance, this new role adds another layer to the prominence of stability guarantees.

VI. Conclusion

As a protection tool against the political risks that an international energy investment may face, stability provisions have been utilised for more than 80 years. They were originally initiated as a way to strengthen concession contracts against expropriation and nationalisation. However, with ensuing developments in the international investment arena, the manners of interventions by the host states have also changed, hence the need for modified stability provisions. In order to cope with the new challenges and needs, various types of stability provisions have been produced. These provisions comprise five different types: freezing clauses, intangibility clauses, economic balancing clauses, allocation of burden clauses and hybrid clauses; indeed, there is a great variety of denomination styles in the literature. This actually makes the analysis difficult, because the same clause might be referred to under a number of different names. This book has employed a broad meaning for the stability provision and does not limit it to merely freezing types.

There is almost a consensus among scholars and arbitral practice regarding the validity of stability provisions. The vast majority of scholars deem these provisions to be valid, while acknowledging the permanent sovereignty over natural resources principle. This principle does not necessarily conflict with any undertaking on the part of host states, and they can thus mutually exist. Undertaking an obligation by freely negotiating a contractual clause is considered the execution of permanent sovereignty itself. Alongside this discussion, arbitral courts have consistently decided on the validity of the stability provisions, even if their views on the practical effects of these provisions differ.

An international investor may find the stability guarantee within various legal sources, such as international investment contracts, legal stability agreements, national laws of the host states and international investment agreements. A contractual stability clause is more attractive to an investor due to the underlying negotiations phase. Through the negotiations, an investor might ask for the specific assurances that it needs.

However, there is no negotiation aspect to stability provisions that are a part of national legislation and are offered by the host state on a unilateral basis. A government has every right to alter its own legislation, and what is given through this procedure can be taken back as well. In this sense, the scope of the protection offered by a stability provision through domestic legislation is thus narrower than the associated contractual scope; however, this is only true when there is no treaty protection available to the investor. If an investor cannot resort to the investment treaty arbitration, the changes under domestic laws might not result in a redress. If it can appeal to the investment arbitration, however, a stability provision under domestic legislation becomes an important protection instrument, as will be discussed in the following chapters.

On the other hand, international investment agreements provide a broader protection to investors. These treaties are employed to deliver stability and protection to the investment. However, the stability offered by treaties is different from both contractual and legislative stability. In the latter, there is an explicit provision upon which the investor relies and in which the investor finds the boundaries of the stability guarantee to be granted. In contrast, treaties do not grant explicit and specific assurances to investors, but rather propose a broad framework through their substantive standards. One of the most important substantive standards of treaties with respect to this study is the FET standard. It has the closest conjunction with other forms of stability guarantee. Thus, the following chapter will analyse the FET standard, and particularly the legitimate expectations principle under that standard, in depth.

4

Backgrounds of Two Contentious Concepts: Fair and Equitable Treatment Standard and Legitimate Expectations

I. Introduction

Since the start of this millennium, the investment treaty arbitration scene has witnessed the growing application of certain pre-existing concepts. The most important of these is the fair and equitable treatment (FET) standard. Present in almost every treaty, its vague meaning and the vast authority it leaves to tribunals to define its meaning and content have ensured that the FET standard has taken centre stage in debates on international investment treaty operation.

While FET is a contentious concept in itself, it is the legitimate expectations principle, as the most important component of the FET standard, that has added to this controversy among scholars and arbitral tribunals. Even though the legitimate expectations principle is one of the concepts that investors have relied on in the majority of recent cases, it has been argued by some scholars that its use has not been justified under international investment law. This chapter will argue, on the contrary, that the use of the legitimate expectations principle by investment arbitral tribunals is completely justified.

It will be shown that there are two major views with regard to the roots of this principle under international investment law, and indeed that they both justify its use. The first view finds the principle's roots in domestic laws and argues that it is sufficiently widely recognised and applied to enjoy a general principle of law status. The second view, on the other hand, asserts that the legitimate expectations principle is derived from good faith, which is itself a general principle of law. This chapter argues that whichever approach one chooses, one can justify the use of the principle by arbitral tribunals. This is so because arbitral tribunals are not bound by the interpretation or application of a legal principle under domestic laws, but rather can adapt those principles in line with the requirements of investment law and apply them accordingly.

Since the legitimate expectations principle is predominantly applied under the FET standard, this chapter will start with a discussion of FET. Several issues surrounding the FET standard will be presented. However, they will not be scrutinised in depth. They will instead be discussed with the intention of introducing the standard under which the legitimate expectations principle is applied by investment treaty tribunals. Since this is an ongoing and rooted debate, this chapter will not repeat everything that has already been considered; instead, it will refer to these main comprehensive studies.

The main aim of this chapter is to present the roots of the legitimate expectations principle upon which the analyses in the following chapters will be built. It will be shown that the application of this principle is justified under international investment law.

II. The Fair and Equitable Treatment Standard

A. The Historical Background of the FET Standard

Even though the FET standard has been around for a long time in international legal documents, it was only after the year 2000 that arbitral tribunals started to utilise it frequently.[1]

From the 1940s onwards, this concept features – although not in the same wording – in various agreements and treaties, such as the 1948 Havana Charter[2] for the establishment of an International Trade Organisation and the United States Friendship, Commerce and Navigation treaties that were signed in the following years.[3]

Starting from the 1960s, this concept in its current form began to be discussed at the international level with the help of the adoption of the 1967 Draft Convention on the Protection of Foreign Property (Draft OECD (Organisation for Economic Co-operation and Development) Convention) and with the beginning of the bilateral investment treaty (BIT) programmes enacted by various countries, including Germany, Switzerland and Belgium.[4]

Most of the OECD countries considered the Draft OECD Convention a starting point in their international investment agreement negotiations, and thus incorporated this standard into their treaties.[5] Article 1(a) of the Draft OECD Convention reads: 'Each party shall at all times ensure fair and equitable treatment to the property of the nationals of the other Parties.'[6] With the proliferation

---

[1] R Dolzer and C Schreuer, *Principles of International Investment Law* (Oxford University Press, 2012) 130.

[2] Never entered into force.

[3] K Leite, 'The Fair and Equitable Treatment Standard: Search for Better Balance in International Investment Agreements' (2016) 32(1) *American University International Law Review* 363, 370.

[4] KJ Vandevelde, 'A Unified Theory of Fair and Equitable Treatment' (2010) 43(1) *New york University Journal of International Law and Politics* 43, 45.

[5] UNCTAD, 'Fair and Equitable Treatment: A Sequel' (United Nations, 2012) 5.

[6] OECD Draft Convention on the Protection of Foreign Property, 1967, Art 1(a) www.oecd.org/investment/internationalinvestmentagreements/39286571.pdf.

of BITs, the FET standard has become a regular feature of treaty practice[7] and has been included in the vast majority of BITs.[8] However, this does not mean that the FET standard was a favourite clause on which investors based their claims when pleading before arbitral tribunals. It was not until 1997 that the first arbitral award which discussed an FET claim was rendered.[9] Since then, the FET standard has become the most relied upon and the most promising basis for a claim by investors, and it is currently hard to find a case based on an investment treaty that has not attempted to invoke it.[10] Its broad content increases the chances of success in a claim where other standards might fail.[11] Yet, despite this, there has been no consensus on the content, meaning and scope of this standard among the parties to treaties or, indeed, among scholars and arbitrators.

This book will not delve into those discussions in depth. There are already several books[12] which deal exclusively with the FET and many articles and book chapters on these issues. The following sections will mention the most frequently discussed issues regarding the FET purely to set the scene for the legitimate expectations topic and provide detailed references where needed.

B. How to Define FET?

The meaning of this notion has created huge controversy and various interpretations because the legal documents in which the FET standard is found do not provide an associated definition.[13] While governments have pushed for a narrowing of its interpretation, investors have often aspired to an expansive approach in

---

[7] Though there are variations among the texts of these clauses in BITs, there is no unanimity. For details, see A Newcombe and L Paradell, *Law and Practice of Investment Treaties: Standards of Treatment* (Kluwer Law International, 2009) 257–61. An UNCTAD study identifies seven different categories of the FET standard found on BITs, see UNCTAD, 'Bilateral Investment Treaties 1995–2006: Trends in Investment Rulemaking' (United Nations, 2007) 30–32.

[8] OECD, 'Fair and Equitable Treatment Standard in International Investment Law' (OECD Publishing, 2004) 5; P Dumberry, 'Has the Fair and Equitable Treatment Standard Become a Rule of Customary International Law?' (2017) 8(1) *Journal of International Dispute Settlement* 155, 156.

[9] I Tudor, *The Fair and Equitable Treatment Standard in the International Law of Foreign Investment* (Oxford University Press, 2008) 3.

[10] C Schreuer, 'Fair and Equitable Treatment in Arbitral Practice' (2005) 6(3) *Journal of World Investment & Trade* 357, 357. UNCTAD, 'Fair and Equitable Treatment', 1; R Dolzer, 'Fair and Equitable Treatment: A Key Standard in Investment Treaties' (2005) 39(1) *The International Lawyer* 87, 87; A Diehl, *The Core Standard of International Investment Protection: Fair and Equitable Treatment* (Kluwer Law International, 2012) 8.

[11] Newcombe and Paradell, *Standards of Treatment*, 254.

[12] R Kläger, *'Fair and Equitable Treatment' in International Investment Law* (Cambridge University Press, 2011); M Paparinskis, *The International Minimum Standard and Fair and Equitable Treatment* (Oxford University Press, 2013); P Dumberry, *The Fair and Equitable Treatment Standard: A Guide to NAFTA Case Law on Article 1105* (Kluwer Law International, 2013); Diehl, *Core Standard*; Tudor, *The FET Standard*.

[13] JW Salacuse, *The Law of Investment Treaties* (Oxford University Press, 2015) 241; A Saravanan and SR Subramanian, *Role of Domestic Courts in the Settlement of Investor–State Disputes: The Indian Scenario* (Springer, 2020) 15.

defining the standard so that they could concentrate their arguments from various angles under one claim.[14]

Since the meaning of the FET notion has historically been vague, this has created a vast playing field for investors to base any of their claims on this standard.[15] As the widely cited *Waste Management v Mexico* award states, 'Evidently the standard is to some extent a flexible one which must be adapted to the circumstances of each case'.[16] It can be argued that this flexibility helped to increase the standard's popularity among investors. In the same vein, Judge Schwebel opined that 'the meaning of what is fair and equitable is defined when that standard is applied to a set of specific facts'.[17]

On the other hand, the inclusion of this claim in almost every case and the fact that there was no explicit definition resulted in a vast number of different interpretations by arbitral tribunals. Since there had been no jurisprudence on the meaning of the term 'fair and equitable' pre-2000, arbitral tribunals had to undertake the challenge to provide a reasonable interpretation of this notion.[18] One scholar has argued that this vagueness was intentionally created with the purpose of providing adjudicators with a quasi-legislative authority so that they could adjust its content in line with the aims of the treaty in question.[19]

In an attempt to define the notion in general, an United Nations Conference on Trade and Development (UNCTAD) study observes that

> 'fair and equitable treatment' requires an attitude to governance based on an unbiased set of rules that should be applied with a view to doing justice to all interested parties that may be affected by a State's decision in question, including the host State's population at large.[20]

However, this definition is as elusive as the majority of other such attempts and has no practical utility with respect to the dispute resolution process. Another UNCTAD report also acknowledges this issue and provides that

> [t]here is a great deal of uncertainty concerning the precise meaning of the concept, because the notions of 'fairness' and 'equity' do not connote a clear set of legal prescriptions in international investment law and allow for a significant degree of subjective judgment.[21]

---

[14] B Choudhury, 'Evolution or Devolution? Defining Fair and Equitable Treatment in International Investment Law' (2005) 6(2) *Journal of World Investment & Trade* 297, 297.

[15] KJ Vandevelde, *Bilateral Investment Treaties: History, Policy and Interpretation* (Oxford University Press, 2010) 203.

[16] *Waste Management, Inc v United Mexican States*, Award, ICSID Case No ARB(AF)/00/3, 30 April 2004, para 99.

[17] *MTD Equity Sdn Bhd and MTD Chile SA v Republic of Chile*, Award, ICSID Case No ARB/01/7, 25 May 2004, para 109.

[18] Dolzer, 'FET: A Key Standard', 88.

[19] CH Brower II, 'Investor–State Disputes under NAFTA: The Empire Strikes Back' (2001) 40(1) *Columbia Journal of Transnational Law* 43, 56.

[20] UNCTAD, 'Fair and Equitable Treatment', 6.

[21] UNCTAD, 'Investment Policy Framework for Sustainable Development' (United Nations, 2015) 83.

Similarly, Muchlinski states that

> the standard is case specific and requires a flexible approach given that it offers a general point of departure in formulating an argument that the foreign investor has not been well treated by reason of discriminatory or other unfair measures that have been taken against its interests.[22]

The pursuit of giving the FET standard a meaning has also produced a discussion as to whether its meaning equates to the minimum standard of treatment of customary international law or it is an independent, more rigorous treaty standard with an autonomous meaning.[23] However, this ongoing debate is beyond the scope of this book. Suffice it to say that it is possible to witness treaty practice, arbitral jurisdiction and scholarly literature that favour either of these views. Nevertheless, arbitrators are also seemingly moving away from this theoretical discussion in their cases and starting to consider unfolding specific features of the FET standard in order to determine its contours.[24]

Even though there are numerous scholarly writings[25] which discuss the meaning of the FET, they all conclude with an almost identical statement, which is

[22] PT Muchlinski, *Multinational Enterprises and the Law* (Oxford University Press, 2007) 639.

[23] For detailed discussion on this issue, see in general Dumberry, 'Has the FET Become Customary Law?'; N Bernasconi-Osterwalder, 'Giving Arbitrators Carte Blanche – Fair and Equitable Treatment in Investment Treaties' in CL Lim (ed), *Alternative Visions of the International Law on Foreign Investment: Essays in Honour of Muthucumaraswamy Sornarajah* (Cambridge University Press, 2016); Leite, 'Search for Better Balance'; G Bücheler, *Proportionality in Investor–State Arbitration* (Oxford University Press, 2015) 182–86; M Valenti, 'The Protection of General Interests of Host States in the Application of the Fair and Equitable Treatment Standard' in G Sacerdoti (ed), *General Interests of Host States in International Investment Law* (Cambridge University Press, 2014); C Campbell, 'House of Cards: The Relevance of Legitimate Expectations under Fair and Equitable Treatment Provisions in Investment Treaty Law' (2013) 30(4) *Journal of International Arbitration* 361; J Haynes, 'The Evolving Nature of the Fair and Equitable Treatment (FET) Standard: Challenging Its Increasing Pervasiveness in Light of Developing Countries' Concerns – The Case for Regulatory Rebalancing' (2013) 14(1) *Journal of World Investment & Trade* 114; Diehl, *Core Standard*; J Stone, 'Arbitrariness, the Fair and Equitable Treatment Standard and the International Law of Investment' (2012) 25(1) *Leiden Journal of International Law* 77; AR Sureda, *Investment Treaty Arbitration: Judging under Uncertainty* (Cambridge University Press, 2012); MK Bronfman, 'Fair and Equitable Treatment: An Evolving Standard' (2005) 38(150) *Estudios Internacionales* 89; Kläger, *Fair and Equitable Treatment*; JR Picherack, 'The Expanding Scope of the Fair and Equitable Treatment Standard: Have Recent Tribunals Gone Too Far?' (2008) 9(4) *Journal of World Investment & Trade* 255; Tudor, *The FET Standard*; J Kalicki and S Medeiros, 'Fair, Equitable and Ambiguous: What Is Fair and Equitable Treatment in International Investment Law?' (2007) 22(1) *ICSID Review – Foreign Investment Law Journal* 24; G Mayeda, 'Playing Fair: The Meaning of Fair and Equitable Treatment in Bilateral Investment Treaties' (2007) 41(2) *Journal of World Trade* 273; RH Kreindler, 'Fair and Equitable Treatment – A Comparative International Law Approach' (2006) 3(3) *Transnational Dispute Management* 1; Dolzer, 'FET: A Key Standard'; CC Kirkman, 'Fair and Equitable Treatment: Methanex v United States and the Narrowing Scope of NAFTA Article 1105' (2002) 34(1) *Law and Policy in International Business* 343; S Vasciannie, 'The Fair and Equitable Treatment Standard in International Investment Law and Practice' (2000) 70(1) *British Yearbook of International Law* 99.

[24] UNCTAD, 'Fair and Equitable Treatment', 59.

[25] Choudhury, 'Evolution or Devolution?'; Mayeda, 'The Meaning of FET'; Kalicki and Medeiros, 'Fair, Equitable and Ambiguous'; Bernasconi-Osterwalder, 'Giving Arbitrators Carte Blanche – Fair and Equitable Treatment in Investment Treaties'; Haynes, 'The Evolving Nature of the FET Standard'; R Dolzer, 'Fair and Equitable Treatment: Today's Contours' (2013) 12(1) *Santa Clara Journal of*

that there has been no consensus on the definition of the term. Earlier arbitral tribunals were similarly unable to develop a comprehensive and applicable methodology regarding the application of the FET standard by employing traditional means of treaty interpretation, such as referral to the Vienna Convention on the Law of Treaties.[26] The interpretation of the ordinary meaning of the standard (that is, the meaning of the terms 'fair' and 'equitable') does not lead to an applicable consolidated result and fails to demonstrate the normative content of the FET.[27] As Vasciannie notes, 'the words "fair and equitable treatment", in their plain meaning, do not refer to an established body of law or to existing legal precedents'.[28]

Instead of trying to infer a direct meaning, the methodology to use to find a coherent application should be to reveal the subgroups or components of the standard and to follow a casuistic approach.[29] Indeed, this methodology has become one of the main approaches that arbitral tribunals and scholars follow when analysing the FET standard.

However, there is also no unanimity in the debate as to what constitutes an FET standard and there are various interpretations that broaden its scope to as many as eight principles.[30] It is considered by some to be a flexible and ever-expanding standard.[31]

C. Components of the FET Standard

The quest to provide a definition of the FET standard has forced arbitral tribunals to dismantle the standard in order to determine its components. This ongoing arbitral practice has produced some recurring themes.

For example, Choudhury, in her 2005 article, indicated that the emerging themes in arbitral practice comprise the requirements of transparency, due process, a breach of legitimate expectations, arbitrary or discriminatory conduct, acting beyond the scope of legal authority and good faith.[32]

Vandevelde, by reviewing numerous arbitral awards, identified five main principles that constitute the FET standard and classified them as: reasonableness,

International Law 7; Campbell, 'House of Cards'; K Yannaca-Small, 'Fair and Equitable Treatment Standard: Recent Developments' in A Reinisch (ed), *Standards of Investment Protection* (Oxford University Press, 2008).

[26] SW Schill, 'Fair and Equitable Treatment, the Rule of Law and Comparative Public Law' in SW Schill (ed), *International Investment Law and Comparative Public Law* (Oxford University Press, 2010) 155.

[27] ibid.

[28] Vasciannie, 'FET Standard', 103.

[29] Dolzer, 'Today's Contours', 14.

[30] D Gaukrodger, 'The Balance between Investor Protection and the Right to Regulate in Investment Treaties: A Scoping Paper' (2017) OECD Working Papers on International Investment 2017/02.

[31] K Yannaca-Small, 'Fair and Equitable Treatment Standard' in K Yannaca-Small (ed), *Arbitration under International Investment Agreements: A Guide to the Key Issues* (Oxford University Press, 2010) 385.

[32] Choudhury, 'Evolution or Devolution?', 302–16.

non-discrimination, consistency (he considers legitimate expectations to constitute a part of consistency), transparency and due process.[33] In addition to these, he also mentions the good faith principle, but does not consider it a core principle.[34]

Schill, on the other hand, interprets FET to embrace seven elements and lists these as:

[T]he requirement of stability, predictability, and consistency of the legal framework; the principle of legality; the protection of legitimate expectations; procedural due process and denial of justice; substantive due process and protection against discrimination and arbitrariness; transparency; and the principle of reasonableness and proportionality.[35]

According to the aforementioned 2012 UNCTAD report, legitimate expectations, prohibition of arbitrariness, denial of justice and due process, discriminatory treatment and abusive treatment (coercion, duress and harassment) are to be considered instances of state conduct that might lead to violation of the FET standard.[36]

Lastly, Dolzer, in a later article, specified eight components of FET as: good faith; legitimate expectations; due process; transparency; freedom from harassment and coercion; prohibition of arbitrary treatment; failure to readjust equilibrium; and unilateralism in the adaptation of terms.[37]

It should be noted that these classifications are mostly based on the stances of arbitral tribunals, using an ex post approach. However, it is also possible to witness some contemporary legal documents that deal with this issue ex ante and provide the components of FET in the treaty text.[38]

By looking at the arbitral jurisprudence and the newly emerging treaty practice, it can be said that this methodology of defining the contours of the FET standard via its constituents is well established and likely to continue.

This arbitral practice of breaking FET into its fragments is not accepted by all without objection, of course. It is submitted that arbitral tribunals have expanded the scope of the FET standard to the detriment of states, especially developing states.[39] Moreover, the consequences of this practice have been put on a par with

---

[33] Vandevelde, 'A Unified Theory', 53–96.
[34] ibid 97.
[35] Schill, 'Fair and Equitable Treatment', 159–60.
[36] UNCTAD, 'Fair and Equitable Treatment', 61–83.
[37] Dolzer, 'Today's Contours', 16–32.
[38] For instance, Art 8.10 of the Comprehensive Economic and Trade Agreement (CETA) between Canada and the EU defines the FET standard by reference to its components. Instead of leaving the definition process to arbitral tribunals, the treaty deals with this issue in advance. This can be seen from Art 8.10.2: '2. A Party breaches the obligation of fair and equitable treatment referenced in paragraph 1 if a measure or series of measures constitutes: (a) denial of justice in criminal, civil or administrative proceedings; (b) fundamental breach of due process, including a fundamental breach of transparency, in judicial and administrative proceedings; (c) manifest arbitrariness; (d) targeted discrimination on manifestly wrongful grounds, such as gender, race or religious belief; (e) abusive treatment of investors, such as coercion, duress and harassment; or (f) a breach of any further elements of the fair and equitable treatment obligation adopted by the Parties in accordance with paragraph 3 of this Article'.
[39] Picherack, 'The Expanding Scope of the FET Standard', 291.

strict liability and it was argued that arbitral tribunals are eager to hold states liable, even if their acts are for the purposes of legitimate and objective regulation.[40] On top of this, Kläger argues that a casuistic approach alone does not provide the necessary guidance to arbitrators when there is a difficult case with new, different facts from the previous ones which constitute the existing lines of jurisprudence.[41] Thus, he opines that:

> A doctrinal approach that amounts to nothing more than the categorisation of lines of jurisprudence, in order to simplify fair and equitable treatment by the specification of factors and fact situations possibly indicating a breach of the standard, is unable to guide arbitrators in difficult cases. This is because such a lowering of complexity will never lead to a scheme that is detailed enough so as to cover all difficult cases. Therefore, a comprehensive doctrinal concept needs to go beyond a mere analysis of case law and be capable of indicating, in difficult cases as well, what justificatory arguments are admissible.[42]

Within the context of this study, elements of FET other than legitimate expectations will not be discussed since the legitimate expectations principle has been chosen as the focal point of this book due to its growing importance in the investment treaty arbitration jurisprudence.

III. Investors' Legitimate Expectations

A. The Legitimate Expectations Principle under Domestic Laws

This section will not attempt to conduct a comparative analysis of the domestic laws presented below, nor will it try to analyse the application and scope of the doctrine in any of these national legal systems in any depth. By giving some examples, this section will purely attempt to demonstrate that this doctrine was present under numerous domestic legal systems long before it was adopted by arbitral tribunals. It is important to discuss these national laws in order to determine the legal source of the concept applied by arbitral tribunals and to identify whether this principle can be accepted as a general principle of law. Since there are several arguments against the use of the principle by arbitral tribunals,[43] it is necessary first to examine the understanding of the principle under domestic laws. This will help to conclude whether its application by arbitral tribunals is justified.

Ahmed and Perry describe the protection provided by the legitimate expectations principle under administrative law simply as: 'When you have a "legitimate

---

[40] ibid 290–91.
[41] Kläger, *Fair and Equitable Treatment*, 120.
[42] ibid 121.
[43] See s IIIB of the present chapter.

expectation" that a public body will exercise its discretion in some way, you may be entitled to the law's protection if that "expectation" is disappointed.'[44] In other words, 'the doctrine of legitimate expectations is essentially about getting public bodies to do what they said they would do'.[45] The main justification for protecting legitimate expectations is said to be sustaining the trust between the governed and the governor.[46]

The legitimate expectations principle is recognised under numerous domestic legal systems[47] and it has become a 'central principle of administrative law'.[48] This principle can be seen in the laws of Germany, Australia, Canada, the UK, New Zealand, Netherlands, Belgium, Denmark, Italy, Greece, Switzerland, Spain, Portugal, Japan, Hong Kong, Singapore, India, Kenya, Colombia, Venezuela and the EU as a supranational system.[49] The doctrine has also started to be applied in some other Latin American countries (eg Argentina, Brazil and Chile), although not in a widespread manner.[50] However, there is no uniform application; rather, it takes a variety of guises under the aforementioned legal systems.[51]

Craig, while discussing its existence under European law, opines: 'The connected concepts of legal certainty and legitimate expectations are to be found in all the legal systems of the Member States which make up the Community, although their precise legal content may vary from one system to another.'[52]

It is possible to trace the concept of the legitimate expectations principle under the common law system back to 1969, to the *Schmidt v Secretary of State*

---

[44] F Ahmed and A Perry, 'The Coherence of the Doctrine of Legitimate Expectations' (2014) 73(1) *CLJ* 61, 61.

[45] ibid 67.

[46] C Forsyth, 'Legitimate Expectations Revisited' (2011) 16(4) *Judicial Review* 429, 430.

[47] See in general SJ Schønberg, *Legitimate Expectations in Administrative Law* (Oxford University Press, 2000).

[48] D Barak-Erez, 'The Doctrine of Legitimate Expectations and the Distinction between the Reliance and Expectation Interests' (2005) 11(5) *European Public Law* 583, 584.

[49] J Schwarze, *European Administrative Law* (Sweet & Maxwell, 1992) 867–937; Schønberg, *Legitimate Expectations*, 3; HA Mairal, 'Legitimate Expectations and Informal Administrative Representations' in SW Schill (ed), *International Investment Law and Comparative Public Law* (Oxford University Press, 2010) 416; C Brown, 'The Protection of Legitimate Expectations as a "General Principle of Law": Some Preliminary Thoughts' (2009) 6(1) *Transnational Dispute Management* 1, 4; S Hamamoto, 'Protection of the Investor's Legitimate Expectations: Intersection of a Treaty Obligation and a General Principle of Law' in W Shan and J Su (eds), *China and International Investment Law: Twenty Years of ICSID Membership* (Brill Nijhoff, 2014) 165; N Monebhurrun, 'Gold Reserve Inc v Bolivarian Republic of Venezuela: Enshrining Legitimate Expectations as a General Principle of International Law?' (2015) 32(5) *Journal of International Arbitration* 551, 557; S Jhaveri, 'Contrasting Responses to the "Coughlan Moment": Legitimate Expectations in Hong Kong and Singapore' in M Groves and G Weeks (eds), *Legitimate Expectations in the Common Law World* (Hart Publishing, 2017).

[50] Mairal, 'Legitimate Expectations', 417.

[51] S Fietta, 'The "Legitimate Expectations" Principle under Article 1105 NAFTA' (2006) 7(3) *Journal of World Investment & Trade* 423, 424; T Zeyl, 'Charting the Wrong Course: The Doctrine of Legitimate Expectations in Investment Treaty Law' (2011) 49(1) *Alberta Law Review* 203, 207.

[52] PP Craig, 'Substantive Legitimate Expectations in Domestic and Community Law' (1996) 55(2) *CLJ* 289, 304.

for Home Affairs case, where Lord Denning first introduced it into English Law in his judgment.[53] Hlophe, analysing Lord Denning's approach, states: 'According to this concept a "legitimate expectation" entitles the complainant to be heard before an adverse decision is made against him. It is not necessary to show that the decision affects his pre-existing right(s).'[54] Even though the principle was known to German jurisprudence at that time, Lord Denning made no mention of any source in his use of the concept; further, in a letter to Forsyth, he said that it had come out of his own head and not from any other jurisdiction.[55] Reynolds states that the reasons why legitimate expectations are protected under English law are explained within the judiciary as 'the importance of ensuring "fairness", and to prevent decision makers from "abusing their power".'[56]

It is stated that the protection of legitimate expectations under common law tradition was initially merely procedural and excluded any substantive protection.[57] However, this stance of English law only providing a procedural protection seems to be developing gradually to the point where substantive protection is also embraced in specific circumstances.[58]

According to Barak-Erez:

> The procedural protection of legitimate expectations requires the authorities, having created a legitimate expectation regarding a particular policy or action, to adopt a proceeding providing the individual concerned with the right to a hearing or to participation in another procedure, such as a consultation. This protection of legitimate expectations is procedural in the sense that it does not relate to the substance or the merits of the final decision adopted by the authorities.[59]

Procedural protection basically means to be heard and to be consulted prior to reaching an administrative decision.[60] Substantive protection, on the other hand, is broad in scope and might lead to the revocation of the public body's act that frustrated the legitimate expectations. Tribunals are capable of reviewing the content of administrative decisions with a substantive approach.[61]

When the protection is procedural, the decision that affected the private party is set aside until the concerned party is given an opportunity to state its case, after

---

[53] C Forsyth, 'The Provenance and Protection of Legitimate Expectations' (1988) 47(2) *CLJ* 238, 238; J Hlophe, 'Legitimate Expectation and Natural Justice: English, Australian and South African Law' (1987) 104(1) *South African Law Journal* 165, 165.

[54] Hlophe, 'Legitimate Expectation', 165.

[55] Forsyth, 'Provenance and Protection', 241.

[56] P Reynolds, 'Legitimate Expectations and the Protection of Trust in Public Officials' (2011) 2 *PL* 330, 331.

[57] APG Pandya and A Moody, 'Legitimate Expectations in Investment Treaty Arbitration: An Unclear Future' (2010) 15(1) *Tilburg Law Review* 93, 98; Hamamoto, 'Legitimate Expectations', 160.

[58] M Potestà, 'Legitimate Expectations in Investment Treaty Law: Understanding the Roots and the Limits of a Controversial Concept' (2013) 28(1) *ICSID Review – Foreign Investment Law Journal* 88, 96; Hamamoto, 'Legitimate Expectations', 163; Zeyl, 'Charting the Wrong Course', 212.

[59] Barak-Erez, 'Legitimate Expectations', 594.

[60] A Brown, 'Justifying Compensation for Frustrated Legitimate Expectations' (2011) 30(6) *Law and Philosophy* 699, 702.

[61] Zeyl, 'Charting the Wrong Course', 205.

which the initial decision might be enforced as is, amended or abandoned.[62] If the protection is substantive, 'the new decision is definitely set aside or, in other cases, it is maintained but compensatory damages are awarded to the private party'.[63]

In Germany, legitimate expectations are protected as a constitutional norm under the principle of *Vertrauensschutz* (protection of trust)[64] and its application dates back to just after the approval of the *Grundgesetz* in 1949.[65] This principle aims to protect everyone who trusts the legality of a public administrative decision and it applies concurrently with other principles, such as transparency, predictability and legal certainty.[66] It not only applies to decisions or representations made by public authorities, but can also be used to overturn legislative measures.[67] This means that the protection provided under this principle is not only procedural, but also encompasses substantive protection.

This approach in German law is considered to be one of the clearest and widest applications of the principle.[68] Zeyl argues that the German position is 'the most expansive of all jurisdictions when it comes to recognizing substantive legitimate expectations'.[69] According to the European Court of Justice, *Vertrauensschutz* is the underlying concept to the legitimate expectations principle.[70]

It is possible to present more examples from various countries that adopt and apply the legitimate expectations principle in their domestic laws.[71] However, for the purposes of this chapter, suffice it to note that the application of the principle is more restricted in some countries, such as Italy,[72] broader in others, such as Germany, or is explicitly not adopted in still others, such as France (though there are other principles that effectively provide the same protection).[73] Even though there are some differences in the scope of its application or in its denomination, it has been a widely recognised doctrine under numerous domestic laws for decades.

---

[62] Mairal, 'Legitimate Expectations', 414.

[63] ibid 415.

[64] E Snodgrass, 'Protecting Investors' Legitimate Expectations – Recognizing and Delimiting a General Principle' (2006) 21(1) *ICSID Review – Foreign Investment Law Journal* 1, 26.

[65] K Rennert, 'The Protection of Legitimate Expectations under German Administrative Law' (Seminar on the Protection of Legitimate Expectations in Administrative Law and EU Law, 2016) 3.

[66] M Schröder, 'Administrative Law in Germany' in R Seerden and F Stroink (eds), *Administrative Law of the European Union, its Member States and the United States: A Comparative Analysis* (Intersentia, 2002) 119.

[67] Brown, 'Legitimate Expectations', 5.

[68] Forsyth, 'Provenance and Protection', 262; Schwarze, *European Administrative Law*, 869.

[69] Zeyl, 'Charting the Wrong Course', 216.

[70] Reynolds, 'Legitimate Expectations', 341.

[71] For detailed discussion of the principle under domestic jurisdictions, see in general Snodgrass, 'Legitimate Expectations'; Zeyl, 'Charting the Wrong Course'; Schönberg, *Legitimate Expectations*; Hamamoto, 'Legitimate Expectations'; Potestà, 'Legitimate Expectations'; S Felix, 'The Protection of Substantive Legitimate Expectations in Administrative Law' (2006) 18(1) *Sri Lanka Journal of International Law* 69; Craig, 'Legitimate Expectations'.

[72] Schwarze, *European Administrative Law*, 911–18.

[73] Brown, 'Legitimate Expectations', 5; Snodgrass, 'Legitimate Expectations', 27.

B. The Legitimate Expectations Principle under Investment Treaty Law

The application history of the legitimate expectations principle under the investment treaty law regime is relatively recent compared to domestic law. Even though the *SPP v Egypt* case (1992) was the first arbitral decision to include an approach based on the need to protect the investor's expectations,[74] the *Técnicas Medioambientales Tecmed, SA v Mexico* award (*Tecmed*) in 2003 is considered the first arbitral award to expressly outline the scope of the legitimate expectations of investors in relation to the FET standard.[75] The Tribunal stated in that award that:

> 154. The Arbitral Tribunal considers that this provision of the Agreement, in light of the good faith principle established by international law, requires the Contracting Parties to provide to international investments treatment that does not affect the *basic expectations* that were taken into account by the foreign investor to make the investment. The foreign investor *expects* the host State to act in a consistent manner, free from ambiguity and totally transparently in its relations with the foreign investor, so that it may know beforehand any and all rules and regulations that will govern its investments, as well as the goals of the relevant policies and administrative practices or directives, to be able to plan its investment and comply with such regulations …[76]

Even though the principle has been used in numerous contexts by arbitral tribunals, such as under the umbrella clause or as part of an expropriation analysis,[77] it is as a component of the FET standard that we mostly come across it. Especially after the *Tecmed* award, the use of the breach of investors' legitimate expectations has proliferated in claims. Both investors and arbitral tribunals have furthered the principle using the *Tecmed* award as a starting point. Since that award, the principle has become the 'dominant element'[78] of the FET standard, and the majority of the cases that deal with alleged breaches of the FET standard have scrutinised legitimate expectations claims as an integral part of their analyses.[79] Today, the legitimate expectations principle is considered the most important component of the FET standard[80] and it has become an 'independent basis for a claim under the fair and equitable treatment standard'.[81] This view is sufficiently prevalent among

---

[74] Hamamoto, 'Legitimate Expectations', 142.

[75] Zeyl, 'Charting the Wrong Course', 220; T Wongkaew, 'The Transplantation of Legitimate Expectations in Investment Treaty Arbitration: A Critique' in S Lalani and RP Lazo (eds), *The Role of the State in Investor–State Arbitration* (Brill Nijhoff, 2014) 75.

[76] *Técnicas Medioambientales Tecmed, SA v The United Mexican States*, Award, ICSID Case No ARB (AF)/00/2, 29 May 2003, para 154 (emphasis added).

[77] Snodgrass, 'Legitimate Expectations', 54.

[78] *Saluka Investments BV v The Czech Republic*, Partial Award, PCA Case No 2001-04, 17 March 2006, para 302.

[79] J Bonnitcha, *Substantive Protection under Investment Treaties: A Legal and Economic Analysis* (Cambridge University Press, 2014) 167.

[80] TJ Westcott, 'Recent Practice on Fair and Equitable Treatment' (2007) 8(3) *Journal of World Investment & Trade* 409, 414.

[81] Yannaca-Small, 'FET Standard', 398.

arbitral decisions that tribunals now spend more time scrutinising the scope and outlines of the legitimate expectations principle instead of discussing whether it is actually an element of the FET.[82]

References to the principle by arbitral tribunals have been abundant and this may cause confusion, since there are three main ways in which arbitral tribunals have referred to the principle.[83] The first, according to Newcombe and Paradell, is that the principle 'refers to expectations arising from the foreign investor's reliance on specific host state conduct, usually oral or written representations or commitments made by the host state relating to an investment'.[84] The second way that tribunals refer to this principle encompasses a stable and predictable legal and administrative framework.[85] The last way, as a more general approach, was used by the *Saluka* Tribunal and refers to the 'expectation that the conduct of the host State subsequent to the investment will be fair and equitable'.[86]

Unlike some of its domestic applications, substantive protection of legitimate expectations is a concept that is both rooted and consistently recognised under investment treaty jurisprudence.[87] It has been applied more broadly than English law's earlier procedural protection approach under investment treaty arbitration,[88] though it would be pointless just to have a procedural protection without having access to a compensatory remedy for the purposes of an investment treaty claim.[89]

However, this attitude of arbitral tribunals giving the principle a substantive protection scope cannot escape criticism. Sornarajah, for example, asserts on this point:

> The fair and equitable treatment standard has now been reinterpreted to include a substantive rule relating to legitimate expectations. The result is as if a stabilisation clause, though not negotiated by the parties, is driven into every foreign investment transaction as the expectations created at the commencement of the contract are frozen all the time.[90]

According to him, if the legitimate expectations principle is used as a substantive rule, this would lead to inflexibility in the event of a dramatic change in circumstances and would eventually harm the states.[91] It is argued that since there are a variety of applications of the principle in domestic jurisdictions, substantive protection is not recognised by all and, therefore, arbitral tribunals should not

---

[82] Bonnitcha, *Substantive Protection*, 162.
[83] Newcombe and Paradell, *Standards of Treatment*, 279.
[84] ibid.
[85] ibid 280.
[86] ibid.
[87] Zeyl, 'Charting the Wrong Course', 219.
[88] Pandya and Moody, 'Legitimate Expectations', 105.
[89] Potestà, 'Legitimate Expectations', 95.
[90] M Sornarajah, 'Evolution or Revolution in International Investment Arbitration? The Descent into Normlessness' in C Brown and K Miles (eds), *Evolution in Investment Treaty Law and Arbitration* (Cambridge University Press, 2011) 651.
[91] ibid.

adopt this principle in its broad sense.[92] It is believed by some that arbitrators' subjective approaches show wide discretion in the application of the legitimate expectations principle.[93]

In a similar vein, arbitrator Pedro Nikken, in his separate opinion in the *Suez v Argentina* case, stated:

> I find, indeed, that the development of the doctrine of legitimate expectations is the result of the interaction of the claims of investors and their acceptance by arbitral tribunals, buttressed by the presumed moral authority of the decided cases. I believe that the standard of fair and equitable treatment has been interpreted so broadly that it results in arbitral tribunals imposing upon the Parties obligations that do not arise in any way from the terms that the Parties themselves used to define their commitments. Indeed, more attention has been paid to what the claimants have considered the scope of their rights than what the Parties defined as the extent of their obligations.[94]

In a much-cited separate opinion in the *Thunderbird* case regarding the evolution of the legitimate expectations principle, the late Thomas Waelde stated:

> One can observe over the last years a significant growth in the role and scope of the legitimate expectation principle, from an earlier function as a subsidiary interpretative principle to reinforce a particular interpretative approach chosen, to its current role as a self-standing subcategory and independent basis for a claim under the 'fair and equitable standard' ...[95]

Again, the *Thunderbird* Tribunal explained that the concept within the NAFTA framework relates to a situation

> where a Contracting Party's conduct creates reasonable and justifiable expectations on the part of an investor (or investment) to act in reliance on said conduct, such that a failure by the NAFTA Party to honour those expectations could cause the investor (or investment) to suffer damages.[96]

Legitimate expectations doctrine maintains and increases its importance simultaneously with its utilisation by the investors in the investment treaty arbitrations. Dolzer, considering this matter, opines that: 'The topic of legitimate expectations will likely remain in the foreground of the FET rule. The further definition of this central topic remains the most important component in the development of the FET standard.'[97]

---

[92] Zeyl, 'Charting the Wrong Course', 234.

[93] NM Perrone, 'The Emerging Global Right to Investment: Understanding the Reasoning behind Foreign Investor Rights' (2017) 8(4) *Journal of International Dispute Settlement* 673, 690.

[94] *Suez, Sociedad General de Aguas de Barcelona, SA and Vivendi Universal, SA v Argentine Republic*, Separate Opinion of Arbitrator Pedro Nikken, ICSID Case No ARB/03/19, 30 July 2010, para 27.

[95] *International Thunderbird Gaming Corporation v The United Mexican States*, Separate Opinion of Thomas Waelde, UNCITRAL, 1 December 2005, para 37.

[96] *International Thunderbird Gaming Corporation v The United Mexican States*, Award, UNCITRAL, 26 January 2006, para 147.

[97] Dolzer, 'Today's Contours', 33.

As Dolzer states, since the principle is a relatively new one, its definition and scope still remain ambiguous and contentious under international investment law. Legitimate expectations is not a notion that is referred to in treaties under the FET provisions, but rather is one of the components of the classification created by arbitral tribunals.[98] However, most (but not all) arbitral tribunals have not, until recently, attempted to conduct a systematic analysis and to provide a justification for the use of the principle. Instead, they have chosen to follow the line of reasoning used in previous awards which did not include an in-depth analysis of the origins or the legal justification of the principle.[99] Some more recent awards have tried to provide a justification for the use of the principle.[100] Nonetheless, this does not remove the ambiguity or the need for further clarification. Therefore, the need to provide a scholarly rationalisation of the constant utilisation of the principle by arbitral tribunals arises.

One of the main discussions regarding the principle other than its content is its source. There are two main justifications asserted in relation to the principle's roots. One view argues that even though the *Tecmed* Tribunal and some subsequent ones did not mention domestic laws as the main source of the principle, it is nevertheless derived from these domestic jurisdictions.[101] In order for this domestic principle to be applied in an investment treaty arbitration, it must enjoy a general principle of law status and therefore the arguments concentrate on deciding whether or not the legitimate expectations principle has achieved a general principle of law position.

The second view, in contrast, argues that the legitimate expectations principle as applied by arbitral tribunals is derived from the good faith principle under international law. Therefore, there is no need to discuss the position of the principle within domestic jurisdictions and the tribunals are free to interpret the principle in relation to the treaty standards. The following sections will analyse these two main lines of justifications in order to reveal the origins of the principle.

(i) General Principles of Law Approach

As stated above, even though arbitral tribunals do not state it explicitly, it is argued by the majority of scholars that the legitimate expectations principle is mainly derived from the domestic administrative jurisdictions. Section IIIA has already touched upon some applications of the principle under various domestic laws. The question here is whether its application under these domestic laws could be considered to provide the status of a general principle. If so, the utilisation of the principle by arbitral tribunals can be justified on those grounds.

---

[98] UNCTAD, 'Fair and Equitable Treatment', 9.
[99] Potestà, 'Legitimate Expectations', 89–90.
[100] *Gold Reserve Inc v Bolivarian Republic of Venezuela*, Award, ICSID Case No ARB(AF)/09/1, 22 September 2014.
[101] Wongkaew, 'Transplantation', 76.

This approach considers the application of the principle under diverse domestic legal systems and attempts to extract general principles of law in order to justify its application under international treaty arbitration. According to Kläger, if domestic legal systems can generate universally applicable general principles of law, then those general principles would be directly applicable to an investment dispute and there will be no need to refer to them as an argumentative tool for the construction of a norm.[102] While some treaties include a direct reference to general principles of law as the applicable law, others do not explicitly refer to them but, instead, refer to principles of international law which indeed encompass general principles of law.[103]

A general principle of law is determined by evaluating whether it has achieved a wide-ranging character, whether it is recognised by domestic legal jurisdictions and whether it is applicable in international law.[104] If a principle satisfies these requirements, then it might be considered a general principle of law. The issue here is whether the mere existence of the principle under national laws would be adequate to be considered a general principle or whether its application should also be taken into account.[105] Diehl argues on this matter that it is impossible to define the exact status and application of a general principle under all domestic jurisdictions, and therefore the mere existence of a principle should be enough for it to be granted a general principle status.[106] While establishing a general principle, it is important to present inductive proof of its existence and this proof should be based on an elaborative examination of the major representative domestic legal systems.[107]

General principles are subsidiary in nature and 'international tribunals tend to use them to fill remaining gaps in treaty and customary law laws'.[108] Snodgrass determines the function of general principles of law to be as follows:

> The primary function of general principles of law in the international legal system is to facilitate the resolution of disputes by managing the interplay of other, usually customary or conventional, norms to knit together the sometimes patchy fabric of international law into a comprehensive system capable of resolving disputes.[109]

While attempting to determine from where the doctrine of legitimate expectations arises, one might look at the issue of the sources of law under international law. According to Article 38(1) of the Statute of the International Court of Justice,

---

[102] Kläger, *Fair and Equitable Treatment*, 128.
[103] T Gazzini, 'General Principles of Law in the Field of Foreign Investment' (2009) 10(1) *Journal of World Investment & Trade* 103, 112.
[104] M Hirsch, 'Sources of International Investment Law' (International Law Association Study Group on the Role of Soft Law Instruments in International Investment Law, 2011) 13–14.
[105] Diehl, *Core Standard*, 167.
[106] ibid 168.
[107] C Schreuer et al, *The ICSID Convention: A Commentary* (Cambridge University Press, 2009) 610.
[108] Hirsch, 'Sources', 17.
[109] Snodgrass, 'Legitimate Expectations', 11.

the main sources might be international conventions, customary international law or the general principles of law recognised by civilised nations.[110] Even though Article 38 deals with settling disputes between states, it 'provides important indications that are pervasive of all fields of international law including foreign investment law'.[111] The first two sources (treaties and custom) are created through the interaction of states, and therefore general principles of law are especially beneficial in fields that involve non-state actors, such as investment relationships.[112] In addition to this, Article 42(1) of the ICSID Convention could also be taken as a reference to the general principles of law to which an arbitrator can apply as a source of law.[113]

If each of these sources were evaluated, it would be clear that there is no explicit mention of the legitimate expectations principle under any bilateral or multilateral treaties in force, nor is the principle established under customary international law.[114] Thus, the only rational justification for the use of this principle would be to consider it under the general principles of law.

So, the test that should be conducted at this point is to assess whether the legitimate expectations principle has reached the level of a general principle. Regarding this debate, there are three major views in the doctrine. The first argues that it bears all the requirements and has achieved the status of a general principle of law. The second claims that there is no general principle of law protecting the legitimate expectations and it is merely an invention[115] of the arbitral tribunals. The last approach asserts that there is an emerging general principle of law.[116] The latter two will be analysed next, then the section will conclude with a discussion of the first view.

As a harsh critic of the idea that the legitimate expectations principle has achieved the status of general principle of law, Sornarajah opines that

> [i]t is an error to state that there is a general principle of law that violations of legitimate expectations give rise to substantive remedies. That does not appear to be the case, in English law at any rate. It is unlikely that such a rule can be maintained in any system. Yet, it is precisely such a rule that has been developed in the recent ICSID cases which declare it to be a substantive rule, justifying the award of damages for its breach.[117]

At the same time, he does not contend with the procedural legitimate expectations protection being recognised as a general principle of law.[118] In a similar vein, it

---

[110] United Nations, *Statute of the International Court of Justice*, entered into force 24 October 1945, Art 38(1)(c).

[111] Gazzini, 'General Principles', 103.

[112] Schreuer et al, *A Commentary*, 608.

[113] Tudor, *The FET Standard*, 86.

[114] Brown, 'Legitimate Expectations', 3; Campbell, 'House of Cards', 379.

[115] Campbell, 'House of Cards', 379.

[116] Potestà, 'Legitimate Expectations', 98.

[117] M Sornarajah, *The International Law on Foreign Investment* (Cambridge University Press, 2010) 355.

[118] ibid 354.

has also been submitted by Zeyl that acknowledging legitimate expectations as a general principle is a 'misstatement of law' that contravenes the requirement of a general principle to be based on wide acceptance by domestic jurisdictions.[119] In addition to these views, Costamagna argues that the selective approach to domestic laws and the fact that the differences between them are disregarded by the proponents of the general principle of law argument renders the argument methodologically problematic.[120]

While Sornarajah at least recognises procedural protection as a general principle, Campbell, in a more rigid way, urges the requirement to protect the legitimate expectations to be disavowed and calls the concept built by arbitral tribunals 'a house of cards'.[121] As the reason for this, he argues that the states would not have committed themselves to the level of the standard required by the legitimate expectations principle under the FET today had they known it earlier.[122] However, this argument, to say the least, is unfounded. It has already been discussed earlier in this chapter that there are a good majority of domestic laws that recognise the concept of legitimate expectations in one way or another. As these states already have the principle under their domestic laws, it is thus incoherent to argue that they would oppose the concept under international jurisdiction. Moreover, again as argued before, general principles of law are recognised as a source of international law, and if a principle has reached the status of a general principle, it does not matter whether it falls short of the requirements or anticipations of a certain state; it is applicable under international law.

Another argument from Sornarajah is that there is no support for this principle under treaties and therefore it cannot be used in arbitral decisions.[123] However, this is the whole idea of resorting to the general principles of law as a source of international law. Since there is no mention of the legitimate expectations principle in treaties, the tribunals refer to the general principles of law in pursuit of finding an applicable principle to the case at hand in order to reach a fair decision.

As a representative of the moderate view, Potestà concludes that there is 'an emerging general principle of protection of legitimate expectations'.[124] However, it should be noted that this is a very prudent and neutral conclusion that is reached purely to be on the safe side of the debate. In practice, this does not mean any applicable approach. Since the main discussion regarding this issue is whether to apply this principle in investment treaty arbitrations as an important component of the FET standard or otherwise, this moderate approach does not add anything to the discussion. He has also not presented any sources other than the general

---

[119] Zeyl, 'Charting the Wrong Course', 234.
[120] F Costamagna, 'Protecting Foreign Investments in Public Services: Regulatory Stability at Any Cost?' (2017) 17(3) *Global Jurist* 1, 5.
[121] Campbell, 'House of Cards', 379.
[122] ibid.
[123] ibid 379.
[124] Potestà, 'Legitimate Expectations', 98.

principle of law as the justification behind the application of the principle in investment treaty law. It is difficult to see from this approach how the utilisation of the principle by arbitral tribunals is justified if there is no general principle right now, only an emerging one. Suggesting that there is an emerging principle means that the arbitral tribunals that employ this doctrine today base their arguments on a non-existent principle.

On the other hand, some scholars and tribunals have argued that the legitimate expectations principle is a general principle of law which justifies its use by arbitral tribunals.[125] There are several extensive and comprehensive works that deal with the domestic applications of the legitimate expectations principle.[126] As mentioned earlier, it is beyond the scope of this book to scrutinise these domestic laws in detail. However, as discussed in section IIIA, the principle is sufficiently widespread among domestic jurisdictions to be recognised as a general principle of law.[127] In addition to the domestic legal systems, the legitimate expectations principle is recognised as a general principle of law by EU law and the European Court of Justice.[128] Waelde, after conducting a comparative analysis of the principle, concluded that

> under developed systems of administrative law, a citizen – even more so an investor – should be protected against unexpected and detrimental changes of policy if the investor has carried out significant investment with a reasonable, public-authority initiated assurance in the stability of such policy.[129]

Although it is possible to witness some variance between the applications of the legitimate expectations principle under different domestic laws, this should not be an obstacle to its acceptance as a general principle of law.[130] This has been the issue for a number of other principles, such as the doctrine of abuse of rights or *res judicata*, where their applications in domestic jurisdictions differ but they are still recognised as general principles of law.[131] Indeed, this approach has also been upheld by other branches of international law. Carpanelli, paraphrasing what Judge Shahabuddeen argued in an International Criminal Tribunal judgment, states that

> general principles of law would not amount to generalizations reached by the application of comparative law but to particularizations of a common underlying sense of what

---

[125] See in general Brown, 'Legitimate Expectations'; Snodgrass, 'Legitimate Expectations'; Monebhurrun, 'Enshrining Legitimate Expectations'; Hamamoto, 'Legitimate Expectations'.
[126] Schønberg, *Legitimate Expectations*; Schwarze, *European Administrative Law*; M Groves and G Weeks (eds), *Legitimate Expectations in the Common Law World* (Hart Publishing, 2017); PP Craig, *EU Administrative Law* (Oxford University Press, 2012); Mairal, 'Legitimate Expectations'.
[127] SW Schill, 'General Principles of Law and International Investment Law' in T Gazzini and E de Brabandere (eds), *International Investment Law: The Sources of Rights and Obligations* (Martinus Nijhoff Publishers, 2012) 168–69.
[128] Fietta, 'Legitimate Expectations', 424.
[129] *Thunderbird v Mexico*, Separate Opinion of Thomas Waelde, para 30.
[130] Brown, 'Legitimate Expectations', 6.
[131] ibid.

is just in the circumstances; as a consequence, an international tribunal may select an interpretation, even if it is at variance with that of some legal systems.[132]

Mann asserts on this point that universality is not a requirement of a general principle of law; it is enough that 'the principle pervades the municipal law of nations in general'.[133] Also, it is impossible for these rules to be completely identical between various domestic laws and that, when searching for a general principle, the similarities should be looked for instead.[134] As Snodgrass states:

> [A] general principle may be identified when different rules in different legal systems reflect the same principle, despite differences in points of detail, as when legal systems reach similar outcomes in similar cases, even if by different routes of legal reasoning.[135]

Even if there are different approaches to the legitimate expectations principle as a doctrinal matter under domestic jurisdictions, the outcomes seem to be consistent.[136]

Considering these approaches together, one might conclude that the legitimate expectations principle has reached the level of a general principle of law and, therefore, can be applied by arbitral tribunals as a component of the FET standard. Its application is not groundless, despite what Campbell[137] and Zeyl[138] argue in their articles.

It is true that there is variance between the application of the principle under some domestic jurisdictions and under investment arbitration. However, this is something that originates from the very nature of these two systems. The main principles and purposes underlying domestic administrative laws and international investment law are different in essence, and this requires different approaches to the same doctrines.[139] International investment law 'tends to privilege regulatory certainty for investors over more complex understanding of the rule of law and parliamentary sovereignty: concepts which are carefully balanced in domestic administrative law'.[140] Applying the legitimate expectations principle under the international investment law in the exact same way as it is applied under domestic administrative laws would undermine the objectives of the former since they operate in different contexts.[141] Also, these common principles of domestic laws are generally not concrete enough to be applied directly as is, and therefore

---

[132] E Carpanelli, 'General Principles of International Law: Struggling with a Slippery Concept' in L Pineschi (ed), *General Principles of Law – The Role of the Judiciary* (Springer, 2012) 126.

[133] FA Mann, 'Reflections on a Commercial Law of Nations' (1957) 33 *British Yearbook of International Law* 20, 38–39.

[134] ibid 39.

[135] Snodgrass, 'Legitimate Expectations', 22.

[136] Gaukrodger, 'A Scoping Paper', 27.

[137] Campbell, 'House of Cards'.

[138] Zeyl, 'Charting the Wrong Course'.

[139] Z Meyers, 'Adapting Legitimate Expectations to International Investment Law: A Defence of Arbitral Tribunals' Approach' (2014) 11(3) *Transnational Dispute Management* 1, 38.

[140] ibid.

[141] ibid 39.

require adaptation.[142] An international judge does not have to apply a general principle in the same way as domestic principles apply; rather,

> he has the creative task of maintaining the essential features of the general principles while at the same time finding the appropriate solution for the international legal relation upon which he has to pass judgment. The norm which he applies is a norm of international law, taken from principles observed in domestic legal orders and adapted by him to the particular needs of international relations.[143]

The divergence that Meyers speaks of is not dramatic, and is limited to a certain degree. Vicuña states that 'in the light of a number of recent decisions, "fair and equitable treatment" is not really different from legitimate expectation as developed, for example, by the English courts and also recently by the World Bank Administrative Tribunal'.[144] So, even though there are some differences in the application of the principle, ultimately, the way it is recognised by arbitral tribunals in the form of a component of the FET standard and the way it is understood by domestic jurisdictions are not two completely different principles.

(ii) Good Faith Approach

Even though arbitral tribunals do not mention domestic laws as a means of justification for their use of the legitimate expectations principle, they have made several references to the good faith principle in connection with its juridical roots.[145] According to this approach, arbitral tribunals base their decisions, when they employ the legitimate expectations principle, on the good faith principle of international law. In this view, unlike the previous one, there is no discussion as to whether the legitimate expectations principle is itself a general principle of law; rather, the main issue here is whether it is a part of a well-recognised general principle of law, namely good faith.

Indeed, the good faith principle is considered one of the most pervasive and fundamental general principles of law.[146] Due to its practical implications and content, good faith duly resembles a 'Swiss army knife' among other principles.[147] This section will not discuss the status of the good faith principle, since it is firmly

---

[142] H Mosler, 'General Principles of Law' in R Bernhardt (ed), *Encyclopedia of Public International Law* (North-Holland, 1995) 517.

[143] ibid.

[144] FO Vicuña, 'Foreign Investment Law: How Customary Is Custom?' (2005) 38(148) *Estudios Internacionales* 79, 83.

[145] Wongkaew, 'Transplantation', 76.

[146] See in general AD Mitchell, M Sornarajah and T Voon (eds), *Good Faith and International Economic Law* (Oxford University Press, 2015); R Kolb, *Good Faith in International Law* (Hart Publishing, 2017); B Cheng, *General Principles of Law as Applied by International Courts and Tribunals* (Cambridge University Press, 2006); M Panizzon, *Good Faith in the Jurisprudence of the WTO: The Protection of Legitimate Expectations, Good Faith Interpretation and Fair Dispute Settlement* (Hart Publishing, 2006).

[147] AR Ziegler and J Baumgartner, 'Good Faith as a General Principle of (International) Law' in AD Mitchell, M Sornarajah and T Voon (eds), *Good Faith and International Economic Law* (Oxford University Press, 2015) 9.

established under international law as a general principle. Rather, it will scrutinise it only in relation to the legitimate expectations principle.

There are several arbitral tribunals that expressly attach the legitimate expectations principle to the good faith principle. The *Tecmed* award, as quoted above, articulated that not affecting the basic expectations of the investors is a required component of the FET standard, which is recognised 'in light of the good faith principle established by international law'.[148] The very same approach was subsequently quoted and employed by another Tribunal, *Eureko v Poland*, in 2005.[149]

This was followed by the *Thunderbird* award; when defining legitimate expectations, the tribunal initially resorted to 'the good faith principle of international customary law'.[150] In his separate opinion of the same case, Waelde opined that the legitimate expectations principle is 'considered to be part of the "good faith" principle which is a guiding principle (also a general principle of international law)'.[151]

Likewise, the Tribunal in *Total v Argentina* stated:

> Since the concept of legitimate expectations is based on the requirement of good faith, one of the general principles referred to in Article 38(1)(c) of the Statute of the International Court of Justice as a source of international law, the Tribunal believes that a comparative analysis of the protection of legitimate expectations in domestic jurisdictions is justified at this point.[152]

However, the *Total* Tribunal proceeded with a comparative analysis of domestic jurisdictions after this argument. It should have argued and justified the reasons why the legitimate expectations principle is encapsulated by the good faith principle instead of resorting to domestic applications.

In *Saluka v Czech Republic*, the Tribunal also formed a connection between legitimate expectations and good faith by stating: 'the expectations of foreign investors certainly include the observation by the host State of such well-established fundamental standards as good faith, due process, and non-discrimination'.[153]

In 2011, in *El Paso v Argentina*, the Tribunal also recognised the relationship between the two, stating:

> [T]he legitimate expectations of the investors have generally been considered central in the definition of FET, whatever its scope. There is an overwhelming trend to consider the touchstone of fair and equitable treatment to be found in the legitimate and reasonable expectations of the Parties, which derive from the obligation of good faith.[154]

---

[148] *Tecmed v Mexico*, Award, para 154.

[149] *Eureko BV v Republic of Poland*, Partial Award, UNCITRAL, 19 August 2005, para 235.

[150] *Thunderbird v Mexico*, Award, para 147.

[151] *Thunderbird v Mexico*, Separate Opinion of Thomas Waelde, para 25.

[152] *Total SA v The Argentine Republic*, Decision on Liability, ICSID Case No ARB/04/01, 27 December 2010, para 128 (emphasis added).

[153] *Saluka v Czech*, Partial Award, para 303.

[154] *El Paso Energy International Company v The Argentine Republic*, Award, ICSID Case No ARB/03/15, 31 October 2011, para 348.

Apart from investment treaty jurisprudence, protection of legitimate expectations is also considered to be similar to the good faith principle in EU law and World Trade Organization (WTO) law and practice. The *Total* Tribunal notes that the recognition of the legitimate expectations principle in the European Union is 'explicitly based on the international law principle of good faith'.[155] Panizzon, in her detailed work on the WTO, discusses the relationship between the protection of legitimate expectations (PLE) and the good faith principle, explaining that 'the PLE is a self-standing good faith principle which the WTO Panels, and even earlier, the GATT 47 adjudicators directly applied as a "well-established GATT principle". Because PLE is considered an expression of good faith, under Article 31 VCLT ...'[156]

In addition to the above, there are a number of scholarly writings that recognise the protection of legitimate expectations as a part of good faith. It is submitted that the legitimate expectations principle is essentially an expression of the good faith principle[157] and propounds the conclusion that legitimate expectations must be protected.[158] Al-Faruque, in his extensive work on stability, states that 'fulfilment of contractual promise and performance of a contract in good faith has sometimes been expressed as a requirement of "reasonable expectation of the parties"'.[159] Kolb also identifies the legitimate expectations principle as one of 'the main functions of the principle of good faith'.[160] In a similar vein, according to Maniruzzaman, the protection of legitimate expectations principle is fundamentally based on good faith in international investment law.[161] Lastly, Dajic states that 'the legitimate expectation has become the normative and more defined expression of the good faith obligation of the host states'.[162]

In contrast, Sornarajah argues that finding the roots of the protection of legitimate expectations principle in good faith is not plausible since

> the finding of bad faith in the circumstances of investment law would be difficult even if the host state had applied its own law incorrectly. In terms of international law, it is a particularly serious matter to attribute bad faith to a state.[163]

---

[155] *Total v Argentina*, Decision on Liability, para 130.
[156] Panizzon, *Good Faith*, 127.
[157] Newcombe and Paradell, *Standards of Treatment*, 277.
[158] DG Henriques, 'Pathological Arbitration Clauses, Good Faith and the Protection of Legitimate Expectations' (2015) 31(2) *Arbitration International* 349, 357.
[159] A Al Faruque, 'Stability in Petroleum Contracts: Rhetoric and Reality' (PhD Thesis, University of Dundee, 2005), 28.
[160] Kolb, *Good Faith*, 255.
[161] AFM Maniruzzaman, 'The Concept of Good Faith in International Investment Disputes – The Arbitrator's Dilemma' (2012) (89) *Amicus Curiae* 16.
[162] S Dajic, 'Mapping the Good Faith Principle in International Investment Arbitration: Assessment of Its Substantive and Procedural Value' (2012) 46(3) *Proceedings of Novi Sad Faculty of Law* 207, 214.
[163] M Sornarajah, *Resistance and Change in the International Law on Foreign Investment* (Cambridge University Press, 2015) 257.

Moreover, he purports that the arbitral tribunals have referred to the good faith principle as the source of legitimate expectations with the aim of escaping from criticism that they create a new doctrine.[164] It is argued that the arbitral tribunals have not been successful in explaining how the good faith principle encompasses an obligation to protect the legitimate expectations of investors.[165] Indeed, this criticism is fair since none of the arbitral tribunals have attempted to properly explain the relationship between the legitimate expectations and the good faith principles.

One of the main problematic issues of recognising the good faith principle as the basis of legitimate expectations is related to the liability of a host state. If we accept the assertion that the legitimate expectations principle arises out of the good faith principle, then there should be no liability on the part of a host state when the expectations of an investor are hindered by an act of that state conducted in good faith, as Walter argues.[166] However, investment tribunals have found that even when the host state acts in good faith, its acts might frustrate the legitimate expectations of an investor, and thus nevertheless lead to a breach of the FET standard.[167] In order to resolve this problem, Walter suggests that the good faith principle be used merely as a guiding principle in defining the contours of the FET standard, which includes the duty to protect investors' legitimate expectations instead of deriving the legitimate expectations principle directly from good faith.[168]

However, this argument is not the final point in the discussions regarding good faith, since there is not just one uniform understanding and application of the good faith principle; rather, its conceptualisation and application vary across international courts and legal traditions.[169] The issue of whether the principle of good faith can be utilised as an autonomous source of obligation remains dubious.[170] It is possible to witness various approaches within the contexts of the International Court of Justice, the WTO or the investment treaty jurisprudence.[171] While some consider it to be a principle that only underlies an obligation such as the FET[172] without creating duties in itself, others claim that it might be considered a stand-alone instrument that is capable of creating obligations for the state party on its own. Kolb considers the former view as being too narrow and argues that even the good faith principle has mainly played an intermediary role, and has been

---

[164] ibid 257–58.
[165] Wongkaew, 'Transplantation', 82.
[166] A Walter, 'The Investor's Expectations in International Investment Arbitration' (2009) 6(1) *Transnational Dispute Management* 1, 29.
[167] Dolzer and Schreuer, *Principles*, 158.
[168] Walter, 'The Investor's Expectations', 30.
[169] Dajic, 'Good Faith', 209.
[170] Ziegler and Baumgartner, 'Good Faith', 14.
[171] ibid 14–17.
[172] OECD, 'FET', 40; Choudhury, 'Evolution or Devolution?', 317; Schreuer, 'FET in Arbitral Practice', 384; Diehl, *Core Standard*, 357.

applied through other principles. This does not negate its capability of being of direct application itself to certain cases.[173] On this last point, Cremades notes: 'In many arbitration awards, the general principles of law and, specifically, of *good faith, are not only guides, but rather the specific basis for the claims*.'[174] According to Gehne and Brillo: 'From an international public law perspective, the principle of good faith could also be invoked independently of the FET standard.'[175]

As can be seen, it is possible to witness arbitral decisions and scholarly writings that support either of these views. This section will not attempt to take this discussion any further apart from showing that both of these approaches are widely available in practice. It is not possible to contain the good faith principle within the purview of only one line of thought. After all, as Paparinskis appropriately opined, 'good faith operates in many guises in the international legal order. A principle and its different particularizations may play different roles at different stages of legal reasoning.'[176]

(iii) Analysis of the Two Approaches

It can be seen from this analysis that there is strong evidence to support both of the above-mentioned approaches as the source of the legitimate expectations principle under investment treaty law. An arbitral tribunal might choose one of these views while deciding on a potential breach of the legitimate expectations of an investor, and there is enough evidence to justify its use of that path. This is indeed something that strengthens the position of the legitimate expectations principle. Davies suggests that even if the legitimate expectations principle is not considered a general principle of law, arbitral tribunals might still attribute significant weight to it in the interpretation process were the principle to be recognised by the legal systems of the state parties to an investment treaty arbitration.[177]

As for the reason behind this variance, one might consider the wide existence of numerous legal principles that serve the same purpose and lead to the same outcome as the legitimate expectations principle. Thus, it is acceptable for different tribunals consisting of arbitrators from various legal backgrounds to approach the same issue from diverse perspectives. It is entirely reasonable for them to use various principles as the point of departure for their analyses.

---

[173] Kolb, *Good Faith*, 29–31.

[174] BM Cremades, 'Good Faith in International Arbitration' (2012) 27(4) *American University International Law Review* 761, 788 (emphasis added).

[175] K Gehne and R Brillo, 'Stabilization Clauses in International Investment Law: Beyond Balancing and Fair and Equitable Treatment' (NCCR Trade Regulation, 2014).

[176] M Paparinskis, 'Good Faith and Fair and Equitable Treatment in International Investment Law' in AD Mitchell, M Sornarajah and T Voon (eds), *Good Faith and International Economic Law* (Oxford University Press, 2015) 145.

[177] A Davies, 'Investment Treaty Law Interpretation, Fair and Equitable Treatment and Legitimate Expectations' (2018) 15(3) *Manchester Journal of International Economic Law* 314, 330–35.

It should be noted from a practical point of view that these two approaches do not create any significant differences in the principle's application; they are both legally acceptable sources. It does not matter from which source a tribunal benefits as long as the contours of the applied principle are determined properly. Dajic, on the issue of the relationship between good faith and the legitimate expectations principle, states:

> Due to a vague and ambiguous wording of the FET in general, and inclusion of a separate substantive obligations under its chapeaux in particular, the good faith argument is closer to an autonomous standard in the international investment law. Whether good faith principle produced legitimate expectations standard, or vice versa, becomes irrelevant as neither of them has been explicitly envisaged in a number of BITs.[178]

Whichever path an arbitral tribunal chooses, it leads to the application of the legitimate expectations principle to the case at hand. For example, the above-mentioned *Total* Tribunal could have followed the argument that legitimate expectations was a part of the general principles of law itself. It undertook the comparative analysis of the domestic laws and then concluded that the legitimate expectations principle was a part of good faith. The outcome probably would not have been different had the tribunal recognised the legitimate expectations as a general principle because, after determining the source of the principle, the tribunal must still define its contours and content. However, there still remains an open question: do these two different approaches affect the definition or the scope of the principle? This book will not discuss this issue since it requires an in-depth analysis of the two principles (good faith and legitimate expectations). An in-depth analysis of their roots, similarities and differences should be conducted in order to reveal the real association between the two principles within the international investment law context.

An important issue to raise here is that arbitral tribunals have not discussed these sources widely. We cannot deduce from the above-mentioned cases why any particular path should necessarily be followed. We can understand that there is enough evidence to justify each of these approaches separately. However, it is not possible to construe why one particular approach should be preferred over another. Whether the arbitral tribunals should engage with such an extensive analysis is also another aspect of the issue. It is unreasonable to ask such a thing from every tribunal; however, the tribunals also bear the responsibility of justifying their decisions. So, they should be able to cite some credible authorities even if they do not engage with that analysis themselves.

Even though it is more plausible for some to restrict the scope of the good faith principle to that of a guiding principle only, investment treaty jurisprudence has not explicitly rejected its recognition as an autonomous source of obligation. There are no reasonable grounds on which to wage war against the use of the legitimate expectations principle in international investment law, while the principle is sufficiently widely recognised under domestic jurisdictions. Instead, authors and arbitral tribunals should give weight to defining the contours and content of the

---

[178] Dajic, 'Good Faith', 215.

legitimate expectations principle. Only in this way could a consistent and well-defined application of the principle be possible.

C. Why Protect Legitimate Expectations?

As already shown, arbitral tribunals have endeavoured to justify the legitimate expectations principle on the grounds of other international law principles. However, the main rationale behind the protection of legitimate expectations has not been discussed in depth.[179]

One of the reasons for this negligence might be the premise of tribunals that, since the principle has been existent for a fairly long time, its rationale is already obvious and there is little cause for discussion. Even though this might be the case, the tribunals should still have explored and clarified this further in their decisions because domestic administrative law and international investment law are two separate legal areas, and the application of any given principle does not necessarily need to be the same in these two.

Similar to the position of Dupuy and Dupuy that 'it is a commonly accepted moral standard that a unilateral promise must be upheld',[180] Wongkaew also attempts to explain the rationale behind protecting legitimate expectations by developing a theory on the 'moral philosophy of promise'.[181] However, instead of merely contending that there is a moral duty for host states to honour their promises, he takes another path and employs the moral aspect in explaining why a promise would create an obligation.[182] Accordingly, the moral obligation of a host state to keep a promise arises out of the detrimental reliance by the investor on that promise.[183]

Indeed, explaining the rationale underlying the legitimate expectations principle by means of detrimental reliance has been an old practice under domestic laws.[184] Schønberg states that 'The reliance theory argues that legitimate expectations should be protected because to do otherwise would inflict harm on

---

[179] T Wongkaew, *Protection of Legitimate Expectations in Investment Treaty Arbitration: A Theory of Detrimental Reliance* (Cambridge University Press, 2019) 4; F Dupuy and PM Dupuy, 'What to Expect from Legitimate Expectations? A Critical Appraisal and Look Into the Future of the "Legitimate Expectations" Doctrine in International Investment Law' in MA Raouf, P Leboulanger and NG Ziadé (eds), *Festschrift Ahmed Sadek El-Kosheri – From the Arab World to the Globalization of International Law and Arbitration* (Kluwer Law International, 2015) 274.

[180] Dupuy and Dupuy, 'What to Expect from Legitimate Expectations?', 275.

[181] Wongkaew, *Legitimate Expectations*, 9.

[182] ibid 59.

[183] 'The reliance theory of promise states that when the promisor induces the promisee to rely on his or her representation and the promisee does rely on it to his or her detriment, the promisor will be responsible for rectifying that harm.' For more detailed discussion on detrimental reliance theory, see ibid 134–71.

[184] A Siwy, 'Indirect Expropriation and the Legitimate Expectations of the Investor' in C Klausegger et al (eds), *Austrian Arbitration Yearbook 2007* (CH Beck/Stämpfli/Manz, 2007) 370; Snodgrass, 'Legitimate Expectations', 44; Barak-Erez, 'Legitimate Expectations'; Schønberg, *Legitimate Expectations*, 9–12.

individuals who rely upon such expectations'.[185] Actually, the reliance here is not on the 'expectations', but rather on the 'promise or assurance' of the state.

Adopting this detrimental reliance approach from domestic laws and adapting it to the investment law would actually be an appropriate way of answering the question 'Why should legitimate expectations be protected?' In this way, arbitral tribunals will have an analytical framework while holding host states responsible for not respecting the legitimate expectations of investors.

IV. Conclusion

Probably the most important and effective legal instrument of the last decade in investment treaty jurisprudence has been the FET standard. Arising out of its vague wording, there are still ongoing debates regarding the definition and the content of the standard. Nevertheless, it is also possible to witness a particular approach gaining weight in defining the FET among arbitral tribunals and authors: that is, to specify the components of the standard in order to determine its scope.

This pursuit of defining the components has produced several approaches. Some of them tend to subdivide the standard into as many as eight different headings. However, there is one principle that is recognised as an essential part of the FET standard in almost all of these various approaches, namely the legitimate expectations principle.

Even though the legitimate expectations principle is a concept that is widely recognised both by domestic jurisdictions and arbitral jurisprudence, its roots and scope have been the two major focal points of recent debate on this subject. This chapter has attempted to identify the former: that is, the origins of the legitimate expectations principle. In this regard, the study has found that there are two major lines of thought concerning the justification of the use of the standard by arbitral tribunals. The principle is either considered a general principle of law which derives from domestic laws or a part of the general principle of good faith; indeed, there is enough evidence to support either view. Since the principle is recognised and applied by a wide range of states, it might be recognised as a general principle of law. Again, since the good faith principle is a part of the general principles of law, by acknowledging the legitimate expectations principle as a component of the good faith principle, it is justified from a legal perspective to utilise it in investment treaty disputes. However, it should be noted that the arbitral tribunals have, to date, failed to explain the theoretical relationship between good faith and legitimate expectations.

---

[185] Schønberg, *Legitimate Expectations*, 9.

5

The Legitimate Expectations Principle in Investment Treaty Arbitration: Current Status and Contours

I. Introduction

There are two major schools of thought in the interpretation and application of the legitimate expectations principle, among both scholars and arbitrators. While members of the first school strive to narrow down the scope and application of the principle, those of the latter call for a broader approach. The first school of thought argues that only specific assurances can create legitimate expectations. The second school of thought, on the other hand, does not limit these sources to the specific ones only. This book argues that the legitimate expectations principle should be interpreted in its wider form so that it provides more comprehensive protection to investors and secures the stable investment environment that they aspire to.

This approach is directly relevant to the main argument of the research, which is that while the stability concept, through stabilisation provisions, reinforces legitimate expectations claims before an arbitral tribunal, this applies the other way around as well. That is to say, the presence of the legitimate expectations principle under the fair and equitable treatment (FET) standard inherently imposes a duty on the host states to provide and secure a stable legal framework. Failing to uphold the duty of stability might, in turn, result in a breach of legitimate expectations. This leads to the conclusion that legitimate expectations might be created even in the absence of specific stability undertakings by host states.

This chapter is designed to present the current and latest state of the scope and understanding of the legitimate expectations principle under investment treaty arbitration jurisprudence. As already mentioned, the contours of the principle are not clear and fixed, but rather are still developing. One of the main problems that this book deals with is ambiguity and inconsistency in the application of the legitimate expectations principle. Hence, this chapter aims to clarify its contours and show the direction that should be taken by arbitral tribunals when examining legitimate expectations. It is important to clarify the limits of the principle because an inconsistent application would also harm the stability aspirations of investors. The first thing to do is to present the demarcations of the principle, before revealing its relationship with the stability concept.

It is important to conduct an in-depth analysis of the scope of legitimate expectations in order to determine the link between the assurance given and the expectations created. The legitimate expectations principle has a direct relevance to the stability concept and it must be construed and applied in a way that enhances investment protection. This chapter explains that the legitimate expectations principle still finds application in its wider form before arbitral tribunals and that this approach should be followed by future tribunals as well.

The following sections will analyse the three sources by which a legitimate expectation can be created, namely through contracts, representations, and the legal and regulatory framework of a host state. It will be argued that there is sufficient evidence to suggest that a legitimate expectation might be based on any of these sources provided that it fulfils certain requirements. The framework presented in this chapter will form the basis for the analysis presented in the following chapter, in which the stability concept and the legitimate expectations principle will be tied together.

Keeping the scope of the legitimate expectations principle wide is particularly essential to investment protection in the energy industry. Since it is a highly regulated sector with a wide range of legislation, decrees, licences and contracts included within it, foreign investors make their decisions by simultaneously taking all of these aspects into account. Therefore, their expectations are also based on various legal sources in combination. The legitimate expectations doctrine should thus also take this cumulative aspect of international energy investments into account.

The three main questions that will be answered in the next section in relation to legitimate expectations are what, when and how questions. *What* are the sources that create legitimate expectations? *When* must these expectations be in place? *How* can an expectation be considered legitimate?

II. What Creates Legitimate Expectations?

In the previous chapter, it was argued that whether the legitimate expectations principle applied under investment treaty arbitration originates from domestic laws or a good faith principle does not generate a significant difference with respect to arbitral practice. It is the arbitral tribunals themselves who will define its contours within the context of investment law. Since simply transplanting the doctrine from domestic laws to international investment law and applying it in the exact same way without any customisation would undermine the objectives of investment law,[1] arbitral tribunals have a duty to detect, define and develop the principle in accordance with the needs of international investment law.

---

[1] Z Meyers, 'Adapting Legitimate Expectations to International Investment Law: A Defence of Arbitral Tribunals' Approach' (2014) 11(3) *Transnational Dispute Management* 1, 38–39.

Therefore, it is essential to answer the question in the title in connection with arbitral decisions and present some suggestions on how to improve its application further.

There are certain elements that a foreign investor takes into account both in the course of the investment decision and in its day-to-day business in the concerned host state which eventually might lead to the creation of legitimate expectations on the investor's side.[2] Even though it is still a controversial area,[3] it can be seen from the arbitral jurisprudence that there are three major legal sources that have a potential to generate a legitimate expectation. These are: contractual undertakings, administrative representations and promises, and the general legislative and regulatory framework prevalent in a host state.

This section will attempt to analyse how these different sources create legitimate expectations and what requirements must be met to be granted a protection.

A. Contractual Undertakings

A relatively less challenged protection provided by the legitimate expectations principle is associated with the contracts, ie international investment contracts (or state contracts) within the scope of this book. Contracts, being one of the main tools of an international investment relationship, govern the investment process from its very beginning until its end. Contracts are utilised in every legal system in order to provide legal stability and predictability to the legal relationship between the parties.[4] With contracts, investors' legitimate expectations are formalised.[5]

The importance of a contract especially in international energy investments, is more visible since they possess particular characteristics.[6] The rights, obligations and all sorts of other aspects surrounding an investment are included in contracts and generate legal rules under international investment law,[7] thus creating a basis for legitimate expectations.

The significance of a contract in creating a legitimate expectation has been endorsed by several arbitral tribunals. In *Continental v Argentina*, the Tribunal emphasised that contracts deserve more scrutiny when assessing the legitimate expectations because they create 'legal rights and therefore expectations of

---

[2] I Tudor, *The Fair and Equitable Treatment Standard in the International Law of Foreign Investment* (Oxford University Press, 2008) 164.

[3] SA Bandali, 'Understanding FET: The Case for Protecting Contract-Based Legitimate Expectations' in IA Laird et al (eds), *Investment Treaty Arbitration and International Law*, vol 7 (JurisNet, 2014) 133.

[4] C Schreuer, 'Fair and Equitable Treatment (FET): Interactions with Other Standards' (2007) 4(5) *Transnational Dispute Management* 1, 18.

[5] TW Waelde and A Kolo, 'Environmental Regulation, Investment Protection and "Regulatory Taking" in International Law' (2001) 50(04) *International & Comparative Law Quarterly* 811, 844.

[6] See ch 2.

[7] P Dumberry, 'International Investment Contracts' in E de Brabandere and T Gazzini (eds), *International Investment Law: The Sources of Rights and Obligations* (Martinus Nijhoff Publishers, 2012) 219.

compliance'.[8] In *Suez (InterAgua) v Argentina*, the Tribunal referred to a concession contract as 'a document which certainly reflects in detail the Claimants' legitimate expectations'.[9] Along the same lines, the Tribunal in *Total v Argentina* noted that:

> The expectation of the investor is undoubtedly 'legitimate', and hence subject to protection under the fair and equitable treatment clause, if the host State has explicitly assumed a specific legal obligation for the future, such as by contracts, concessions or stabilisation clauses on which the investor is therefore entitled to rely as a matter of law.[10]

It is argued that the legitimate expectations arising out of contracts should be subject to the highest level of protection since they 'reflect the carefully negotiated balance achieved by the opposing parties and could be said to crystallize the parties' expectations'.[11] The fact that a contract is a product of negotiations between the parties places it at a higher level with respect to the expectations created. Indeed, this is particularly relevant to upstream petroleum investments, where the parties, in defining the rights and obligations, heavily rely on contracts drafted after lengthy negotiations. The main reason that a contract might be deemed the source of a legitimate expectation is that the bargain struck in a contract embodies 'a set of advantages and benefits which must be adhered to and preserved'.[12] It is those advantages and benefits that create the expectation from the investor's perspective. In *Occidental v Ecuador*, the Tribunal found that a subsequent law which changed the contractual framework that had been agreed on breached the FET standard. It stated that the investor 'was justified in expecting that this contractual framework would be respected and certainly not modified unilaterally by the Respondent'.[13]

It is quite obvious that an investor expects the host state to respect the contract concluded between them. However, this mere contractual expectation – or, in other words, hope – does not create a basis for a legitimate expectations claim under the FET standard in the event of a breach.[14] This means that even though an anticipation might be legitimate from a contractual perspective, it does not have to be a legitimate expectation as understood by the FET standard.[15]

---

[8] *Continental Casualty Company v The Argentine Republic*, Award, ICSID Case No ARB/03/9, 5 September 2008, para 261.

[9] *Suez, Sociedad General de Aguas de Barcelona SA and InterAguas Servicios Integrales del Agua SA v The Argentine Republic*, Decision on Liability, ICSID Case No ARB/03/17, 30 July 2010, para 212.

[10] *Total v Argentina*, Decision on Liability, para 117.

[11] M Potestà, 'Legitimate Expectations in Investment Treaty Law: Understanding the Roots and the Limits of a Controversial Concept' (2013) 28(1) *ICSID Review – Foreign Investment Law Journal* 88, 103.

[12] SKB Asante, 'Stability of Contractual Relations in the Transnational Investment Process' (1979) 28(3) *International & Comparative Law Quarterly* 401, 404.

[13] *Occidental Petroleum Corporation and Occidental Exploration and Production Company v The Republic of Ecuador*, Award, ICSID Case No ARB/06/11, 5 October 2012, para 526.

[14] J Bonnitcha, *Substantive Protection under Investment Treaties: A Legal and Economic Analysis* (Cambridge University Press, 2014) 182.

[15] JO Voss, *Impact of Investment Treaties on Contracts between Host States and Foreign Investors* (Martinus Nijhoff Publishers, 2010) 207.

In this regard, the *Parkerings v Lithuania* Tribunal stated:

> It is evident that not every hope amounts to an expectation under international law. The expectation a party to an agreement may have of the regular fulfilment of the obligation by the other party is not necessarily an expectation protected by international law. In other words, contracts involve intrinsic expectations from each party that do not amount to expectations as understood in international law. Indeed, the party whose contractual expectations are frustrated should, under specific conditions, seek redress before a national tribunal.[16]

Accordingly, a simple breach of the contract by the host state does not directly amount to the frustration of the FET standard.

(i) Breach of Contractual Expectations versus Breach of the Legitimate Expectations under the FET Standard

Not every contractual expectation is protected by international law under the FET standard.[17] Indeed, a treaty claim and a contract claim are conceptually two different matters by virtue of their underlying legal documents and the content of the rights included in such documents.[18] As aptly put by Crawford:

> At the level of the merits it must be borne in mind that the investment contract is itself an allocation of risks and opportunities, and that that allocation is relevant in determining, in particular, whether there has been fair and equitable treatment under the BIT [bilateral investment treaty]. In particular, the doctrine of legitimate expectations should not be used as a substitute for the actual arrangements agreed between the parties, or as a supervening and overriding source of the applicable law.[19]

Even though there are some arbitral decisions that keep the threshold relatively low on this issue and say that a contractual breach will equate to a breach under treaty,[20] the recent arbitral jurisprudence and scholarly views demonstrate that the mere obstruction of expectations arising from contracts is not automatically protected under the legitimate expectations principle of the FET standard; rather, this would require the presence of some additional factors.[21] According to Judge Schwebel, for example, while an ordinary commercial breach by a host state does not amount

[16] *Parkerings-Compagniet AS v Republic of Lithuania*, Award, ICSID Case No ARB/05/8, 11 September 2007, para 344.

[17] PM Blyschak, 'Arbitrating Overseas Oil and Gas Disputes: Breaches of Contract versus Breaches of Treaty' (2010) 27(6) *Journal of International Arbitration* 579, 592.

[18] Voss, *Impact of Investment Treaties*, 161.

[19] J Crawford, 'Treaty and Contract in Investment Arbitration' (2008) 24(3) *Arbitration International* 351, 374.

[20] *SGS Société Générale de Surveillance SA v Republic of the Philippines*, Decision of the Tribunal on Objections to Jurisdiction, ICSID Case No ARB/02/62, 9 January 2004; *Noble Ventures, Inc. v Romania*, Award, ICSID Case No ARB/01/11, 12 October 2005.

[21] Potestà, 'Legitimate Expectations', 102.

to a violation of international law, 'the use of the sovereign authority of a State, contrary to the expectations of the parties, to abrogate or violate a contract with an alien, is a violation of international law'.[22] Similarly, Carlston argues that when a contract termination is 'effected by the exercise of sovereign power instead of claimed contractual right, there is very considerable authority for the proposition that international responsibility to the state of the concessionaire directly and immediately arises'.[23]

In line with the *Parkerings* award mentioned above, Sasson emphasised that 'a breach of contract cannot be automatically equated to a violation of the fair and equitable treatment standard, unless the treaty expressly includes breach of contract as a basis for such a violation'.[24] In *Gustav v Ghana*, the Tribunal further upheld the *Parkerings* approach by stating that 'It is important to emphasise that the existence of legitimate expectations and the existence of contractual rights are two separate issues'.[25] If the contractual rights were to be linked strictly to the legitimate expectations protection, this would render the FET standard into a broadly applied umbrella clause, which is implausible.[26] Instead of the legitimate expectations principle framework, contractual rights must be protected under the contract framework.[27]

As affirmed by the *CMS v Argentina* award:

> [N]ot all contract breaches result in breaches of the Treaty. The standard of protection of the treaty will be engaged only when there is a specific breach of treaty rights and obligations or a violation of contract rights protected under the treaty. Purely commercial aspects of a contract might not be protected by the treaty in some situations, but the protection is likely to be available when there is significant interference by governments or public agencies with the rights of the investor.[28]

So, what is needed for the breach of a contractual right to amount to a breach of the FET standard as based upon the legitimate expectations principle is significant interference on the part of a host state which uses some of its prerogatives and sovereign power. This interference must be serious and material enough to prevent any trivial misconduct on the part of a public official from falling under the jurisdiction of an investment treaty tribunal.[29] For instance, if an official delays

---

[22] S Schwebel, 'On Whether the Breach by a State of a Contract with an Alien Is a Breach of International Law', *Justice in International Law: Selected Writings* (Cambridge University Press, 1994) 431–32.

[23] KS Carlston, 'Concession Agreements and Nationalization' (1958) 52(2) *American Journal of International Law* 260, 261.

[24] M Sasson, *Substantive Law in Investment Treaty Arbitration: The Unsettled Relationship between International Law and Municipal Law* (Kluwer Law International, 2017) 217.

[25] *Gustav F W Hamester GmbH & Co KG v Republic of Ghana*, Award, ICSID Case No ARB/07/24, 18 June 2010, para 335.

[26] Schreuer, 'FET: Interactions with Other Standards', 18.

[27] S Montt, *State Liability in Investment Treaty Arbitration: Global Constitutional and Administrative Law in the BIT Generation* (Hart Publishing, 2009) 363.

[28] *CMS Gas Transmission Company v The Argentine Republic*, Award, ICSID Case No ARB/01/8, 12 May 2005, para 299.

[29] *Thunderbird v Mexico*, Separate Opinion of Thomas Waelde, para 14.

or cancels a payment arising from the contract in his personal capacity, this would not equate to the violation of the FET standard unless there were some additional, aggravating factor. There should be 'wilful refusals by a government authority to evade agreements with foreign investors, or actions in bad faith in the course of contractual performance'.[30]

In *Duke v Ecuador*, the Tribunal stated that the contract breaches in question that related to Electroquil in that case (imposing contractual fines, non-payment of interest, etc) were of the type that could be conducted by any of the parties without resorting to sovereign power, and therefore did not amount to violation of the FET standard.[31] While finding a breach of the legitimate expectations of the investor based on its contractual rights, the Tribunal in *Eureko v Poland* also concluded that the Republic of Poland 'by the conduct of organs of the State, acted not for cause but for purely arbitrary reasons linked to the interplay of Polish politics and nationalistic reasons of a discriminatory character'.[32] Furthermore, the Tribunal considered the acts of Poland as 'outrageous' and 'shocking'.[33]

In the same vein, the Tribunal in *Impregilo v Pakistan* stated:

> In order that the alleged breach of contract may constitute a violation of the BIT, it must be the result of behaviour going beyond that which an ordinary contracting party could adopt. Only the State in the exercise of its sovereign authority ('puissance publique'), and not as a contracting party, may breach the obligations assumed under the BIT. In other words, the investment protection treaty only provides a remedy to the investor where the investor proves that the alleged damages were a consequence of the behaviour of the Host State acting in breach of the obligations it had assumed under the treaty.[34]

Schreuer argues that searching for a sovereign act by the host state might not be the best way to evaluate this issue and suggests that what should be done instead is to test 'whether the investor's legitimate expectations regarding a secure and stable legal framework are affected'.[35] The *Rumeli v Kazakhstan* award is a good example of such an approach. In that award, the Tribunal found that Kazakhstan's breach of the investment contract amounted to a breach of the BIT since 'the decision was arbitrary, unfair, unjust, lacked in due process and did not respect the investor's reasonable and legitimate expectations'.[36]

There is an approach that suggests that a contract is the basis of investor expectations and that any breach of that contract by the use of sovereign prerogatives might amount to the liability of a state under the FET standard of a treaty. On the

---

[30] JW Salacuse, *The Law of Investment Treaties* (Oxford University Press, 2015) 259.
[31] *Duke Energy Electroquil Partners & Electroquil SA v Republic of Ecuador*, Award, ICSID Case No ARB/04/19, 18 August 2008, para 348.
[32] *Eureko v Poland*, Partial Award, para 233.
[33] ibid para 234.
[34] *Impregilo SpA v Islamic Republic of Pakistan*, Decision on Jurisdiction, ICSID Case No ARB/03/3, 22 April 2005, para 260 (footnote omitted).
[35] Schreuer, 'FET: Interactions with Other Standards', 20.
[36] *Rumeli Telekom AS and Telsim Mobil Telekomunikasyon Hizmetleri AS v Republic of Kazakhstan*, Award, ICSID Case No ARB/05/16, 29 July 2008, para 615.

other hand, there is a view that propounds a more direct and general approach, and suggests a review of the effect of that contractual breach on the legal framework surrounding the investment relationship. Whichever approach one chooses, it is certain that whether a contractual breach amounts to the violation of the FET standard should be evaluated on a case-by-case basis by the arbitral tribunals. It is also well established that a contractual breach will always lead to a violation of the FET standard under certain conditions.

B. Administrative Representations and Promises

One of the sources that creates legitimate expectations that has often been relied on by investors in arbitral cases is an administrative representation or promise. This is considered to be the most specific form of the legitimate expectations.[37] While some suggest that legitimate expectations should be confined to representations only, this would contravene the widely acknowledged references made to the general legal and regulatory framework and other surrounding circumstances in the arbitral jurisprudence.[38] Hence, this will be examined as one of the sources of legitimate expectations, rather than the only one.

These representations might either be explicit or implicit,[39] and may take any of several forms, such as oral statements, presentations and various types of written statements – and even the silence of a host state administration might be considered under certain circumstances.[40] The *Gold Reserve v Venezuela* Tribunal concluded that the expectations of the Claimant were reinforced 'by the absence of any warnings or formal notice from Respondent.'[41] So, a host state, by abstaining from issuing any warnings, might also create legitimate expectations on the investor's side.

Further, the *Invesmart v Czech* Tribunal opined that 'internal governmental discussions' might also form the basis of legitimate expectations if they are later disclosed to the investor.[42] While the administrative representation might be a formal one, taking the character of a regulation or an administrative decision, it might well be an informal one too.[43] Dolzer and Schreuer opine that 'Undertakings

---

[37] A Newcombe and L Paradell, *Law and Practice of Investment Treaties: Standards of Treatment* (Kluwer Law International, 2009) 279.

[38] R Dolzer, 'Fair and Equitable Treatment: Today's Contours' (2013) 12(1) *Santa Clara Journal of International Law* 7, 23–24.

[39] C Schreuer, 'Fair and Equitable Treatment in Arbitral Practice' (2005) 6(3) *Journal of World Investment & Trade* 357, 374.

[40] HA Mairal, 'Legitimate Expectations and Informal Administrative Representations' in SW Schill (ed), *International Investment Law and Comparative Public Law* (Oxford University Press, 2010) 433–34.

[41] *Gold Reserve v Venezuela*, Award, para 579.

[42] *Invesmart, BV v The Czech Republic*, Award, UNCITRAL, 26 June 2009, para 253.

[43] Mairal, 'Legitimate Expectations', 414.

and representations made explicitly or implicitly by the host state are the strongest basis for legitimate expectations.'[44]

As a relatively early case, the *Waste Management v Mexico* award recognised the impact of the administrative representations on creating a legitimate expectation by stating while applying the FET standard that 'it is relevant that the treatment is in breach of representations made by the host State which were reasonably relied on by the claimant'.[45] The *Parkerings* award affirms this approach, stating: 'The expectation is legitimate if the investor received an explicit promise or guaranty from the host-State, or if implicitly, the host-State made assurances or representation that the investor took into account in making the investment.'[46] Waelde, in his separate opinion, concluded, after reviewing some previous cases on legitimate expectations, that 'conduct, informal, oral or general assurances can give rise to or support the existence of a legitimate expectation.'[47] In *National Grid v Argentina*, the Tribunal also submitted, after reviewing the case law, that the FET standard 'protects the reasonable expectations of the investor at the time it made the investment and which were based on representations, commitments or specific conditions offered by the State concerned.'[48]

It is also possible to witness analyses of legitimate expectations created by administrative representations in recent arbitral awards. In 2016, the *Crystallex v Venezuela* award stated:

> A legitimate expectation may arise in cases where the Administration has made a promise or representation to an investor as to a substantive benefit, on which the investor has relied in making its investment, and which later was frustrated by the conduct of the Administration.[49]

Again, in the same year, an important point regarding representations was raised by Professor Tawil in his dissenting opinion in the *Charanne v Spain* case. He argued that in the event of more than one representation being present, there might be a legitimate expectation generated by the combination of those representations, even if each representation in isolation does not possess the required weight to create a legitimate expectation.[50]

What is common to these approaches is that the investor is required to have relied on these administrative representations in order to claim the existence of a legitimate expectation. The reliance here is evaluated on the basis of making an

---

[44] R Dolzer and C Schreuer, *Principles of International Investment Law* (Oxford University Press, 2012) 145.

[45] *Waste Management v Mexico*, Award, para 98.

[46] *Parkerings v Lithuania*, Award, para 331.

[47] *Thunderbird v Mexico*, Separate Opinion of Thomas Waelde, para 32.

[48] *National Grid PLC v The Argentine Republic*, Award, UNCITRAL, 3 November 2008, para 173.

[49] *Crystallex International Corporation v Bolivarian Republic of Venezuela*, Award, ICSID Case No ARB(AF)/11/2, 4 April 2016, para 547.

[50] *Charanne BV and Construction Investments SARL v The Kingdom of Spain*, Dissenting Opinion of Guido Santiago Tawil, Unofficial English translation provided by McDermott Will & Emery Rechtsanwälte Steuerberater LLP, SCC Case No 062/2012, 21 January 2016, para 6.

initial investment or expanding an existing investment.[51] However, this reliance should be reasonable, and there is no legitimate expectation if the assurance in question was given in response to misleading or inaccurate information initially provided by the investor.[52]

According to Dupuy and Dupuy, it is uncontroversial that when a host state makes a promise to an investor upon which the investor significantly relies when making their investment and then subsequently breaches that promise, this would lead to an associated responsibility of the host state under the FET standard.[53] Even though they summarise the issue in such a simple way, it does not always work so seamlessly in practice. There are several controversial points as to the form that these representations and promises should take and the extent of the legitimate expectations that they create.

(i) Requirement of Specificity

According to one view of the investment treaty arbitration jurisprudence which endorses the representation approach, not every administrative representation is capable of generating a legitimate expectation. There is the requirement of a level of specificity that they must adhere to. However, the required level of specificity is not uniform and there are several approaches to this issue. What is mainly seen from the arbitral jurisprudence is that the tribunals will commonly only examine the representation or promise at hand to decide whether it satisfies the specificity requirement or otherwise and abstain from propounding a comprehensive formulation on how to define the specificity.

In *Crystallex v Venezuela*, the Tribunal indicated that 'To be able to give rise to such legitimate expectations, such promise or representation – addressed to the individual investor – must be sufficiently specific, ie it must be precise as to its content and clear as to its form'.[54] The claimant in this case, Crystallex, argued that it had legitimate expectations on the issuance of the environmental permit, which would allow it to develop the mining project based on some of the assurances it had received from the government officials. Among those assurances were a 'generic statement by the Ministry of Mines in June 2005 that the Permit was "well on track"'[55] and a statement 'by the President of the Commission of Mines of the National Assembly, Deputy Ricardo Gutiérrez, and the Mayor of

[51] Newcombe and Paradell, *Standards of Treatment*, 279.
[52] S Fietta, 'The "Legitimate Expectations" Principle under Article 1105 NAFTA' (2006) 7(3) *Journal of World Investment & Trade* 423, 432.
[53] F Dupuy and PM Dupuy, 'What to Expect from Legitimate Expectations? A Critical Appraisal and Look Into the Future of the "Legitimate Expectations" Doctrine in International Investment Law' in MA Raouf, P Leboulanger and NG Ziadé (eds), *Festschrift Ahmed Sadek El-Kosheri – From the Arab World to the Globalization of International Law and Arbitration* (Kluwer Law International, 2015) 289–90.
[54] *Crystallex v Venezuela*, Award, para 547.
[55] ibid para 553.

Sifontes, expressing their joint support for the commencement of the Las Cristinas Project.[56] The Tribunal rejected these claims by stating that these officials were not in a position to decide on and affect the outcome of the permit, hence no legitimate expectations were existent on this basis.[57] Furthermore, the Tribunal also rejected Crystallex's legitimate expectations claim based on the statements of an official in the National Assembly meeting since 'such vague statements do not meet the level of specificity required to create legitimate expectations'.[58]

However, the Tribunal took a different approach to a letter sent to Crystallex from the Office of Permission of the Ministry of Environment. Even though the letter was not the official accreditation of the project, it evidently pointed out that the evaluation was approved by the Office and the permit would be handed over.[59] The Tribunal concluded that 'at that time, a positive decision by the Administration towards the granting of the Permit had been taken',[60] and considered the letter a specific positive representation in clear and precise terms.[61] Therefore, the Tribunal decided that Crystallex had legitimate expectations based on this letter and its expectations were frustrated by the subsequent decisions of the administration.

The *Charanne v Spain* award of 2016 concerned the change of the regime regulating the photovoltaic generation sector in Spain. The claimants argued that after inducing their investments, the host state had changed the special regimes proposed by several royal decrees that provided certain benefits and upon which they had relied while making the investment. In addition to this, the claimants submitted that the Government of Spain had initiated an investment promotion campaign called 'The Sun Can Be All Yours' and had produced some documents and prospectuses in which potential high returns from these special tariffs were publicised. After the change in these tariffs, the claimants argued that their legitimate expectations had been frustrated. The Tribunal concluded that these promotion documents were 'not specific enough to have generated an expectation' of tariffs remaining untouched throughout the course of the investment.[62]

Regarding the royal decrees, the Tribunal stated that, even though they 'were directed to a limited group of investors, it does not make them to be commitments specifically directed at each investor'.[63] While the Tribunal did accept the claimants' approach regarding the legitimate expectations being present 'even in the absence of specific commitments, when the receiving State performs acts incompatible with a criterion of economic reasonableness, with public interest or with

---

[56] ibid para 554.
[57] ibid.
[58] ibid para 555.
[59] ibid para 562.
[60] ibid.
[61] ibid para 563.
[62] *Charanne BV and Construction Investments SARL v The Kingdom of Spain*, Award, Unofficial English translation provided by Mena Chambers, SCC Case No 062/2012, 21 January 2016, para 497.
[63] ibid para 493.

the principle of proportionality', it concluded nevertheless that the changes in the regulatory regime did not amount to an unreasonable or disproportionate act.[64]

However, two years after the *Charanne v Spain* award, another arbitral tribunal had to decide on similar issues. In 2018, in *Novenergia v Spain*, the Tribunal appraised the issue in a different way. Even though there were additional regulatory changes in the *Novenergia v Spain* case, and indeed those changes played a significant role in the outcome, it is only the approach of the Tribunal to the government's promotion campaign that will be discussed in this part. Unlike the approach taken by the *Charanne v Spain* Tribunal, the tariff information provided in the prospectuses of 'The Sun Can Be All Yours' was not considered unspecific and not ignored by the *Novenergia v Spain* Tribunal. On the contrary, the Tribunal, referring to the prospectuses, stated: 'the above statements were also aimed at incentivising companies to invest heavily in the Spanish electricity sector and formed part of the basis for the Claimant's investment'.[65] This latter approach can be considered an endorsement of the dissenting approach of Professor Tawil in the *Charanne v Spain* case, where he argued that the regime provided by the royal decrees should be considered together with the information laid down in the prospectuses when assessing the existence of legitimate expectations.[66]

In the *Saint-Gobain v Venezuela* case, the Tribunal strongly suggested that 'a legitimate expectation can be created only by specific promises or commitments made by the State'.[67] The *PSEG v Turkey* Tribunal also had clearly stated that general investment promotion policy announcements of a government cannot be deemed a specific promise towards an investor's project and therefore cannot create a legitimate expectation.[68]

In the *Frontier v Czech Republic* case, while discussing the letters sent by the Ministry of Industry and Trade to the claimant in which the Ministry explicitly stated that it could not intervene in the dispute that the claimant was in, 'the Tribunal [found] that the relevant statements do not exhibit the level of specificity necessary to generate legitimate expectations' and concluded that there was no undertaking by the Ministry that could create a legitimate expectation.[69] The *White Industries v India* Tribunal also concluded that some encouraging remarks from Indian officials and statements about India being a safe place for an investment or having similar laws to Australia were vague and general representations that could not give rise to legitimate expectations.[70]

---

[64] ibid paras 513–15.

[65] *Novenergia II – Energy & Environment (SCA) (Grand Duchy of Luxembourg), SICAR v The Kingdom of Spain*, Final Arbitral Award, SCC Case No 2015/063, 15 February 2018, para 669.

[66] *Charanne v Spain*, Dissenting Opinion Tawil, para 6.

[67] *Saint-Gobain Performance Plastics Europe v Bolivarian Republic of Venezuela*, Decision on Liability and the Principles of Quantum, ICSID Case No ARB/12/13, 30 December 2016, para 531.

[68] *PSEG Global Inc and Konya Ilgin Elektrik Üretim ve Ticaret Limited Sirketi v Republic of Turkey*, Award, ICSID Case No ARB/02/5, 19 January 2007, para 243.

[69] *Frontier Petroleum Services Ltd v The Czech Republic*, Final Award, UNCITRAL, 12 November 2010, para 468.

[70] *White Industries Australia Limited v The Republic of India*, Final Award, UNCITRAL, 30 November 2011, para 10.3.17.

Similarly, in the *Mamidoil v Albania* case, the claimant argued that it had had several meetings with high government officials and had received assurances regarding their investment during those meetings. However, the Tribunal did not take these claims into account while analysing the existence of legitimate expectations because 'all of these representations were made orally, without written confirmation, and are therefore not in evidence beyond the testimony of the witnesses'.[71] The Tribunal also added that it did not doubt that the meetings took place or that the claimant was encouraged in general terms; however, it said, 'all of these friendly discussions remained on the level of verbal exchanges; none resulted in an agreed letter of intent, in any type of formal representations or in recorded minutes of meetings'.[72]

Earlier, the *Total v Argentina* Tribunal had emphasised that if the public authorities in a host state assume a legal obligation through conduct or by declaration and make the investor believe in the existence of such an obligation, then the legitimate expectations of the investor would be protected.[73] In addition to this, it also underscored the requirement of specificity by stating: 'Representations made by the host State are enforceable and justify the investor's reliance only when they are specifically addressed to a particular investor.'[74] However, the Tribunal did not entirely rule out the possibility of a legitimate expectation being present in the absence of a 'specific declaration to the addressee', and considered the specificity requirement to be a strengthening factor in the claim.[75]

On the issue of how to determine a specific commitment, the *El Paso v Argentina* Tribunal argued that there is no common definition of specific commitments and they should be determined on a case-by-case basis.[76] So, the level of specificity required for the creation of a legitimate expectation is not completely predetermined; rather, the tribunals should decide whether a commitment fulfils the specificity requirement.

Yet, the *El Paso* Tribunal provided a template and opined that a commitment might be specific with respect to its addressee or its object and purpose.[77] This was later stated as being 'precise as to its content and clear as to its form' by the *Crystallex v Venezuela* Tribunal.[78] According to this categorisation, a commitment in a contract or in a letter of intent or a verbal promise in a business meeting might be considered specific enough in terms of its addressee since these are made directly to the investors.[79] Also, 'a commitment can be considered specific if its precise object was to give a real guarantee of stability to the investor'.[80]

---

[71] *Mamidoil v Albania*, Award, para 152.
[72] ibid para 409.
[73] *Total v Argentina*, Decision on Liability, para 118.
[74] ibid para 119.
[75] ibid para 121.
[76] *El Paso v Argentina*, Award, para 375.
[77] ibid.
[78] *Crystallex v Venezuela*, Award, para 547.
[79] *El Paso v Argentina*, Award, para 376.
[80] ibid para 377.

In accordance with this approach, a repetitive general statement in various forms might be able to create a legitimate expectation.[81] This view was later followed by Professor Tawil in his separate opinion as discussed above.

The arbitral tribunals that take representations into account while deciding on the existence of a legitimate expectation agree that there might be a legitimate expectation if the host state had provided assurances about maintaining the prevailing regulatory framework.[82]

However, several issues with the requirement of specificity remain ambiguous. The arbitral tribunals do not explain why an administrative representation must be specific in order to create a legitimate expectation. With respect to this issue, some authors argue that the legitimate expectations principle is derived from several doctrines, such as estoppel, promissory obligations or unilateral acts, which entail a certain level of specificity, hence the same level of specificity is also required by the legitimate expectations doctrine.[83] Though, as discussed in the previous chapter, there are several explanations with regard to the roots of the legitimate expectations concept, numerous tribunals acknowledge the good faith principle as its source. When the good faith principle is accepted as the basis, the arguments asserted above in relation to the specificity requirement become irrelevant and the question as to why a representation should be specific remains unanswered.

Schønberg, while discussing legitimate expectations under administrative law, notes that when 'a public authority makes a general representation about the procedure or policy it will follow in relation to a certain type of decision, but subsequently departs from the procedure or policy in the particular case', this also might be considered frustration of legitimate expectations in accordance with the Rule of Law theory.[84] It is also not required under English jurisprudence for a representation to be directed at the individual claiming a legitimate expectation.[85] So, under administrative laws, it is possible to witness some cases that do not require the same level of specificity as an investment treaty arbitration.

Most tribunals demand some form of specificity and clarity to the representations to be able to create a legitimate expectation, but they do not provide the reasoning for this demand, nor do they determine the level of that specificity. It seems in practice that determining whether an administrative representation or assurance bears the necessary level of specificity is left entirely to the arbitral tribunal's subjective approach, which adds to the inconsistency of investment treaty arbitration.

---

[81] ibid.

[82] Bonnitcha, *Substantive Protection*, 179.

[83] T Wongkaew, 'The Transplantation of Legitimate Expectations in Investment Treaty Arbitration: A Critique' in S Lalani and RP Lazo (eds), *The Role of the State in Investor–State Arbitration* (Brill Nijhoff, 2014) 93.

[84] SJ Schønberg, *Legitimate Expectations in Administrative Law* (Oxford University Press, 2000) 15.

[85] E Snodgrass, 'Protecting Investors' Legitimate Expectations – Recognizing and Delimiting a General Principle' (2006) 21(1) *ICSID Review – Foreign Investment Law Journal* 1, 33.

Since the tribunals do not provide reasoning for the requirement of specificity and there is no unanimous approach as to what a specific representation might mean, tribunals should cease demanding this as a prerequisite for identifying the existence of a legitimate expectation and start focusing on the ability of the representation in question to create a legitimate expectation. Instead of viewing the specificity requirement as absolute, the real effect of the representation on inducing the investment should be evaluated.[86]

The word 'relevant' might be employed instead of the word 'specific' as well. The representations must be relevant to the investment and the investor. Without doubt, there must be a level of relevance between the representation provided and the investment made; however, this does not imply that the representation must be specifically directed towards a certain investor in a strict form. If it is to be used anyway, the word 'specific' should be understood as being precise about the guarantee that is provided by the representation. It is the specificity of the expectation created, not the representation made. If the instrument that provides the assurance is closely associated with an investment, then this might create legitimate expectations even if not directed towards a particular investor.[87]

This view can also be derived from some recent awards. The *Micula v Romania* award focuses on the expectation created rather than the form of the representation, stating: 'This promise, assurance of representation may have been issued generally or specifically, but it must have created a specific and reasonable expectation in the investor.'[88]

The *Electrabel v Hungary* Tribunal also did not consider a specific representation to be indispensable and maintained that there might be a legitimate expectation even in the absence of a specific representation. However, in this case, the investor should be able to present its reasonable reliance on the representation in question.[89] This view is also later quoted and endorsed by the Tribunal in *Novenergia v Spain* in 2018.[90]

As Reisman and Arsanjani aptly stated:

> Where statements are made either orally or distributed in writing in either hard copy or on-line, clearly promising certain conditions or treatment for foreign investors and such statements are made public and are made repeatedly and foreign investors relied on them, and governments do not retrieve or qualify those statements of commitment before the conclusion of contracts with foreign investors, they should, in our view, bind the state.[91]

---

[86] Meyers, 'Adapting Legitimate Expectations', 36.

[87] A Davies, 'Investment Treaty Law Interpretation, Fair and Equitable Treatment and Legitimate Expectations' (2018) 15(3) *Manchester Journal of International Economic Law* 314, 323–26.

[88] *Ioan Micula, Viorel Micula, SC European Food SA, SC Starmill SRL and SC Multipack SRL v Romania*, Award, ICSID Case No ARB/05/20, 11 December 2013, para 671.

[89] *Electrabel SA v Hungary*, Award, ICSID Case No ARB/07/19, 25 November 2015, para 155.

[90] *Novenergia v Spain*, Award, para 650.

[91] WM Reisman and MH Arsanjani, 'The Question of Unilateral Governmental Statements as Applicable Law in Investment Disputes' (2004) 19(2) *ICSID Review – Foreign Investment Law Journal* 328, 343.

Jose Alvarez has argued that arbitral awards are not clear on the issue of whether a representation must be directed towards a certain investor or whether an investor can rely on a public representation that is available to everyone.[92] This still being relevant, it can be said that the idea of taking representations into account even if they are not addressed to a specific investor has been growing in the arbitral jurisprudence. More weight is being given to the expectations created by a representation, rather than to the way in which the representation is communicated to an investor.

An accumulation of various formal or informal representations of different types should be able to give rise to a legitimate expectation even if they are not specifically directed towards a known investor. This is also evident from the approach that discusses the ability of a general legal framework to create legitimate expectations, which will be analysed later in this chapter.

(ii) Informal Representations

The form that an administrative representation should take in order to create a legitimate expectation is another contentious issue relating to this subject.[93] Under EU law, informal statements can create legitimate expectations as well as formal decisions.[94] As Schønberg states: 'informal representations such as advice given to citizens and circulars setting out administrative policy are also an important part of the information on the basis of which lives are planned and choices made'.[95]

Within the scope of administrative law, promises that do not enjoy a formal status, public announcements of the administration concerning its legal view or policy on an issue, or repeated administrative practices might create a legitimate expectation.[96] An informal representation might be any form of administrative conduct other than formally constituted regulatory documents or a properly conducted governmental act.[97]

Within the context of international investment law, Waelde argued that informal assurances can give rise to a legitimate expectation, but the associated threshold would be higher than the specific representations that enjoy an official character.[98] Thus, an early deduction would be that informal administrative

---

[92] JE Alvarez, *The Public International Law Regime Governing International Investment* (Brill Nijhoff, 2011) 208.

[93] B Scharaw, *The Protection of Foreign Investments in Mongolia: Treaties, Domestic Law and Contracts on Investments in International Comparison and Arbitral Practice* (Springer International Publishing, 2018) 79.

[94] Snodgrass, 'Legitimate Expectations', 32.

[95] Schønberg, *Legitimate Expectations*, 107.

[96] D Barak-Erez, 'The Doctrine of Legitimate Expectations and the Distinction between the Reliance and Expectation Interests' (2005) 11(5) *European Public Law* 583, 593.

[97] Mairal, 'Legitimate Expectations', 415.

[98] *Thunderbird v Mexico*, Separate Opinion of Thomas Waelde, para 32.

assurances are also capable of creating legitimate expectations for investors, but will be subject to more scrutiny.[99]

One of the earliest arbitral decisions regarding this issue can be found in *Southern Pacific Properties v Egypt.*[100] Even though the dispute was not related to a treaty or the FET standard, the Tribunal's approach towards informal representations is worth reviewing. The Tribunal in this case concluded that even though the acts of the Egyptian officials might be null and void under Egyptian law, the investor's reliance on these acts was adequate to create legitimate expectations under international law.[101] Even though a representation is inconsistent with local laws, it might still create legitimate expectations if the investor had clean hands while relying on that representation.[102]

There are no recent arbitral decisions regarding an ultra vires act's ability to give rise to legitimate expectations. However, it is argued that several domestic administrative laws accept that it is possible, in principle, for an ultra vires representation to create a legitimate expectation.[103] It is also argued from an international investment law perspective that arbitral tribunals, when faced with such an administrative representation, should evaluate whether it was difficult for the investor to spot the unlawfulness of the representation prior to relying on it.[104] This is easier to detect in the case of formal representations since an adequate due diligence would reveal whether the administration's act was lawful. However, it would be more difficult for an investor to determine whether an informal representation is ultra vires or not. In this case, the informal representation might be considered the basis for a legitimate expectation if it is provided by a competent official and is not explicitly against the law.[105] This view is also consistent with the suggestion made by Reisman and Arsanjani: 'Even if such statements and declarations were inconsistent with domestic law ... they could be binding as a matter of international law.'[106] Customary international law holds a state responsible for the ultra vires acts of their state organs.[107]

Taking informal representations into account while determining whether a legitimate expectation exists or not brings another problem with it, which is the potential detrimental effect on government behaviour. If the scope of the informal

---

[99] A Siwy, 'Indirect Expropriation and the Legitimate Expectations of the Investor' in C Klausegger et al (eds), *Austrian Arbitration Yearbook 2007* (CH Beck/Stämpfli/Manz, 2007) 372.

[100] *Southern Pacific Properties (Middle East) Limited v Arab Republic of Egypt*, Award, ICSID Case No ARB/84/3, 20 May 1992.

[101] ibid para 83.

[102] Newcombe and Paradell, *Standards of Treatment*, 282.

[103] Snodgrass, 'Legitimate Expectations', 39; A Diehl, *The Core Standard of International Investment Protection: Fair and Equitable Treatment* (Kluwer Law International, 2012) 402.

[104] Diehl, *Core Standard*, 405.

[105] *Thunderbird v Mexico*, Separate Opinion of Thomas Waelde, para 93.

[106] Reisman and Arsanjani, 'Unilateral Governmental Statements', 343.

[107] C Annacker, 'Role of Investors' Legitimate Expectations in Defense of Investment Treaty Claims' in AK Bjorklund (ed), *Yearbook on International Investment Law & Policy* (Oxford University Press, 2015) 236.

representations is kept wide, governments or officials might abstain from providing information, advice, statements or their own views about a certain project in case such information as they provide might be used against their state in a legitimate expectations claim in the future.[108] This can be considered a micro-version of *regulatory chill*. At the same time, however, representations of an informal character provide more incentives to the potential investors since they secure another guarantee to rely on in the future.[109]

(iii) Political Statements

The value that should be attributed to political statements in assessing legitimate expectations is not highly contested among arbitral tribunals. There are several cases where the statements of politicians were evaluated. The prevailing view argues that political statements are not of any particular importance when it comes to creating a legitimate expectation.

The *Continental v Argentina* Tribunal, while rejecting the breach of the legitimate expectations claim, asserted that 'political statements have the least legal value, regrettably but notoriously so'.[110] This view was also later quoted and endorsed by the *Mamidoil v Albania* Tribunal.[111] The *El Paso v Argentina* Tribunal followed the same line of reasoning and explicitly stated that 'a declaration made by the President of the Republic clearly must be viewed by everyone as a political statement' to which only limited confidence should be ascribed.[112]

Sornarajah provided a legal opinion for the same case in which he argues that the statements of the President can only be seen as a promotional activity to induce investment: 'they cannot create legal obligations unless and until more formal rights are secured in the context of negotiations'.[113] Abi-Saab, in his separate opinion in the *Micula v Romania* case, remarks that in order for a legitimate expectation to arise from a representation, it 'has to bear the makings of an identifiable legal commitment towards the specific investor', and such a commitment could not be derived from general political statements.[114]

The claimant in the *Bayindir v Pakistan* case argued that the then Prime Minister Nawaz Sharif provided repeated assurances regarding Pakistan's commitment to the claimant's highway construction project, on which it claimed that it had relied.[115] However, the Tribunal decided that the claimant had been aware

---

[108] D Gaukrodger, 'The Balance between Investor Protection and the Right to Regulate in Investment Treaties: A Scoping Paper' (2017) OECD Working Papers on International Investment 2017/02.
[109] ibid.
[110] *Continental v Argentina*, Award, para 261.
[111] *Mamidoil v Albania*, Award, para 643.
[112] *El Paso v Argentina*, Award, para 395.
[113] *El Paso v Argentina*, Legal Opinion of M Sornarajah, para 58.
[114] *Micula v Romania*, Separate Opinion of Georges Abi-Saab, paras 3–5.
[115] *Bayindir Insaat Turizm Ticaret Ve Sanayi AS v Islamic Republic of Pakistan*, Award, ICSID Case No ARB/03/29, 27 August 2009, para 194.

of the political environment of the country and the potential for a change in its government, so it should have known that its project was linked to these political shifts and the assurances given by a prime minister whose position was already on shaky ground could not be regarded as producing legitimate expectations.[116]

Another view, albeit a minority one, recognises the political statements as a potential source of the legitimate expectations claim. As already mentioned above, Reisman and Arsanjani concluded that 'general international law recognizes the competence of state officials to bind their states by unilateral statements without regard to such internal authorizations'.[117] It has already been noted that informal representations are capable of creating legitimate expectations. In this case, however, some tribunals and scholars make the distinction between an informal representation and a political statement, attributing a lack of confidence to the latter. It is not clear on what basis this distinction is made, however.

There is also evidence from the arbitral jurisprudence where political statements are not completely overlooked. For instance, the *MTD v Chile*[118] Tribunal made several references to the President of Chile's statements at a dinner where he acclaims and praises the investment in dispute, though the weight of these references in the Tribunal's analysis of the legitimate expectations of the investor is not known.[119] The *Ece v Czech* Tribunal also discussed some assurances given by the mayor of a city on which the claimant argues that it had relied.[120] In its decision, the Tribunal concluded that the mayor only assured the investor that it would not be treated unfairly, and that this kind of statement falls short of a promise that might create a legitimate expectation.[121] Even though these examples do not demonstrate that statements by politicians can play a significant role in creating legitimate expectations, they surely prove that their statements are not trivial. In particular, the way that the *Ece v Czech* Tribunal analysed the mayor's statements indicates that had those statements included a different approach, they could have created legitimate expectations.

It is also confusing to see that several arbitral tribunals take negative political statements towards the investors into account while evaluating legitimate expectations or the dispute in general. In the *Biwater v Tanzania* case, the claimant argued that it had a legitimate expectation from the government not to take a negative position against the investor/investment (City Water) and not to taint its image in the eyes of the public.[122] This argument was built upon a series of negative public statements from the Minister of Water and Livestock Development of

---

[116] ibid.

[117] Reisman and Arsanjani, 'Unilateral Governmental Statements', 338.

[118] *MTD v Chile*, Award.

[119] Potestà, 'Legitimate Expectations', 107.

[120] *ECE Projektmanagement International GmbH and Kommanditgesellschaft PANTA Achtungsechzigste Grundstücksgesellschaft mbH & Co v The Czech Republic*, Award, PCA Case No 2010-5, 19 September 2013, para 4.770.

[121] ibid.

[122] *Biwater Gauff v Tanzania*, Award, para 552.

Tanzania against the investor. The Tribunal stated: 'In May 2005, the Republic's attitude dramatically changed. Far from seeking to manage the public's expectations, the Minister acted in such a way as to undermine the public's confidence in City Water.'[123] Even though the respondent relied on previous cases and accordingly stated that there were no examples of negative public statements being taken into account while assessing a claimed breach of the FET standard, the Tribunal disagreed with this approach and held that the Minister's statements amounted to an 'unwarranted interference' and polarised public opinion further while inflaming the situation, which eventually led to termination of the contract outwith its regular process.[124] The Tribunal therefore concluded that 'in acting in such a way in May 2005, the Republic did not comply with the fair and equitable treatment principle'.[125]

So, what is to be seen from the latter approach is that statements made by politicians are also considered to be a significant factor in determining the existence of legitimate expectations by some. Even though the prevailing approach considers political statements unreliable and lacking legal value, several other awards and scholarly works prove that they might play an important role under certain circumstances. If such political statements have no legal value at all, the tribunals should not even have discussed them; however, they did not choose to leave them out of the equation. Moreover, as seen from the *Biwater* award, a politician's negative statements towards an investor can be used to prove a breach. This shows that a political statement might well be regarded as the basis of a legitimate expectation, and it is not true to claim that they have no legal value at all.

The problem might be arising from the definition of a political statement. The awards that express a lack of confidence in political statements do not specify the associated scope. They do not specify what should be considered a political statement and what should not. Should we consider every statement from every political figure to constitute a political statement and attribute no confidence to them whatsoever? Such an approach would not be compatible with the realities of an investment environment, especially of the energy sector, where the other side of the relationship is often high-ranking officials, members of governments and politicians. Instead of ignoring political statements entirely and presuming that they are unreliable, the role that they might have played in inducing the investment and the reliance placed by investors on those statements should be examined. Even if a political statement is considered to lack legal weight in and of itself, it can nevertheless act as an assisting factor to a claim. Political statements might also be of particular relevance in interpreting the intentions of a host state on a certain issue.

---

[123] ibid para 624.
[124] ibid para 627.
[125] ibid para 628.

C. Legal and Regulatory Framework Prevalent in a Host State

The last source that creates legitimate expectations is the legislative and regulatory framework of the host state. While predictability and stability of the legal framework of a host state is considered a significant requirement of the FET standard,[126] it is also acknowledged as a basis for legitimate expectations. According to this view, a specific commitment or a government promise is not needed for the creation of legitimate expectations.[127] The state of the law in a host country prior to the investment being realised constitutes the framework upon which legitimate expectations can be built.[128] This legal and regulatory framework would include legislation, treaties, guarantees given in decrees and licences.[129]

The legal framework of the host state is an important determinant in an investor's investment decisions,[130] and for this reason the FET standard provides protection to investors regarding the rights acquired under domestic laws and the associated legitimate expectations concerning the execution of those rights.[131] An investor expects that legal and fiscal frameworks surrounding the investment will remain stable for a certain duration.[132] Since energy investments in particular are 'long-term, high risk, capital intensive and highly dependent on the exercise of government's regulatory power',[133] the stability of the legal framework becomes more relevant in these types of investment.

As Salacuse rightly points out: 'when a state has created certain expectations through its laws and acts that have led the investor to invest, it is generally considered unfair for the state to take subsequent actions that fundamentally deny or frustrate those expectations'.[134] When the host state generates legal and regulatory circumstances that encourage investors and upon which an investor relies, their later frustration might cause a breach of legitimate expectations.[135]

This approach is now a well-established arbitral practice, having been taken in numerous decisions of earlier arbitral tribunals.[136] Several recent arbitral awards,

---

[126] M Jacob and SW Schill, 'Fair and Equitable Treatment: Content, Practice, Method' (2017) Amsterdam Center for International Law Research Paper No 2017-20 https://ssrn.com/abstract=2933425.

[127] V Poiedynok, O Kolohoida and I Lukach, 'The Doctrine of Legitimate Expectations: Need for Limits' (2017) VIII(5) *Journal of Advanced Research in Law and Economics* 1604, 1605; UNCTAD, 'Fair and Equitable Treatment: A Sequel' (United Nations, 2012) 69.

[128] R Dolzer, 'Fair and Equitable Treatment: A Key Standard in Investment Treaties' (2005) 39(1) *International Lawyer* 87, 103.

[129] Dolzer and Schreuer, *Principles*, 145.

[130] Tudor, *The FET Standard*, 103.

[131] Newcombe and Paradell, *Standards of Treatment*, 279.

[132] Waelde and Kolo, 'Environmental Regulation', 819.

[133] ibid.

[134] Salacuse, *The Law of Investment Treaties*, 254.

[135] APG Pandya and A Moody, 'Legitimate Expectations in Investment Treaty Arbitration: An Unclear Future' (2010) 15(1) *Tilburg Law Review* 93, 105–06.

[136] *Toto Costruzioni Generali SpA v Republic of Lebanon*, Award, ICSID Case No ARB/07/12, 7 June 2012; *Impregilo SpA v Argentine Republic*, Award, ICSID Case No ARB/07/17, 21 June 2011;

some of which will be discussed below, have also endorsed the idea that the legal and regulatory framework could be a basis for legitimate expectations.

The *Novenergia v Spain* Tribunal remarked that 'The legitimate expectations of an investor has generally been considered to be grounded in the legal order of the host State as it stands at the time the investor acquires or makes the investment'.[137] In a similar approach, the *Murphy v Ecuador* Tribunal declared that 'An investor may hold legitimate expectations based on an objective assessment of the legal framework absent specific representations or promises made by the State to the investor'.[138] Tawil, in his dissenting opinion in *Charanne v Spain*, upheld the same view, stating that

> the creation of legitimate expectations in an investor is not limited solely to the exist-
> ence of a 'specific commitment' – either contractual in nature or founded in statements
> or specific conditions declared by the receiving State – but it can also derive from, or be
> based on, the legal system in force at the time of the investment.[139]

As already mentioned in previous sections, the *Electrabel v Hungary* Tribunal also established that even though a specific assurance would increase the level of legitimacy of an expectation, it is not an indispensable element of the legiti-mate expectations principle and an investor might also base its expectations on a law.[140] In the same vein, the *Frontier v Czech* Tribunal indicated that 'The investor may rely on that legal framework as well as on representations and undertakings made by the host state including those in legislation, treaties, decrees, licenses, and contracts'.[141]

The legal framework of a host state is considered an integral part of the invest-ment environment as an investor does not base its investment solely on the contractual commitments, disregarding the surrounding legal factors. Gary Born, in his dissenting opinion in the *JSW Solar v Czech* case, demonstrates this aspect of an investment clearly by stating:

> In contemporary market economies, operating under the rule of law, it is both common-
> place and essential for states to be able to provide undertakings to private parties by way
> of 'general' legislative or regulatory instruments. In many circumstances, modern states

---

El Paso v Argentina, Award; *Suez (InterAgua) v Argentina*, Decision on Liability; *National Grid v Argentina*, Award; *CMS v Argentina*, Award; *Continental v Argentina*, Award; *Duke v Ecuador*, Award; *Sempra Energy International v Argentine Republic*, Award, ICSID Case No ARB/02/16, 28 September 2007; *Enron Corporation and Ponderosa Assets, LP v Argentine Republic*, Award, ICSID Case No ARB/01/3, 22 May 2007; *LG&E Energy Corp, LG&E Capital Corp and LG&E International, Inc v Argentine Republic*, Decision on Liability, ICSID Case No ARB/02/1, 3 October 2006; *Occidental v Ecuador*, Final Award (2004).
    [137] *Novenergia v Spain*, Award, para 532.
    [138] *Murphy Exploration & Production Company International v The Republic of Ecuador*, Partial Final Award, PCA Case No 2012-16, 6 May 2016, para 249.
    [139] *Charanne v Spain*, Dissenting Opinion of Tawil, para 5.
    [140] *Electrabel v Hungary*, Award, para 155.
    [141] *Frontier v Czech*, Final Award, para 285.

cannot as a practical matter negotiate contracts with large numbers of parties, but must instead regulate the conduct of private parties through legislation and regulations.[142]

Every time this facet of a legal framework having the capability of creating legitimate expectations is raised, a caveat always accompanies it: the acknowledgement of a host state's entitlement to alter its legislative and regulatory framework. Nearly every arbitral award commences its analysis of legitimate expectations by stating this fact, even though they might end up with different judgments. This statement is no more than a declaration of the theoretical aspect of state sovereignty. Arbitral tribunals concede that the states are sovereign entities and can alter their own legislation as they wish.

The *Impregilo v Argentina* Tribunal held the view that 'The legitimate expectations of foreign investors cannot be that the State will never modify the legal framework'.[143] Similarly, the *El Paso* Tribunal stated that 'it is unthinkable that a State could make a general commitment to all foreign investors never to change its legislation whatever the circumstances, and it would be unreasonable for an investor to rely on such a freeze'.[144] Likewise, the *Mamidoil v Albania* Tribunal stated that the FET standard 'recognizes a State's legitimate interest and right to change conditions reasonably for public policy purposes'.[145] In the same vein, the *Micula v Romania* Tribunal opined that 'The state has a right to regulate, and investors must expect that the legislation will change, absent a stabilization clause or other specific assurance giving rise to a legitimate expectation of stability'.[146] Even Gary Born, who drafted a powerful dissent in the *JSW Solar v Czech* case and found a breach of legitimate expectations, agreed that 'the obligation of fair and equitable treatment does not generally prevent a state from altering its legislative or regulatory regimes in response to changing economic, technological or other circumstances'.[147] The *Crystallex v Venezuela* Tribunal required an 'abuse of power' in the application of a law to find a breach of legitimate expectations of the investor. Otherwise, it contended:

> Laws are general and impersonal in nature; they will usually leave some degree of discretion to the state agencies for the making of their case-specific decisions and, in fact, are rarely unconditional in their provisions so that the investor would have difficulty founding an actual expectation akin to a vested right.[148]

The Tribunal in the *Eiser v Spain* case also concluded that there is a need to protect the reliance of an investor on a favourable regulatory regime that was intended to

---

[142] *Jürgen Wirtgen, Stefan Wirtgen, Gisela Wirtgen and JSW Solar (zwei) GmbH & Co KG v The Czech Republic*, Dissenting Opinion of Gary Born, PCA Case No 2014-03, 11 October 2017, para 15.

[143] *Impregilo v Argentina*, Award, para 291.

[144] *El Paso v Argentina*, Award, para 372.

[145] *Mamidoil v Albania*, Award, para 703.

[146] *Micula v Romania*, Award, para 666.

[147] *JSW Solar v Czech*, Gary Born, para 7.

[148] *Crystallex v Venezuela*, Award, para 552.

attract the investment, while acknowledging that this cannot mean freezing the regulatory regime.[149]

It is crystal clear from the above examples that a host state's entitlement to change its legislative and regulatory environment is well established and undisputed by arbitral tribunals.[150] It is an undeniable fact that the legal and regulatory framework of a host state cannot be completely muted. However, accepting this principle does not have a big effect in practice. Both groups of tribunals that find a breach of legitimate expectations or rejecting the claims agree on this principle. There is no tribunal which explicitly states that the host states cannot change their laws. The issue is, however, far from solely acknowledging this principle; it is about weighing the effects of the alteration of the legal and regulatory framework on the investor.

Therefore, the arbitral jurisprudence, while acknowledging this right, introduces certain restrictions to it at the same time. As the *ADC v Hungary* Tribunal aptly suggested: 'while a sovereign State possesses the inherent right to regulate its domestic affairs, the exercise of such right is not unlimited and must have its boundaries'.[151] These boundaries are identified in various ways by arbitral tribunals and some of those limitations require that the change must be 'reasonably justifiable by public policies'[152] and should not 'manifestly violate the requirements of consistency, transparency, even-handedness and non-discrimination',[153] alteration of the legal framework should not be total and unreasonable,[154] the modification should not be unreasonable,[155] application of the laws should not be arbitrary or non-transparent,[156] modifications should not be made 'specifically to prejudice' the investment,[157] the host state should not have a 'discriminatory and disproportionate attitude' against the investor,[158] the new measures should not be 'outside the acceptable margin of change'[159] and the host state should not act 'unfairly, unreasonably or inequitably in the exercise of its legislative power'.[160] The *Toto v Lebanon* Tribunal also declares that discriminatory or drastic changes in the key features of the investment might amount to a breach.[161]

---

[149] *Eiser Infrastructure Limited and Energía Solar Luxembourg SÁRL v Kingdom of Spain*, Award, ICSID Case No ARB/13/36, 4 May 2017, para 382.

[150] For a thorough analysis of a State's right to regulate, see A Titi, *The Right to Regulate in International Investment Law* (Nomos/Hart Publishing, 2014).

[151] *ADC Affiliate Limited and ADC & ADMC Management Limited v The Republic of Hungary*, Award of the Tribunal, ICSID Case No ARB/03/16, 2 October 2006, para 423.

[152] *Saluka v Czech*, Partial Award, para 307.

[153] ibid.

[154] *El Paso v Argentina*, Award, para 374; *Eiser v Spain*, Award, para 363.

[155] *Impregilo v Argentina*, Award, para 291.

[156] *Crystallex v Venezuela*, Award, para 552.

[157] *Parkerings v Lithuania*, Award, para 337.

[158] *Renée Rose Levy de Levi v The Republic of Peru*, Award, ICSID Case No ARB/10/17, 26 February 2014, para 332.

[159] *El Paso v Argentina*, Award, para 402.

[160] *Parkerings v Lithuania*, Award, para 332.

[161] *Toto v Lebanon*, Award, para 244.

Potestà, by analysing arbitral practice, identified four different situations where a change in the legal or regulatory framework would entail a breach of legitimate expectations even in the absence of a specific assurance: the extent of the change; the way the alteration arises; the discriminatory effect of the change; and the unreasonable nature of the alteration.[162] As seen from the above examples, every tribunal adopts its own approach to the issue in line with the facts of the cases at hand, and it is almost impossible to create a blanket threshold that would cover each and every situation a tribunal might come across.[163]

What can be derived from this is that even if it is theoretically recognised that states are sovereign and can alter their laws without restriction, a duty to compensate the investor arises when they perform this right to the detriment of investors' legitimate expectations. It is not a question of whether a host state's legal framework could be totally frozen; rather, it is about identifying the boundaries of a modification so that it does not upset the legitimate expectations of an investor.[164] The host states must know that their legal orders constitute a source for legitimate expectations and make their future alterations bearing those expectations in mind.[165] This was also the view held by the *Micula v Romania* Tribunal, which proposed that

> the state may always change its legislation, being aware and thus taking into consideration that: (i) an investor's legitimate expectations must be protected; (ii) the state's conduct must be substantively proper (eg not arbitrary or discriminatory); and (iii) the state's conduct must be procedurally proper (eg in compliance with due process and fair administration).[166]

The *Total v Argentina* Tribunal considered the legitimate expectations claims arising from legislation or regulations of the host states as the most difficult cases coming before them since there is a significant need to be able to distinguish between a legitimate expectation to a stable legal framework and the regulatory space of the host state.[167] It argued that a legitimate expectation might be based on a legislative and regulatory framework as long as the framework in question is 'inherently prospective'.[168] However, this approach was later criticised by Dolzer on the basis that the Tribunal excluded rules on tariffs or taxes from the scope of a 'prospective regulation', and failed to present a persuasive explanation for its stance.[169] It should come as no surprise that this view, as propounded by the *Total* Tribunal, has not found much support in the arbitral jurisprudence because

---

[162] Potestà, 'Legitimate Expectations', 117.
[163] ibid.
[164] Waelde and Kolo, 'Environmental Regulation', 825.
[165] Dolzer and Schreuer, *Principles*, 146; S Hamamoto, 'Protection of the Investor's Legitimate Expectations: Intersection of a Treaty Obligation and a General Principle of Law' in W Shan and J Su (eds), *China and International Investment Law: Twenty Years of ICSID Membership* (Brill Nijhoff, 2014) 149.
[166] *Micula v Romania*, Award, para 529.
[167] *Total v Argentina*, Decision on Liability, para 122.
[168] ibid.
[169] Dolzer, 'Today's Contours', 24.

distinguishing the laws as prospective and non-prospective would add further complexity to a tribunal's analysis.

While there are various critics of the legitimate expectations principle,[170] Sornarajah is one of those who propose a more radical interpretation. He claims that general promises (be they in legislation or in another form) of host states towards potential investors cannot create legitimate expectations.[171] However, arguing that the legal and regulatory framework of a host state has no relevance to creating legitimate expectations would amount to rejecting the fundamental aim of an investment treaty, which is to secure a stable and predictable legal framework.[172] This view also disregards the realities of an investment environment where legislation plays a significant role in inducing the investment.[173] It is well recognised under international law that states can undertake binding commitments in their legislation without having the need for a contract or for a specifically directed representation to be present.[174] It is also equally unreasonable to expect the investor to stipulate every detail regarding the stability of the legal framework in its contract. Some aspects of the investment relationship should be left to the general legal framework, otherwise the contract negotiations would consume a large amount of time and money. So, the argument that the legal order cannot create legitimate expectations seems implausible.

Montt, taking a more moderate view, contends that a legitimate expectation based on the legal and regulatory framework is the 'weakest version' of all.[175] While this statement might be true under certain circumstances, it would be the safest position to abstain from such a generalisation. After all, it depends on the guarantees provided by the framework in question, the extent of the conduct of the host state and the reliance based on that guarantee on the part of the investor. Clear legislation that prescribes a certain level of stability and which is used to induce the investment might play a more significant role than any of the other sources mentioned above if the investor had completely and reasonably relied upon it.

Another interesting point that should be noted was raised by the counsel for the claimant in the *Blusun v Italy* case. The counsel there, while criticising the approach of the *Charanne* Tribunal, stated:

> [T]he language [in Charanne] that seems to suggest that an investor can't base a legitimate expectation on a provision of law is unfathomable, because the law is the most

---

[170] T Zeyl, 'Charting the Wrong Course: The Doctrine of Legitimate Expectations in Investment Treaty Law' (2011) 49(1) *Alberta Law Review* 203; C Campbell, 'House of Cards: The Relevance of Legitimate Expectations under Fair and Equitable Treatment Provisions in Investment Treaty Law' (2013) 30(4) *Journal of International Arbitration* 361.

[171] M Sornarajah, *Resistance and Change in the International Law on Foreign Investment* (Cambridge University Press, 2015) 273.

[172] Dolzer, 'Today's Contours', 23.

[173] R Supapa, 'The Protection of Upstream Energy Contracts under Investment Treaty Arbitration: A Study of the Interaction between Contract and Treaty Instruments' (PhD Thesis, University of Aberdeen, 2014), 252; D Zannoni, 'The Legitimate Expectation of Regulatory Stability under the Energy Charter Treaty' (2020) 33(2) *Leiden Journal of International Law* 451, 8.

[174] *JSW Solar v Czech*, Gary Born, para 11; Siwy, 'Legitimate Expectations', 371.

[175] Montt, *State Liability*, 360.

formal statement on which any investor can base an expectation. How can it possibly be that some kind of representation made informally to an investor is more significant in terms of international law analysis than a representation that is made in the form of a law?[176]

Indeed, this is a legitimate question that needs to be responded to by those arbitral tribunals that completely disregard the legal framework as the basis of legitimate expectations. The difference between a contract and a law is evident; while the former is a product of negotiations between the relevant parties and contains more specific details and undertakings about the issue in question, the latter is often aimed at a more general audience and adopts a broader approach. However, this is not clear when it comes to the difference between an administrative representation and a law. Arbitral tribunals also do not explicitly articulate why a representation should prevail over a law in creating legitimate expectations.

It is true that 'international arbitrators are not necessarily bound by the hierarchy of norms or legal sources spelled out in any national constitution or legal system'.[177] However, in this particular issue, the hierarchy of norms approach can be used to inform the analysis of an arbitral tribunal. Even if an administrative representation is capable of creating a legal right, then the laws, in theory, should have a stronger effect.

Even though there are several arbitral awards, as discussed above, that follow a narrower approach and attempt to confine the legitimate expectations principle to the specific undertakings of a host state only, recent arbitral awards show that it is accepted by a good number of scholars and tribunals that the legal and regulatory framework prevalent in a host state could also be recognised as a basis for legitimate expectations. One thing to bear in mind is that host states are entitled to modify their legal and regulatory frameworks, even if this is financially detrimental to foreign investors. However, this alteration should not have a significantly drastic effect on the investment.[178]

III. Temporal Requirement of Legitimate Expectations

As already evident from the previous sections, not all expectations will be protected by the legitimate expectations principle. Alongside the other associated requirements, there is also a temporal prerequisite for an expectation to be considered legitimate and granted protection under the FET standard. The time that the expectations exist matters in assessing the legitimacy of the investors' reliance on

---

[176] *Blusun SA, Jean-Pierre Lecorcier and Michael Stein v Italian Republic*, Award, ICSID Case No ARB/14/3, 27 December 2016, para 370.
[177] HAG Naón, 'Should International Commercial Arbitrators Declare a Law Unconstitutional?' in DD Caron et al (eds), *Practising Virtue: Inside International Arbitration* (Oxford University Press, 2015) 314.
[178] M Campbell, L Shore and M Weiniger, *International Investment Arbitration: Substantive Principles* (Oxford University Press, 2017) 312.

a given source. Schreuer and Kriebaum, after analysing several earlier arbitral awards, produced an authoritative text on the issue of the time during which investors' legitimate expectations might possibly be created.[179] Their conclusive approach has since been upheld by numerous arbitral tribunals. According to them, the main point in time when a legitimate expectation could be created is the time at which the investment is made.[180] This is applicable to all the kinds of sources mentioned above. Those assurances in any form must already be in place at the time the investment is realised in order to generate a legitimate expectation.

In one of the more recent awards, the *Novenergia v Spain* Tribunal concluded that 'an investor's legitimate expectations are based on the host State's legal framework and on any representations or undertakings by the host State *at the time the investor makes the investment*'.[181] Likewise, the *JSW Solar v Czech* Tribunal suggested that 'legitimate expectations can only arise if the investor relies on the representations made by the State *at the time of its investment*'.[182] In the same vein, the *Crystallex v Venezuela* Tribunal indicated that 'It is rather trite to note that the investor may consider the regulatory framework *at the time of the decision to invest*'.[183] Similarly, the *Mamidoil v Albania* Tribunal declared that

> the Tribunal holds that legitimate expectations can only arise *at the time the investment is made*. Investors base their plans on circumstances and conditions as they find them, and they can only rely on conditions as they exist at that period.[184]

Equally, the *Frontier v Czech* Tribunal, after citing the previous arbitral awards, concluded that those awards

> have pointed out that a foreign investor has to make its business decisions and shape its expectations on the basis of the law and the factual situation prevailing in the country *as it stands at the time of the investment*.[185]

Lastly, the *Invesmart v Czech* Tribunal, while elaborating more on the issue, decided that an investor cannot retrospectively rely on certain documents which were unknown to it at the time it made the investment but were later disclosed during the arbitral process.[186] They can be used to reinforce the already existing legitimate expectations claims based on other assurances, but cannot form the main basis of a legitimate expectations claim.[187]

It is also clear that an investor is bound by the prevailing legal framework of a host state at the time of its investment and cannot claim a breach based on

---

[179] C Schreuer and U Kriebaum, 'At What Time Must Legitimate Expectations Exist?' in J Werner and AH Ali (eds), *A Liber Amicorum: Thomas Wälde – Law Beyond Conventional Thought* (CMP Publishing, 2009).

[180] ibid 266.

[181] *Novenergia v Spain*, Award, para 662 (emphasis added).

[182] *JSW Solar v Czech*, Award, para 436 (emphasis added).

[183] *Crystallex v Venezuela*, Award, para 552 (emphasis added).

[184] *Mamidoil v Albania*, Award, para 695 (emphasis added).

[185] *Frontier v Czech*, Final Award, para 287 (emphasis added).

[186] *Invesmart v Czech*, Award, para 253.

[187] ibid.

the 'subsequent faithful application' of that framework unless there is an explicit specific undertaking to the contrary.[188]

Arbitral jurisprudence and scholarly works show that this approach is now established practice. When a specific time of the investment can be determined, that would be recognised as the relevant time. The *Novenergia v Spain* case is an example of this, where the Tribunal determined the time of investment as 13 September 2007.[189]

However, the problematic issue is that an investment does not always take place in a specific, instant moment in time. Rather, it is often a combined process comprising several different steps, activities and transactions that extend over time.[190] Therefore, this complex feature and the various steps to an investment should be taken into account when determining legitimate expectations.[191] In addition to the initial investment stage, the future phases of 'expansion, development or reorganisation of the investment' must also be observed.[192] One important caveat to this approach might be that a new business decision should be substantial enough to be able to create legitimate expectations. Not every new business decision would amount to the level of significance required by the legitimate expectations principle.

In *Crystallex v Venezuela*, the claimant argued that its legitimate expectations arose in three different moments in time, namely at the time of its initial investment, upon receipt of a letter from the Ministry of Environment in May 2007 approving the project, and between 2008 and the government takeover in 2011.[193] The Tribunal, while rejecting the first and last claims, agreed with the second one, and even though the investor had already made a significant investment by that date, the Tribunal recognised the letter sent from the Ministry as capable of creating legitimate expectations because the claimant 'continued to invest throughout the process, and made investments after the 16 May 2007 letter'.[194]

A significant advancement on this widely recognised approach was recently brought by the *Urbaser v Argentina* Tribunal, which stated:

> The guarantee provided by the fair and equitable treatment standard protects the investor's rights and expectations in their content as they existed at the time the allegedly unfair or inequitable treatment occurred. When the expectations covered by the fair and equitable treatment protection originated at an earlier moment, they are protected only as long as they remained the same until the time such treatment had been applied.[195]

---

[188] Campbell et al, *International Investment Arbitration*, 309.
[189] *Novenergia v Spain*, Award, para 662.
[190] Schreuer and Kriebaum, 'At What Time Must Legitimate Expectations Exist?', 269.
[191] ibid.
[192] ibid.
[193] *Crystallex v Venezuela*, Award, para 549.
[194] ibid para 557.
[195] *Urbaser SA and Consorcio de Aguas Bilbao Bizkaia, Bilbao Biskaia Ur Partzuergoa v The Argentine Republic*, Award, ICSID Case No ARB/07/26, 8 December 2016, para 630.

This view of the Tribunal should indeed be considered the crux of the matter. Legitimate expectations at the time an investment is made should be seen as the upper limit of expectations that are relevant. These expectations might have changed during the course of the investment, and indeed some of them might even have been accomplished. An investor cannot base its legitimate expectations on subsequent assurances given by a host state to other investors or favourable changes made to the legal framework unless it relies on the subsequent assurances and modifications by making substantial expansions or business decisions with regard to its initial investment. Therefore, the earliest point in time for an expectation to be recognised as legitimate would be the time when the investment is initially made or when a subsequent 'decisive step' is taken.[196] In both situations, however, this expectation must still be relevant at the time the breach occurs. The mere existence of legitimate expectations by the time the investment is made does not secure its protection by the time the breach occurs since the expectations must be perpetual.

To summarise, legitimate expectations might be generated:

1. by the time the initial investment is made; or
2. any time within the duration of the investment following a new condition presented by host states provided that a subsequent substantial decisive step is taken with the required reliance on the new conditions.

It is also important to note again that these expectations must still exist at the time of the claimed breach in order to be protected.

IV. How Can an Expectation be Considered Legitimate?

The requirements for an expectation to be considered legitimate have already been discussed under the previous sections, albeit in a slightly random manner. This section will bring those pieces together and present them in a more cohesive form.

There are two recurrent themes in the assessment of the legitimacy of an expectation: reliance and reasonableness. In order for an expectation to be considered legitimate and granted protection under the FET standard, it must bear these two qualifications. As the *Micula v Romania* Tribunal clearly indicated, the investor who claims that its legitimate expectations have been breached must establish that: (i) the host state made a promise or assurance; (ii) the investor relied on that promise or assurance; and (iii) the reliance was reasonable.[197]

---

[196] Schreuer and Kriebaum, 'At What Time Must Legitimate Expectations Exist?', 276.
[197] *Micula v Romania*, Award, para 668.

A. Reliance

It is submitted that, under the investment treaty arbitration setting, reliance on an assurance confirms the legitimacy of an expectation.[198] Reliance should be understood as either making an initial investment or expanding an already existent one.[199] An investor will be redressed due to the infringement of its legitimate expectations only if it had relied on that expectation while making the investment.[200]

Numerous arbitral awards have emphasised the necessity of reliance in order to confer legitimacy to an expectation. The *Eiser v Spain* Tribunal submitted that 'regulatory regimes cannot be radically altered as applied to existing investments in ways that deprive investors who *invested in reliance on those regimes* of their investment's value'.[201] The *Crystallex v Venezuela* Tribunal explicitly stated that 'it is the *investor's reliance on a promise* which may prompt, or contribute to, its decision to invest and proceed with that investment, and which makes in turn the expectation worthy of legal protection'.[202] In a similar vein, the *Duke v Ecuador* Tribunal suggests that 'expectations must arise from the conditions that the State offered the investor and the latter *must have relied upon them* when deciding to invest'.[203] The *Parkerings v Lithuania* Tribunal also followed the same line of thought and concluded that an expectation is legitimate if the investor takes the assurances given by the host state into account while investing.[204] The *LG&E v Argentina* Tribunal provides another example to this end whereby it states that: 'the fair and equitable treatment analysis involves consideration of the investor's expectations when making its investment *in reliance on the protections to be granted* by the host State'.[205] Lastly, in one of the earliest cases, the *Tecmed v Mexico* Tribunal declared:

> The foreign investor also expects the host State to act consistently, ie without arbitrarily revoking any preexisting decisions or permits issued by the State *that were relied upon by the investor to assume its commitments* as well as to plan and launch its commercial and business activities.[206]

However, there is no requirement for an investment to be concluded solely on the basis of relying on a single assurance that creates legitimate expectations. As the *Micula* Tribunal aptly put it:

> Businessmen do not invest on the basis of one single consideration, no matter how important. In the Tribunal's view, that expectation must be a determining factor in an investor's decision to invest, or in the manner or magnitude of its investments.[207]

[198] Snodgrass, 'Legitimate Expectations', 45.
[199] Newcombe and Paradell, *Standards of Treatment*, 279.
[200] Bonnitcha, *Substantive Protection*, 182; Dolzer, 'Today's Contours', 20.
[201] *Eiser v Spain*, Award, para 382 (emphasis added).
[202] *Crystallex v Venezuela*, Award, para 557 (emphasis added).
[203] *Duke v Ecuador*, Award, para 340 (emphasis added).
[204] *Parkerings v Lithuania*, Award, para 331.
[205] *LG&E v Argentina*, Decision on Liability, para 127 (emphasis added).
[206] *Tecmed v Mexico*, Award, para 154 (emphasis added).
[207] *Micula v Romania*, Award, para 672.

As can be seen from these illustrations, the prerequisite of reliance on the assurance has been consistently recognised by arbitral tribunals throughout the years. In addition to the temporal dimension discussed under the previous section, reliance also looms large in determining the legitimacy of an expectation. However, even though an investor has relied on an assurance in a timely manner, this is not sufficient to render the expectation legitimate. That reliance, in addition to being timely, must also be reasonable.

B. Reasonableness

For an expectation to be considered legitimate, the investor's reliance on an assurance must be reasonable, both objectively and subjectively, with respect to the circumstances of the case.[208] The *Saluka* Tribunal stated that the investors' expectations 'must rise to the level of legitimacy and reasonableness in light of the circumstances' in order to be protected.[209] The *Charanne* Tribunal also recently required the expectation to be reasonable in that particular case.[210] While these cases did not explicitly state what might be considered reasonable, the *Total* Tribunal stated that an investor might expect the host state to act within the limits of economic rationality, public interest and proportionality, and deemed any expectations based on these principles to be reasonable.[211] The reasonableness test is an assessment of the facts related to the dispute.[212]

The intention of the host state is immaterial while measuring the capability of conduct sufficient to generate legitimate expectations. This was expressly stated by the *Micula* Tribunal as follows: 'It is irrelevant whether the state in fact wished to commit itself; it is sufficient that it acted in a manner that would reasonably be understood to create such an appearance.'[213] This approach was also recently upheld by the *Novenergia* Tribunal.[214] Even if a host state had not aimed at that particular outcome, if an objective assessment of the state conduct allows the investor to understand it in a certain way, then legitimate expectations will become relevant. This objective assessment of the said conduct is the duty of the arbitrators to discharge.

In this regard, an investor's knowledge of the facts concerning the guarantees provided by a host state and the precise content of such assurances are the two fundamental factors in the determination of the reasonableness aspect.[215] For an objective assessment, the tribunal should look for an answer to the question of

---

[208] Diehl, *Core Standard*, 428; Snodgrass, 'Legitimate Expectations', 41; Campbell et al, *International Investment Arbitration*, 317.

[209] *Saluka v Czech*, Partial Award, para 304.

[210] *Charanne v Spain*, Award, para 495.

[211] *Total v Argentina*, Decision on Liability, para 333.

[212] *Micula v Romania*, Award, para 669.

[213] ibid.

[214] *Novenergia v Spain*, Award, para 652.

[215] Fietta, 'Legitimate Expectations', 432.

whether the investor's conduct or decisions prior to making its investment were those of a diligent or prudent investor.[216]

Investor diligence is considered a key aspect in determining the reasonableness of the legitimate expectations.[217] This examination of diligence should be made regardless of the expectation's source.[218] According to the *Isolux v Spain* Tribunal, extensive legal due diligence is not a prerequisite to an acknowledgement of the reasonableness of the expectation, but rather a general knowledge regarding the legal framework of the host state which every prudent investor should know is considered sufficient.[219] In a similar vein, the latest *Masdar v Spain* award states that an 'appropriate due diligence' is required to establish a legitimate expectations claim.[220]

What is required here is not an in-depth and extensive legal inquiry into the legal framework of the host state, but rather a certain level of knowledge about the existing laws. Waelde, while dissenting from his colleagues in the *Thunderbird* case, stated:

> They imply a very high level of due diligence, of knowledge of local conditions and of government risk to be taken by the investor. I rather see the government as responsible for providing a clear message and of sticking to the message once given and as reasonably understood by the investor. They view the investor as having a duty to be close to perfect in its dealings with the government, I consider the government to have a duty to be transparent and consistent, and as responsible for the message conveyed: ie how such conduct was reasonably understood by the investor.[221]

A breach of legitimate expectations claim cannot be asserted if the investor has not undertaken any kind of legal survey regarding the laws of the host state. However, it should also be noted that if the modifications were not foreseeable regardless of due diligence, then the investor should not be refused protection solely on the basis of its lack of conducting due diligence.

The due diligence requirement should also be analysed objectively by taking the surrounding circumstances into account at the time of the investment. The level of diligence that an investor must satisfy is contingent upon the country's context and the business risk associated with its investment.[222]

---

[216] FM Palombino, *Fair and Equitable Treatment and the Fabric of General Principles* (Asser Press, 2018) 91.

[217] JE Viñuales, 'Investor Diligence in Investment Arbitration: Sources and Arguments' (2017) 32(2) *ICSID Review – Foreign Investment Law Journal* 346, 362; AFM Maniruzzaman, 'The Pursuit of Stability in International Energy Investment Contracts: A Critical Appraisal of the Emerging Trends' (2008) 1(2) *Journal of World Energy Law & Business* 121, 151.

[218] Potestà, 'Legitimate Expectations', 119.

[219] *Isolux Netherlands, BV v Kingdom of Spain*, Final Award, SCC Case V2013/153, 17 July 2016, para 781 (free translation), cited in *JSW Solar v Czech*, Gary Born, para 100.

[220] *Masdar Solar & Wind Cooperatief UA v Kingdom of Spain*, Award, ICSID Case No ARB/14/1, 16 May 2018, para 494.

[221] *Thunderbird v Mexico*, Separate Opinion of Thomas Waelde, para6.

[222] AR Sureda, *Investment Treaty Arbitration: Judging under Uncertainty* (Cambridge University Press, 2012) 79.

As for objective consideration, the *Duke v Ecuador* Award emphasised that:

> The assessment of the reasonableness or legitimacy must take into account all circumstances, including not only the facts surrounding the investment, but also the political, socioeconomic, cultural and historical conditions prevailing in the host State.[223]

This view was later followed in the *Bayindir v Pakistan* case, where the Tribunal stated that the investor 'could not reasonably have ignored the volatility of the political conditions prevailing in Pakistan'.[224]

According to this approach, not every host state would be considered the same with respect to the expectations created. Both Tudor and Potestà argue that an investor cannot reasonably expect the same level of legal stability or administrative efficiency from a developing country as it could from a developed one.[225] However, in my opinion, this developed versus developing rhetoric should be abandoned because it is clear that the level of development of a host state is not of particular importance when it comes to unilateral interventions. Recent renewable energy disputes in Spain, Italy and the Czech Republic and the arguments in several scholarly works[226] provide suitable evidence that the regulatory risk does not belong solely to developing states.

The reasonableness of an expectation should not be assessed with respect to the level of development of the host state; rather, it should be evaluated based on the facts surrounding the investment. As an example, a developing host state's stability guarantees, as based on its legal framework and recurring representations, might render the investors' expectations more reasonable than the expectations arising from a developed host state's legal environment without the offer of an explicit assurance.

While examining the reasonableness of the investor's expectations, the *Micula v Romania* Tribunal assessed the issue within the context of Romania's accession to the EU in order to determine whether it was reasonable for the investor to think that the incentives provided by Romania were compatible with EU law.[227] As can also be seen from this example, the reasonableness of the reliance should be evaluated within the context of each particular case; there is no uniform approach that can be adopted.

The subjective aspect, on the other hand, focuses on the investor's prior knowledge of a potential risk or change in circumstances. If the investor had already known that there was a certain obstacle to the realisation of its expectations, if the assurance provided by the host state to the investor was based on misinformation

---

[223] *Duke v Ecuador*, Award, para 340.
[224] *Bayindir v Pakistan*, Award, para 193.
[225] Tudor, *The FET Standard*, 165; Potestà, 'Legitimate Expectations', 118.
[226] See ch 2, s VA.
[227] *Micula v Romania*, Award, para 690.

or if the investor's conduct was in bad faith or fraudulent, then it would not be reasonable for the investor to rely on that expectation.[228]

V. A Test to Identify Legitimate Expectations

Taking all the above-mentioned aspects of legitimate expectations into account, an assessment to identify a legitimate expectation shall be presented. First of all, what should be of the utmost importance is not the source of a legitimate expectation, but rather the expectation created by that source and the way this is communicated to the investor. Therefore, before focusing on the form of an expectation's source, its content should first be evaluated. It should be a presupposition that any of these above-discussed sources are at least in theory capable of creating legitimate expectations. In order to evaluate the practical effect, the expectations generated might be assessed.

A legitimate expectation might arise from any kind of legal or regulatory source, be it binding or non-binding. Since the legitimate expectations principle is being applied as a component of the FET standard, it should also bear the same requirements and characteristics that the FET standard bears. There is no such argument in the arbitral awards or scholarly works that the FET can only be breached when a contract is involved. On the contrary, the FET standard provides a broader protection which takes the legal framework as a whole into account, and this is one of the reasons for its popularity. Gary Born explains this in his *Antaris v Czech* dissent in clear terms:

> Similarly, the fair and equitable treatment doctrine is directed towards the protection of the legitimate expectations of investors. There is no requirement that those expectations arise only from contractual instruments, or 'specific' representations; indeed, as noted above, fair and equitable treatment analysis focuses on a state's overall legal framework. The decisive question is not the form of a state's representations but whether the content and character of those representations is sufficiently clear to give rise to legitimate investor expectations that the state will abide by its commitments.[229]

This would be an appropriate approach in order to eliminate the divergent applications of the legitimate expectations principle in the arbitral jurisprudence. The important points to be considered are as follows:

1. *Inducement Effect:* Was the assurance communicated to the investor put in place in order to attract the investor to the host state? This should be an

---

[228] FM Téllez, 'Conditions and Criteria for the Protection of Legitimate Expectations under International Investment Law: 2012 ICSID Review Student Writing Competition' (2012) 27(2) *ICSID Review – Foreign Investment Law Journal* 432, 3; Fietta, 'Legitimate Expectations', 432; Supapa, 'Upstream Energy Contracts', 264.

[229] *Antaris GMBH and Dr Michael Göde v The Czech Republic*, Dissenting Opinion of Gary Born, PCA Case No 2014-01, 2 May 2018, para 45 (footnote omitted).

important factor to consider when evaluating the existence of a legitimate expectation. If a legal framework or a representation which provides certain guarantees has been put in place and utilised specifically to attract the investor to invest, then this might be readily considered a legitimate basis for the expectations of the investor.[230] It can be said that an assurance that is aimed directly at inducing the investor to invest should be recognised as having the highest potential to generate legitimate expectations. It does not have to be aimed at a single investor; rather, if the content of the assurance includes a manifest inducement objective, any investor would be entitled to rely on it.[231] However, this is not an indispensable requirement for the recognition of legitimate expectations. Even without the existence of an active inducement, the investor might have legitimate expectations.

2. *Clarity and Relevance of the Commitment:* It should be assessed whether the assurance is clear enough with regard to its content and meaning. This is to be understood as the mere interpretation of the source in question. No matter how an assurance is communicated to the investor, be it through a representation or through legislation, what should be evaluated is whether it clearly and explicitly provides a benefit to the investor. The simple wording of the guarantee provided by the host state or the act conducted should be in conformance with the result deduced and relied upon by the investor in an objective manner. As already discussed above, the guarantee upon which the investor relies must be relevant to the investment made. A causal link between the assurance provided and the investment made is necessary.[232] An investor cannot legitimately rely on a commitment provided by the host state under a different framework or for different types of investments.

3. *Cumulative Effect:* International investments, especially those in the energy sector, are based on several layers of different legal and economic considerations. An investor does not treat each and every variable separately, but rather takes them into account in a cumulative manner. This is particularly visible in the legal aspect, where an investor looks into the general legal and regulatory framework, which consists of contracts, legislation, regulations, licences and administrative representations, altogether, not separately. The energy sector, being highly regulated, should be analysed in its entirety. Therefore, it is the duty of arbitral tribunals to take the legal framework of a host state into account as a whole. Instead of focusing purely on a contract or a certain administrative representation, what should be done is to take the legal framework in question into account entirely and decide whether a legitimate

---

[230] Jacob and Schill, 'Content, Practice, Method', 26; A Boute, 'Combating Climate Change through Investment Arbitration' (2012) 35(3) *Fordham International Law Journal* 613, 636.

[231] YS Selivanova, 'Changes in Renewables Support Policy and Investment Protection under the Energy Charter Treaty: Analysis of Jurisprudence and Outlook for the Current Arbitration Cases' (2018) 33(2) *ICSID Review – Foreign Investment Law Journal* 433, 442; UNCTAD, 'Fair and Equitable Treatment', 69.

[232] Annacker, 'Legitimate Expectations', 233.

expectation might be created from cumulative legal sources. If it is possible for a legitimate expectation to arise and it is reasonable for an investor to rely on it, and if the investor has actually relied on that cumulative framework, then those expectations must be protected against subsequent disruptions. As an illustration, if legislation is not sufficiently explicit and clear to deduce a direct assurance to the investor, successive administrative representations clarifying that legislation should be taken into account as a decisive factor.

4. *Reasonable Reliance on Time:* If the initial investment or the following substantial investment decisions are not made by taking the assurances provided by the host state into account, then there can be no legitimate expectations. There must be an assurance upon which the investor must have reasonably, and in a timely fashion, relied upon. Reasonableness is not a fixed concept within the meaning of legitimate expectations, but rather depends on the circumstances of each case. So, there is no one-size-fits-all approach to the assessment of reasonableness. For the subjective assessment, a tribunal should examine whether the claimant investor actually holds an expectation; for the objective assessment, it should consider whether it was objectively reasonable to rely on that expectation.[233]

These could be seen as the main points to consider while determining the existence of a legitimate expectation. However, contractual clauses and guarantees can be distinguished from other assurances by their very nature. Since a contract already creates a legal framework in which the parties concretise their expectations, contractual expectations could be more readily noticed without having to resort to these points separately and specifically.

VI. Conclusion

A breach of legitimate expectations claim comprises three major components: an assurance provided by the host state; a reasonable reliance on that assurance by the investor; and a subsequent alteration of that assurance. The assurance in question might be provided in several forms: as a contractual clause; as an administrative representation; or as part of a general legal and regulatory framework of the host state.

The current arbitral jurisprudence shows that the investors' legitimate expectations must be protected against unilateral subsequent changes of the host states if the investor had reasonably and in a timely manner relied on a guarantee. If an investor had not taken those assurances into account while investing or expanding its already existing investment, then there would be no legitimate expectations.

---

[233] S Maynard, 'Legitimate Expectations and the Interpretation of the "Legal Stability Obligation"' (2016) 1(1) *European Investment Law and Arbitration Review* 99, 112.

Even though some arbitral tribunals and scholars argue that the scope of application of the principle should be kept narrow, it is evident from the majority of the latest arbitral decisions that this narrow approach is not widely favoured. Tribunals are more inclined to uphold the view that legitimate expectations might be created by a wide range of legal sources.

While assessing the existence of a legitimate expectation, the source of the disputed assurance should not be the first element examined. Rather, the content of the assurance delivered by the host state should be evaluated first in order to determine whether it is capable of creating an expectation. This becomes especially important where several guarantees are not individually sufficient to create legitimate expectations, but are able to generate legitimate expectations when assessed together.

The legitimate expectations principle is still a developing concept under international investment law. This chapter, by analysing the latest awards and literature, has shown that applying the principle in its wider form is the path that should be followed in analyses of legitimate expectations. Since BITs are put in place to provide investors with a secure and stable investment environment, standards under BITs should be interpreted in line with this objective. Therefore, the FET standard and the legitimate expectation principle under that standard should be utilised in such a way as to grant more comprehensive protection to investors. This could be achieved by allowing investors to base their expectations on any of the above-mentioned sources instead of restricting the scope of application of the principle.

International energy investments, due to their special characteristics, such as being large, capital-intensive projects in commercial terms and playing a significant role in host state politics, are mostly regulated by a combination of legal sources and are typically under considerable public scrutiny. Therefore, the legitimate expectations principle remains of value and is a significant recourse to claimants in arbitrations about energy investments which have fallen victim to regulatory risks. A stable legal framework requires – among other things – a broad approach to the application of the legitimate expectations principle.

6

Legitimate Expectations and Stability: The Interplay

I. Introduction

So far, this book has discussed the stability concept with respect to international energy investments, the stabilisation provisions, the fair and equitable treatment (FET) standard and the doctrine of legitimate expectations, and its current appraisal by arbitral tribunals under these headings. In this chapter, the two concepts that are at the core of this book, stability and legitimate expectations, will be brought together in order to present a protection framework relevant to international energy investors. Building upon the previous chapters, this chapter will analyse the stability provisions separately through the lens of legitimate expectations.

The focus will be on two aspects of the nexus between the concepts. The first aspect is the relationship between already existent stability commitments and legitimate expectations. These are the legitimate expectations created by the stability provisions.

The commitment that provides the most expansive protection is a contractual stabilisation clause. When there is a contractual stability provision, arbitral tribunals readily accept the existence of legitimate expectations in the event of a subsequent detrimental alteration.

The second is the stability provision found under domestic legislation. Even though these provisions are seen as less effective in the traditional stability literature, they are nevertheless able to offer a significant degree of protection to investors when a host state modifies its legal framework. When they are considered in conjunction with the legitimate expectations principle, they are of substantial importance during the dispute resolution process and thus should not be overlooked. The effect of legislative stability commitments is especially visible from the latest renewable energy cases involving Spain.

The last commitment is the administrative stability aspect. Although the stability literature does not discuss them as a part of the stability concept, what can be derived from the legitimate expectations case law and the literature is that a stability assurance given by means of administrative representations could well be considered a guarantee worthy of protection.

The second aspect of the nexus between stability and legitimate expectations is the protection of the latter in the absence of an explicit stability guarantee in any of the forms mentioned above. Even if there is no explicit stability provision, there might be a legitimate expectation on the part of the investor to stability. Within the context of the Energy Charter Treaty (ECT) or any other bilateral investment treaty (BIT), there is a duty for a host state to maintain a stable legal framework. If a host state cannot provide a stable investment environment and this were to impair the investment, then it might be held responsible for a breach of the legitimate expectations of investors.

II. Legitimate Expectations 'from' Stability

The first aspect of the nexus between legitimate expectations and the stability concept that this book identifies is framed with the 'from stability' term. Under this relationship, the legitimate expectations of investors are based upon an already existing stability guarantee provided earlier by a host state.

For this aspect to be applicable in disputes, the prerequisite is the existence of an explicit stabilisation provision in any form prior to an investment being realised. First, there must be a stability assurance provided by the host state, then the investor should have reasonably relied on that assurance while making its investment. In this case, the stabilisation provisions play a substantial role in determining the existence of a legitimate expectation and strengthening the breach of legitimate expectations claims before an arbitral tribunal.

Under this section of the chapter, different forms of stability provisions will be analysed with regard to the expectations that are based upon them. The sources of stabilisation provisions that were discussed in chapter three will be reviewed here through the legitimate expectations perspective. The question of how each of these sources are considered or should be considered by arbitral tribunals with respect to the legitimate expectations principle will be the focal point of the following sections. The role that a stability provision plays in the evaluation of the legitimate expectations principle will be analysed in depth.

A. Contractual Stability and Legitimate Expectations

As discussed in the previous chapter, contractual undertakings create the highest level of legitimate expectations.[1] However, as discussed previously, not every breach of contractual clauses attracts protection under the FET standard; rather, some additional requirements are needed.[2] With the existence of a contractual stabilisation clause, on the other hand, the contract might already be considered internationalised and thus be subject to international law without any further

---

[1] See ch 5, s IIA.
[2] See ch 5, s IIA(i).

requirements.[3] It is clear from the implications of a stabilisation clause that its breach includes the exercise of a sovereign power, the additional requirement for the treaty protection.[4] Therefore, the inclusion of a stabilisation clause in an investment contract would bring the contract under the treaty protection, and hence the legitimate expectations principle under the FET standard.

An United Nations Conference on Trade and Development (UNCTAD) study observes that 'an investor may derive legitimate expectations … from … specific commitments addressed to it personally, for example, in the form of a stabilization clause'.[5]

Even though there are not many arbitral awards that directly deal with a contractual stabilisation clause, several arbitral tribunals have nevertheless mentioned the importance of stabilisation clauses when evaluating legitimate expectations.

The *Parkerings* Tribunal stated that if an investor received an explicit promise in the form of a stabilisation clause, then its expectations would be legitimate.[6] As noted in the previous chapter, the *Total* Tribunal considered an expectation 'undoubtedly legitimate' if it is based on a stabilisation clause.[7] Likewise, the *AES v Hungary* Tribunal observed that a stabilisation clause 'could legitimately have made the investor believe that no change in the law would occur'.[8] Similarly, the *Paushok v Mongolia* Tribunal pointed out that in order to have a legitimate expectation that the taxes would not increase in the future, the investor must have already obtained a stability agreement.[9] In the same vein, the *Micula* Tribunal stated that 'Investors must expect that the legislation will change from time to time, absent a stabilization clause or other specific assurances giving rise to a legitimate expectation of stabilization', and this was later further endorsed by the *Eiser* Tribunal.[10] The *Charanne* Tribunal also did not find a breach of legitimate expectations on the basis of the lack of a specific commitment, such as a stabilisation clause directed towards the investors.[11] Had there been a contractual stabilisation clause, the Tribunal would have granted a protection based on legitimate expectations. While evaluating the breach of a legitimate expectations claim, the *Perenco v Ecuador* Tribunal expressly stated that 'the Tribunal would have little difficulty

---

[3] See ch 3, s IVA(i).

[4] J Gjuzi, *Stabilization Clauses in International Investment Law: A Sustainable Development Approach* (Springer, 2018) 335.

[5] UNCTAD, 'Fair and Equitable Treatment: A Sequel' (United Nations, 2012) 69.

[6] *Parkerings-Compagniet AS v Republic of Lithuania*, Award, ICSID Case No ARB/05/8, 11 September 2007, paras 331–32.

[7] *Total SA v The Argentine Republic*, Decision on Liability, ICSID Case No ARB/04/01, 27 December 2010, para 117.

[8] *AES Summit Generation Limited and AES-Tisza Erömü Kft v The Republic of Hungary*, Award, ICSID Case No ARB/07/22, 23 September 2010, para 9.3.31.

[9] *Sergei Paushok, CJSC Golden East Company and CJSC Vostokneftegaz Company v The Government of Mongolia*, Award on Jurisdiction and Liability, UNCITRAL, 28 April 2011, para 302.

[10] *Micula v Romania*, Award, para 529; *Eiser v Spain*, Award, para 362.

[11] *Charanne v Spain*, Award, para 490.

holding that a fully stabilised contract that did not admit of any future legislative or other change cannot be changed unilaterally.'[12]

A contractual stabilisation clause could be considered the most specific assurance with respect to its addressee and content given to the investors by the host states. Therefore, the approach that confines the legitimate expectations principle purely to specific guarantees would also be satisfied in the existence of a contractual stability provision.[13]

As Cameron rightly put: 'If a stabilization clause is included in a contract, it may be argued that this grant by the state alone creates the expectation that the law will not be changed.'[14] This was also noted previously by Weil when he opined, in relation to the stabilisation clauses, that: 'In subscribing to a protection clause, the host government has thus created to the benefit of the other contracting party a legitimate expectation, which the government may not subsequently frustrate without infringing the principle of good faith.'[15]

A stabilisation clause definitely bolsters the legitimate expectations of the investor.[16] The link between contractual stabilisation provisions and the legitimate expectations principle has been consistently recognised by arbitral tribunals.[17]

It is worth noting that when there is a contractual stability provision, the arbitral tribunal's analysis should not be guided by the reliance of the investor or the extent of the change itself. These are considerations undertaken by tribunals when there is no explicit contractual stabilisation clause available. The mere existence of a contractual stability provision would be enough to fulfil the reasonable reliance requirement. The investor does not have to show its actual reliance on the said clause in order to be protected by the principle. Likewise, a tribunal's analysis should not focus overly on the extent of the unilateral alteration by the host state. Rather, any kind of detrimental deviation from the stabilised legal framework would be enough to upset investors' legitimate expectations.

It is true that the existence of a contractual stabilisation clause raises investors' expectations, but, as will be seen in the following sections, a contractual

---

[12] *Perenco Ecuador Ltd v The Republic of Ecuador*, Decision on Remaining Issues of Jurisdiction and on Liability, ICSID Case No ARB/08/6, 12 September 2014, para 593.

[13] R Supapa, 'The Protection of Upstream Energy Contracts under Investment Treaty Arbitration: A Study of the Interaction between Contract and Treaty Instruments' (PhD Thesis, University of Aberdeen, 2014), 267.

[14] PD Cameron, *International Energy Investment Law: The Pursuit of Stability* (Oxford University Press, 2010) 66.

[15] P Weil, 'Les Clauses de Stabilisation ou d'intangibilité Insérées dans les Accords de Développement Économique' in *Mélanges offerts à Charles Rousseau* (Pedone, 1974) 326, cited in W Peter, 'Stabilization Clauses in State Contracts' (1998) (8) *International Business Law Journal* 875, 885.

[16] O Osasu, 'Legitimate Expectations and Political Risk: Lessons from Investment Arbitration for Energy Investors' (2013) (6) *International Energy Law Review* 249, 262; AFM Maniruzzaman, 'National Laws Providing for Stability of International Investment Contracts: A Comparative Perspective' (2007) 8(2) *Journal of World Investment & Trade* 233, 237.

[17] L Mistelis, 'Contractual Mechanisms for Stability in Energy Contracts' in M Scherer (ed), *International Arbitration in the Energy Sector* (Oxford University Press, 2018) 168.

stabilisation clause is not indispensable in generating legitimate expectations in the way that some tribunals have suggested.[18]

In a nutshell, the existence of a contractual stabilisation clause, in the event of a subsequent unilateral alteration of the legal framework, would function as a presumption of the existence of legitimate expectations and tribunals would accordingly grant a treaty protection. A legitimate expectation claim arising from a contractual stability provision would require the highest level of protection and the lowest level of scrutiny. The protection in this case would be greater because 'the investor has been able to bargain that commitment individually'.[19] Since long-term energy investment contracts are drafted in a bespoke manner by taking the specific stability needs of the investors into account,[20] they are readily accepted as a basis for legitimate expectations.

However, as has already been analysed in chapter three, stabilisation clauses are not uniform, but rather appear in contracts and laws in numerous different forms. How, then, should these various forms be treated with respect to their capability of creating legitimate expectations?

(i) Which Stabilisation Clause?

The analysis in this subsection will draw upon the stabilisation clause classifications provided in chapter three, and discuss whether they might be considered as having the capability of creating legitimate expectations. Five different types of stabilisation clauses were identified in chapter three, and these will be grouped under two headings as traditional clauses (freezing and intangibility) and contemporary clauses (economic balancing, allocation of burden and hybrid).

What is mostly seen from arbitral practice and scholarly works is that when stabilisation clauses are mentioned within the context of legitimate expectations, they refer to a situation where the host state unilaterally alters the legal framework regulating the investment. In this case, the focus is mostly on traditional types of stabilisation clause. If there is a traditional type of stability provision in the contract, this would definitely lead to the creation of legitimate expectations. A freezing clause and an intangibility clause both aim to prevent a host state from modifying certain aspects of the legal framework.[21]

On the other hand, the so-called contemporary types of stabilisation clause do not attempt to achieve the same result as the traditional ones. Rather, they acknowledge the changeability of the economic conditions of the investment and attempt to rebalance the equilibrium. Their main objective is thus not to prevent

[18] Supapa, 'Upstream Energy Contracts', 256.
[19] M Potestà, 'Legitimate Expectations in Investment Treaty Law: Understanding the Roots and the Limits of a Controversial Concept' (2013) 28(1) *ICSID Review – Foreign Investment Law Journal* 88, 114.
[20] Mistelis, 'Stability', 154.
[21] See ch 3, s IIIC.

the host state from altering its legal framework, unlike traditional clauses. So, the question that arises here is whether a contractual clause which has already stipulated a change in circumstances might give rise to legitimate expectations.

This issue was discussed in the *Ulysseas v Ecuador*[22] case. Article 24 of the Licence Contract that was subject to dispute is as follows:

> TWENTY-FOUR: INDEMNIFICATION PAID TO THE PERMIT HOLDER.
>
> Article two hundred seventy-one of the Constitution of the Republic of Ecuador stipulates that the State, through the GRANTOR, may establish special guarantees and security assurances to the investor to ensure that the agreements will not be modified by laws or other provisions of any type which have an impact on their clauses. *If laws or standards are enacted which prejudice the investor or change the contract clauses, the State will pay the investor the respective compensation for damages caused by those situations, in such a way as to at all times restore and maintain the economic and financial stability which would have been in effect if the acts or decisions had not occurred.*[23]

This is an economic equilibrium clause, and the Tribunal, by utilising the Article in its analysis of legitimate expectations, indicated that the claimant should have expected a change.[24] The Tribunal explicitly stated:

> In effect, this provision shows that Claimant had accepted in September 2006 that changes might be introduced to laws 'or other provisions of any nature' which 'would prejudice the investor' and that, should this occur, compensation would be paid for damages so caused to it.[25]

The Tribunal, therefore, did not find a legitimate expectation on the investor's side regarding the stability of the regulatory framework; on the contrary, the economic equilibrium clause was considered an indication of a possible change that the investor should have expected.

In addition to this, the Tribunal observed that there was a contractual right on the part of the investor to request compensation in the event of a detrimental change and that, by bringing the dispute before a treaty tribunal, the claimant has waived this right.[26] Indeed, the investor should have pursued its contractual right to an economic equilibrium first. There could have been a successful legitimate expectations claim had the investor first tried the contractual mechanism but failed to resolve the dispute due to the host state's behaviour resulting from exercising its sovereign authority. This would then have elevated the contractual dispute to the treaty level and the legitimate expectations of the claimant could have been protected. This was exactly the issue in the *Impregilo v Argentina* case, where the Tribunal found a breach of the FET standard, which it linked to

---

[22] *Ulysseas, Inc v The Republic of Ecuador*, Final Award, PCA Case No 2009-19, 12 June 2012.
[23] ibid para 229 (emphasis added).
[24] PD Cameron, 'In Search of Investment Stability' in K Talus (ed), *Research Handbook on International Energy Law* (Edward Elgar Publishing, 2014) 144.
[25] *Ulysseas v Ecuador*, Final Award, para 258.
[26] ibid.

legitimate expectations, and stated that 'Argentina, by failing to restore a reasonable equilibrium in the concession, aggravated its situation to such extent as to constitute a breach of its duty under the BIT to afford a fair and equitable treatment to Impregilo's investment.'[27]

This was also the consideration put forward by an earlier award. The *AES* Tribunal commented that there was a 'Change in Law'[28] clause under the power purchase agreement between the parties by which it was made clear that 'a change in the law could occur that could make the obligations under the agreement become illegal, unenforceable or impossible to perform.'[29] Therefore, the *AES* Tribunal also concluded that the investor was aware of a possible change in law and could not have a legitimate expectation of stability. The *Electrabel* Tribunal dealt with a similar clause and concluded that the power purchase agreement disputed in the case included a clause whereby the agreement could have been terminated without compensation: 'if any obligation became unlawful to perform due to [a] change in law.'[30] The rather long clauses in these two cases included some form of rebalancing and renegotiation provisions. What is common to the tribunals' analyses is that since a change had already been anticipated in a contractual clause, an investor could not have legitimately expected the law to stay intact.

So, according to the type of stabilisation clause, the treatment that an investor might legitimately expect can be determined. If the clause is of the traditional type, then the investor might legitimately expect that the legal framework will not be altered, or, if the clause is of the contemporary type, it might expect a renegotiation or rebalancing after a change occurs.[31] However, an investor cannot legitimately expect the laws not to be changed if there is a modern type of clause.[32] As the above-mentioned Tribunal also suggested, any type of contractual stability clause that stipulates a change in the future cannot be utilised to argue for a frozen legal framework. Only the ones which aim to freeze a certain part of the legal and regulatory framework applicable to the investment might be considered as having the effect of creating legitimate expectations outright.

While the adaptation/renegotiation type of stability clauses have been considered a better approach in terms of achieving a flexible and sustainable relationship between host states and investors,[33] they do not seem to be of help within the

---

[27] *Impregilo v Argentina*, Award, para 331.

[28] *AES v Hungary*, Award, para 4.10.

[29] ibid para 9.3.32.

[30] *Electrabel v Hungary*, Award, para 157.

[31] Cameron, *International Energy Investment Law*, 66.

[32] It can expect the change not to be detrimental to the economic bargain struck at the outset, but if it is, then some renegotiation or readjustment is to be anticipated to restore the disturbed equilibrium.

[33] M Mansour and C Nakhle, 'Fiscal Stabilization in Oil and Gas Contracts: Evidence and Implications' (2016) www.oxfordenergy.org/publications/fiscal-stabilization-in-oil-and-gas-contracts-evidence-and-implications/; DE Omukoro, 'Examining Contractual Stability Measures in Light of Emerging Risks: Revisiting the Stabilisation Clause Debate' (2012–15) 24 *Sri Lanka Journal of International Law* 85, 87; M Erkan, *International Energy Investment Law: Stability through Contractual Clauses*

context of legitimate expectations once a dispute arises. A traditional, freezing type of clause would be directly protected under the legitimate expectations principle. Even though the recent stability literature promotes adaptation/renegotiation clauses over classic stability provisions, it should be kept in mind that they will provide a narrower protection within the legitimate expectations framework when a unilateral alteration is undertaken by the host state and the dispute comes before an arbitral tribunal.

(ii) Legal Stability Agreements: Where do they Stand?

Apart from a contractual stabilisation clause embedded in an investment agreement, there is also the Latin American innovation of a stability contract, namely the legal stability agreement (LSA).[34] In its form, this is no more than any other contract between host states and international investors. However, there are certain aspects which render it distinct from an ordinary contractual stabilisation clause. These are the negotiation element and procedural differences.

As discussed in the previous chapter,[35] arbitral tribunals consider contractual undertakings as bearing the highest level of protection under the legitimate expectations principle by virtue of the negotiation element that is included. According to this, a contractual undertaking requires wider protection because the provisions were negotiated with the freewill of both parties and both parties had agreed on the terms in the wake of these lengthy discussions.

However, even though an LSA is an agreement, they are mostly not negotiated between a host state and an investor, but are standard documents with standard terms that apply in the exact same way to all investors who fulfil certain requirements. So, the question is whether the lack of negotiation between parties to an LSA would affect the legitimate expectations created, or otherwise. Should an LSA be considered as having the same effect as a contractual stabilisation clause with respect to the expectations created?

Regarding the procedural differences, Vielleville and Vasani suggest that 'because the authorization to enter into LSAs and, in some the cases, the approval process applicable to specific LSAs arise from legislative acts, LSAs enjoy a stronger

(Kluwer Law International, 2011) 166–77; L Cotula, 'Pushing the Boundaries vs Striking a Balance: The Scope and Interpretation of Stabilization Clauses in Light of the Duke v Peru Award' (2010) 11(1) *Journal of World Investment & Trade* 27, 28; Cameron, *International Energy Investment Law*, 84; A Al Faruque, 'Renegotiation and Adaptation of Petroleum Contracts: The Quest for Equilibrium and Stability' (2008) 9(2) *Journal of World Investment & Trade* 113, 145; P Bernardini, 'Stabilization and Adaptation in Oil and Gas Investments' (2008) 1(1) *Journal of World Energy Law & Business* 98, 102; L Cotula, 'Reconciling Regulatory Stability and Evolution of Environmental Standards in Investment Contracts: Towards a Rethink of Stabilization Clauses' (2008) 1(2) *Journal of World Energy Law & Business* 158, 178.
[34] See ch 3, s IVB.
[35] See ch 5, s IIA.

legal platform than stabilization clauses'.[36] As discussed in chapter three,[37] LSAs might be offered through a legislative act in some states. In such cases there would be an agreement between an investor and the host state body which is later turned into a law. This suggests that there is a twofold endorsement of the stability that the host state offers to the investor. Therefore, an LSA in this form would easily create legitimate expectations to be protected, just like a contractual stabilisation clause.

In addition to this, since LSAs are specifically created to attract investors,[38] the stability expectations of the investors would be reasonable and protected if they had invested relying on that assurance. Consequently, an LSA would create a high level of legitimate expectations to be protected, even though it lacked a negotiation aspect. Their particular use in attracting foreign investors and explicitly providing for stability would create legitimate expectations.

B. Stability Commitments in Domestic Legislation and Legitimate Expectations

The second aspect in which the nexus between stability and legitimate expectations is visible is the situation where an explicit stability provision is provided under the legal and regulatory framework of the host state.

As discussed in chapter three, it is common for host states to offer stability guarantees in their own domestic legislation.[39] The traditional stability literature considers the stability provisions found under a domestic legal framework to be less effective, of limited value and non-binding.[40] Waelde and Ndi commented on this issue in the following way: 'in view of the sensitivity of this issue and the principle of interpreting waivers of sovereignty restrictively, we contend that a stabilization promise made only in legislation is not sufficient to assume an explicit, formal, and binding stabilization agreement'.[41] In a similar vein, Cameron states that

---

[36] DE Vielleville and BS Vasani, 'Sovereignty over Natural Resources versus Rights under Investment Contracts: Which One Prevails?' (2008) 5(2) *Transnational Dispute Management* 1, 14.

[37] See ch 3, s IVB.

[38] A Pereira, 'Legal Stability Contracts in Colombia: An Appropriate Incentive for Investments?' (2013) 12(2) *Richmond Journal of Global Law and Business* 237.

[39] See ch 3, s IVC.

[40] P Daniel and EM Sunley, 'Contractual Assurances of Fiscal Stability' in P Daniel, M Keen and C McPherson (eds), *The Taxation of Petroleum and Minerals: Principles, Problems and Practice* (Routledge, 2010) 406; Maniruzzaman, 'National Laws', 237; K Tienhaara, 'Unilateral Commitments to Investment Protection: Does the Promise of Stability Restrict Environmental Policy Development?' (2006) 17(1) *Yearbook of International Environmental Law* 139, 149; A Al Faruque, 'Stability in Petroleum Contracts: Rhetoric and Reality' (PhD Thesis, University of Dundee, 2005), 199; TW Waelde and G Ndi, 'Fiscal Regime Stability and Issues of State Sovereignty' in J Otto (ed), *Taxation of Mineral Enterprises* (Graham & Trotman, 1995) 240.

[41] TW Waelde and G Ndi, 'Stabilizing International Investment Commitments: International Law versus Contract Interpretation' (1996) 31 *Texas International Law Journal* 215, 240.

'These attempts to grant additional stability by legislative means may indeed act as little more than a comfort factor to the foreign investor',[42] though he also acknowledges that they might be used to bolster the investor's legitimate expectations claim.[43]

It is true that when evaluated as a stand-alone provision, a law or regulation which contains a stability guarantee might not mean anything more than any other legal provision under legislation. It falls under the sovereign authority of a host state and it might then be subject to subsequent alteration.

However, as this book shows, when a stability promise under domestic legislation is evaluated through the lens of the legitimate expectations principle, its effect proves to be much higher than anticipated by the traditional literature. The protection granted by arbitral tribunals within the investment treaty framework proves that a stability commitment under domestic legislation might also provide significant protection to the investor by creating legitimate expectations.

Neuhaus argues that stability provisions granted under national laws have the sole purpose of inducing investment and their main objective is to address the stability of the legal framework only, and therefore they must be honoured by the host state.[44]

Recent renewable energy cases involving Spain, the Czech Republic and Italy provide useful insights regarding the nexus between stability commitments under a domestic legal framework and the legitimate expectations principle.

(i) Spanish Renewables Cases

In order to achieve the EU's renewable energy targets and its own energy strategy interests, Spain introduced a 'special regime' with respect to the renewable energy sector starting from 1997, by enacting Law 54/1997.[45] The main reason for this special regime was to encourage electricity production from renewable sources, especially solar energy.[46] Spain has regulated the generation of electricity from renewable sources mainly by means of laws, royal decree laws, regulations and royal decrees.[47] As a part of this regime, Spain established a system of premiums and fixed tariffs.[48] With this initial framework, Spain provided solar energy

---

[42] Cameron, *International Energy Investment Law*, 63.

[43] ibid.

[44] JE Neuhaus, 'The Enforceability of Legislative Stabilization Clauses' in DD Caron et al (eds), *Practising Virtue: Inside International Arbitration* (Oxford University Press, 2015) 325.

[45] *Masdar Solar & Wind Cooperatief UA v Kingdom of Spain*, Award, ICSID Case No ARB/14/1, 16 May 2018, paras 103–37.

[46] *Antin Infrastructure Services Luxembourg SÁRL and Antin Energia Termosolar BV v Kingdom of Spain*, Award, ICSID Case No ARB/13/31, 15 June 2018, para 77.

[47] T Dromgool and DY Enguix, 'The Fair and Equitable Treatment Standard and the Revocation of Feed in Tariffs – Foreign Renewable Energy Investments in Crisis-Struck Spain' in V Mauerhofer (ed), *Legal Aspects of Sustainable Development: Horizontal and Sectorial Policy Issues* (Springer International Publishing, 2016) 393.

[48] *Charanne v Spain*, Award, para 79.

producers with a feed-in tariff (FiT) for a 25-year period.[49] This was the most generous incentive regime for renewables among all EU Member States.[50]

Royal Decree (RD) 661/2007 was the most significant tool in this incentive scheme since it allowed producers to either 'sell the electricity to the system at a fixed FiT in eurocents per kWh' or 'sell the electricity on the wholesale market and receive a premium in eurocents per kWh'.[51] With RD 661/2007, solar photovoltaic (PV) deployment levels witnessed a spike.[52]

After attracting a high number of foreign investors with those incentives, Spain subsequently introduced certain measures, starting from 2008, due to the tariff deficit caused by the economic crisis and following a reduction in electricity consumption.[53] Those amendments included inter alia a reduction in tariff levels, a cap on the operating hours eligible to FiT payments and a new special tax for electricity generation.[54]

After 2013, Spain abolished the initial framework entirely and replaced it with a new scheme, which it also started to apply to already existing facilities.[55] This led to a situation where the differences between conventional and renewable producers with regard to grid access and dispatch that were created by the 'special regime' were repealed.[56] These legislative alterations affected the profitability of the investments to a large extent. Therefore, numerous cases have been brought before arbitral tribunals under the ECT.[57]

The importance of these Spanish cases is that some tribunals have considered the stability commitments provided under royal decrees to form the basis of legitimate expectations on the part of investors. Some of those provisions and the analyses of the tribunals will be discussed below.

The facts and applicable legal framework of these cases differ from one another, yet certain aspects remain the same. This section will not analyse the facts that led to the decisions in depth and will not provide a holistic analysis of each case. Rather, it will restrict the discussion to the ability of stability assurances granted by the domestic legal framework to create legitimate expectations. Not all of the cases from Spain are discussed here; some have been left out because they do not include such a wide discussion of stability as the ones that are selected.

---

[49] N Lavranos and C Verburg, 'Renewable Energy Investment Disputes: Recent Developments and Implications for Prospective Energy Market Reforms' in MM Roggenkamp and C Banet (eds), *European Energy Law Report XII* (Intersentia, 2018) 68.

[50] C Otero García-Castrillón, 'Spain and Investment Arbitration: The Renewable Energy Explosion' (Centre for International Governance Innovation, 2016) 3.

[51] A Noilhac, 'Renewable Energy Investment Cases against Spain and the Quest for Regulatory Consistency' (2020) 71 *Questions of International Law* 21, 25.

[52] P del Rio and P Mir-Artigues, 'A Cautionary Tale: Spain's Solar PV Investment Bubble' (International Institute for Sustainable Development, 2014) 10.

[53] Otero García-Castrillón, 'Spain and Investment', 4.

[54] del Rio and Mir-Artigues, 'A Cautionary Tale', 16.

[55] Lavranos and Verburg, 'Renewable Energy', 69.

[56] Noilhac, 'Renewable Energy Investment Cases', 25.

[57] As of December 2020, 47 cases have been brought against Spain under the ECT according to the list provided in www.energychartertreaty.org/cases/list-of-cases/.

In the *Masdar* case, there were two royal decrees which included stability commitments according to the analysis of the Tribunal: RD 1614/2010[58] and RD 661/2007.[59] It was argued that 'The State guaranteed the stability of the benefits, if the investors fulfilled a certain number of conditions, both procedural and substantial, during a certain window of time'.[60]

The Tribunal found that the claimant had placed particular reliance on the stabilisation clauses provided under the general regulations while making its investment.[61]

The Tribunal here undertook a twofold analysis regarding the creation of legitimate expectations. It indicated that there are two main schools of thought regarding the legitimate expectations principle. The first considers that a commitment based on a general legal framework might be sufficient to create legitimate expectations, whereas the second argues that there must be a specific commitment.[62] The Tribunal then concluded that, from the perspective of the first school of thought, the stabilisation provisions found under the royal decrees were sufficient to create legitimate expectations worthy of protection.[63] From the second viewpoint, the Tribunal also argued that there were sufficient specific commitments in addition to the stabilisation provision under RD 661/2007 to satisfy the requirements of this school.[64]

So, the Tribunal acknowledged that a stability commitment granted under a royal decree is a basis for legitimate expectations and concluded that Spain was in breach of the FET obligations under the ECT.

---

[58] *Masdar v Spain*, Award, para 502. Article 4 of RD1614/2010 reads: 'For solar thermoelectric technology facilities that fall under Royal Decree 661/2007 of 25 May, revisions of tariffs, premiums and upper and lower limits referred to in article 44.3 of the aforementioned Royal Decree, shall not affect facilities registered definitively in the Administrative Registry of production facilities entitled to the special regime that is maintained by the Directorate General for Energy and Mining Policy as of 7 May 2009, nor those that were to have been registered in the Remuneration Preassignment Registry under the fourth transitional provision of Royal Decree-Law 6/2009 of 30 April, and that meet the obligation envisaged in its article 4.8, extended until 31 December 2013 for those facilities associated to phase 4 envisaged in the Agreement of the Council of Ministers of 13 November 2009.'

[59] *Masdar v Spain*. Award, para 500.
Article 44(3) of RD661/2007: 'During the year 2010, on sight of the results of the monitoring reports on the degree of fulfilment of the Renewable Energies Plan (PER) 2005–2010, and of the Energy Efficiency and Savings Strategy in Spain (E4), together with such new targets as may be included in the subsequent Renewable Energies Plan 2011–2020, there shall be a review of the tariffs, premiums, supplements and lower and upper limits defined in this Royal Decree with regard to the costs associated with each of these technologies, the degree of participation of the special regime in covering the demand and its impact upon the technical and economic management of the system, and a reasonable rate of profitability shall always be guaranteed with reference to the cost of money in the capital markets. Subsequently a further review shall be performed every four years, maintaining the same criteria as previously. The revisions to the regulated tariff and the upper and lower limits indicated in this paragraph shall not affect facilities for which the deed of commissioning shall have been granted prior to 1 January of the second year following the year in which the revision shall have been performed.'

[60] ibid para 512.
[61] ibid paras 500–03.
[62] ibid para 490.
[63] ibid para 503.
[64] ibid para 521.

The *Antin* Tribunal also considered the legal and economic regime established by RD 661/2007 to be a stability commitment emplaced to attract investment in the renewables sector.[65] The Tribunal supported its argument by relying on further statements included in government reports, press releases and presentations which emphasised the stability objective of RD 661/2007.[66] Alongside this, as in the *Masdar* award, certain provisions of RD 1614/2010 were also considered to constitute a stability guarantee by the *Antin* Tribunal.[67] In addition to the explicit stability promises under the provisions of royal decrees, the Tribunal assessed their general objectives and found that they were aimed at stabilising the applicable regime. The Tribunal referred to the preambles of RD 661/2007 and RD 1614/2010, and concluded that they expressly provided for the stability of the sector.[68] The Tribunal concluded:

> In the present case, the preamble of the royal decrees enacted by the Spanish Government – specifically RD 661/2007 and RD 1614/2010 – reflect the Respondent's intention to provide for and guarantee the stability of the legal and economic regime applicable to RE projects.[69]

The *Novenergia* case asserted a similar approach with regard to the royal decrees. After stating that the claimant had made its investment in reliance on the framework provided by RD 661/2007, the Tribunal added that 'The commitment from the Kingdom of Spain could not have been clearer'.[70] With respect to Spain's argument about the alleged failure of the investor to conduct an adequate due diligence, the Tribunal stated that '... also because RD 661/2007 was so adamantly clear that its understanding by common readers did not require a particularly sophisticated analysis'.[71] Again, this Tribunal also concluded that RD 661/2007 contained a stability guarantee for the FiT, and therefore the investor's expectations were legitimate.[72]

In the *NextEra*[73] case, the Tribunal stated that the investor cannot rely on a regulatory framework that is based on a piece of legislation that might be subject to change.[74] Then, it continues with discussing the claimant's arguments separately and finds that they do not generate legitimate expectations individually.[75] The Tribunal adds that 'While none of these claims individually constitute a basis for Claimants' legitimate expectations claim, they do provide context for that claim'.[76]

---

[65] *Antin v Spain*, Award, para 540.
[66] ibid para 543.
[67] ibid para 546.
[68] ibid paras 543–46.
[69] ibid para 548.
[70] *Novenergia v Spain*, Award, para 667.
[71] ibid para 679.
[72] ibid para 681.
[73] *NextEra Energy Global Holdings BV and NextEra Energy Spain Holdings BV v Kingdom of Spain*, Decision on Jurisdiction, Liability and Quantum Principles, ICSID Case No ARB/14/11, 12 March 2019.
[74] ibid para 584.
[75] ibid paras 585–86.
[76] ibid para 587.

The Tribunal stressed that the claimant could not have expected the freezing of the regime created by RD 661/2007, but it came to the conclusion, by taking surrounding circumstances into account as well, that the investor 'had a legitimate expectation that the regulatory regime in RD 661/2007 would not be changed in a way that would undermine the security and viability of their investment'.[77]

The most important evidence that created legitimate expectations according to the Tribunal was the statements made by Spanish officials to the investor.[78] In particular, there were letters from government officials to the investor which emphasised that the new framework would continue providing stability and legal security to the investments.[79] With regard to these letters, a significant comment was made by the Tribunal: 'The Tribunal does not see these as "commitments" by Spain, but "legitimate expectations" can exist in the absence of actual formal commitments.'[80] Since these letters mentioned 'guarantees' and 'preserving' the conditions, the Tribunal concluded, also by taking the wider context into consideration, that the investor could have had legitimate expectations and that Spain violated these expectations and the FET standard under the ECT.[81]

The Tribunal in *9Ren*[82] followed the UNCTAD view that legitimate expectations might be generated by general rules set forth to attract foreign investors, and that they do not have to be specifically addressed to a known investor or consider RD 661/2007 as such.[83] It further asserted that:

> There is no doubt that an enforceable 'legitimate expectation' requires a clear and specific commitment, but in the view of this Tribunal there is no reason in principle why such a commitment of the requisite clarity and specificity cannot be made in the regulation itself where (as here) such a commitment is made for the purpose of inducing investment, which succeeded in attracting the Claimant's investment and once made resulted in losses to the Claimant.[84]

So, after accepting RD 661/2007 as a source that might create legitimate expectations, the Tribunal assessed its content and concluded that it included a 'regulatory guarantee of price stability'.[85] The Tribunal repeatedly made it clear in several points under the award that RD 661/2007 included a stabilisation guarantee. It further concluded that the investor had reasonable and legitimate expectations of tariff stability, but that Spain's unilateral actions and alterations had violated the FET requirement under the ECT.[86]

---

[77] ibid para 596.
[78] ibid para 590.
[79] ibid para 592.
[80] ibid.
[81] ibid para 596–601.
[82] *9REN Holding Sarl v Kingdom of Spain*, Award, ICSID Case No ARB/15/15, 31 May 2019.
[83] ibid para 294.
[84] ibid para 295.
[85] ibid para 311.
[86] ibid paras 307–11.

The *SolEs*[87] Tribunal started its analysis with the features of PV plants and emphasised that they cannot compete with conventional generators without receiving some kind of subsidy or incentive.[88] The Tribunal also mentioned their capital-intensive character and the long recovery duration of the spent capital.[89] The Tribunal made these assessments in order to show that Spain was aware of these characteristics when it designed the 'special regime'.

Since the claimant in this case did not claim that Spain had violated a stability obligation separate from the FET requirement, the Tribunal did not undertake an analysis as to whether this legal framework included a stabilisation provision.[90] What the Tribunal did instead was to refer to the *Eiser* Tribunal's assessment about the FET standard embracing a stability requirement.[91] Relying on this aspect, the Tribunal found a breach of the legitimate expectations of the investor and thus the FET standard under the ECT.[92]

The *InfraRed*[93] case was concluded immediately after the *SolEs* case. The *InfraRed* case was also related to legitimate expectations and stability issues. The Tribunal stated that 'a legitimate expectation of stability (ie immutability) can only arise in the presence of a specific commitment tendered directly to the investor or industry sector at issue'.[94] After setting the threshold, it moved on to analyse whether there was a specific commitment from Spain to the investors.

Here, the *InfraRed* Tribunal started its analysis with the previous awards, including *Charanne, Isolux, Eiser* and *Novenergia*. After assessing these other awards, the Tribunal concluded that there was no promise from Spain to 'freeze' its laws, regulations and rules related to the 'Original Regulatory Framework'.[95] However, there were certain documents and actions which could be considered as specific commitments of stability, such as the exchange of letters of waiver, the enactment of RD 1614/2010 and some resolutions directed at the investors in the sector.[96]

The *InfraRed* Tribunal mentions that press releases from several government/administrative bodies of Spain about certain actions taken by it explicitly include references to a guarantee of stability.[97] It also used the public remarks of Spain's Secretary of State for Energy and later Spain's Minister of Energy on this matter as reinforcing evidence on the existence of specific guarantees.[98] Taking these

---

[87] *SolEs Badajoz GmbH v Kingdom of Spain*, Award, ICSID Case No ARB/15/38, 31 July 2019.
[88] ibid para 415.
[89] ibid.
[90] ibid para 314.
[91] ibid para 315.
[92] ibid para 462.
[93] *InfraRed Environmental Infrastructure GP Limited and others v Kingdom of Spain*, Award, ICSID Case No ARB/14/12, 2 August 2019.
[94] ibid para 366.
[95] ibid para 406.
[96] ibid para 409.
[97] ibid para 424.
[98] ibid para 426.

specific commitments for stability into account, the Tribunal found that Spain had breached its FET obligation under the ECT.[99]

An award delivered after this was from the *OperaFund*[100] case, where the Tribunal expressed that there was a stabilisation assurance under Article 44(3) of RD 661/2007 and added that 'Indeed, it is hard to imagine a more explicit stabilization assurance than the one mentioned in Article 44(3)' in a split decision.[101] The Tribunal made an interesting analysis, while acknowledging the State's right to regulate:

> Taken in this context, Article 44(3) of RD 661/2007 contained an express stability commitment that served its purpose of inducing investment in part by shielding investors in Claimants' position from legislative or regulatory changes (including the ones complained of in this matter). The Tribunal, thus, respects the legislative authority of the Respondent State by giving effect to each of the terms in Article 44(3) of RD 661/2007, including its assurance that 'revisions ... shall not affect facilities for which the functioning certificate had been granted[.]' The Claimants must have been able to rely on the measures aimed at encouraging the use of renewable and other new technologies and at inducing and protecting their investment.[102]

Here, the Tribunal states that it concedes Spain's right to regulate and it is exactly for this reason that the provisions of a royal decree produced by that state should be taken into account. According to that royal decree, Spain promised the stability of the legal framework and this should be respected.

The *OperaFund* Tribunal relied largely on the previous awards from the *Novenergia* and *Antin* cases, and found a breach of the legitimate expectations of the investor, which led to the violation of the FET standard under the ECT.[103]

One of the last awards of 2019 in relation to these Spanish cases was the *Stadtwerke*[104] case, where the majority of the Tribunal rejected treaty violation claims of the investors. Unlike the previous awards discussed above, the majority in this case did not see a stabilisation provision under Article 44(3) of RD 661/2007.[105] In addition to this, the Tribunal also did not attach any weight to the representations by certain Spanish agencies, such as CNE and InvestInSpain, arguing that these institutions did not have any authority to express binding stability commitments on behalf of Spain.[106]

The majority made the following comment with regard to these representations:

> It is clear that an investor cannot reasonably rely on PowerPoint presentations from Spanish agencies with no regulatory powers to base their expectations in relation to the

---

[99] ibid para 455.
[100] *OperaFund Eco-Invest SICAV PLC and Schwab Holding AG v Kingdom of Spain*, Award, ICSID Case No ARB/15/36, 6 September 2019.
[101] ibid para 485.
[102] ibid.
[103] ibid para 490.
[104] *Stadtwerke München GmbH, RWE Innogy GmbH, and others v Kingdom of Spain*, Award, ICSID Case No ARB/15/1, 2 December 2019.
[105] ibid para 282.
[106] ibid para 285–86.

legal regime for investments in Spain. Legitimate expectations must be grounded in the law and not based upon promotional literature about what the law says.[107]

The majority rejected many points raised by the claimant in relation to the stabilisation issue and concluded that there was no stability guarantee, and that the expectations of the investor were not reasonable or legitimate.[108]

Unlike many of the tribunals discussed above, the *Stadtwerke* majority applied a very strict and narrow understanding of the legitimate expectations and stability principles. Kaj Hober, a member of the Tribunal, did not agree with the majority's decision with regard to the FET standard and dissented.[109] Hober states that a legitimate expectation does not have to be based on a guarantee or a commitment, but they arise from the legal and regulatory framework prevalent in a host state and also from the statements and acts of that state or its representatives.[110] He refers to the statements and representations made by different government bodies of Spain which all explain and clarify the stability of the regime created under RD 661/2007.[111] It can be seen from his analysis that Hober prefers to align with the reasoning in previous awards which found a breach of legitimate expectations.

The year 2020 also saw new Spanish awards, some of which are discussed below.[112] The first award of 2020 to be analysed here is the split *Watkins*[113] case, where the majority found a breach of legitimate expectations of the investor and the FET provision under the ECT.[114] In the reasoning used to reach this conclusion, the Tribunal considered Article 44(3) of RD 661/2007 to be an explicit stabilisation commitment.[115] It added that Spain was not under any obligation to offer this stability commitment, but did so in order to attract investments, and the investor actually relied on this assurance.[116]

The Tribunal also took into account several representations (promotion materials) made by different government bodies while assessing the existence of legitimate expectations.[117] Since there was an explicit stability assurance and other representations indicating this stability aspect, investors had legitimate expectations to envisage the continuance of the conditions applicable to them. When these were altered, investors' legitimate expectations were violated. The route that the *Watkins* Tribunal followed was also similar to many previous ones.

---

[107] ibid para 287.

[108] ibid para 308.

[109] *Stadtwerke München GmbH, RWE Innogy GmbH, and others v Kingdom of Spain*, Dissenting Opinion of Professor Kaj Hober, ICSID Case No ARB/15/1, 2 December 2019.

[110] ibid para 10.

[111] ibid para 12.

[112] Even though the *Hydro* case also includes a legitimate expectations discussion, it will not be covered here since its factual background is different from the ones discussed here. For details of that case, see *Hydro Energy 1 Sàrl and Hydroxana Sweden AB v Kingdom of Spain*, Decision on Jurisdiction, Liability and Directions on Quantum, ICSID Case No ARB/15/42, 9 March 2020.

[113] *Watkins Holdings Sàrl and others v Kingdom of Spain*, Award, ICSID Case No ARB/15/44, 21 January 2020.

[114] ibid para 538.

[115] ibid para 526.

[116] ibid para 528.

[117] ibid para 532.

The *PV Investors*[118] case was another one where the Tribunal did not agree with the claimant's argument that Article 44(3) of RD 661/2007 included a stabilisation provision.[119] A small but relevant part of the Tribunal's analysis is as follows:

> At the outset, it must be recalled that, as an act of general regulation, RD 661/2007 was subject to the power of the legislative bodies of Spain to change the applicable rules according to constitutional procedures and principles governing law-making. It is correct that Article 44.3 states that certain revisions that may occur in the future under that decree would not affect existing installations. However, that mere statement in and of itself does not make of Article 44.3 a stabilization commitment according to which the State guaranteed that future legislative or regulatory change would not affect the investment. Moreover, Article 44.3 cannot be read in isolation but must be viewed in the context of the entirety of the Spanish regulatory framework. This context includes a number of important elements.[120]

As can be seen here, the Tribunal acknowledged that Article 44(3) indeed included a provision about the future changes not affecting the existing installations. Yet, it did not consider this to be a stability promise. According to the Tribunal, the underlying reason for this was that there was an older version of RD 661/2007, ie RD 463/2004, which included a similar provision to Article 44(3), yet Spain was able to introduce alterations to that prior framework without having any issues.[121] Also, the Tribunal considered that the representations by the Spanish government or the campaigns launched to attract foreign investments could not be seen as assurances that the incentives regime under RD 661/2007 would not be altered.[122]

Even though the arbitrators are totally different in these two cases and the outcomes are also different, the approaches of the *PV Investors* Tribunal and the *Stadtwerke* Tribunal to the stabilisation provision and the representation issues are strikingly similar. One of the reasons why they both did not consider Article 44(3) of RD 661/2007 to constitute a stabilisation promise is that there was a similar provision in the previous royal decree and the Spanish government could still change it. Without delving into the issue as to whether Article 44(3) is actually a stabilisation provision or not, it should be stated that the method employed by these two tribunals in delineating stabilisation provisions seems flawed: just because a government is able to alter a legal document does not and cannot define its essence.

As discussed in chapter three, a stability assurance might be given under the legal framework of a host state. The effect and the weight that the investment arbitration tribunal will attribute to that domestic legal provision in the event of a dispute might, of course, change. The host state, as a sovereign entity, can alter its laws, but this does not change the fact that the actual provision in the legal

---

[118] *The PV Investors v Kingdom of Spain*, Final Award, PCA Case No 2012-14, 28 February 2020.
[119] ibid para 600.
[120] ibid para 601.
[121] ibid para 602.
[122] ibid, paras 614–15.

document might still be a stabilisation provision. Of course, the tribunals do not solely rely on this argument when deciding there is no stability promise, but the flaw restricted to this approach should be noted as well.

The claimant in the *Eiser* case had also argued prior to the cases above that Article 44(3) of RD 661/2007 included a stabilisation clause upon which it had relied when making its investment.[123] However, the Tribunal stated that 'the Tribunal does not accept Claimants' contention that RD 661/2007 gave them immutable economic rights that could not be altered by changes in the regulatory regime'.[124] Even though the *Eiser* Tribunal did not acknowledge RD 661/2007 as a stability guarantee, it found a breach of the investor's legitimate expectations based on the general requirement of stability under the ECT.[125]

The *Foresight v Spain* case was rendered in November 2018[126] and followed a similar line of reasoning as in the *Eiser* case. When assessing RD 661/2007, it quoted the *Eiser* Tribunal's approach and concluded that there was no specific stability assurance under RD 661/2007.[127] However, the Tribunal found a breach of legitimate expectations of the investor due to a fundamental change in the regulatory framework.[128] According to the Tribunal, 'the Claimants had a legitimate expectation that the regulatory framework would not be fundamentally and abruptly altered so as to deprive investors of a significant part of their projected revenues'.[129] Referring to earlier awards, the Tribunal reiterated that the changes occurred were radical and unexpected, and led to a totally different regulatory approach.[130] One of those fundamental changes, according to the Tribunal, was the replacement of the FiT regime set forth in RD 661/2007 with a new one.[131] Even though the Tribunal referred to this as 'guaranteed fixed remuneration',[132] it did not consider this assurance to be a specific stability guarantee as other tribunals had done.

The first award of the Spanish renewables arbitration wave, the split *Charanne* award, also did not acknowledge RD 661/2007 as a 'specific commitment'. Even though this case was limited only to the modifications up to 2010 and did not include the more significant changes after 2013, its analysis of royal decrees is of relevance. The Tribunal argued that although RD 661/2007 was directed towards a limited group of investors, it was not directed specifically to each investor;

---

[123] *Eiser v Spain*, Award, para 357.
[124] ibid para 363.
[125] See s III for a detailed discussion on this issue.
[126] *Foresight Luxembourg Solar 1 SÁRL, Foresight Luxembourg Solar 2 SÁRL, Greentech Energy System A/S, GWM Renewable Energy I SpA and GWM Renewable Energy II SpA v The Kingdom of Spain*, Final Award, SCC Case No 2015/150, 14 November 2018.
[127] ibid para 366.
[128] ibid para 377.
[129] ibid para 388.
[130] ibid para 397.
[131] ibid para 396.
[132] ibid para 396.

therefore, it could not create legitimate expectations.[133] Professor Tawil, however, did not agree with the majority with respect to the effect of RD 661/2007. In his dissent, he expressly argued that, 'pursuant to the declarations under RD 661/07 and 1578/08, the claimants could have "objectively" believed the tariff regime established under each law would remain unaltered'.[134] His analysis regarding the stabilising effect of these decrees has been approved by a number of tribunals in subsequent cases on renewable energy subsidies.

One controversial point in the *Charanne* award was that the Tribunal acknowledged that, based on the good faith principle, 'a State cannot induce an investor to make an investment, hereby generating legitimate expectations, to later ignore the commitments that had generated such expectations'.[135] However, after acknowledging this, the Tribunal insisted on the presence of a specific commitment to find the existence of legitimate expectations, even though this inducement could have been made by legislation or could have been deduced from the regulations and corresponding host state actions.[136]

A noteworthy observation regarding the use of legislative stability commitments as the basis of legitimate expectations is that although the tribunals consider them capable of creating legitimate expectations, they do not rely solely on those guarantees when looking for a breach of the FET. Rather, they rely on all available sources, such as representations, reports and regulations, cumulatively.[137] It is also apparent that while the main stability promise arises from these royal decrees, they are also emphasised and strengthened by reiterations in other sources. It is safe to state that the principal source of legitimate expectations in these cases is the stabilisation provision found under the legal framework regulating the sector. However, in practice, the tribunals have considered the legal framework as a whole and have included other dimensions in their analyses as well.

Another significant observation is that when the tribunals deal with a stability commitment found under the general legal framework, they put more emphasis on the investor's reliance on that stability assurance. Unlike contractual stabilisation clauses, a stability commitment in this form requires more scrutiny from the reliance aspect. Even though there is an express stabilisation provision, reliance on the said assurance becomes essential since it has been granted unilaterally by the host state and is not a product of a negotiation between the parties. An investor who claims a breach of its legitimate expectations arising from a stability commitment under the domestic legal framework must be able to establish its reliance on the said promise clearly.

---

[133] *Charanne v Spain*, Award, para 493.
[134] *Charanne v Spain*, Dissenting Opinion of Tawil, para 6 (footnote omitted).
[135] *Charanne v Spain*, Award, para 486.
[136] T Restrepo, 'Modification of Renewable Energy Support Schemes under the Energy Charter Treaty: Eiser and Charanne in the Context of Climate Change' (2017) 8(1) *Goettingen Journal of International Law* 101, 124–25.
[137] See ch 5, s V.

(ii) The Czech Republic Renewables Cases

The historical background of the Czech cases is similar to that of the Spanish cases. The Czech Republic also first introduced a favourable legal regime for investments in the renewable energy sector, then altered the legal framework regulating those investments and repealed certain incentives due to an unexpected surge in solar power investment. The incentive regime dates back to 1992, when the renewable energy production facilities were exempted from income tax for the following five calendar years after they started to operate.[138] Several subsequent acts, decrees, regulations and public notices were introduced in the following years to enhance and clarify the legal regime on renewable energy.

Up until 2009, there was no significant volume of installed PV plants. However, when the price of PV panels started to decrease, installations accelerated and reached a point where the Czech government found it unfeasible to proceed with the conditions then being offered by its legislative and regulatory framework.[139] Thus, starting from 2010, numerous amendments were made in which some incentives were removed and additional taxes were introduced.[140]

Seven investment treaty arbitrations over these reforms in the solar energy sector were brought against the Czech Republic as of August 2020, of which two had already been concluded on behalf of the Czech Republic and one against. *JSW Solar* was the first award of these investment treaty cases to be made publicly available, and it was followed by the *Antaris* award in May 2018. Both awards were split decisions, with arbitrator Gary Born dissenting. Again, the facts and surrounding circumstances will not be discussed in this section; only the stability commitment and its appraisal by the tribunals will be analysed. A partial award was delivered in December 2017 in the *Natland v Czech Republic* case on similar matters; however, this award still remains unpublished as of August 2020. According to the Investment Arbitration Reporter's report, the Tribunal found a breach of the FET standard based on a stabilisation provision in the legislative framework.[141]

In the *JSW Solar* case, the claimant argued that there was an explicit stabilisation clause under section 6(1)[142] of Act 180 (Act on Promotion) that gave rise

---

[138] *Antaris v Czech*, Award, para 81.

[139] ibid para 120–47.

[140] *JSW Solar v Czech*, Award, para 47–52.

[141] D Charlotin, 'Natland v Czech Republic (Part 2 of 2): On the Merits, Tribunal Finds Stabilisation Commitment in Czech Legislation and Breach of that Commitment with Introduction of Solar Levy' (2018) www.iareporter.com/articles/natland-v-czech-republic-part-2-of-2-on-the-merits-tribunal-finds-stabilisation-commitment-in-czech-legislation-and-breach-of-that-commitment-with-introduction-of-solar-levy/.

[142] *JSW Solar v Czech*, Award, para 23. 'Article 6 of Act 180: Amounts of Prices for Electricity from Renewable Sources and Amounts of Green Bonuses: (1) The Office sets, one calendar year in advance, the purchasing prices for electricity from Renewable Sources (the 'Purchasing Prices'), separately for individual kinds of Renewable Sources, and sets green bonuses, so that a) the conditions are created for the achievement of the indicative target so that the share of electricity produced from Renewable Sources accounts for 8% of gross electricity consumption in 2010 and b) for facilities commissioned 1. after the effective date of this Act, there is attained, with the Support consisting of the Purchasing Prices,

to legitimate expectations and which was subsequently breached by the Czech Republic's unilateral measures.[143] Conversely, the respondent argued that Act 180 did not contain any kind of stabilisation provision.[144] The Tribunal therefore noted that 'The dispute is principally on whether the relevant framework contains a stabilization commitment giving rise to legitimate expectations as claimed by the Claimants.'[145] The issue here, as the majority also stated, was not the effect of a stability commitment, but rather the determination of the existence of such a guarantee. The majority, after reviewing section 6(1) of Act 180, concluded that there was no separate stability guarantee and hence no breach of legitimate expectations.[146]

However, arbitrator Gary Born, in a powerful dissent, challenged the majority's decision and stated that

> the plain language and obvious purposes of Section 6(1) of the Act leave no serious doubt that the Claimants were guaranteed a minimum level of FiTs over a specified statutory period (first 15, later 20, years) for electricity produced by the renewable energy sources that they constructed in the Czech Republic.[147]

According to Born, this article was an explicit stabilisation provision as the claimants claimed and section 6(1)(b)(2) provided a 'fundamentally important guarantee of long-term price stability'.[148]

While the majority argued that the article in question only guaranteed an FiT which 'would be set at a level ensuring a 15 year payback of capital expenses and a return on investment or profit of at least 7 per cent per year over 15 years',[149] dissenting Born and the Claimant argued that it was a stabilisation guarantee which fixes the FiT for at least 15 years at a predetermined price level.[150]

Although a thorough literal analysis of the stability commitment in question is beyond the scope of this book, there is one aspect which relates this issue to the book's main argument. As can be seen from the above approaches, both views accept that there was a guarantee under Act 180 which must have been maintained.

---

a fifteen year payback period on capital expenditures, provided technical and economic parameters are met, such parameters consisting of, in particular, cost per unit of installed capacity, exploitation efficiency of the primary energy content in the Renewable Source, and the period of use of the facility, such parameters being stipulated in an implementing legal regulation, 2. after the effective date of this Act, the amount of revenues per unit of electricity from Renewable Sources, assuming Support in the form of Purchasing Prices, is maintained as the minimum [amount of revenues], for a period of 15 years from the commissioning year of the facility, taking into account the industrial producer price index; the commissioning of a facility is also deemed to include cases involving the completion of a rebuild of the technological part of existing equipment, a change of fuel, or the completion of modernization that raises the technical and ecological standard of an existing facility ...'

[143] ibid para 270.
[144] ibid para 312.
[145] ibid para 270.
[146] ibid para 413.
[147] *JSW Solar v Czech*, Gary Born, para 18.
[148] ibid para 29.
[149] *JSW Solar v Czech*, Award, para 368.
[150] *JSW Solar v Czech*, Gary Born, para 56.

A breach of that stability guarantee would have upset the legitimate expectations of the investor. The majority interpreted Act 180 as including a guarantee of a 15-year payback of capital expenses and an annual return on investment of at least seven per cent over 15 years.[151] On the other hand, Born construed that there was a fixed FiT guarantee for 15 years. The dispute arose out of the fact that a seven per cent return on investment and the fixed FiT would deliver different profits.

What is evident from these approaches is that they both acknowledge the existence of a stability guarantee, albeit to a different extent. The majority did not find a breach of legitimate expectations on the grounds that the guarantees provided under Act 180 were still being met. Had there been a measure that impaired the 15-year payback and seven per cent return, then the majority would also have found a breach of legitimate expectations. This is clear from the majority's statement that 'In the circumstances, as the guarantees given by the Czech Republic continue to be complied with in respect of the Claimants, there can be no breach of the Claimants' legitimate expectations'.[152]

Even though the Tribunal could not find a breach in the *JSW Solar* case, what can be deduced from it is that it acknowledged in principle that a stabilisation provision found under domestic legislation might create legitimate expectations to be protected in the event of a breach by the host state. The only issue here was that the majority was not convinced about the extent of the stability guarantee provided. While the award seems to be a decision against the broad application of the legitimate expectations principle at the outset, it inherently reinforces the position taken by several other tribunals, scholars and this book.

The background and facts of the *Antaris* case were similar to the ones in the *JSW Solar* case. While setting out the principles that the Tribunal would follow, the majority stated that '(4) An expectation may arise from what are construed as specific guarantees in legislation'.[153] However, it later narrowed down this statement by adding:

(6) Provisions of general legislation applicable to a plurality of persons or a category of persons, do not create legitimate expectations that there will be no change in the law; and given the State's regulatory powers, in order to rely on legitimate expectations the investor should inquire in advance regarding the prospects of a change in the regulatory framework in light of the then prevailing or reasonably to be expected changes in the economic and social conditions of the host State.[154]

The main consideration of the majority in this case was the time of the investment. By Act 137/2010, which came into force on 20 May 2010, some of the incentives in the FiT regime were removed and the rule that the FiT could not be decreased by more than 5 per cent per year was abolished.[155] However, this was only applicable

---

[151] *JSW Solar v Czech*, Award, para 413.
[152] ibid para 416.
[153] *Antaris v Czech*, Award, para 360.
[154] ibid.
[155] ibid para 94.

to the solar plants connected to the grid after 2011. The investor's four plants in this dispute were constructed and commissioned after May 2010, but before 2011.[156] According to the Czech government,

> the main reason for postponing abolition of the 5 per cent limit until 2011 was to avoid harming projects that were already in progress (but could not be completed in 2009) – not to give licence for even more investors (like the Claimants) to pile in.[157]

According to the Tribunal, the claimant knew that there was a pressing problem arising from the surge in solar power investment and that the market it was entering, in effect, was a bubble.[158] Even though the investor knew all these issues regarding the solar market, it nevertheless invested in the Czech Republic to take advantage of the incentives regime before it was reduced, starting from 2011.[159] The majority stated that it was clear from mid-2010 that the Czech government could introduce taxation measures to cope with the solar boom.[160]

Taking all these circumstances into account, the Tribunal concluded that the investor 'was essentially an opportunistic investor who saw a window of opportunity and who was aware, or should have been aware, that dealing with the solar boom was a fast-moving and controversial political issue'.[161] It also added that the investment protection regime is not designed to shield this kind of opportunistic investor who takes advantage of laws which it knows are in a state of flux.[162]

Even though the Tribunal considered a promise under domestic legislation as having a significant effect under international law and, in contrast to the *JSW Solar* case, construed the Czech Republic's incentive regime as including a stability promise regarding the FiT to be maintained for a 15-year period,[163] it gave more weight to the claimant's knowledge of the ongoing crisis and therefore rejected its claims.

The Tribunal accepted in theory that a stability provision under domestic legislation might create legitimate expectations to be protected under the FET standard. It also went further and stated that

> to establish a legitimate expectation, there is no requirement that there be an express stabilisation provision, and that it is sufficient for the Claimants to establish an express or implied promise giving rise to a legitimate and reasonable expectation of stability.[164]

However, the Tribunal did not find a breach based on this stability promise by arguing that the investor should have expected a change in these guarantees by mid-2010. The Tribunal did not explicitly spell it out, but its main reason for

---

[156] ibid para 95.
[157] ibid para 417.
[158] ibid paras 433–34.
[159] ibid para 418.
[160] ibid para 425.
[161] ibid para 431.
[162] ibid para 435.
[163] ibid para 366.
[164] ibid para 399.

rejecting the case was the lack of reasonableness in the investor's reliance on the said assurance. There was a stability promise under domestic legislation and it could have created legitimate expectations for the investor had it reasonably relied on that assurance when making its investment. While defining the investor as 'opportunistic', the Tribunal implied that its investment was not the outcome of a reasonable reliance on the assurance in question but rather it was a 'speculative hope', as the Respondent suggested.[165]

Gary Born again cast a dissenting vote in this case, similar to his *JSW Solar* dissent, and argued that the claimant could not have anticipated a reduction in the guaranteed FiTs for solar plants commissioned before 1 January 2011.[166] According to Born, section 6 of Act 180 included an explicit stability provision which must have been upheld by the Czech Republic.[167] He concluded that since there was an explicit stability provision under domestic legislation, repealing that guarantee led to the impairment of the legitimate expectations of the investor and consequently to the violation of the FET standard.[168]

These cases again prove that there is no discussion on whether a stability provision under the general legislative framework could generate legitimate expectations. The answer is affirmative. Just like the Spanish cases, the Czech cases (to date) confirm that a stability provision under domestic legislation might create legitimate expectations that must be protected. As already mentioned in the previous section, when the stability provision is not a contractual one, tribunals tend to give more weight to the reasonable reliance aspect in their analyses. This was also the outcome in the *Antaris* case. In order to be protected under the legitimate expectations principle, not only must there be a stability provision under the legislative framework, but the investor must also be able to prove that it had reasonably relied on that assurance while making its investment.

(iii) Italian Renewables Cases

Having a similar background to the Czech Republic and Spanish cases, there are now seven public Italian awards that deal with renewable energy arbitrations in Italy.[169]

---

[165] ibid para 435.
[166] *Antaris v Czech*, Gary Born, para 71.
[167] ibid para 12.
[168] ibid para 29.
[169] *ESPF Beteiligungs GmbH, ESPF Nr 2 Austria Beteiligungs GmbH, and InfraClass Energie 5 GmbH & Co KG v Italian Republic*, Award, ICSID Case No ARB/16/5, 14 September 2020; *Eskosol S.p.A. in liquidazione v Italian Republic*, Award, ICSID Case No ARB/15/50, 4 September 2020; *Sun Reserve Luxco Holdings Sàrl, Sun Reserve Luxco Holdings II Sàrl and Sun Reserve Luxco Holdings III Sàrl v The Italian Republic*, Final Award, SCC Case No 132/2016, 25 March 2020; *Belenergia SA v Italian Republic*, Award, ICSID Case No ARB/15/40, 6 August 2019; *CEF Energia BV v The Italian Republic*, Award, SCC Case No V2015/158, 16 January 2019; *Greentech Energy Systems A/S, NovEnergia II Energy & Environment (SCA) SICAR, and NovEnergia II Italian Portfolio SA v The Italian Republic*, Award, SCC Case No V2015/095, 23 December 2018; *Blusun v Italy*, Award.

In the 1980s, Italy, similar to Spain and the Czech Republic, began to promote and encourage renewable energy development.[170] In 1991, Italy simplified the authorisation procedure for renewable energy production with Law No 9[171] and established the first fixed FiT in 1992 with regulation CIP 6/92.[172] In 1999, Italy enacted Legislative Decree No 79 (the Bersani Decree), which further encouraged electricity production from renewable sources by prioritising their access to the country's electricity grid.[173]

In order to meet the targets set forth by a number of EU Directives, in 2003 Italy enacted Legislative Decree No 387 to further promote renewable energy sources and encourage investments therein.[174] Then, from 2005 to 2012, Italy enacted a series of incentive schemes for PV plants which are referred to as the *Conto Energia* Decrees.[175] As stated in the *Greentech v Italy* award 'Each of the Conto Energia decrees expressly provided that the tariff premiums, once granted, would be paid for a twenty-year period commencing from the date of a PV plant's entry into operation'.[176] However, starting from 2012, Italy implemented a series of measures which detrimentally affected the investments made.[177] In particular, the measures introduced by Law Decree No 91/2014 (the Spalma-incentivi Decree) were at the centre of the arguments presented in these cases.

Without delving further into the facts of the cases, I will consider the legitimate expectations analyses of the tribunals. The *CEF* Tribunal referred to the *Antaris v Spain* case when determining the contours of the legitimate expectations principle and directly referred-quoted the explanation there.[178] When investigating the origin of the investor's legitimate expectations, the Tribunal referred to seven tariff recognition letters sent to the investor by Gestore dei Servizi Energetici (GSE), a state-owned company that deals with the payment of incentives,[179] after seven sections of the PV plant had been connected to the national electricity grid.[180] All of these letters included the same statements, with only the start dates differing. One of these letters read: 'The incentive tariff will be recognized for a period of twenty years as of the date of entry into operation of the plant: 28/04/2011; the tariff is constant, in current currency, all through the 20-year period.'[181] In addition to these letters, seven GSE agreements[182] had also been concluded between

---

[170] *CEF Energia v Italy*, Award, para 105.
[171] ibid para 106.
[172] ibid para 107.
[173] ibid para 108.
[174] ibid para 110.
[175] ibid.
[176] *Greentech v Italy*, Award, para 109.
[177] ibid para 11.
[178] *CEF Energia v Italy*, Award, para 185.
[179] The state-owned company responsible for paying the incentive tariffs to electricity producers under the *Conto Energia* decrees.
[180] *CEF Energia v Italy*, Award, paras 210–11.
[181] ibid para 211.
[182] Agreements between the investor and the GSE that set forth the specific tariff incentive rate that the PV operator would receive and the specific dates comprising a 20-year period during which the incentive would be paid. See *Greentech v Italy*, Award, para 128.

the parties, and those GSE agreements included a direct reference to the incentives and the 20-year period. So, the legal framework that the investor relied on in this case had comprised decrees, tariff recognition letters and the GSE agreements.[183]

Against this background, the Tribunal stated:

> [A] party in the shoes of Claimant would be left in no doubt but that it was to receive incentives, in constant currency, for a twenty year period, and all pursuant to private law contracts (as this was understood to be the state of Italian law <u>at the time</u> of the making by Claimant of its Enersol investments – indeed the Romani Decree could not have been clearer in that respect to any reasonable reader) which could not be amended save by mutual agreement. This was clearly based on the consistent legal policy of Respondent as manifested in the four Contos and the Romani Decree. No reading, no matter how indulgent, could lead anyone to consider anything other than a clear promise of twenty years of constant currency incentives pursuant to a private law contract.[184]

With this, the Tribunal undertook an objective analysis of legitimate expectations and then moved on to the subjective analysis. In its subjective analysis, the Tribunal underlined the legal due diligence report that the investor had received from a law firm and concluded that the investor's reliance could be understood to have been reasonable.[185]

So, while the Tribunal did not explicitly remark on it, the reasoning behind its decision was mainly based on the existence of stability assurances in the Italian legal framework. It was the stability guarantees under the decrees, tariff recognition letters and GSE agreements that led to the creation of legitimate expectations on the part of the investor. The majority in this case found a breach of legitimate expectations and therefore the FET standard of Article 10(1) ECT.[186]

In the *Greentech* case, the majority also found a breach of the legitimate expectations of the investor. The claimants argued that organs and officials of the Italian Republic gave explicit and implicit assurances, and also informal guarantees, that the incentive tariff rates designated under decrees would remain stable for 20 years.[187] The claimants also alleged that they would not have made the investment in question had there been no stability assurance.[188]

The Tribunal stated: 'At the time of investing, Claimants had been led to believe, reasonably, that the incentive tariffs would remain the same as promised in the Conto Energia decrees, GSE letters and GSE Agreements throughout a twenty-year period.'[189] Even though the Tribunal accepted that Italy faced economic difficulties, this was not sufficient for Italy to justify its alterations.

Referring to the *Parkerings* award, the *Greentech* Tribunal stated that the assurances given by Italy bore the hallmarks of 'an agreement, in the form of a

---

[183] *CEF Energia v Italy*, Award, para 217.
[184] ibid.
[185] *CEF Energia v Italy*, Award, para 225.
[186] ibid para 247.
[187] *Greentech v Italy*, Award, para 408.
[188] ibid para 414.
[189] ibid para 447.

stabilisation clause or otherwise.[190] So, the majority of the Tribunal expressly recognised the assurances given by Italy as stability guarantees.

Another significant point raised by the Tribunal in response to Italy's argument that it has a right to regulate is that, since there were repeated and precise assurances concerning the tariff stability, Italy waived its right to reduce the tariff value and Italy's guarantees must be seen as non-waivable assurances.[191] The Tribunal added: 'Host states certainly retain the sovereign prerogative to amend their laws. However, if the state gives an investor express assurances that no amendment would occur, the investor must be fairly compensated if those assurances are violated.'[192]

The claimant in the *Belenergia* case argued that there were 'explicit and implicit specific commitments toward PV investors through regulatory and contractual instruments' put in place by Italy which were aimed at stabilising the applicable conditions.[193] However, the Tribunal did not consider 'the contractual 20-year term originally applying to feed-in tariffs or the prohibition on unilateral changes' as a stabilisation provision.[194]

According to the Tribunal, 'an investor cannot legitimately expect that the legal and regulatory framework will not change when any prudent investor could have anticipated this change before making its investment'.[195] In relation to the contracts concluded with GSE, the Tribunal stated that the 20-year duration provisions under these contracts were just replicated from the relevant legislation and they were not specifically addressed to the investor.[196] What is more interesting in the Tribunal's analysis is that it argued that 'The contractual prohibition on unilateral changes concerned the GSE and not the Italian legislator'.[197] The approach followed in this case concerning GSE contracts (GSE Conventions) significantly contrasts with the one in the *CEF* case discussed above.

The Tribunal in *Belenergia* also gave weight to the due diligence conducted by the investor in its analysis. The claimant had not undertaken due diligence regarding the regulatory risks in Italy concerning feed-in tariffs and minimum prices.[198] Had the claimant scrutinised the Italian PV laws and regulations, as a prudent investor should do, it would have seen that there was a trend towards reducing the incentives, according to the Tribunal.[199] Consequently, the investor's claim that it had legitimate expectations was denied.

SunReserve was the first publicly available case of 2020 and it was heard by an Arbitration Institute of the Stockholm Chamber of Commerce (SCC) Tribunal.

---

[190] ibid para 452.
[191] ibid para 450.
[192] ibid para 452.
[193] *Belenergia v Italy*, Award, para 573.
[194] ibid para 580.
[195] ibid para 584.
[196] ibid para 580.
[197] ibid.
[198] ibid para 585.
[199] ibid para 587.

The Tribunal, when starting its analysis, acknowledged that stability and transparency were the ECT's priority objectives.[200] It also further noted that 'it is also important to note that as part of this general obligation to maintain stability and transparency in the legal framework, host States are also required to generally create a favourable environment for investments'.[201]

The claimant argued here that its legitimate expectations were based on the general regulatory framework of Italy and also the specific assurances given by the GSE with tariff confirmation letters and contracts.[202] According to the Tribunal, there was no requirement of specific or explicit commitments for the creation of legitimate expectations.[203] However, in the absence of a stabilisation provision, states cannot be asked to freeze their legal and regulatory framework.[204]

The Tribunal also undertook a discussion about the temporal requirement[205] of legitimate expectations and, while agreeing that an investment might be made in multiple stages, it added that it is the investor who must establish the exact points in time when there is a legitimate expectation generated by the host state and relied upon by the investor.[206]

After setting the standards that would apply to the case, the Tribunal continued with its analysis of whether any of the subsequent state behaviours frustrated the investor's legitimate expectations. While doing so, it analysed the overall regulatory framework, the Conto Energia Decrees and several representations made by the government officials.[207] It should be noted here that this Tribunal did not see GSE letters and contracts relevant for the legitimate expectations analysis for eight of its nine power plants since these post-dated the investor's decision to invest.[208]

The Tribunal could not find any stability promises for the continuation of the guaranteed payments for 20 years under the above-mentioned framework.[209] When assessing the public statements of government officials, the Tribunal stated that

> [g]iven that the overall regulatory regime in Italy, including the Conto Energia Decrees, did not create expectations of the incentive tariffs being fixed in time for 20 years, the public statements corresponding to this regulatory regime could also not have created such an expectation.[210]

The Tribunal recognised that these statements and representations might create legitimate expectations, but only if they are aligned with the regulatory framework

---

[200] *SunReserve v Italy*, Final Award, para 680.
[201] ibid para 684.
[202] ibid para 594.
[203] ibid para 699.
[204] ibid para 702.
[205] See ch 5, s III for this discussion.
[206] *SunReserve v Italy*, Final Award, para 723.
[207] ibid para 788.
[208] ibid para 781.
[209] ibid para 805.
[210] ibid para 816.

and they cannot create further binding obligations on the state other than the ones already existing under the legal regime in place.[211]

With respect to the ninth power plant, the Tribunal also assessed the effect of the GSE tariff confirmation letter and contract, and concluded that these 'cannot create any commitments or expectations above and beyond the administrative or public acts that they are sourced in'.[212] Consequently, the Tribunal concluded that there was no breach of legitimate expectations of the investor.

The *Eskosol* Tribunal also rejected the claims that there was a breach of legitimate expectations. The claimant argued that the terms of Conto Energia III, public statements of government officials and some representations delivered directly to it created legitimate expectations to be protected.[213]

The Tribunal's position regarding the representations was as follows:

> It is well established that when a 'specific commitment' has been made to a particular investor regarding the legal framework applicable to its investment, changes in that framework can give rise to a violation of the fair and equitable treatment standard, provided the investor has relied on that commitment to make investments protected by the treaty.[214]

It was also recognised by the Tribunal that it was possible that a clear commitment towards a certain group of investors by state officials might create legitimate expectations.[215]

However, the Tribunal could not find any specific representations towards the investor and did not consider the public statements of government officials as explicit guarantees that the applicable legal regime would be stable and unchanged.[216]

The Tribunal, recognising the existence of such a debate in the arbitral jurisprudence, did not delve into the discussion whether a legal and regulatory framework alone might create legitimate expectations without additional representations or guarantees, because it found that Conto Energia III, which constituted the basis of the claimant's argument in this respect, was not applicable to the investor anyway.[217]

The last publicly available award of 2020 was from the *ESPF* case, where the majority of the Tribunal found a breach of the legitimate expectations principle and the FET clause under the ECT. While the Tribunal acknowledged a state's inherent right to regulate, it also affirmed that exercising this right might again be restricted by certain commitments and undertakings by that same state.[218]

---

[211] ibid para 817.
[212] ibid para 823.
[213] *Eskosol v Italy*, Award, para 423.
[214] ibid para 425.
[215] ibid para 432.
[216] ibid paras 430–36.
[217] ibid paras 439–42.
[218] *ESPF v Italy*, Award, para 418.

According to the claimant's argument, the Conto Energia framework generated legitimate expectations that the incentives and tariffs would be stable for a duration of 20 years.[219] In line with the investor's claims, the Tribunal also agreed that 'The Conto Energia Decrees, the GSE Letters and GSE Agreements all specify the tariff rates for which a qualifying producer is entitled for the term of 20 years'.[220]

The Tribunal's analysis of the inducement effect is also noteworthy:

> It is undisputed in this case that the object and purpose of Italy's Conto Energia regime was to induce investment in its developing PV sector ahead of when that investment would otherwise occur in light of the high cost of investment prevalent at the time. Italy had complete control over how it designed its scheme and opted for a regime that provided numerous incentives and support for these investments. The main defining feature was the incentive tariff scheme, which provided a constant income stream over the expected life of the investment.[221]

The majority of the Tribunal agreed that there was a need for a clear and specific undertaking for the creation of legitimate expectations and a specific commitment might be made under the general legal framework.[222] The majority added that 'The clear and specific guarantee in the Conto Energia Decrees satisfies the requisite degree of specificity needed in order for legitimate expectations to arise from legislation'.[223]

The Tribunal in this case undertook a detailed analysis of legitimate expectations based on the legal framework prevalent in a host state. The following comments in this regard are also worthy of notice:

> Legitimate expectations are based on the investor's objective understanding of the legal framework within which the investor has made its investment or, in other words, what a reasonable investor at the time would have expected. Such legal framework includes the host state's domestic legislation and regulations, as well as its international law obligations, any contractual arrangements concluded between the investor and the state, and the specific representations or undertakings made by the state.[224]

(iv) Discussion

Recent arbitral awards tell us a completely different story from the traditional stability literature. Even though the validity of a stability provision in the domestic legislation has been generally conceded by scholars, its effectiveness has always been contentious. The majority of the recent arbitral jurisprudence acknowledges a stability provision under the general legislative framework as worthy of protection under the legitimate expectations principle, under the FET standard. Even

---

[219] ibid para 446.
[220] ibid para 463.
[221] ibid para 510.
[222] ibid para 512.
[223] ibid para 512.
[224] ibid para 513.

though Hirsch argues that 'legislative or regulatory changes alone are insufficient for generating an obligation to compensate foreign investors harmed by such regulatory changes',[225] the recent arbitral awards discussed above negate this opinion. There are, however, still some awards, albeit only a minority, that follow Hirsch's line of reasoning.

An international energy investor who is in dire need of a stable legal framework throughout a certain period in order to recover the relatively large amounts of capital invested in a host state and generate an expected return might utilise the treaty level protection under the legitimate expectations principle even though it has not secured a contractual stabilisation clause. This is possible through the guarantees provided under the domestic legislation of a host state. The support schemes built upon the domestic legal frameworks are especially important for the renewable energy investments because it is hard to maintain the profitability of those investments without public support.[226]

It is more likely that an arbitral tribunal would grant protection had the assurance in question been used as an incentive tool to lure the investor. If it has been promoted in certain ways to attract the foreign investor, then the tribunals would be more sympathetic towards the investor in the event of a revocation of that guarantee.

One of the most important aspects of the protection of legitimate expectations based on legislative stability guarantees is that the investor must have relied on that assurance while making its investment. The emphasis on reliance in the tribunals' analyses is what makes a legislative stability provision different from a contractual stabilisation clause which has been negotiated individually.

Potestà, while discussing the differences between a contractual stability clause and the general legal framework with regard to the legitimate expectations created, emphasises this individual bargaining aspect and argues that it would be illogical to extend such a specific protection to an investor who has not been able to secure it for themself.[227] However, what should be observed here is that even though the protection granted at the end of the process might be the same, the scrutiny that the two are being subjected to is different. Therefore, it cannot be considered a direct extension of the protection; rather, in order to grant a legitimate expectations protection based on a stability provision under the domestic legislation, tribunals seek additional requirements and elaborate more on the reliance aspect. This is clearly visible in the *Antaris* case, where even though the Tribunal had accepted the existence of an explicit stability provision, it did not grant a protection to the investor based on legitimate expectations, arguing that its reliance on that assurance was only to exploit the system and was not reasonable.

---

[225] M Hirsch, 'Between Fair and Equitable Treatment and Stabilization Clause: Stable Legal Environment and Regulatory Change in International Investment Law' (2011) 12(6) *Journal of World Investment & Trade* 783, 792.

[226] A Boute, 'Combating Climate Change through Investment Arbitration' (2012) 35(3) *Fordham International Law Journal* 613, 638.

[227] Potestà, 'Legitimate Expectations', 114.

Another significant conclusion that can be drawn from the above-mentioned awards is that the cumulative effect[228] of all the available documents in creating legitimate expectations is the approach preferred by arbitral tribunals. Both the tribunals finding a breach of legitimate expectations and those not finding a breach evaluate the stability provisions found under domestic legislation in conjunction with other available instruments that intend to clarify the meaning of such a provision. A stability provision under domestic legislation is not analysed in a vacuum. Representations, politicians' comments, press releases, reports, policy documents, action plans and all other relevant documents or sources are evaluated together, either in order to give meaning to the main stability provision or to reinforce the effect of that provision.

Selivanova argues within the renewables context that even if the conditions change and there is an additional cost burden on energy consumers, the responsibility for this risk lies with the host state and not the investor.[229] Therefore, this additional cost must be borne by the host state and the legitimate expectations of the investors must be respected. Not every negative change for the host state justifies its alteration of the investment environment.

Consequently, it is clear from the recent arbitral awards that a stability provision under domestic legislation is capable of creating legitimate expectations that are to be protected under the FET standard in the event of a breach. It is adequately justified for an international investor to rely on a stability assurance under the general legal framework when making its investment. A legislative stabilisation provision becomes a significant tool when it is utilised in conjunction with the legitimate expectations principle.

It can also be argued that a stability provision under domestic legislation might be seen as an enticement tool, which, in turn, produces legitimate expectations that need to be protected. The mere existence of a stabilisation provision under the national laws could be considered an incentive directed towards the potential investors because, as discussed in chapter three, the main rationale behind the birth of these clauses is to provide assurance to the investors. The *Antin* award argues that 'the expectations of the investor need to originate from some affirmative action of the State',[230] and the inclusion of these stability provisions under domestic legislation should be regarded as an affirmative action by the host state.

However, there is one crucial issue about the identification of stabilisation provisions under domestic legislation. It can be seen from several awards discussed above as well that the same legal provision, the same article in a law or regulation, is considered a stability promise by some tribunals and not by some others. This is not related to its effect; it is only related to its characterisation. Some tribunals have

---

[228] See ch 5, s V.
[229] YS Selivanova, 'Changes in Renewables Support Policy and Investment Protection under the Energy Charter Treaty: Analysis of Jurisprudence and Outlook for the Current Arbitration Cases' (2018) 33(2) *ICSID Review – Foreign Investment Law Journal* 433, 447.
[230] *Antin v Spain*, Award, para 538.

accepted the existence of a stabilisation clause but have given a different effect or weight to it within the whole investment scope. This is understandable, and should not create major problems. However, after reading the same text, if one tribunal decides that it is a stabilisation clause and the other decides that it is not, then there emerges a significant problem. It can also be seen from these divergent approaches that a pressing need is that what constitutes a stabilisation provision within a domestic legal and regulatory framework must be discussed in more detail. There should be some standards to make it easier to identify a stabilisation clause within a domestic legal framework, just as there is in the contractual sphere.

As for the specificity aspect, what should be taken into consideration is the capability of an assurance to create legitimate expectations, as discussed in the previous chapter.[231] Even though a stability guarantee in domestic law is not directed towards an identifiable, specific investor, its content should be considered relevant enough to create legitimate expectations if an investor relies on it.

C. Administrative Stability Guarantee: A New Concept?

In the traditional stability literature, there is no concept such as administrative stability. However, when the host government behaviour is analysed in conjunction with the legitimate expectations principle, there is a need to focus on this new concept. Could there be an administrative stability guarantee that might give rise to legitimate expectations? Is it possible to consider assurances provided by representations as a new type of stability guarantee? If so, what would their effect be in creating legitimate expectations?

As discussed in the previous chapter, administrative representations can surely create legitimate expectations on the investor side. In view of this fact, this book argues that if an administrative assurance, in any form, provided by the host state includes a reference to the stability of the legal and regulatory framework, then this should be called an 'administrative stability guarantee', which might create legitimate expectations. Conceptualising these types of administrative acts under this name would make it easier for arbitral tribunals to analyse the dispute in a step-by-step manner. An arbitral tribunal would look at the stability provisions under contracts, under legislative frameworks or under administrative frameworks to find out whether a legitimate expectation exists.

As stated by the *El Paso v Argentina* Tribunal, what makes a host state commitment worthy of protection under the legitimate expectations principle is not its character of being legally binding, but rather its character of being specific.[232] The Tribunal adds that if the main aim of such a commitment is to provide a real assurance of stability to the investor, then this should be considered specific enough to

---

[231] See ch 5, s II.
[232] *El Paso v Argentina*, Award, para 376.

be protected.[233] Hence, an administrative stability guarantee need not be legally binding in order to be taken into account by arbitral tribunals.

An example of the administrative stability assurance can be given from the recent Spanish cases. In 2005, a ministerial organ, the Institute for Diversification and Saving of Energy, started publishing a series of documents about its campaign programme under the name 'The Sun Can Be All Yours' and continued publishing new versions of that document in subsequent years.[234] This was aimed at incentivising foreign investors to invest in Spain's solar power sector. There were several references to the stability of the legal framework and the incentives regime in the documents.[235] If the legal value of such a prospectus were to be analysed in a vacuum, the conclusion reached would be that it was simply an unbinding administrative representation. However, when it is evaluated through the legitimate expectations perspective, it becomes a noteworthy instrument that can be used to prove the existence of legitimate expectations.

So, the stability concept in its widest form comprises administrative stability guarantees as well. In particular, these should not be overlooked when evaluating the legitimate expectations principle.

III. Legitimate Expectations 'to' Stability

So far, this chapter has analysed the legitimate expectations created by pre-existing stability guarantees offered within the broad legal framework surrounding the investment. This section, in contrast, will focus on the general stability obligation of host states that stems from investment treaties.

It has already been demonstrated in the previous chapter that legitimate expectations might arise from the legal framework prevalent in a host state.[236] This section will not repeat that argument; rather, it will discuss the rationale underlying this approach. It has already been argued that if there is an explicit stability provision under the domestic legal framework, it might create legitimate expectations. Another case is the situation where there is no stability provision under domestic law. Legitimate expectations to stability under those circumstances emerge from the investment treaties. This approach provides a more permissive view of the legitimate expectations principle and is consistent with the stability aspirations of the investors.[237]

The questions to be answered in this section are: why do investors have legitimate expectations to regulatory stability even in the absence of an explicit stability

---

[233] ibid para 377.
[234] *Novenergia v Spain*, Award, paras 112–17.
[235] ibid para 556.
[236] See ch 5, s IIC.
[237] J Bonnitcha, *Substantive Protection under Investment Treaties: A Legal and Economic Analysis* (Cambridge University Press, 2014) 184.

undertaking by the host state; what happens if there is no inducement or encouragement involved in any of the laws or regulations that the investor relies on; and what is it in an investment treaty that gives rise to legitimate expectations of stability?

A. Investment Treaties and Stability

It is well established in the literature that the main impetus underpinning international investment treaties is to secure a stable legal framework and protect investments from potential detrimental host government actions.[238] This very essence of the investment treaty is a significant factor that encourages investors to invest in a given host state, especially investors in the energy sector, who conclude their investments with a long-term outlook and whose investments' viability depends on the level of stability in that host state.[239] One of the major aims of an investment treaty is to produce an incentive for new investments.[240]

While the stability of the legal framework in which an international energy investor concludes its investment can be ensured through contractual means, as already discussed, it can equally be ensured by means of investment treaty standards.[241] It is argued that when the stability at the treaty level increases, the need for stability at the contractual level decreases.[242] Irrespective of a stabilisation provision being present in the investment contract, investment treaties might play a role in providing a stable investment environment.[243] According to the *Occidental* Tribunal, 'there is certainly an obligation not to alter the legal and business environment in which the investment has been made'[244] under international law. As Cameron notes, when a dispute arises, an international energy

---

[238] T Gazzini, *Interpretation of International Investment Treaties* (Hart Publishing, 2016) 34; P Bekker and A Ogawa, 'The Impact of Bilateral Investment Treaty (BIT) Proliferation on Demand for Investment Insurance: Reassessing Political Risk Insurance after the "BIT Bang"' (2013) 28(2) *ICSID Review – Foreign Investment Law Journal* 314, 338; Cameron, *International Energy Investment Law*, 146–47; JW Salacuse and NP Sullivan, 'Do BITs Really Work?: An Evaluation of Bilateral Investment Treaties and their Grand Bargain' in KP Sauvant and LE Sachs (eds), *The Effect of Treaties on Foreign Direct Investment: Bilateral Investment Treaties, Double Taxation Treaties, and Investment Flows* (Oxford University Press, 2009) 118; WM Reisman and RD Sloane, 'Indirect Expropriation and Its Valuation in the BIT Generation' (2004) 74(1) *British Yearbook of International Law* 115, 144.

[239] R Dolzer, 'Fair and Equitable Treatment: Today's Contours' (2013) 12(1) *Santa Clara Journal of International Law* 7, 23; I Tudor, *The Fair and Equitable Treatment Standard in the International Law of Foreign Investment* (Oxford University Press, 2008) 169.

[240] R Dolzer and M Stevens, *Bilateral Investment Treaties* (Kluwer Law International, 1995) 12.

[241] Mistelis, 'Stability', 155.

[242] ibid.

[243] AFM Maniruzzaman, 'The Pursuit of Stability in International Energy Investment Contracts: A Critical Appraisal of the Emerging Trends' (2008) 1(2) *Journal of World Energy Law & Business* 121, 147.

[244] *Occidental v Ecuador*, Final Award (2004), para 191.

investor should consider 'whether it wishes to pursue a claim against a host state on the basis of a contractual breach or a violation of a provision in a BIT or both'.[245]

As clearly stated by Salacuse and Sullivan: 'Most BITs pursue the objective of investment protection by establishing rules about the host country's treatment of foreign investment and processes for enforcing these rules'.[246] It is also to be seen from the provisions of BITs that these instruments are designed to protect investments, insomuch that Vandevelde refers to BITs as 'investment protection agreements'.[247]

However, the treatment that the investor will receive might change according to the language of the treaty text. Even though most of these treaties hold a similar approach to the FET standard, there can be slight differences in their texts as well. While certain BITs refer to the stability concept in their preambles or within their texts, some of them do not contain any such reference at all.

The FET provisions found in investment treaties should also be interpreted in light of the purpose of the treaty.[248] This was made clear under Article 31(1) of the 1969 Vienna Convention on the Law of Treaties. The interpretation standard there was set out as follows: '1. A treaty shall be interpreted in good faith in accordance with the ordinary meaning to be given to the terms of the treaty in their context and in the light of its object and purpose'.[249]

According to this, when the FET standard and its components are to be interpreted, this should be in line with the context of the investment treaty in question and its object and purpose. Many tribunals have relied upon the titles of treaties and their preambles in order to determine their object and purpose.[250] This approach of interpreting the object and purpose of a treaty through its preamble has been a popular one.[251] Following this approach, numerous tribunals have concluded 'that the object and purpose of the treaty was to promote and protect investments'.[252] Along the same line, Newcombe and Paradell have also stated: 'In looking at object and purpose and, with it, the title and preamble of BITs, tribunals have noted that the purpose of BITs is to protect investments and investors'.[253]

---

[245] Cameron, *International Energy Investment Law*, 149.

[246] Salacuse and Sullivan, 'Do BITs Really Work?', 122.

[247] KJ Vandevelde, *Bilateral Investment Treaties: History, Policy, and Interpretation* (Oxford University Press, 2010) 5.

[248] F Costamagna, 'Protecting Foreign Investments in Public Services: Regulatory Stability at Any Cost?' (2017) 17(3) *Global Jurist* 1, 5.

[249] United Nations, *Vienna Convention on the Law of Treaties*, entered into force 27 January 1980, Art 31(1).

[250] For detailed analysis of treaty interpretation through preambles, see TH Yen, *The Interpretation of Investment Treaties* (Brill Nijhoff, 2014); MH Hulme, 'Preambles in Treaty Interpretation' (2016) 164(5) *University of Pennsylvania Law Review* 1281.

[251] C Schreuer, 'Diversity and Harmonization of Treaty Interpretation in Investment Arbitration' in M Fitzmaurice, O Elias and P Merkouris (eds), *Treaty Interpretation and the Vienna Convention on the Law of Treaties: 30 Years on* (Martinus Nijhoff Publishers, 2010) 131.

[252] Yen, *The Interpretation of Investment Treaties*, 62.

[253] A Newcombe and L Paradell, *Law and Practice of Investment Treaties: Standards of Treatment* (Kluwer Law International, 2009) 114.

Several tribunals have interpreted the treaty standards by reference to their preambles. The *SGS v Philippines* Tribunal stated:

> According to the preamble it is intended 'to create and maintain favourable conditions for investments by investors of one Contracting Party in the territory of the other'. It is legitimate to resolve uncertainties in its interpretation so as to favour the protection of covered investments.[254]

This approach was also employed by the *Lemire v Ukraine*[255] Tribunal. While discussing the meaning of the FET standard found under the USA–Ukraine BIT, the Tribunal noted that the words used in treaties must be interpreted in line with their contexts. Accordingly, the Tribunal stated:

> The context of Article II.3 is to be found in the Preamble of the BIT, in which the contracting parties state 'that fair and equitable treatment of investment is desirable in order to maintain a stable framework for investment ...'. The FET standard is thus closely tied to the notion of legitimate expectations – actions or omissions by Ukraine are contrary to the FET standard if they frustrate legitimate and reasonable expectations on which the investor relied at the time when he made the investment.[256]

A similar approach was set forth earlier in the *Occidental v Ecuador* case, where the Tribunal referred to the preamble of the USA–Ecuador BIT in order to tie the stability concept to the FET standard.[257] The Tribunal stated:

> Although fair and equitable treatment is not defined in the Treaty, the Preamble clearly records the agreement of the parties that such treatment 'is desirable in order to maintain a stable framework for investment and maximum effective utilization of economic resources'. The stability of the legal and business framework is thus an essential element of fair and equitable treatment.[258]

Likewise, the *CMS v Argentina* Tribunal expressly noted that since the stability objective was mentioned under the preamble of the BIT between the USA and Argentina, a stable investment environment was an essential element of the FET standard.[259] The same treaty preamble was also evaluated along the same lines in the *LG&E v Argentina* case.[260]

However, Potestà argues that a reference to stability in the preamble is not adequate to create legitimate expectations of stability and to establish a burden on the host state,[261] though he does not provide solid reasoning for this argument. Since the FET standard does not have an explicit and undisputed meaning,

---

[254] *SGS v Philippines*, Decision of the Tribunal on the Objections to Jurisdiction, para 116.
[255] *Joseph Charles Lemire v Ukraine*, Decision on Jurisdiction and Liability, ICSID Case No ARB/06/18, 14 January 2010.
[256] ibid para 264 (footnote omitted).
[257] *Occidental v Ecuador*, Final Award (2004), para 183.
[258] ibid.
[259] *CMS v Argentina*, Award, para 274.
[260] *LG&E v Argentina*, Decision on Liability, para 124.
[261] Potestà, 'Legitimate Expectations', 113.

it is the tribunals' duty to interpret it. As stated above, the Vienna Convention establishes the methods for treaty interpretation, and looking at the context, object and purpose of a treaty is one of those methods. If the stability aspiration can be deduced from those elements, as was the issue in the cases mentioned above, then the host states must observe the investors' legitimate expectations to stability and grant protection to the investor in the event of a significant modification in investment conditions.

It is true that the FET provision does not entail a stabilisation clause.[262] However, this should not mean that a host state that signed an investment treaty can alter its investment environment without any restrictions. Its modifications should be in conformity with its undertakings under a treaty.

This section goes hand in hand with section IIC of the previous chapter, where the effect of the legal and regulatory framework on creating legitimate expectations was discussed. In the previous section of this chapter,[263] it was shown that the general legal framework might be the basis of legitimate expectations if there is an explicit stability provision. If not, it is still possible to create legitimate expectations of stability by relying on the general legal framework of a host state.

The main rationale underlying this approach is the close connection between the concepts of legitimate expectations and stability. Dolzer notes in this regard that 'The FET standard with its focus on legitimate expectations appropriately reflects the connection between the flow of investments and legal stability'.[264] Similarly, Krzykowski et al suggest that 'It cannot be overlooked that the principle of reasonable and legitimate expectations is related to the obligation of securing a stable and predictable legal framework'.[265]

Indeed, the stability requirement under the FET standard has been evaluated and put into effect by reference to the legitimate expectations principle.[266] As noted by the *Duke v Ecuador* Tribunal, 'The stability of the legal and business environment is directly linked to the investor's justified expectations'.[267] Along the same lines, the *Frontier* Tribunal also stated, after acknowledging the close relationship between legitimate expectations and stability, that

> [s]tability means that the investor's legitimate expectations based on this legal framework and on any undertakings and representations made explicitly or implicitly by the host state will be protected. The investor may rely on that legal framework as well as on representations and undertakings made by the host state including those in legislation, treaties, decrees, licenses, and contracts.[268]

---

[262] Hirsch, 'FET and Stabilization', 806.
[263] See ch 6, s IIB.
[264] Dolzer, 'Today's Contours', 23.
[265] M Krzykowski, M Marianski and J Ziety, 'Principle of Reasonable and Legitimate Expectations in International Law as a Premise for Investments in the Energy Sector' (2020) *International Environmental Agreements: Politics, Law and Economics* https://doi.org/10.1007/s10784-020-09471-x.
[266] S Maynard, 'Legitimate Expectations and the Interpretation of the "Legal Stability Obligation"' (2016) 1(1) *European Investment Law and Arbitration Review* 99, 99.
[267] *Duke v Ecuador*, Award, para 340.
[268] *Frontier v Czech*, Final Award, para 285.

B. Energy Charter Treaty in Perspective

The ECT is widely considered the most noteworthy multilateral instrument for promoting cooperation and investment in the energy sector.[269] As stated in Article 2 of the ECT, the purpose of the treaty is to establish 'a legal framework in order to promote long-term cooperation in the energy field, based on complementarities and mutual benefits, in accordance with the objectives and principles of the Charter'.[270] Although this statement refers to the cooperation between signatory states, its implementation is nevertheless directly related to individual investors. In order to maintain this long-term cooperation, contracting parties must provide a certain level of treatment to the investors of other nationals, as designated under several standards of the treaty. This desire to maintain a long-term cooperation implicitly embraces the requirement of stability as well.[271]

Article 10(1) of the ECT lays down a significant obligation which is in close connection with the central issue of this book. Accordingly:

> Each Contracting Party shall, in accordance with the provisions of this Treaty, encourage and create stable, equitable, favourable and transparent conditions for Investors of other Contracting Parties to make Investments in its Area. Such conditions shall include a commitment to accord at all times to Investments of Investors of other Contracting Parties fair and equitable treatment.[272]

Even though the main purpose behind investment treaties is to maintain stability, this is not always explicitly stated in their texts. The ECT, on the other hand, expressly imposes a duty on host states to create a stable investment environment. This requirement of creating 'stable conditions' has also been subjected to scrutiny by several arbitral tribunals.

One of the latest awards based on the ECT, the *Antin* award, allocates a large space to this discussion and it would be appropriate to quote the Tribunal's full consideration here:

> The Tribunal deems it important to emphasize that the content and scope of the FET standard must be assessed within the context of the Treaty in which it is found. Reference to decisions on the stability of a regime based on treaties whose text is substantially different and where no specific obligation of stability is contained may be of no assistance in the interpretation of this specific feature of the ECT. Not only does the ECT expressly state that its purpose is to provide a legal framework to promote long-term cooperation in the energy field in accordance with the objectives and principles of the

---

[269] E Gaillard, 'Investments and Investors Covered by the Energy Charter Treaty' in C Ribeiro (ed), *Investment Arbitration and the Energy Charter Treaty* (JurisNet, 2006) 55; TW Waelde, 'Investment Arbitration under the Energy Charter Treaty – From Dispute Settlement to Treaty Implementation' (1996) 12(4) *Arbitration International* 429, 429.

[270] Energy Charter Treaty, Art 2.

[271] *Eiser v Spain*, Award, para 378.

[272] Energy Charter Treaty, Art 10(1).

Charter – which stresses the need for a stable and transparent legal framework, – it also contains a specific obligation – as opposed to a mere declaration in the preamble, and with language that suggests an imperative and not merely a recommendation – to encourage and create stable conditions for investments. Regardless of how the relationship between stability of the legal framework and the obligation to accord FET is conceived, it seems clear that, in the context of the ECT, the concepts are associated in a manner that merits their joined assessment. In fact, it seems undisputed that the ECT's FET standard includes the obligation to provide a stable and predictable legal framework for investments (footnotes omitted).[273]

According to this, the stability requirement is considered an integral element of the FET standard, and especially of the legitimate expectations component. This approach is also consistent with the characterisation proposed by Dolzer and Schreuer when they assessed these two concepts together.[274]

Similarly, the *Foresight v Spain* Tribunal noted the following: 'The Tribunal agrees with the Claimants that a State's duty under the FET standard to ensure a stable legal and regulatory framework "arises when the State has generated 'legitimate expectations' of such stability on the part of investors".[275]

The claimant in the *Novenergia* case argued that the requirement under Article 10(1) is a distinct and fully fledged stability standard.[276] However, the Tribunal rejected this argument and noted that the stability requirement under the ECT is not a separate obligation, but rather is 'simply an illustration of the obligation to respect the investor's legitimate expectations through the FET standard'.[277]

The *AES v Hungary* Tribunal also analysed the requirement to maintain stable conditions under the ECT and noted that it was a complex task to assess the scope of stability that should be provided since it would depend on the 'specific circumstances that surrounds the investor's decision to invest and the measure taken by the state in the public interest'.[278] It concluded that since there was no specific assurance from Hungary, such as a stabilisation clause, the investor could not have legitimately expected that no change would occur.[279] However, the approach adopted by the Tribunal here has its shortcomings within the context of the ECT. There is an explicit stability requirement under Article 10(1) of the ECT, which, as discussed above, could be put into effect by means of the legitimate expectations principle. The stability prerequisite under Article 10(1) is not a recommendation; on the contrary, it is an obligation.[280] The ECT does not enunciate that this stability

---

[273] *Antin v Spain*, Award, para 533.
[274] R Dolzer and C Schreuer, *Principles of International Investment Law* (Oxford University Press, 2012) 145.
[275] *Foresight v Spain*, Final Award, para 352.
[276] *Novenergia v Spain*, Award, para 562.
[277] ibid para 646.
[278] *AES v Hungary*, Award, para 9.3.30.
[279] ibid para 9.3.33.
[280] *Antin v Spain*, Award, para 525.

condition hinges upon a specific assurance; rather, it is a general duty imposed on host states. Therefore, arbitral tribunals should not be looking for a specific assurance in order to give effect to the stability requirement. As correctly noted by the *AES* Tribunal, this requirement is not a stabilisation clause.[281] However, this fact does not mean that there is no obligation on the host states to provide a certain level of stability.

Within the ECT context, the protection of the legitimate expectations requirement embraces the maintenance of a stable investment environment. Therefore, legitimate expectations might arise from the general legal framework as well. The arbitral approach which extends the coverage of legitimate expectations to the general legal framework could be said to be correct in this regard. The justification for legitimate expectations to be based on the general legal framework even if there is no explicit stability undertaking arises from this standard of the ECT.

However, in the absence of an explicit stability guarantee, the stability requirement under Article 10(1) would provide a lower level of protection. This is because a state cannot be precluded from altering its legal framework and the stability requirement under this article is not a stabilisation clause as stated by the *AES* Tribunal.[282] The *Plama* Tribunal followed a similar line of reasoning when it stated: '

> [T]he Tribunal believes that the ECT does not protect investors against any and all changes in the host country's laws. Under the fair and equitable treatment standard the investor is only protected if (at least) reasonable and justifiable expectations were created in that regard.[283]

So, what kind of a stability analysis is required by arbitral tribunals under these circumstances? In response to this issue, Coop and Seif note that the tribunal must scrutinise '(i) the purpose and context of the regulatory measures; and (ii) the extent of the interference of those measures with the legitimate expectations of the investor(s).'[284]

C. Discussion

It can be deduced from the above discussion that there is a requirement to maintain a certain level of stable investment environment upon host states under investment treaties. This obligation arises directly from the investment treaties themselves. It makes no difference whether this requirement is expressly stated

---

[281] *AES v Hungary*, Award, para 9.3.29.
[282] ibid.
[283] *Plama Consortium Limited v Republic of Bulgaria*, Award, ICSID Case No ARB/03/24, 27 August 2008, para 219.
[284] G Coop and I Seif, 'ECT and States' Right to Regulate' in M Scherer (ed), *International Arbitration in the Energy Sector* (Oxford University Press, 2018) 234.

in the treaty text or otherwise. The inherent characteristics of investment treaties allow such an inference.

Therefore, as discussed in the previous chapter,[285] the legitimate expectations of investors to stability might be based on the general legal framework prevalent in a host state. However, the level of stability that an investor might legitimately expect changes in this case. As the *Foresight* Tribunal notes, in the absence of an explicit stability provision, the investor cannot expect that there would be no changes at all; nevertheless, it is the investor's legitimate expectation that 'the regulatory framework would not be fundamentally and abruptly altered so as to deprive investors of a significant part of their projected revenues'.[286]

Without an explicit stability provision, the investor's legitimate expectations would be limited, and it would require more scrutiny by the tribunals. It is argued that in the absence of an explicit stability guarantee, the extent of the regulatory change that is permissible not to breach the legitimate expectations becomes unclear.[287]

The requirement of stability in the absence of an explicit stability assurance was highlighted in an earlier decision of the *PSEG v Turkey* case. The Tribunal there found a breach of the FET provision based on continuous legislative changes.[288] It did not base its decision on the legitimate expectations principle; however, the Tribunal stated that continually changing legal framework constituted a 'roller-coaster effect'[289] on the investor's side and stability could not exist under such circumstances.[290] There was no stabilisation clause in this case and the Tribunal's approach also proves that a certain level of stability is a treaty requirement.

As noted by the *Masdar* Tribunal, 'If the general legislation is to be regarded as a source of an investor's legitimate expectations, the investor must demonstrate that it has exercised appropriate due diligence and that it has familiarised itself with the existing laws'.[291]

Likewise, the *Parkerings* Tribunal also urges the investor to undertake due diligence and requires the expectations to be reasonable in light of the surrounding circumstances.[292] It is the investor's duty to analyse the legal system correctly; there would be no breaches of the FET standard had the investor misunderstood or misinterpreted the prevailing legal system and hence generated subjective expectations.[293]

---

[285] See ch 5, s IIC.

[286] *Foresight v Spain*, Final Award, para 388.

[287] F Ortino, 'The Obligation of Regulatory Stability in the Fair and Equitable Treatment Standard: How Far Have We Come?' (2018) 21(4) *Journal of International Economic Law* 845, 846.

[288] *PSEG v Turkey*, Award, para 250.

[289] ibid.

[290] ibid para 254.

[291] *Masdar v Spain*, Award, para 494.

[292] *Parkerings v Lithuania*, Award, para 333.

[293] M Kaldunski, 'The Element of Risk in International Investment Arbitration' (2011) 13(1/2) *International Community Law Review* 111, 115.

The *Eiser* Tribunal, by analysing the ECT within its context and taking its objectives into account, concluded that the level of stability that an investor might legitimately expect without an explicit stability provision corresponds only to preventing fundamental and radical alterations.[294]

Ortino, after assessing the arbitral tribunals' approaches, identifies two forms of stability obligation under the FET standard in the absence of a stabilisation clause as 'strict' and 'soft' stability obligations. With regard to the strict form, any change in the general legal framework that affects the investor detrimentally would mean a breach of the stability obligation and hence the FET standard.[295] However, this approach would be akin to reading a stabilisation clause into every FET provision under a treaty, which is not sensible. He also adds that this was an earlier approach and has now been overtaken by arbitral awards that reject the strict stability obligation.[296]

According to the soft form of stability obligation, which is now the prevailing approach,[297] not every detrimental change would lead to a breach; rather, the tribunal would analyse the merit and magnitude of the regulatory changes in question.[298] However, he submits that although the claimants always argue that the regulatory changes that they face are radical, arbitral tribunals fail to specify what kind of change would constitute one with sufficiently drastic effects to constitute a breach of the FET.[299] Even though Ortino criticises arbitral tribunals for not providing a universal criterion and leaving ambiguous the issue of which regulatory change would mean a radical one, in my view, this should be the path that tribunals should follow. This is mainly because each of these investment disputes has its own characteristics and should be analysed within its own context. While a regulatory change might result in drastic effects under certain circumstances, it might not lead to the same consequences in another context. Therefore, this should be determined by arbitral tribunals on a case-by-case basis, taking all surrounding circumstances into account.

So, it is not a question of whether there is an inherent legitimate expectation to stability under international investment agreements, but, rather, one about the level of scrutiny that the investor's reliance and the host state's alteration would be subject to. There might be legitimate expectations to stability on the investor side even in the absence of an explicit stability provision or an active inducement provided by the host state. In this case, the tribunal would evaluate the reasonable reliance aspect in more detail. At the same time, the tribunal would look at the host state's conduct to determine whether that change falls outside the acceptable

---

[294] *Eiser v Spain*, Award, para 382.
[295] Ortino, 'Regulatory Stability', 849.
[296] ibid 854.
[297] ibid 857.
[298] ibid 849.
[299] ibid 860.

margin of change.[300] This approach is considered to provide the weakest form of protection to the investor in the event of a change to the legal framework.[301]

IV. Conclusion

This chapter has shown that there is a concrete link between the stability and legitimate expectations concepts. These two are interconnected – and, indeed, their interaction is visible – on several layers. When the stability concept is referred to within an international energy investment setting, this mostly indicates one of its substantive forms, such as a contractual stabilisation clause or a legislative provision. These clauses are the main and the most widespread means of providing stability to an energy investment. However, it is contentious whether these provisions actually achieve what they aim to in practice. As discussed in the previous chapters, stability clauses cannot constrain a host state from altering its legal and regulatory framework. Therefore, their importance becomes more visible when a dispute arises. A stabilisation clause plays a significant role during the dispute resolution process.

It is well established in arbitral practice that the existence of an explicit contractual stabilisation clause would lead directly to a breach of legitimate expectations and therefore of the FET standard of a treaty in the event of a detrimental change in the host state regulatory framework. This interaction of contractual stabilisation clauses with the legitimate expectations principle reveals a new dimension to the investment protection mechanism. Nonetheless, the type of stabilisation clause matters when assessing the legitimate expectations created. If the clause in question is a traditional, freezing type, then a legitimate expectation would be assumed to be present. However, if the clause is what this book has previously called a contemporary one, which already prescribes a change in the legal environment, then a mere change of the legal framework would not mean a direct breach of legitimate expectations.

This chapter has argued that this conclusion is also valid for legislative stability commitments. If the legal and regulatory framework of a host state comprises an explicit stability guarantee, then the host state must respect the fact of an investor who invested based on its reliance on that assurance. This is a divergence from the traditional stabilisation literature, where the legislative stability commitments are mostly considered ineffective. This finding is especially significant for international energy investors, who cannot completely rely on contractual mechanisms due to certain features of the sector. As can be seen from the recent Spanish, Italian

---

[300] *Antaris v Czech*, Award.
[301] Gjuzi, *Stabilization*, 339; Potestà, 'Legitimate Expectations', 115.

and Czech cases cited in this chapter, the current arbitral understanding of the relationship between stability guarantees and legitimate expectations encompasses the stability provisions provided by domestic laws or regulations as well. These are considered significant assurances put in place in order to induce the foreign investor, and therefore a high level of importance is attributed to such provisions.

The substantive stability guarantee provided by an administrative act or representation is also of relevance when determining the existence of legitimate expectations to be protected. An administrative stability assurance does not fall under the traditional understanding of stabilisation provisions, but this should also be considered as a separate form of stability which might give rise to legitimate expectations.

While it is less contentious that the stability provisions in various forms might create legitimate expectations to be protected, the issue of whether an investor might legitimately expect a stable legal framework even in the absence of an explicit stability guarantee is more contentious. The expansive view on this issue is that there is an inherent stability obligation for host states under the investment treaties independently of their texts. This is so because one the main aims of investment treaties is to provide a stable investment environment for the investors. Based on this reason, a host state must maintain a certain level of stability and an investor might rely on the general legal framework even if there is no stability provision. However, finding a legitimate expectation in this case is harder than in the former cases. Without an explicit stability assurance, an investor cannot legitimately expect that the laws will not change at all. The threshold for finding legitimate expectations becomes higher and the scrutiny that the investors are being subjected to becomes more detailed. In this case, arbitral tribunals are more interested in the reasonable reliance aspect of the investor and the magnitude of the change introduced by the host state. If the investor had reasonably relied on the general legal framework and the changes are beyond certain acceptable standards, then there might be a breach of legitimate expectations to stability.

7

Concluding Remarks

I. General Conclusions

The main focal point of this book has been the stability concept in international energy investments and its relationship with the legitimate expectations principle found under the fair and equitable treatment (FET) standard in investment treaties. The stability commitments have been commented upon many times in the literature, but there was a gap on their utilisation within the context of investment treaty protection. The use of the stability concept in conjunction with the legitimate expectations principle would provide valuable insight into the investment protection mechanisms. Therefore, the question posed in this book was designed to explore the interplay between these two concepts in order to fill that gap. This book has attempted to show international energy investors the existing investment treaty protection mechanisms in relation to the stability concept.

The book has found that there is a close reciprocal relationship between the legitimate expectations principle and the stability concept. It has been observed that while a contractual, legislative or administrative stabilisation guarantee reinforces the strength of the arguments based on the legitimate expectations principle during the arbitration process, an investor may also argue that the host state is obliged to provide a stable investment environment even in the absence of such explicit stabilisation guarantees. This requirement arises directly out of investment treaties.

This last chapter will summarise the conclusions and the main findings of the book. In this first section, a brief overview of the significant points discussed in this study will be presented. The next section will present the main contributions and findings of the book. The last section will provide several recommendations for international energy investors and arbitral tribunals.

A. International Energy Investments and Political Risk

International energy investments constitute a large portion of both global investments and investment disputes. Since energy projects are generally capital-intensive and of long duration, states need international investment in this particular area.

International energy investments play a significant role in the development of international investment law. This book advances the understanding of the legitimate expectations principle and the stability concept with reference to international energy investments. Even though international energy investments are part of the general international investment regime, they also bear certain specific characteristics which drag them into a niche area under international investment law.[1]

One of the characteristics that places international energy investments in a different position to other types of investments is the political risk prevalent in the energy industry. Political risk has been identified as one of the most, if not the most, important risks that international energy investments face. There are several categories of political risk, but this study is confined to unilateral modifications by host states, or in other words, regulatory risks.

Since the party that an international energy investor deals with most often is a sovereign state, this brings along certain challenges. Host states, regardless of their development level, might unilaterally alter the investment environment that an investor has invested in. While host states introduce incentives in order to lure investors to their energy sector, they might change their welcoming attitude once the investment has been made. There are several reasons why a host state might act in such a manner. It might be because of the economic difficulties that the host state faces or the public pressure that the government encounters, or a change of government might lead to a new political stance. It was the changing economic conditions in the latest renewable energy investment arbitrations in Spain, Italy and the Czech Republic that triggered the relevant governments to introduce new measures.[2]

Obsolescing bargain is also another significant concept that is closely relevant to international energy investments.[3] Even if none of the reasons mentioned above exist, host states might simply intervene in the investment environment solely by virtue of the shifting bargaining power. Once a large portion of an investment is completed, the bargaining power shifts towards the host state and they begin to introduce new measures, thinking that the investor cannot leave the country easily. Since the realisation of obsolescing bargain hinges upon the fixed assets of the investor, energy sector and energy investors are highly susceptible to this concept.

Whatever the motive behind the unilateral actions of host states is, the result is mostly the same, which is damage or loss on the investor side. In order to protect its investment from such detrimental interferences, investors rely on certain protection mechanisms. The stability concept is one of the most important tools that an international energy investor counts on in order to protect its investment.

---

[1] See ch 2.
[2] See ch 6, s II.
[3] See ch 2, s VC.

B. Stability

Stability, within the context of international energy investments, is a broad concept that comprises various legal tools, such as contractual clauses, laws and regulations, and administrative assurances. It is closely related to energy investments insomuch that the first examples of stability provisions can be found in international energy investment agreements from many decades ago.[4]

An international energy investor deems stability highly important because of the fact that its investment's profitability depends on the continuance of the conditions in existence at the time that the investment was made.[5] In order to keep those conditions the same, investors rely on certain mechanisms, one of which is stability.

There are two main rationales behind the use of stability provisions: protection and promotion. It is the protection that it provides against political risks that makes a stability provision important and desirable for an energy investor. On the other hand, host states utilise these assurances as an incentive towards potential investors and they attempt to lure those investors into their countries with the help of stability provisions. Even though Frank disagrees with the promotion role of stability provisions and argues that there is no correlation between a stability assurance and the investment made,[6] the claimants in the cases discussed in previous chapters assert that they relied on the stability guarantees offered by the host state and that they would not have made their investment had there been no such guarantee.

Even though there are some theoretical discussions over the validity of stability provisions in the literature,[7] this is no longer a concern of arbitral tribunals, as can be seen from recent cases. They do not discuss whether these assurances are valid under international law, but, rather, discuss the scope and effect of such guarantees and their position in investment treaties. A stability guarantee offered in any form (contract, legislation, representation) has a legal value under international investment law and can be used in building a case.

One of the problems that can be seen from the stability literature is that there are numerous types of stability provisions and various different names for the same or similar approaches. This poses a problem when conducting a rigorous analysis. However, it does not create any particular complications for arbitral tribunals, since they are mostly interested in the content of the assurance and not the form. Yet, the distinction between traditional and contemporary stability provisions is a

---

[4] See ch 3, s IIIA.
[5] F Costamagna, 'Protecting Foreign Investments in Public Services: Regulatory Stability at Any Cost?' (2017) 17(3) *Global Jurist* 1, 1.
[6] S Frank, 'Stabilisation Clauses and Foreign Direct Investment: Presumptions versus Realities' (2015) 16(1) *Journal of World Investment & Trade* 88.
[7] See ch 3, s IIID.

significant one, as discussed earlier.[8] While traditional stability provisions attempt to freeze the legal framework of a host state in part or in whole, modern ones have the objective of adjusting the investment relationship in line with the changing conditions.

Within the investment protection context, stabilisation provisions can be used in two ways by investors: first, as a preventive and deterrent tool against host states' unilateral actions; and secondly, as a tool to prove and reinforce the legitimate expectations claims of an investor during the investment arbitration process. We do not know, and it is not easy to measure, how effective these provisions as a preventive tool actually are; however, we can assess their effectiveness as a reinforcement tool in the arbitration process.

Accordingly, as this book has also argued, even though the stability provisions may not be sufficiently effective in preventing host states from altering their legal frameworks, they are one of the most effective tools in proving a breach of the legitimate expectations principle, hence the FET standard of investment treaties.

C. Legitimate Expectations

The legitimate expectations principle has long been present in many domestic laws.[9] It has mainly been considered an administrative law principle by those legal systems. The key rationale behind this principle was said to be that of maintaining and protecting the trust between the governor and the governed.[10]

Its application under investment treaty law in relation to the FET standard is relatively recent, and started with the famous *Tecmed* award in 2003. However, the Tribunal did not conduct an in-depth analysis on the roots of the principle. The subsequent tribunals that applied the principle in their cases also chose not to comment on the source of their transplanting the doctrine into investment treaty law.[11] In fact, this is not as imperative an issue as some suggest. It does not matter from where arbitral tribunals borrowed the principle; rather, the important aspect is how they give scope and content to it. If their application is consistent with the requirements of treaty provisions and international investment law, then the debate over the roots of a principle would be pointless.

Starting from 2003, the legitimate expectations principle has gradually become the most important component of the FET standard. Since there is no explicit definition of the term 'fair and equitable' under investment treaties, it is the arbitral tribunals' duty to interpret and ascribe a meaning to this term. After many arbitrators have conducted this practice, it is now well established that the legitimate

---

[8] See ch 6, s IIA(i).

[9] See ch 4, s IIIA.

[10] C Forsyth, 'Legitimate Expectations Revisited' (2011) 16(4) *Judicial Review* 429, 430.

[11] For a detailed discussion, see T Wongkaew, 'The Transplantation of Legitimate Expectations in Investment Treaty Arbitration: A Critique' in S Lalani and RP Lazo (eds), *The Role of the State in Investor–State Arbitration* (Brill Nijhoff, 2014).

expectations principle constitutes the dominant element[12] of the FET standard. Today, it is almost impossible to find a breach of an FET claim without an argument based on legitimate expectations. One of the reasons behind the popularity of this principle among investors might be its flexible and wide scope. That is, since the legitimate expectations principle encompasses anything from administrative representations to domestic legal frameworks, it becomes easier for investors to place their arguments and cases under this principle.

The legitimate expectations principle, as understood by investment treaty law and applied by arbitral tribunals, has two main strands. The first is the narrow approach, according to which legitimate expectations arise only out of specific assurances. The second is the broad approach, which, as is evident from its name, considers any form of assurance capable of creating legitimate expectations on the investor's side. The key difference between the two approaches is the significance attributed to the specificity issue.

This book has advocated that the broad approach be followed because only in this way will the stability aspirations of investors be duly fulfilled. It is important especially for international energy investments that arbitral tribunals follow the broad approach because an energy investment process, due to its characteristics, requires an interaction with many domestic laws, regulations, administrative decisions and government officials. If an energy investor cannot rely on the assurances they provide, it becomes nearly impossible to conclude and maintain that investment. At one point, an investor will have to take the laws or administrative representations of a host state into account instead of trying to include every aspect in its contract.

As this book has established, legitimate expectations might be based on three sources: contracts; administrative representations and assurances; and the general legal and regulatory framework of a host state. An investor would be able to build its expectations on any of these sources while investing in a host state. Explicit or implicit assurances given by host states from any of these above-mentioned sources could be the subject of legitimate expectations. Of course, this would not occur without any boundaries and restrictions.

In order for an expectation to be legitimate under the FET standard, it must satisfy certain thresholds. An investor must be able to prove that there was an assurance given by the host state and that it relied on that assurance while making its investment in a reasonable and timely manner.[13] If one of these does not exist, then there will be no legitimate expectations. While assessing the existence of legitimate expectations, arbitral tribunals should look for the cumulative effect of the assurances granted by host states. It might not be possible sometimes for only one representation or law provision to create legitimate expectations for investors; however, when more than one guarantee is present in various forms, or there are

---

[12] *Saluka v Czech*, Partial Award, para 302.
[13] See ch 5, s IV.

several other statements and clarifications over an assurance, these might create legitimate expectations to be protected and therefore they must be taken into account in a cumulative manner. Even if these cannot create legitimate expectations separately, their combined effect might indicate a more powerful promise.

The analysis of the link between the stability concept and the legitimate expectations principle has been the most important aspect of this book. Accordingly, it has been shown that stability provisions, be they contractual, legislative or administrative, have a reinforcing effect in the legitimate expectations claims of investors. If there is a stability provision granted by a host state, then this would create legitimate expectations on the investor's side. Renewable energy investment arbitrations from Spain, the Czech Republic and Italy show that a stability provision in the general legal framework of a host state creates legitimate expectations to be protected under the FET standards of investment treaties. If a host state introduces stability assurances on certain matters and modifies these after the investment has been made, this act would violate the investment treaties and the damage that the investor is exposed to must be compensated. This book has designated this approach as 'legitimate expectations from stability'.[14]

The research conducted over the link between these concepts has revealed that even if there is no explicit stability undertaking by a host state in one of the above-mentioned forms, they might still be required to maintain a certain level of stability based on their commitments under investment treaties. International investors have 'legitimate expectations to stability' in this regard.[15] Since the main idea behind investment treaties is to provide and maintain a stable legal framework, investors might argue that their legitimate expectations have been frustrated due to the alterations made by host states.[16] This will require more scrutiny by arbitral tribunals, however, who will analyse the magnitude of the change and the extent of its detrimental effect on the investor.

II. Main Findings

This book, by analysing and combining the legitimate expectations and stability concepts together, has demonstrated several significant findings and contributions to the literature.

First, this book has analysed stability as a broad concept and identified the motives that create the need for stability amongst international energy investors. Political risk has been identified as a major factor contributing to the instability of energy investments. It has been found that political risk is not a concern of developing states solely; rather, developed states also tend to unilaterally alter their legal

---

[14] See ch 6, s II.
[15] See ch 6, s III.
[16] See ch 6, s IIIA.

frameworks when they find it appropriate to do so. This is evident from the latest renewable energy investment disputes in Spain, the Czech Republic and Italy.[17]

While the traditional stability literature praises stabilisation clauses as one of the most efficient protection mechanisms available against political risk, it is argued and shown by this book that the legitimate expectations principle can be utilised as an additional layer of protection and convert contractual or legislative stabilisation provisions into a more effective tool in the dispute resolution phase.

A noteworthy finding of this book is that while stabilisation provisions still maintain their importance as an investment protection tool, they also bear a growing significance within the legitimate expectations context. Contractual stabilisation clauses are still considered by international energy investors as essential protection against regulatory risk. In addition, while the traditional stabilisation literature considers the legislative stability provisions to be less effective than contractual stabilisation clauses/provisions, this study shows that they can also provide significant protection when utilised in conjunction with the legitimate expectations principle. It is well established by the recent arbitral awards that an explicit stabilisation provision under the domestic legislation of a host state might also create legitimate expectations to be protected.[18]

This book finds that an explicit stability assurance, be it as part of a contract, a representation or a piece of legislation, is highly significant in reinforcing legitimate expectations claims before an arbitral tribunal. Legitimate expectations are easily created by existing stability provisions. Therefore, this book suggests that it is essential for an international energy investor to try to secure some kind of stability provision and rely on it while making its investment.

Second, it has been shown that a traditional or freezing type of contractual stabilisation clause is much more effective in a legitimate expectations claim than a contemporary or adaptation type of stability provision. The main reason behind this is that arbitral tribunals consider modern stabilisation clauses to be premises to any potential change in the future. When the equilibrium of the investment changes, this does not constitute a direct breach of the legitimate expectations principle if the stabilisation clause in question is a contemporary one. The investor must first follow the rebalancing procedures stipulated in the contract, and if the host state obstructs that process by using its sovereign power, only then might the investor claim a breach of its legitimate expectations.

If the contractual stability clause is of the traditional freezing type, this would outright create legitimate expectations to be protected because the host state explicitly assures the investor that there will be no change in the investment legal framework.

Third, this book has argued that even though there are several debates in the literature regarding the roots of the legitimate expectations principle under the

---

[17] See ch 6.
[18] See ch 6.

FET standard, this does not have any practical effect on its application.[19] Whether the principle stems from domestic laws, and therefore is applied as a part of general principles of law, or from the good faith principle, which is in and of itself a general principle of law, does not bear any significance with respect to its application by arbitral tribunals. There is enough evidence to support both views, and it is adequately justified for arbitral tribunals to utilise this concept in their cases as a component of the FET standard. The contours of the legitimate expectations principle are being clarified by arbitral jurisprudence – as they should be, since the tribunals are not bound by the application of a principle under domestic laws. It has been observed that arbitral tribunals also no longer deal with the roots of the legitimate expectations principle discussion, but rather focus on the principle's scope and content.

Fourth, this book has provided an in-depth analysis of the legitimate expectations principle under investment treaty jurisprudence. By introducing the latest understanding of the concept by arbitral tribunals, the book demonstrates the current contours of the legitimate expectations principle and identifies two major schools of thought – wide and narrow – with regard to the application of the principle. While the narrow understanding insists on a specific undertaking (eg a contract) by the host states being in place so as to generate legitimate expectations, the wide approach asserts that general legislative framework and administrative representations are also adequate to create legitimate expectations and there is no need to look for a specific guarantee.

Based on this, the book has argued that the principle should be applied in its wider form in order to provide and secure the stability that is required by international energy investors. The research shows that a growing number of recent arbitral decisions have also taken this path and consider a stability guarantee provided under any form as being capable of generating legitimate expectations. Accordingly, legitimate expectations might be created by contracts, the general legal framework of a host state or its administrative representations. The form of a guarantee is not important; it is the content of that guarantee which should be scrutinised when assessing whether legitimate expectations exist.

It has been argued by some scholars that the current wide application of the legitimate expectations principle under the FET standard is not justified.[20] However, this book shows that there is a strong link between the stability concept and the legitimate expectations principle which justifies its use under the FET standard. Since one of the main aims of any bilateral investment treaty is to guarantee a stable investment legal framework on the part of a host state, the FET standard and the legitimate expectations principle should be evaluated in line

---

[19] See ch 4.

[20] M Sornarajah, *Resistance and Change in the International Law on Foreign Investment* (Cambridge University Press, 2015) 256–99; C Campbell, 'House of Cards: The Relevance of Legitimate Expectations under Fair and Equitable Treatment Provisions in Investment Treaty Law' (2013) 30(4) *Journal of International Arbitration* 361.

with the stability requirements.[21] A fair and equitable host state treatment would include providing a stable investment environment to the investor.

It has also been presented that domestic laws and administrative representations play a significant role in attracting foreign investors. An instrument used to lure the investor into a host state must also be recognised as a substantial factor in terms of creating legitimate expectations. In the energy industry in particular, it is not always possible to put every aspect of an investment into a contract. Therefore, many things are left to the general legal frameworks of host states upon which investors might rely while making their investments.

Fifth, this book, unlike the traditional stability literature, argues that there is a new layer of stability assurance which should be taken into account when making an investment: administrative stability.[22] The book has argued that administrative representations play a significant role in creating legitimate expectations. When a stability assurance is communicated to the investor through an administrative representation, the investor might claim a breach of its legitimate expectations based on that representation in the event of a subsequent change. This is neither a contractual clause nor legislation; it is simply a representation from the host state administration that can be given in various forms. The book argues that the stability concept, in its wider form, also encompasses the administrative stability phenomenon.

Even though an administrative representation might create legitimate expectations to be respected in its own right, not every representation will have the same value before an arbitral tribunal. An explicit, written statement that includes a stability assurance is evaluated in a different manner to a political statement or an informal representation by an arbitral tribunal. However, this does not mean that they have no value at all. Tribunals tend to analyse the issue at hand holistically, and they use these kinds of representations as reinforcing factors. As Professor Tawil suggested, even if only one representation might not be enough in itself to create legitimate expectations, sometimes the combination of more than one representation in the same case might generate legitimate expectations.[23]

Sixth, it is clear from the analyses in this book that stability and legitimate expectations concepts are not and should not be evaluated as distinct principles. Rather, the stability concept is immanent in the legitimate expectations principle. This can be seen from the discussion in section III of chapter six, where the obligation of a host state to provide a stable legal framework under the legitimate expectations principle is presented. Accordingly, host states are required to maintain a certain level of stability even if they have not granted explicit stability assurances to their investors. This obligation originates from investment treaties. It is up to arbitral tribunals to determine the level of stability that host states

---

[21] See ch 6, s III.
[22] See ch 6, s IIC.
[23] See ch 5, s IIB.

must provide in this situation. There should not be a one-size-fits-all approach by arbitral tribunals because every arbitral case will have its own unique characteristics and the approach designated should be in line with those features.

Maynard suggested that the two concepts of stability and legitimate expectations should be treated separately, arguing that this might lead to greater clarity in terms of their scope and content.[24] However, this book has argued that the stability concept within the investment treaty context can be better understood by reference to the legitimate expectations principle. It has been shown that the most effective use of these concepts for international energy investors can be ensured through their utilisation in conjunction with one another. An international energy investor would receive a wider protection based on an investment treaty if it chose to rely on the relationship between legitimate expectations and stability.

III. Recommendations

This book has identified several noteworthy points for international energy investors and arbitral tribunals, which are as follows.

- Contractual stabilisation clauses still maintain their importance for an international energy investor. Therefore, investors should endeavour to secure a contractual stabilisation clause first. As stated above, the type of contractual clause that an investor chooses will have a direct effect on the outcome in a dispute resolution process. An international energy investor should decide what type of clause to choose before making its investment. If it prioritises maintaining the relationship with the host state, contemporary stability provisions might be a good choice, since they provide for a flexible form which allows the parties to redress the balance should it deteriorate. However, if the investor's main aim is to secure the fastest and widest protection based on that stability provision, then a freezing type would prove to be more useful. If securing a contractual stability provision is not possible, then the investor should look for any other type of stability guarantee that the host state offers, and they should take that guarantee into account and rely on that assurance in an explicit and clear manner when making their investment.

- Even though the development level of a host state might indicate a certain degree of rule of law and security for investments, this is not a guarantee that the host state will never alter its investment conditions unilaterally. An investor should be aware that any host state, irrespective of it being a developed or developing one, might change its legal framework and affect the investment detrimentally. Bearing this fact in mind will help investors to seek assurances for their investments beforehand.

---

[24] S Maynard, 'Legitimate Expectations and the Interpretation of the "Legal Stability Obligation"' (2016) 1(1) *European Investment Law and Arbitration Review* 99.

- Conducting due diligence, especially over the stability guarantees offered by host states under their general legal framework, would be helpful for investors during the arbitration process while arguing for the existence of legitimate expectations. If the investor does not conduct any general due diligence, this might weigh against them during the arbitration. This due diligence does not have to be extensive. However, in order to determine whether an expectation is reasonable, arbitral tribunals will look for the existence of due diligence.

- Arbitral tribunals should now strive to sharpen the scope and content of the legitimate expectations principle and avoid inconsistent applications. Consistency is a key factor to stability. In order to secure the stability that international energy investors aspire to, arbitral tribunals should continue following the wide approach. There is a trend towards this path which can be witnessed in the latest renewable energy investment arbitrations, but what is needed is a continuous and consistent application.

BIBLIOGRAPHY

Ahmed, F and Perry, A, 'The Coherence of the Doctrine of Legitimate Expectations' (2014) 73(1) *CLJ* 61.

Al Emadi, TAQ, 'Stabilization Clauses in International Joint Venture Agreements' (2010) 3 *International Energy Law Review* 54.

Al Faruque, A, 'Stability in Petroleum Contracts: Rhetoric and Reality' (PhD Thesis, University of Dundee, 2005).

——, 'The Rationale and Instrumentalities for Stability in Long-Term State Contracts' (2006) 7(1) *Journal of World Investment & Trade* 85.

——, 'Validity and Efficacy of Stabilisation Clauses: Legal Protection vs Functional Value' (2006) 23(4) *Journal of International Arbitration* 317.

——, 'Typologies, Efficacy and Political Economy of Stabilisation Clauses: A Critical Appraisal' (2007) 5(4) *Oil, Gas & Energy Law* 1.

——, 'Renegotiation and Adaptation of Petroleum Contracts: The Quest for Equilibrium and Stability' (2008) 9(2) *Journal of World Investment & Trade* 113.

——, *Petroleum Contracts: Stability and Risk Management in Developing Countries* (Bangladesh Institute of Law and International Affairs, 2011).

Al Khalifa, HR, 'Negotiating and Arbitrating against Government Entities' (2003) 19(5) *Construction Law Journal* 258.

Alexander, F, 'Comment on Articles on Stabilization by Piero Bernardini, Lorenzo Cotula and AFM Maniruzzaman' (2009) 2(3) *Journal of World Energy Law & Business* 243.

Alkahtani, F, 'Legal Protection of Foreign Direct Investment in Saudi Arabia' (PhD Thesis, Newcastle University, 2010).

Allison, RC, *Protecting against the Expropriation Risk in Investing Abroad* (Matthew Bender, 1988).

Alvarez, JE, *The Public International Law Regime Governing International Investment* (Brill Nijhoff, 2011).

Annacker, C, 'Role of Investors' Legitimate Expectations in Defense of Investment Treaty Claims' in AK Bjorklund (ed), *Yearbook on International Investment Law & Policy* (Oxford University Press, 2015).

Asante, SKB, 'Stability of Contractual Relations in the Transnational Investment Process' (1979) 28(3) *International & Comparative Law Quarterly* 401.

Asqari, Z, 'Investor's Legitimate Expectations and the Interests of the Host State in Foreign Investment' (2014) 4(12) *Asian Economic and Financial Review* 1906.

Aven, T and Renn, O, 'On Risk Defined as an Event Where the Outcome Is Uncertain' (2009) 12(1) *Journal of Risk Research* 1.

Bandali, SA, 'Understanding FET: The Case for Protecting Contract-Based Legitimate Expectations' in IA Laird et al (eds), *Investment Treaty Arbitration and International Law*, vol 7 (JurisNet, 2014).

Barak-Erez, D, 'The Doctrine of Legitimate Expectations and the Distinction between the Reliance and Expectation Interests' (2005) 11(5) *European Public Law* 583.

Bauerle Danzman, S, 'Contracting with Whom? The Differential Effects of Investment Treaties on FDI' (2016) 42(3) *International Interactions* 452.

Bazrafkan, A and Herwig, A, 'Reinterpreting the Fair and Equitable Treatment Provision in International Investment Agreements as a New and More Legitimate Way to Manage Risks' (2016) 7(2) *European Journal of Risk Regulation* 439.

Bekker, P and Ogawa, A, 'The Impact of Bilateral Investment Treaty (BIT) Proliferation on Demand for Investment Insurance: Reassessing Political Risk Insurance after the "BIT Bang"' (2013) 28(2) *ICSID Review – Foreign Investment Law Journal* 314.

Bellantuono, G, 'The Misguided Quest for Regulatory Stability in the Renewable Energy Sector' (2017) 10(4) *Journal of World Energy Law & Business* 274.

Berger, KP, 'Renegotiation and Adaption of International Investment Contracts: The Role of Contract Drafters and Arbitrators' (2003) 36 *Vanderbilt Journal of Transnational Law* 1347.

Berlin, A and Berlin, AI, 'Managing Political Risk in the Oil and Gas Industries' (2004) 1(1) *Transnational Dispute Management* 1.

Bernardini, P, 'The Renegotiation of the Investment Contract' (1998) 13(2) *ICSID Review – Foreign Investment Law Journal* 411.

——, 'Investment Protection under Bilateral Investment Treaties and Investment Contracts' (2001) 2(2) *Journal of World Investment & Trade* 235.

——, 'Stabilization and Adaptation in Oil and Gas Investments' (2008) 1(1) *Journal of World Energy Law & Business* 98.

——, 'Reforming Investor–State Dispute Settlement: The Need to Balance Both Parties' Interests' (2017) 32(1) *ICSID Review – Foreign Investment Law Journal* 38.

Bernasconi-Osterwalder, N, 'Giving Arbitrators Carte Blanche – Fair and Equitable Treatment in Investment Treaties' in CL Lim (ed), *Alternative Visions of the International Law on Foreign Investment: Essays in Honour of Muthucumaraswamy Sornarajah* (Cambridge University Press, 2016).

Bishop, RD, 'International Arbitration of Petroleum Disputes: The Development of a Lex Petrolea' (1998) 23 *Yearbook Commercial Arbitration* 1131.

Bishop RD, Dimitroff, SD and Miles, CS, 'Strategic Options Available When Catastrophe Strikes the Major International Energy Project' (2001) 36(4) *Texas International Law Journal* 635.

Bishop, RD, Roché, EQ and McBrearty, S, 'The Breadth and Complexity of the International Energy Industry' in JW Rowley, RD Bishop and G Kaiser (eds), *The Guide to Energy Arbitrations* (Global Arbitration Review, 2017).

Blyschak, PM, 'Arbitrating Overseas Oil and Gas Disputes: Breaches of Contract versus Breaches of Treaty' (2010) 27(6) *Journal of International Arbitration* 579.

Bonnitcha, J, *Substantive Protection under Investment Treaties: A Legal and Economic Analysis* (Cambridge University Press, 2014).

Boulos, AJ, 'Assessing Political Risk: A Supplement to the IPAA International Primer' (2003) www.ipaa.org/wp-content/uploads/2017/01/PoliticalRisk.pdf.

Boute, A, 'Combating Climate Change through Investment Arbitration' (2012) 35(3) *Fordham International Law Journal* 613.

Bowman, J, 'Dispute Resolution Planning for the Oil and Gas Industry' (2001) 16(2) *ICSID Review – Foreign Investment Law Journal* 332.

BP, 'BP Energy Outlook 2018' (2018) www.bp.com/content/dam/bp/en/corporate/pdf/energy-economics/energy-outlook/bp-energy-outlook-2018.pdf.

Bradbrook, A, 'Energy Law as an Academic Discipline' (1996) 14(2) *Journal of Energy and Natural Resources Law* 193.

Bronfman, MK, 'Fair and Equitable Treatment: An Evolving Standard' (2005) 38(150) *Estudios Internacionales* 89.

Brower, CH, II, 'Investor–State Disputes under NAFTA: The Empire Strikes Back' (2001) 40(1) *Columbia Journal of Transnational Law* 43.

Brown, A, 'Justifying Compensation for Frustrated Legitimate Expectations' (2011) 30(6) *Law and Philosophy* 699.

Brown, C, 'The Protection of Legitimate Expectations as a "General Principle of Law": Some Preliminary Thoughts' (2009) 6(1) *Transnational Dispute Management* 1.

Bücheler, G, *Proportionality in Investor-State Arbitration* (Oxford University Press, 2015).

Caliskan, Y, 'Dispute Settlement in International Investment Law' in Y Aksar (ed), *International Economic Law through Dispute Settlement Mechanisms* (Martinus Nijhoff Publishers, 2011).

——, 'ICSID Jurisdiction: Whose Dictionary Will Be Used for the Definition of "Investment" and the "Scope of Consent"' in C Sural and E Omeroglu (eds), *Foreign Investment Law* (Seckin, 2016).

Cameron, PD, 'Stabilisation in Investment Contracts and Changes of Rules in Host Countries: Tools for Oil & Gas Investors' (AIPN, 2006) www.international-arbitration-attorney.com/wp-content/uploads/arbitrationlaw4-Stabilisation-Paper.pdf.

——, 'Stability of Contract in the International Energy Industry' (2009) 27(3) *Journal of Energy and Natural Resources Law* 305.

——, *International Energy Investment Law: The Pursuit of Stability* (Oxford University Press, 2010).

——, 'Reflections on Sovereignty over Natural Resources and the Enforcement of Stabilization Clauses' in KP Sauvant (ed), *Yearbook on International Investment Law & Policy 2011–2012* (Oxford University Press, 2013).

——, 'In Search of Investment Stability' in K Talus (ed), *Research Handbook on International Energy Law* (Edward Elgar Publishing, 2014).

——, 'Investment Cycles and the Rule of Law in the International Oil and Gas Industry: Some Reflections on Changing Investor–State Relationships' (2016) 38(3) *Houston Journal of International Law* 755.

——, 'Stabilization and the Impact of Changing Patterns of Energy Investment' (2017) 10(5) *Journal of World Energy Law & Business* 389.

Cameron, PD and Kolo, A, 'What Is Energy Investment Law and Why Does It Matter?' (2012) EI Source Book Working Paper.

Campbell, C, 'House of Cards: The Relevance of Legitimate Expectations under Fair and Equitable Treatment Provisions in Investment Treaty Law' (2013) 30(4) *Journal of International Arbitration* 361.

Campbell, M, Shore, L and Weiniger, M, *International Investment Arbitration: Substantive Principles* (Oxford University Press, 2017).

Cantegreil, J, 'The Audacity of the Texaco/Calasiatic Award: René-Jean Dupuy and the Internationalization of Foreign Investment Law' (2011) 22(2) *European Journal of International Law* 441.

Carlston, KS, 'Concession Agreements and Nationalization' (1958) 52(2) *American Journal of International Law* 260.

Carpanelli, E, 'General Principles of International Law: Struggling with a Slippery Concept' in L Pineschi (ed), *General Principles of Law – The Role of the Judiciary* (Springer, 2012).

Charlotin, D, 'Natland v Czech Republic (Part 2 of 2): On the Merits, Tribunal Finds Stabilisation Commitment in Czech Legislation and Breach of that Commitment with Introduction of Solar Levy' (2018) www.iareporter.com/articles/natland-v-czech-republic-part-2-of-2-on-the-merits-tribunal-finds-stabilisation-commitment-in-czech-legislation-and-breach-of-that-commitment-with-introduction-of-solar-levy/.

Cheng, B, *General Principles of Law as Applied by International Courts and Tribunals* (Cambridge University Press, 2006).

Childs, T, 'The Current State of International Oil and Gas Arbitration' (2018) 13(1) *Texas Journal of Oil, Gas, And Energy Law* 1.

Choudhury, B, 'Evolution or Devolution? Defining Fair and Equitable Treatment in International Investment Law' (2005) 6(2) *Journal of World Investment & Trade* 297.

Chowdhury, SR, 'Permanent Sovereignty and its Impact on Stabilization Clauses, Standards of Compensation and Patterns of Development Co-operation' in K Hossain and SR Chowdhury (eds), *Permanent Sovereignty over Natural Resources in International Law* (Frances Pinter, 1984).

Chynoweth, P, 'Legal Research' in A Knight and L Ruddock (eds), *Advanced Research Methods in the Built Environment* (Wiley-Blackwell, 2008).

Clement-Davies, C, 'Contractual Stability in the Energy Sector: Reconciling the Needs of States and Investors' (2014) (2) *International Energy Law Review* 47.

Click, RW and Weiner, RJ, 'Resource Nationalism Meets the Market: Political Risk and the Value of Petroleum Reserves' (2010) 41 *Journal of International Business Studies* 783.

Coale, MTB, 'Stabilization Clauses in International Petroleum Transactions' (2001) 30(2) *Denver Journal of International Law & Policy* 217.

Comeaux, PE and Kinsella, NS, 'Reducing Political Risk in Developing Countries: Bilateral Investment Treaties, Stabilization Clauses, and MIGA & OPIC Investment Insurance' (1994) 15(1) *New York Law School Journal of International and Comparative Law* 1.

——, *Protecting Foreign Investment under International Law: Legal Aspects of Political Risk* (Oceana Publications, 1997).

Coop, G, 'Introduction' in E de Brabandere and T Gazzini (eds), *Foreign Investment in the Energy Sector: Balancing Private and Public Interests* (Brill Nijhoff, 2014).

Coop, G and Seif, I, 'ECT and States' Right to Regulate' in M Scherer (ed), *International Arbitration in the Energy Sector* (Oxford University Press, 2018).

Costamagna, F, 'Protecting Foreign Investments in Public Services: Regulatory Stability at Any Cost?' (2017) 17(3) *Global Jurist* 1.

Cotula, L, 'Reconciling Regulatory Stability and Evolution of Environmental Standards in Investment Contracts: Towards a Rethink of Stabilization Clauses' (2008) 1(2) *Journal of World Energy Law & Business* 158.

——, 'Pushing the Boundaries vs Striking a Balance: The Scope and Interpretation of Stabilization Clauses in Light of the Duke v Peru Award' (2010) 11(1) *Journal of World Investment & Trade* 27.

Craig, PP, 'Substantive Legitimate Expectations in Domestic and Community Law' (1996) 55(2) *CLJ* 289.

——, *EU Administrative Law* (Oxford University Press, 2012).

Crawford, J, 'Treaty and Contract in Investment Arbitration' (2008) 24(3) *Arbitration International* 351.

——, *Brownlie's Principles of Public International Law* (Oxford University Press, 2012).

Cremades, BM, 'Good Faith in International Arbitration' (2012) 27(4) *American University International Law Review* 761.

Curtis, CT, 'The Legal Security of Economic Development Agreements' (1988) 29(2) *Harvard International Law Journal* 317.

Dajic, S, 'Mapping the Good Faith Principle in International Investment Arbitration: Assessment of Its Substantive and Procedural Value' (2012) 46(3) *Proceedings of Novi Sad Faculty of Law* 207.

Daniel, P and Sunley, EM, 'Contractual Assurances of Fiscal Stability' in P Daniel, M Keen and C McPherson (eds), *The Taxation of Petroleum and Minerals: Principles, Problems and Practice* (Routledge, 2010).

Davies, A, 'Investment Treaty Law Interpretation, Fair and Equitable Treatment and Legitimate Expectations' (2018) 15(3) *Manchester Journal of International Economic Law* 314.

de Brabandere, E, 'The Settlement of Investment Disputes in the Energy Sector' in E de Brabandere and T Gazzini (eds), *Foreign Investment in the Energy Sector: Balancing Private and Public Interests* (Brill Nijhoff, 2014).

de Macedo, JV, 'From Tradition to Modernity: Not Necessarily an Evolution – The Case of Stabilisation and Renegotiation Clauses' (2011) 9(1) *Oil, Gas & Energy Law* 1.

Dekastros, M, 'Portfolio Investment: Reconceptualising the Notion of Investment under the ICSID Convention' (2013) 14(2) *Journal of World Investment & Trade* 286.

del Rio, P and Mir-Artigues, P, 'A Cautionary Tale: Spain's Solar PV Investment Bubble' (International Institute for Sustainable Development, 2014).

Delaume, GR, 'The Proper Law of State Contracts Revisited' (1997) 12(1) *ICSID Review – Foreign Investment Law Journal* 1.

Demirkol, B, 'The Notion of "Investment" in International Investment Law' (2015) 1(1) *Turkish Commercial Law Review* 41.

Diehl, A, *The Core Standard of International Investment Protection: Fair and Equitable Treatment* (Kluwer Law International, 2012).

Dolzer, R, 'Fair and Equitable Treatment: A Key Standard in Investment Treaties' (2005) 39(1) *International Lawyer* 87.

——, 'Fair and Equitable Treatment: Today's Contours' (2013) 12(1) *Santa Clara Journal of International Law* 7.

Dolzer, R and Schreuer, C, *Principles of International Investment Law* (Oxford University Press, 2012).

Dolzer, R and Stevens, M, *Bilateral Investment Treaties* (Kluwer Law International, 1995).

Douglas, Z, *The International Law of Investment Claims* (Cambridge University Press, 2009).

Dromgool, T and Enguix, DY, 'The Fair and Equitable Treatment Standard and the Revocation of Feed in Tariffs – Foreign Renewable Energy Investments in Crisis-Struck Spain' in V Mauerhofer (ed), *Legal Aspects of Sustainable Development: Horizontal and Sectorial Policy Issues* (Springer International Publishing, 2016).

Dumberry, P, 'International Investment Contracts' in E de Brabandere and T Gazzini (eds), *International Investment Law: The Sources of Rights and Obligations* (Martinus Nijhoff Publishers, 2012).

——, *The Fair and Equitable Treatment Standard: A Guide to NAFTA Case Law on Article 1105* (Kluwer Law International, 2013).

——, 'Has the Fair and Equitable Treatment Standard Become a Rule of Customary International Law?' (2017) 8(1) *Journal of International Dispute Settlement* 155.

Dupont, C, Schultz, T and Angin, M, 'Political Risk and Investment Arbitration: An Empirical Study' (2016) 7(1) *Journal of International Dispute Settlement* 136.

Dupont, C et al, 'Types of Political Risk Leading to Investment Arbitrations in the Oil and Gas Sector' (2015) 8(4) *Journal of World Energy Law & Business* 337.

Dupuy, F and Dupuy, PM, 'What to Expect from Legitimate Expectations? A Critical Appraisal and Look into the Future of the "Legitimate Expectations" Doctrine in International Investment Law' in MA Raouf, P Leboulanger and NG Ziadé (eds), *Festschrift Ahmed Sadek El-Kosheri – From the Arab World to the Globalization of International Law and Arbitration* (Kluwer Law International, 2015).

Eden, L, Lenway, S and Schuler, DA, 'From the Obsolescing Bargain to the Political Bargaining Model' (Bush School of Government & Public Service, 2004).

Eljuri, E and Abul-Failat, Y, 'Political Risk Management in Natural Resources Projects in the MENA and the Latin American Regions' (2018) 16(3) *Oil, Gas & Energy Law* 1.

Eljuri, E and Trevino, C, 'Energy Investment Disputes in Latin America: The Pursuit of Stability' (2015) 33(2) *Berkeley Journal of International Law* 306.

El-Kosheri, AS, 'Settling Disputes in the Energy Sector: The Particularity of the Conflict Avoidance Methods Pertaining to Petroleum Agreements' (1996) 11(2) *ICSID Review – Foreign Investment Law Journal* 272.

El-Kosheri, AS and Riad, TF, 'The Law Governing a New Generation of Petroleum Agreements: Changes in the Arbitration Process' (1986) 1(2) *ICSID Review – Foreign Investment Law Journal* 257.

Emeka, JN, 'Anchoring Stabilization Clauses in International Petroleum Contracts' (2008) 42(4) *International Lawyer* 1317.

Erkan, M, *International Energy Investment Law: Stability through Contractual Clauses* (Kluwer Law International, 2011).

Faccio, S, 'The Assessment of the FET Standard between Legitimate Expectations and Economic Impact in the Italian Solar Energy Investment Case Law' (2020) 71 *Questions of International Law* 3.

Fatouros, AA, *Government Guarantees to Foreign Investors* (Columbia University Press, 1962).

——, 'International Law and the Internationalized Contract' (1980) 74 *American Journal of International Law* 134.

Felix, S, 'The Protection of Substantive Legitimate Expectations in Administrative Law' (2006) 18(1) *Sri Lanka Journal of International Law* 69.

Fietta, S, 'The "Legitimate Expectations" Principle under Article 1105 NAFTA' (2006) 7(3) *Journal of World Investment & Trade* 423.

Fitzpatrick, M, 'The Definition and Assessment of Political Risk in International Business: A Review of the Literature' (1983) 8(2) *Academy of Management Review* 249.

Forsyth, C, 'The Provenance and Protection of Legitimate Expectations' (1988) 47(2) *CLJ* 238.

——, 'Legitimate Expectations Revisited' (2011) 16(4) *Judicial Review* 429.

Foster, GK, 'Managing Expropriation Risks in the Energy Sector: Steps for Foreign Investors to Minimise Their Exposure and Maximise Prospects for Recovery When Takings Occur' (2005) 23(1) *Journal of Energy and Natural Resources Law* 36.

Franck, SD, 'The Legitimacy Crisis in Investment Treaty Arbitration: Privatizing Public International Law through Inconsistent Decisions' (2005) 73(4) *Fordham Law Review* 1521.

Frank, S, 'Stabilisation Clauses and Sustainable Development in Developing Countries' (PhD Thesis, University of Nottingham, 2014).

——, 'Stabilisation Clauses and Foreign Direct Investment: Presumptions versus Realities' (2015) 16(1) *Journal of World Investment & Trade* 88.

Gaillard, E, 'Investments and Investors Covered by the Energy Charter Treaty' in C Ribeiro (ed), *Investment Arbitration and the Energy Charter Treaty* (JurisNet, 2006).

——, 'Identify or Define? Reflections on the Evolution of the Concept of Investment in ICSID Practice' in C Binder et al (eds), *International Investment Law for the 21st Century: Essays in Honour of Christoph Schreuer* (Oxford University Press, 2009).

Gallagher, N, 'ECT and Renewable Energy Disputes' in M Scherer (ed), *International Arbitration in the Energy Sector* (Oxford University Press, 2018).

Garcia-Amador, FV, 'State Responsibility in Case of Stabilization Clauses' (1993) 2 *Journal of Transnational Law and Policy* 23.

Gaukrodger, D, 'The Balance between Investor Protection and the Right to Regulate in Investment Treaties: A Scoping Paper' (2017) OECD Working Papers on International Investment 2017/02.

Gazzini, T, 'General Principles of Law in the Field of Foreign Investment' (2009) 10(1) *Journal of World Investment & Trade* 103.

——, *Interpretation of International Investment Treaties* (Hart Publishing, 2016).

Gehne, K and Brillo, R, 'Stabilization Clauses in International Investment Law: Beyond Balancing and Fair and Equitable Treatment' (NCCR Trade Regulation, 2014).

Gjuzi, J, *Stabilization Clauses in International Investment Law: A Sustainable Development Approach* (Springer, 2018).

González, CJM, 'The Convergence of Recent International Investment Awards and Case Law on the Principle of Legitimate Expectations: Towards Common Criteria Regarding Fair and Equitable Treatment?' (2017) 42(3) *European Law Review* 402.

Grabowski, A, 'The Definition of Investment under the ICSID Convention: A Defense of Salini' (2014) 15(1) *Chicago Journal of International Law* 287.

Grisel, F, 'The Sources of Foreign Investment Law' in Z Douglas, J Pauwelyn and JE Vinuales (eds), *The Foundations of International Investment Law: Bringing Theory into Practice* (Oxford University Press, 2014).

Groves, M and Weeks, G (eds), *Legitimate Expectations in the Common Law World* (Hart Publishing, 2017).

Hajzler, C, 'Resource-Based FDI and Expropriation in Developing Economies' (University of Otago, 2010).

Halabi, SF, 'Efficient Contracting between Foreign Investors and Host States: Evidence from Stabilized Clauses' (2011) 31(2) *Northwestern Journal of International Law & Business* 261.

Hamamoto, S, 'Protection of the Investor's Legitimate Expectations: Intersection of a Treaty Obligation and a General Principle of Law' in W Shan and J Su (eds), *China and International Investment Law: Twenty Years of ICSID Membership* (Brill Nijhoff, 2014).

Hamida, WB, 'Two Nebulous ICSID Features: The Notion of Investment and the Scope of Annulment Control: Ad Hoc Committee's Decision in Patrick Mitchell v Democratic Republic of Congo' (2007) 24(3) *Journal of International Arbitration* 287.

Hansen, TB, 'The Legal Effect Given Stabilization Clauses in Economic Development Agreements' (1987) 28 *Virginia Journal of International law* 1015.

Haynes, J, 'The Evolving Nature of the Fair and Equitable Treatment (FET) Standard: Challenging Its Increasing Pervasiveness in Light of Developing Countries' Concerns – The Case for Regulatory Rebalancing' (2013) 14(1) *Journal of World Investment & Trade* 114.

Heffron, RJ et al, 'A Review of Energy Law Education in the UK' (2016) 9(5) *Journal of World Energy Law & Business* 346.

Henriques, DG, 'Pathological Arbitration Clauses, Good Faith and the Protection of Legitimate Expectations' (2015) 31(2) *Arbitration International* 349.

Hirsch, M, 'Between Fair and Equitable Treatment and Stabilization Clause: Stable Legal Environment and Regulatory Change in International Investment Law' (2011) 12(6) *Journal of World Investment & Trade* 783.

——, 'Sources of International Investment Law' (International Law Association Study Group on the Role of Soft Law Instruments in International Investment Law, 2011).

Hiscock, ME, 'The Emerging Legal Concept of Investment' (2009) 27(3) *Penn State International Law Review* 765.

Hlophe, J, 'Legitimate Expectation and Natural Justice: English, Australian and South African Law' (1987) 104(1) *South African Law Journal* 165.

Horn, N, 'Arbitration and the Protection of Foreign Investment: Concepts and Means' in N Horn (ed), *Arbitrating Foreign Investment Disputes: Procedural and Substantive Legal Aspects* (Kluwer Law International, 2004).

Howse, R, 'Freezing Government Policy: Stabilization Clauses in Investment Contracts' (*Investment Treaty News*, 2011) www.iisd.org/itn/2011/04/04/freezing-government-policy-stabilization-clauses-in-investment-contracts-2/.

Hulme, MH, 'Preambles in Treaty Interpretation' (2016) 164(5) *University of Pennsylvania Law Review* 1281.

Hwang, M and Fong Lee Cheng, J, 'Definition of "Investment" – A Voice from the Eye of the Storm' (2011) 1(1) *Asian Journal of International Law* 99.

ICSID, 'The ICSID Caseload – Statistics' (2020) 2020-2 https://icsid.worldbank.org/sites/default/files/publications/The%20ICSID%20Caseload%20Statistics%20%282020-2%20Edition%29%20ENG.pdf.

IEA, 'World Energy Investment Outlook: Special Report' (International Energy Agency, 2014) www.iea.org/reports/world-energy-investment-outlook.

——, 'World Energy Investment 2020' (International Energy Agency, 2020) www.iea.org/reports/world-energy-investment-2020.

——, 'World Energy Outlook 2020' (International Energy Agency, 2020) www.iea.org/reports/world-energy-outlook-2020.

IMF, 'External Debt Statistics: Guide for Compilers and Users – Appendix 3' (International Monetary Fund, 2003) www.imf.org/external/pubs/ft/eds/Eng/Guide/file6.pdf.

——, 'Mongolia: Selected Issues and Statistical Appendix' (International Monetary Fund, 2008).

Jacob, M and Schill, SW, 'Fair and Equitable Treatment: Content, Practice, Method' (2017) Amsterdam Center for International Law Research Paper No 2017-20 https://ssrn.com/abstract=2933425.

Jain, SN, 'Doctrinal and Non-doctrinal Legal Research' (1975) 17(4) *Journal of the Indian Law Institute* 516.

James, RA and Mauel, JG, 'An Integrated Approach to International Energy Investment Protection' (LexisNexis/Matthew Bender, 2007).

Jasimuddin, SM and Maniruzzaman, AFM, 'Resource Nationalism Specter Hovers Over the Oil Industry: The Transnational Corporate Strategy to Tackle Resource Nationalism Risks' (2016) 32(2) *Journal of Applied Business Research* 387.

Jensen, N, 'Political Risk, Democratic Institutions, and Foreign Direct Investment' (2008) 70(4) *Journal of Politics* 1040.

Jensen, NM and Johnston, NP, 'Political Risk, Reputation, and the Resource Curse' (2011) 44(6) *Comparative Political Studies* 662.

Jhaveri, S, 'Contrasting Responses to the "Coughlan Moment": Legitimate Expectations in Hong Kong and Singapore' in M Groves and G Weeks (eds), *Legitimate Expectations in the Common Law World* (Hart Publishing, 2017).

Joffé, G et al, 'Expropriation of Oil and Gas Investments: Historical, Legal and Economic Perspectives in a New Age of Resource Nationalism' (2009) 2(1) *Journal of World Energy Law & Business* 3.

Kachikwu, MK, 'The Changing Face of Political Risk in the Energy Industry' in J Werner and AH Ali (eds), *A Liber Amicorum: Thomas Wälde – Law Beyond Conventional Thought* (CMP Publishing, 2009).

Kaldunski, M, 'The Element of Risk in International Investment Arbitration' (2011) 13(1/2) *International Community Law Review* 111.

Kalicki, J and Medeiros, S, 'Fair, Equitable and Ambiguous: What Is Fair and Equitable Treatment in International Investment Law?' (2007) 22(1) *ICSID Review – Foreign Investment Law Journal* 24.

Karl J, 'FDI in the Energy Sector: Recent Trends and Policy Issues' in E de Brabandere and T Gazzini (eds), *Foreign Investment in the Energy Sector: Balancing Private and Public Interests* (Brill Nijhoff, 2014).

Kethireddy, SR, 'Still the Law of Nations: Legitimate Expectations and the Sovereigntist Turn in International Investment' (2019) 44(2) *Yale Journal of International Law* 315.

Khatchadourian, M, 'Legal Safeguards in Egypt's Petroleum Concession Agreements' (2008) 22(4) *Arab Law Quarterly* 387.

Kirkman, CC, 'Fair and Equitable Treatment: Methanex v United States and the Narrowing Scope of NAFTA Article 1105' (2002) 34(1) *Law and Policy in International Business* 343.

Kissam, LT and Leach, EK, 'Sovereign Expropriation of Property and Abrogation of Concession Contracts' (1959) 28(2) *Fordham Law Review* 177.

Kläger, R, *'Fair and Equitable Treatment' in International Investment Law* (Cambridge University Press, 2011).

Kobrin, SJ, 'Political Risk: A Review and Reconsideration' (Alfred P Sloan School of Management, 1978) Working Paper 998-78 http://dspace.mit.edu/bitstream/handle/1721.1/48801/politicalriskrev00kobr.pdf?s.

Kolb, R, *Good Faith in International Law* (Hart Publishing, 2017).

Kolo, A, 'Managing Political Risk in Transnational Investment Contracts' (University of Dundee, 1994).

——, 'State Regulation of Foreign Property Rights: Between Legitimate Regulation and Nationalisation – An Analysis of Current International Economic Law in Light of the Jurisprudence of the Iran–United States Claims Tribunal' (2004) 1(4) *Transnational Dispute Management* 1.

Krajewski, M, 'The Impact of International Investment Agreements on Energy Regulation' in C Herrmann and JP Terhechte (eds), *European Yearbook of International Economic Law* (Springer, 2012).

Kreindler, RH, 'Fair and Equitable Treatment – A Comparative International Law Approach' (2006) 3(3) *Transnational Dispute Management* 1.

Krishan, D, 'A Notion of ICSID Investment' (2009) 6(1) *Transnational Dispute Management* 1.

Krzykowski, M, Marianski, M and Ziety, J, 'Principle of Reasonable and Legitimate Expectations in International Law as a Premise for Investments in the Energy Sector' (2020) *International Environmental Agreements: Politics, Law and Economics* https://doi.org/10.1007/s10784-020-09471-x.

Kuznetsov AV, 'The Limits of Contractual Stabilization Clauses for Protecting International Oil and Gas Investments Examined through the Prism of the Sakhalin-2 PSA: Mandatory Law, the Umbrella Clause, and the Fair and Equitable Treatment Standard' (2015) 22(2) *Willamette Journal of International Law and Dispute Resolution* 223.

Lavranos, N and Verburg, C, 'Renewable Energy Investment Disputes: Recent Developments and Implications for Prospective Energy Market Reforms' in MM Roggenkamp and C Banet (eds), *European Energy Law Report XII* (Intersentia, 2018).

Lax, HL, *Political Risk in the International Oil and Gas Industry* (International Human Resources Development Corporation, 1983).

LCIA, '2019 Annual Casework Report' (2019) www.lcia.org/media/download.aspx?MediaId=816.

Legum, B and Mouawad, C, 'The Meaning of "Investment" in the ICSID Convention' in PHF Bekker, R Dolzer and M Waibel (eds), *Making Transnational Law Work in the Global Economy: Essays in Honour of Detlev Vagts* (Cambridge University Press, 2010).

Leite, K, 'The Fair and Equitable Treatment Standard: Search for Better Balance in International Investment Agreements' (2016) 32(1) *American University International Law Review* 363.

Lindquist, SA and Cross, FC, 'Stability, Predictability and the Rule of Law: Stare Decisis as Reciprocity Norm' (University of Texas Schoolof Law, 2010).

Lo, MW, 'Legitimate Expectations in a Time of Pandemic: The Host State's Covid-19 Measures, Its Obligations and Possible Defenses under International Investment Agreements' (2020) 13(1) *Contemporary Asia Arbitration Journal* 249.

Lovells International Law Firm and Association of Corporate Counsel, 'Sino-Foreign Oil and Gas Industry: Legal Risk Comparative Analysis' (2005).

Mairal, HA, 'Legitimate Expectations and Informal Administrative Representations' in SW Schill (ed), *International Investment Law and Comparative Public Law* (Oxford University Press, 2010).

Malik, M, 'Definition of Investment in International Investment Agreements' (International Institute for Sustainable Development, 2009) www.iisd.org/publications/definition-investment-international-investment-agreements.

Manciaux, S, 'The Notion of Investment: New Controversies' (2008) 9(6) *Journal of World Investment & Trade* 443.

Maniruzzaman, AFM, 'International Energy Contracts and Cross-Border Pipeline Projects: Stabilization, Renegotiation and Economic Balancing in Changed Circumstances – Some Recent Trends' (2006) 4(4) *Oil, Gas & Energy Law* 1.

——, 'Drafting Stabilization Clauses in International Energy Contracts: Some Pitfalls for the Unwary' (2007) (2) *International Energy Law & Taxation Review* 23.

——, 'National Laws Providing for Stability of International Investment Contracts: A Comparative Perspective' (2007) 8(2) *Journal of World Investment & Trade* 233.

——, 'The Pursuit of Stability in International Energy Investment Contracts: A Critical Appraisal of the Emerging Trends' (2008) 1(2) *Journal of World Energy Law & Business* 121.

——, 'The Issue of Resource Nationalism: Risk Engineering and Dispute Management in the Oil and Gas Industry' (2009) 5(1) *Texas Journal of Oil, Gas, And Energy Law* 79.

——, 'The Concept of Good Faith in International Investment Disputes – The Arbitrator's Dilemma' (2012) (89) *Amicus Curiae* 16.

Mann, FA, 'Reflections on a Commercial Law of Nations' (1957) 33 *British Yearbook of International Law* 20.

——, 'The Consequences of an International Wrong in International and National Law' (1977) 48(1) *British Yearbook of International Law* 1.

——, *Further Studies in International Law* (Clarendon Press, 1990).

Mann, H, 'Stabilization in Investment Contracts: Rethinking the Context, Reformulating the Result' (*Investment Treaty News*, 2011) www.iisd.org/itn/2011/10/07/stabilization-in-investment-contracts-rethinking-the-context-reformulating-the-result/.

Mansour, M and Nakhle, C, 'Fiscal Stabilization in Oil and Gas Contracts: Evidence and Implications' (Oxford Institute for Energy Studies, 2016) www.oxfordenergy.org/publications/fiscal-stabilization-in-oil-and-gas-contracts-evidence-and-implications/.

Martin, AP, 'Reviewing Stability Commitments in Investor–State Agreements: Creating Legitimate Expectations for Sustainable Foreign Investment Policies' (PhD Thesis, University of Surrey, 2012).

——, 'Stability in Contemporary Investment Law: Reconsidering the Role and Shape of Contractual Commitments in Light of Recent Trends' (2013) 10(1) *Manchester Journal of International Economic Law* 38.

Martin, AT, 'Dispute Resolution in the International Energy Sector: An Overview' (2011) 4(4) *Journal of World Energy Law & Business* 332.

Masood, MH, 'International Arbitration of Petroleum Disputes' (PhD Thesis, University of Aberdeen, 2004).

Mato, HT, 'The Role of Stability and Renegotiation in Transnational Petroleum Agreements' (2012) 5(1) *Journal of Politics and Law* 33.

Mayeda, G, 'Playing Fair: The Meaning of Fair and Equitable Treatment in Bilateral Investment Treaties' (2007) 41(2) *Journal of World Trade* 273.

Maynard, S, 'Legitimate Expectations and the Interpretation of the "Legal Stability Obligation"' (2016) 1(1) *European Investment Law and Arbitration Review* 99.

Meyers, Z, 'Adapting Legitimate Expectations to International Investment Law: A Defence of Arbitral Tribunals' Approach' (2014) 11(3) *Transnational Dispute Management* 1.

MIGA, 'World Investment and Political Risk 2009' (World Bank, 2009).

——, 'World Investment and Political Risk 2010' (World Bank, 2010).

——, 'World Investment and Political Risk 2011' (World Bank, 2011).

Mills, A, 'The Balancing (and Unbalancing?) of Interests in International Investment Law and Arbitration' in Z Douglas, J Pauwelyn and JE Viñuales (eds), *The Foundations of International Investment Law: Bringing Theory into Practice* (Oxford University Press, 2014).

Mistelis, L, 'Contractual Mechanisms for Stability in Energy Contracts' in M Scherer (ed), *International Arbitration in the Energy Sector* (Oxford University Press, 2018).

Mitchell, AD, Sornarajah, M and Voon, T (eds), *Good Faith and International Economic Law* (Oxford University Press, 2015).

Mohajeri, E, 'Overview of Political and Regulatory Risks in International Energy Investment' (2013) 11(2) *Oil, Gas & Energy Law* 1.

Monebhurrun, N, 'Gold Reserve Inc v Bolivarian Republic of Venezuela: Enshrining Legitimate Expectations as a General Principle of International Law?' (2015) 32(5) *Journal of International Arbitration* 551.

Montembault, B, 'The Stabilisation of State Contracts Using the Example of Oil Contracts. A Return of the Gods of Olympia?' (2003) 6 *International Business Law Journal* 593.

Montt, S, *State Liability in Investment Treaty Arbitration: Global Constitutional and Administrative Law in the BIT Generation* (Hart Publishing, 2009).

Mortenson, JD, 'The Meaning of "Investment": ICSID's Travaux and the Domain of International Investment Law' (2010) 51(1) *Harvard International Law Journal* 257.

Mosler, H, 'General Principles of Law' in R Bernhardt (ed), *Encyclopedia of Public International Law* (North-Holland, 1995).

Muchlinski, PT, *Multinational Enterprises and the Law* (Oxford University Press, 2007).

Muhammad, N, 'Legitimate Expectations in Investment Treaty Arbitration: Balancing between State's Legitimate Regulatory Functions and Investor's Legitimate Expectations' (PhD Thesis, University of Dundee, 2015).

Naón, HAG, 'Should International Commercial Arbitrators Declare a Law Unconstitutional?' in DD Caron et al (eds), *Practising Virtue: Inside International Arbitration* (Oxford University Press, 2015).

Neuhaus, JE, 'The Enforceability of Legislative Stabilization Clauses' in DD Caron et al (eds), *Practising Virtue: Inside International Arbitration* (Oxford University Press, 2015).

Newcombe, A and Paradell, L, *Law and Practice of Investment Treaties: Standards of Treatment* (Kluwer Law International, 2009).

Noilhac, A, 'Renewable Energy Investment Cases against Spain and the Quest for Regulatory Consistency' (2020) 71 *Questions of International Law* 21.

Norton, JJ, 'An "Environmental" Approach to FDI and Effective Dispute Resolution: The Exhortations of the Monterrey Consensus' in N Horn (ed), *Arbitrating Foreign Investment Disputes: Procedural and Substantive Legal Aspects* (Kluwer Law International, 2004).

Nowak, LM, 'Exploring the Limits of the Concept of Legitimate Expectations in Investment Treaty Law: A Study in Comparative Law and the Development of International Law' (PhD Thesis, SOAS, University of London, 2015).

Nwaokoro, J, 'Enforcing Stabilization of International Energy Contracts' (2010) 3(1) *Journal of World Energy Law & Business* 103.

OECD, 'Fair and Equitable Treatment Standard in International Investment Law' (OECD Publishing, 2004).

——, 'Indirect Expropriation and the Right to Regulate in International Investment Law' (OECD Publishing, 2004).

Omukoro, DE, 'Examining Contractual Stability Measures in Light of Emerging Risks: Revisiting the Stabilisation Clause Debate' (2012–15) 24 *Sri Lanka Journal of International Law* 85.

Ortino, F, 'The Obligation of Regulatory Stability in the Fair and Equitable Treatment Standard: How Far Have We Come?' (2018) 21(4) *Journal of International Economic Law* 845.

Osasu, O, 'Legitimate Expectations and Political Risk: Lessons from Investment Arbitration for Energy Investors' (2013) 6 *International Energy Law Review* 249.

Oshionebo, E, 'Stabilization Clauses in Natural Resource Extraction Contracts: Legal, Economic and Social Implications for Developing Countries' (2010) 10 *Asper Review of International Business and Trade Law* 1.

Otero García-Castrillón, C, 'Spain and Investment Arbitration: The Renewable Energy Explosion' (Centre for International Governance Innovation, 2016).

Paasivirta, E, 'Internationalization and Stabilization of Contracts versus State Sovereignty' (1989) 60(1) *British Yearbook of International Law* 315.

Palombino, FM, *Fair and Equitable Treatment and the Fabric of General Principles* (Asser Press, 2018).

Pandya, APG and Moody, A, 'Legitimate Expectations in Investment Treaty Arbitration: An Unclear Future' (2010) 15(1) *Tilburg Law Review* 93.

Panizzon, M, *Good Faith in the Jurisprudence of the WTO: The Protection of Legitimate Expectations, Good Faith Interpretation and Fair Dispute Settlement* (Hart Publishing, 2006).

Paparinskis, M, *The International Minimum Standard and Fair and Equitable Treatment* (Oxford University Press, 2013).

——, 'Good Faith and Fair and Equitable Treatment in International Investment Law' in AD Mitchell, M Sornarajah and T Voon (eds), *Good Faith and International Economic Law* (Oxford University Press, 2015).

Partasides, C and Martinez, L, 'Of Taxes and Stabilisation' in JW Rowley, RD Bishop and G Kaiser (eds), *The Guide to Energy Arbitrations* (Global Arbitration Review, 2017).

Pate, TJ, 'Evaluating Stabilization Clauses in Venezuela's Strategic Association Agreements for Heavy-Crude Extraction in the Orinoco Belt: The Return of a Forgotten Contractual Risk Reduction Mechanism for the Petroleum Industry' (2009) 40(2) *University of Miami Inter-American Law Review* 347.

Pereira, A, 'Legal Stability Contracts in Colombia: An Appropriate Incentive for Investments?' (2013) 12(2) *Richmond Journal of Global Law and Business* 237.

Perrone, NM, 'The Emerging Global Right to Investment: Understanding the Reasoning behind Foreign Investor Rights' (2017) 8(4) *Journal of International Dispute Settlement* 673.

Peter, W, *Arbitration and Renegotiation of International Investment Agreements* (Kluwer Law International, 1995).

——, 'Stabilization Clauses in State Contracts' (1998) 8 *International Business Law Journal* 875.

Picherack, JR, 'The Expanding Scope of the Fair and Equitable Treatment Standard: Have Recent Tribunals Gone Too Far?' (2008) 9(4) *Journal of World Investment & Trade* 255.

Poiedynok, V, Kolohoida, O and Lukach, I, 'The Doctrine of Legitimate Expectations: Need for Limits' (2017) VIII(5) *Journal of Advanced Research in Law and Economics* 1604.

Potestà, M, 'Legitimate Expectations in Investment Treaty Law: Understanding the Roots and the Limits of a Controversial Concept' (2013) 28(1) *ICSID Review – Foreign Investment Law Journal* 88.

Pusceddu, P, 'Contractual Stability in the Oil and Gas Industry: Stabilization, Renegotiation and Unilateral State's Undertakings' (2014) (2) *International Energy Law Review* 58.

Pusic, N, 'Balancing the Interests between TNCs and Host Developing States: The Role of Law' (PhD Thesis, Institute of Advanced Legal Studies, University of London, 2017).

Radi, Y, 'Balancing the Public and the Private in International Investment Law' in HM Watt and DPF Arroyo (eds), *Private International Law and Global Governance* (Oxford University Press, 2014).

Reed, L and Consedine, S, 'Fair and Equitable Treatment: Legitimate Expectations and Transparency' in M Kinnear et al (eds), *Building International Investment Law: The First 50 Years of ICSID* (Kluwer Law International, 2015).

Reisman, WM and Arsanjani, MH, 'The Question of Unilateral Governmental Statements as Applicable Law in Investment Disputes' (2004) 19(2) *ICSID Review – Foreign Investment Law Journal* 328.

Reisman, WM and Sloane, RD, 'Indirect Expropriation and Its Valuation in the BIT Generation' (2004) 74(1) *British Yearbook of International Law* 115.

Rennert, K, 'The Protection of Legitimate Expectations under German Administrative Law' 2016).

Restrepo, D, Correia, R and Poblacion, J, 'Political Risk and Corporate Investment Decisions' (Universidad Carlos III de Madrid, 2012).

Restrepo, T, 'Modification of Renewable Energy Support Schemes under the Energy Charter Treaty: Eiser and Charanne in the Context of Climate Change' (2017) 8(1) *Goettingen Journal of International Law* 101.

Reynolds, P, 'Legitimate Expectations and the Protection of Trust in Public Officials' (2011) 2 *PL* 330.

Rivkin, DW, Lamb, SJ and Leslie, NK, 'The Future of Investor–State Dispute Settlement in the Energy Sector: Engaging with Climate Change, Human Rights and the Rule of Law' (2015) 8(2) *Journal of World Energy Law & Business* 130.

Rodriguez-Yong, CA, 'Enhancing Legal Certainty in Colombia: The Role of the Andean Community' (2008) 17(2) *Michigan State University College of Law Journal of International Law* 407.

Rodriguez-Yong, CA and Martinez-Munoz, KX, 'The Andean Approach to Stabilisation Clauses' (2013) 6(1) *International Journal of Private Law* 67.

Rubins, N, 'The Notion of "Investment" in International Investment Arbitration' in N Horn (ed), *Arbitrating Foreign Investment Disputes: Procedural and Substantive Legal Aspects* (Kluwer Law International, 2004).

Rubins, N and Kinsella, NS, *International Investment, Political Risk and Dispute Resolution: A Practitioner's Guide* (Oceana Publications, 2005).

Salacuse, JW, *The Three Laws of International Investment: National, Contractual, and International Frameworks for Foreign Capital* (Oxford University Press, 2013).

——, *The Law of Investment Treaties* (Oxford University Press, 2015).

Salacuse, JW and Sullivan, NP, 'Do BITs Really Work?: An Evaluation of Bilateral Investment Treaties and their Grand Bargain' in KP Sauvant and LE Sachs (eds), *The Effect of Treaties on Foreign Direct Investment: Bilateral Investment Treaties, Double Taxation Treaties, and Investment Flows* (Oxford University Press, 2009).

Saravanan, A and Subramanian, SR, *Role of Domestic Courts in the Settlement of Investor–State Disputes: The Indian Scenario* (Springer, 2020).

Sasson, M, *Substantive Law in Investment Treaty Arbitration: The Unsettled Relationship between International Law and Municipal Law* (Kluwer Law International, 2017).

Sattorova M, 'From Expropriation to Non-expropriatory Standards of Treatment: Towards a Unified Concept of an Investment Treaty Breach' (PhD Thesis, University of Birmingham, 2010).

——, 'Defining Investment under the ICSID Convention and BITs: Of Ordinary Meaning, Telos, and Beyond' (2012) 2(2) *Asian Journal of International Law* 267.

Sauvant, KP and Unuvar, G, 'Can Host Countries Have Legitimate Expectations?' (2016) 183 *Columbia FDI Perspectives* http://ccsi.columbia.edu/files/2013/10/No-183-Sauvant-and-%C3%9Cn%C3%BCvar-FINAL.pdf.

Scharaw, B, *The Protection of Foreign Investments in Mongolia: Treaties, Domestic Law, and Contracts on Investments in International Comparison and Arbitral Practice* (Springer International Publishing, 2018).

Scherer, M, 'Introduction' in M Scherer (ed), *International Arbitration in the Energy Sector* (Oxford University Press, 2018).

Schill, SW, 'Fair and Equitable Treatment, the Rule of Law, and Comparative Public Law' in SW Schill (ed), *International Investment Law and Comparative Public Law* (Oxford University Press, 2010).

——, 'General Principles of Law and International Investment Law' in T Gazzini and E de Brabandere (eds), *International Investment Law: The Sources of Rights and Obligations* (Martinus Nijhoff Publishers, 2012).

——, 'Foreign Investment in the Energy Sector: Lessons for International Investment Law' in E de Brabandere and T Gazzini (eds), *Foreign Investment in the Energy Sector: Balancing Private and Public Interests* (Brill Nijhoff, 2014).

Schonberg, SJ, *Legitimate Expectations in Administrative Law* (Oxford University Press, 2000).

Schreuer, C, 'Commentary on the ICSID Convention' (1996) 11(2) *ICSID Review – Foreign Investment Law Journal* 318.

——, 'Fair and Equitable Treatment in Arbitral Practice' (2005) 6(3) *Journal of World Investment & Trade* 357.

——, 'Fair and Equitable Treatment (FET): Interactions with Other Standards' (2007) 4(5) *Transnational Dispute Management* 1.

——, 'Introduction: Interrelationship of Standards' in A Reinisch (ed), *Standards of Investment Protection* (Oxford University Press, 2008).

——, 'Diversity and Harmonization of Treaty Interpretation in Investment Arbitration' in M Fitzmaurice, O Elias and P Merkouris (eds), *Treaty Interpretation and the Vienna Convention on the Law of Treaties: 30 Years On* (Martinus Nijhoff Publishers, 2010).

Schreuer, C and Kriebaum, U, 'At What Time Must Legitimate Expectations Exist?' in J Werner and AH Ali (eds), *A Liber Amicorum: Thomas Wälde – Law beyond Conventional Thought* (CMP Publishing, 2009).

Schreuer, C, Friedland, PD and Park, WW, 'Selected Standards of Treatment Available under the Energy Charter Treaty' in G Coop and C Ribeiro (eds), *Investment Protection and the Energy Charter Treaty* (JurisNet, 2008).

Schreuer, C et al, *The ICSID Convention: A Commentary* (Cambridge University Press, 2009).

Schröder, M, 'Administrative Law in Germany' in R Seerden and F Stroink (eds), *Administrative Law of the European Union, its Member States and the United States: A Comparative Analysis* (Intersentia, 2002).

Schwarze, J, *European Administrative Law* (Sweet & Maxwell, 1992).

Schwebel, S, 'On Whether the Breach by a State of a Contract with an Alien Is a Breach of International Law' in *Justice in International Law: Selected Writings* (Cambridge University Press, 1994).

Selivanova, YS, 'Changes in Renewables Support Policy and Investment Protection under the Energy Charter Treaty: Analysis of Jurisprudence and Outlook for the Current Arbitration Cases' (2018) 33(2) *ICSID Review – Foreign Investment Law Journal* 433.

Shamila, DLF, 'Rationalize of Host State's Regulatory Measures and Protection of Legitimate Expectations of Foreign Investor: Analyzing the State of Necessity in the Investment Treaty Context' (2013) 2(3) *South East Asia Journal of Contemporary Business, Economics and Law* 34.

Shemberg, A, 'Stabilization Clauses and Human Rights: A Research Project Conducted for IFC and the United Nations Special Representative to the Secretary General on Business and Human Rights' (IFC, 2009) www.ifc.org/wps/wcm/connect/0883d81a-e00a-4551-b2b9-46641e5a9bba/Stabilization%2BPaper.pdf?MOD=AJPERES&CACHEID=ROOTWORKSPACE-0883d81a-e00a-4551-b2b9-46641e5a9bba-jqeww2e.

Simoes, FD, 'Charanne and Construction Investments v Spain: Legitimate Expectations and Investments in Renewable Energy' (2017) 26(2) *Review of European, Comparative & International Environmental Law* 174.

Siwy, A, 'Indirect Expropriation and the Legitimate Expectations of the Investor' in C Klausegger et al (eds), *Austrian Arbitration Yearbook 2007* (CH Beck/Stämpfli/Manz, 2007).

Snodgrass, E, 'Protecting Investors' Legitimate Expectations – Recognizing and Delimiting a General Principle' (2006) 21(1) *ICSID Review – Foreign Investment Law Journal* 1.

Solimene, F, 'Political Risk in the Oil and Gas Industry and Legal Tools for Mitigation' (2014) 2 *International Energy Law Review* 81.

Sornarajah, M, 'The Myth of International Contract Law' (1981) 15(3) *Journal of World Trade* 187.

——, *The Settlement of Foreign Investment Disputes* (Kluwer Law International, 2000).

——, *The International Law on Foreign Investment* (Cambridge University Press, 2010).

——, 'Evolution or Revolution in International Investment Arbitration? The Descent into Normlessness' in C Brown and K Miles (eds), *Evolution in Investment Treaty Law and Arbitration* (Cambridge University Press, 2011).

——, *Resistance and Change in the International Law on Foreign Investment* (Cambridge University Press, 2015).

Sottilotta, CE, 'Political Risk: Concepts, Definitions, Challenges' (LUISS School of Government, 2013).

Sourgens, FG, 'Keep the Faith: Investment Protection Following the Denunciation of International Investment Agreements' (2012) 11 *Santa Clara Journal of International Law* 335.

Stone, J, 'Arbitrariness, the Fair and Equitable Treatment Standard, and the International Law of Investment' (2012) 25(1) *Leiden Journal of International Law* 77.

Subedi, SP, *International Investment Law: Reconciling Policy and Principle* (Hart Publishing, 2012).

Supapa, R, 'The Protection of Upstream Energy Contracts under Investment Treaty Arbitration: A Study of the Interaction between Contract and Treaty Instruments' (PhD Thesis, University of Aberdeen, 2014).

Sureda, AR, *Investment Treaty Arbitration: Judging under Uncertainty* (Cambridge University Press, 2012).

Talus, K, *EU Energy Law and Policy: A Critical Account* (Oxford University Press, 2013).

——, 'Internationalization of Energy Law' in K Talus (ed), *Research Handbook on International Energy Law* (Edward Elgar Publishing, 2014).

Talus, K and Heffron, RJ, 'What Is "International Energy Law" or "Energy Law"?' (2018) 16(3) *Oil, Gas & Energy Law* 1.

Talus, K, Looper, S and Otillar, S, 'Lex Petrolea and the Internationalization of Petroleum Agreements: Focus on Host Government Contracts' (2012) 5(3) *Journal of World Energy Law & Business* 181.

Teggi, N, 'Legitimate Expectations in Investment Arbitration: At the End of Its Life Cycle' (2016) 5(1) *Indian Journal of Arbitration Law* 64.

Téllez, FM, 'Conditions and Criteria for the Protection of Legitimate Expectations under International Investment Law: 2012 ICSID Review Student Writing Competition' (2012) 27(2) *ICSID Review – Foreign Investment Law Journal* 432.

Thakur, T, 'Reforming the Investor–State Dispute Settlement Mechanism and the Host State's Right to Regulate: A Critical Assessment' (2020) *Indian Journal of International Law* https://doi.org/10.1007/s40901-020-00111-2.

Tienhaara, K, 'Unilateral Commitments to Investment Protection: Does the Promise of Stability Restrict Environmental Policy Development?' (2006) 17(1) *Yearbook of International Environmental Law* 139.

Tirado, JM, 'Renewable Energy Claims under the Energy Charter Treaty: An Overview' (2015) 12(3) *Transnational Dispute Management* 1.

Titi, A, *The Right to Regulate in International Investment Law* (Nomos/Hart Publishing, 2014).

Tudor, I, *The Fair and Equitable Treatment Standard in the International Law of Foreign Investment* (Oxford University Press, 2008).

Umirdinov, A, 'The End of Hibernation of Stabilization Clause in Investment Arbitration: Reassessing Its Contribution to Sustainable Development' (2015) 43 *Denver Journal of International Law & Policy* 455.

UNCTAD, 'Investment Policy Review of Colombia' (United Nations, 2006).

——, 'Bilateral Investment Treaties 1995–2006: Trends in Investment Rulemaking' (United Nations, 2007).

——, 'World Investment Report: Transnational Corporations, Extractive Industries and Development' (United Nations, 2007).

——, 'Fair and Equitable Treatment: A Sequel' (United Nations, 2012).

——, 'Investment Policy Framework for Sustainable Development' (United Nations, 2015).

Valenti, M, 'The Protection of General Interests of Host States in the Application of the Fair and Equitable Treatment Standard' in G Sacerdoti (ed), *General Interests of Host States in International Investment Law* (Cambridge University Press, 2014).

Valera, JL, 'Political Risks for International Oil Companies Investing in Latin America' (2006) 4(1) *Oil, Gas & Energy Law* 1.

van Aaken, A, 'Perils of Success? The Case of International Investment Protection' (2008) 9(1) *European Business Organization Law Review* 1.

Van de Putte, A, Gates, DF and Holder, AK, 'Political Risk Insurance as an Instrument to Reduce Oil and Gas Investment Risk and Manage Investment Returns' (2012) 5(4) *Journal of World Energy Law & Business* 284.

Vandevelde, KJ, 'Investment Liberalization and Economic Development: The Role of Bilateral Investment Treaties' (1998) 36(3) *Columbia Journal of Transnational Law* 501.

——, 'A Brief History of International Investment Agreements' (2005) 12(1) *UC Davis Journal of International Law & Policy* 157.

——, *Bilateral Investment Treaties: History, Policy, and Interpretation* (Oxford University Press, 2010).

——, 'A Unified Theory of Fair and Equitable Treatment' (2010) 43(1) *New York University Journal of International Law and Politics* 43.

Vanhonnaeker, L, 'Promoting Successful and Sustainable Foreign Direct Investment through Political Risk Mitigation Strategies' (2016) 1(2) *Chinese Journal of Global Governance* 133.

Vargiu, P, 'Beyond Hallmarks and Formal Requirements: A "Jurisprudence Constante" on the Notion of Investment in the ICSID Convention' (2009) 10(5) *Journal of World Investment & Trade* 753.

Varis, O, 'International Energy Investments: Tracking the Legal Concept' (2014) 2(1) *Groningen Journal of International Law* 81.

——, 'Constitutionalisation and Institutionalisation Applied to the International Investment Regime: Toward a Uniform, Consistent and Coherent International Investment Law' (PhD Thesis, University of Dundee, 2018).

——, 'Redefining Energy in the Post-Pandemic Era' (2020) 1(2) *Global Energy Law and Sustainability* 164.

Vasciannie, S, 'The Fair and Equitable Treatment Standard in International Investment Law and Practice' (2000) 70(1) *British Yearbook of International Law* 99.

Verhoosel, G, 'Foreign Direct Investment and Legal Constraints on Domestic Environmental Policies: Striking a Reasonable Balance between Stability and Change' (1997) 29(4) *Law and Policy in International Business* 451.

Vernon, R, 'Long-Run Trends in Concession Contracts' (1967) 61 *Proceedings of the American Society of International Law* 81.

——, *Sovereignty at Bay: The Multinational Spread of US Enterprises* (Longman, 1971).

Vicuña, FO, 'Foreign Investment Law: How Customary Is Custom?' (2005) 38(148) *Estudios Internacionales* 79.

Vielleville, DE and Vasani, BS, 'Sovereignty over Natural Resources versus Rights under Investment Contracts: Which One Prevails?' (2008) 5(2) *Transnational Dispute Management* 1.

Viñuales, JE, 'Investor Diligence in Investment Arbitration: Sources and Arguments' (2017) 32(2) *ICSID Review – Foreign Investment Law Journal* 346.

Voss, JO, *Impact of Investment Treaties on Contracts between Host States and Foreign Investors* (Martinus Nijhoff Publishers, 2010).

Waelde, TW, 'Negotiating for Dispute Settlement in Transnational Mineral Contracts: Current Practice, Trends, and an Evaluation from the Host Country's Perspective' (1977) 7 *Denver Journal of International Law & Policy* 33.

——, 'International Energy Investment' (1996) 17 *Energy Law Journal* 191.

——, 'Investment Arbitration under the Energy Charter Treaty – From Dispute Settlement to Treaty Implementation' (1996) 12(4) *Arbitration International* 429.

——, 'International Investment Law: An Overview of Key Concepts and Methodology' (2007) 4(4) *Transnational Dispute Management* 1.

——, 'Renegotiating Acquired Rights in the Oil and Gas Industries: Industry and Political Cycles Meet the Rule of Law' (2008) 1(1) *Journal of World Energy Law & Business* 55.

——, 'The Role of Arbitration in the Globalisation of Energy Markets: Perspective in the Year 2000' (2008) 6(3) *Oil, Gas & Energy Law* 1.

Waelde, TW and Kolo, A, 'Environmental Regulation, Investment Protection and "Regulatory Taking" in International Law' (2001) 50(4) *International & Comparative Law Quarterly* 811.

Waelde, TW and Ndi, G, 'Fiscal Regime Stability and Issues of State Sovereignty' in J Otto (ed), *Taxation of Mineral Enterprises* (Graham & Trotman, 1995).

——, 'Stabilizing International Investment Commitments: International Law versus Contract Interpretation' (1996) 31 *Texas International Law Journal* 215.

Waibel, M, 'Opening Pandora's Box: Sovereign Bonds in International Arbitration' (2007) 101(4) *American Journal of International Law* 711.

Walter, A, 'The Investor's Expectations in International Investment Arbitration' (2009) 6(1) *Transnational Dispute Management* 1.

Weil, P, 'Les Clauses de Stabilisation ou d'intangibilité Insérées dans les Accords de Développement Économique' in *Mélanges offerts à Charles Rousseau* (Pedone, 1974).

Westcott, TJ, 'Recent Practice on Fair and Equitable Treatment' (2007) 8(3) *Journal of World Investment & Trade* 409.

Williams, SL, 'Political and Other Risk Insurance: OPIC, MIGA, EXIMBANK and other Providers' (1993) 5(1) *Pace International Law Review* 59.

Wilson, JD, 'Understanding Resource Nationalism: Economic Dynamics and Political Institutions' (2015) 21(4) *Contemporary Politics* 399.

Wongkaew, T, 'The Transplantation of Legitimate Expectations in Investment Treaty Arbitration: A Critique' in S Lalani and RP Lazo (eds), *The Role of the State in Investor–State Arbitration* (Brill Nijhoff, 2014).

——, *Protection of Legitimate Expectations in Investment Treaty Arbitration: A Theory of Detrimental Reliance* (Cambridge University Press, 2019).

World Energy Council, 'World Energy Scenarios 2016' (2016) www.worldenergy.org/assets/downloads/World-Energy-Scenarios-2016_Full-Report.pdf.

Xenofontos, A, 'Managing Investor–State Disputes in Upstream Oil and Gas Industry: IOCs' Perspective' (2018) 4 *Oil, Gas & Energy Law* 1.

Yackee, JW, 'Do We Really Need BITs – Toward a Return to Contract in International Investment Law' (2008) 3(1) *Asian Journal of WTO & International Health Law and Policy* 121.

——, 'Political Risk and International Investment Law' (2014) 24 *Duke Journal of Comparative & International Law* 477.

Yala, F, 'The Notion of "Investment" in ICSID Case Law: A Drifting Jurisdictional Requirement? Some "Un-Conventional" Thoughts on Salini, SGS & Mihaly' (2004) 1(4) *Transnational Dispute Management* 1.

Yannaca-Small, K, 'Fair and Equitable Treatment Standard: Recent Developments' in A Reinisch (ed), *Standards of Investment Protection* (Oxford University Press, 2008).

——, 'Fair and Equitable Treatment Standard' in K Yannaca-Small (ed), *Arbitration under International Investment Agreements: A Guide to the Key Issues* (Oxford University Press, 2010).

Yen, TH, *The Interpretation of Investment Treaties* (Brill Nijhoff, 2014).

Zannoni, D, 'The Legitimate Expectation of Regulatory Stability under the Energy Charter Treaty' (2020) 33(2) *Leiden Journal of International Law* 451.

Zeyl, T, 'Charting the Wrong Course: The Doctrine of Legitimate Expectations in Investment Treaty Law' (2011) 49(1) *Alberta Law Review* 203.

Ziegler, AR and Baumgartner, J, 'Good Faith as a General Principle of (International) Law' in AD Mitchell, M Sornarajah and T Voon (eds), *Good Faith and International Economic Law* (Oxford University Press, 2015).

INDEX